DRINK AND SOBRIETY IN VICTORIAN WALES
c. 1820—*c.* 1895

DRINK AND SOBRIETY IN VICTORIAN WALES
c. 1820—c. 1895

W. R. LAMBERT

Distributed in the U.S.A. by

Humanities Press

Atlantic Highlands, N. J.

UNIVERSITY OF WALES PRESS
CARDIFF
1983

166965

British Library Cataloguing in Publication Data

Lambert, W. R.
  Drink and sobriety in Victorian Wales, *c.* 1820 – *c.* 1895.
  1. Temperance—History   2. Temperance societies
  —Wales—History
  I. Title
  178'.1'09429   HV5449.W/

ISBN 0-7083-0845-7

Printed in Wales by
QUALITEX PRINTING LIMITED, CARDIFF

TO MONICA
AND ANNA

PREFACE

Nineteenth-century Wales possessed its own peculiar cultural configuration based on the dominance of religious nonconformity, the widespread use of the Welsh language and the rise of political nationalism after 1868. These three distinguishing characteristics call for and justify a discussion of the nineteenth-century temperance movement in Wales. It is probably true to say that until the last two decades, historians had usually studied the nineteenth century, particularly social class in the nineteenth century, in relation to work rather than leisure; hence their concentration on the conflicting interests of employer and employee; hence also their interest in Chartists and socialists and their relative neglect of humanitarians and temperance reformers. Professor Vincent's claim, however, that popular radicalism was the product of the leisure of Saturday night and Sunday morning, 'the pothouse and the chapel, not of the working week', draws our attention to nineteenth-century movements connected with recreation, one of the most significant of which was the temperance movement. [1]

Temperance or teetotalism appears to most present-day observers as an exceedingly outworn remnant or shibboleth of nonconformity and Liberalism in their heyday. [2] But it played a powerful part in the process of self-betterment of Welsh people in the nineteenth and early-twentieth centuries; with its emphasis on thrift and 'impulse-renunciation', it helped to make many people respectable.

For Britain as a whole, the most scholarly published work on the nineteenth-century temperance movement has been written by Dr. Brian Harrison. In his *Drink and the Victorians. The Temperance Question in England, 1815-1872* (1971), Dr. Harrison became the first historian outside the temperance movement to discuss it at any length. The historiography of the temperance movement had hitherto been dominated by historians inside the movement who, to a considerable extent, produced histories which are jejune and otiose. These historians tended to treat their material in the form of uncritical narrative, much of which is anecdotal and antiquarian in character. They presented temperance reformers as plaster saints and, in general, pulled far too many punches. There were, however, occasional nuggets amongst the dross; P. T. Winskill and Dawson

vii

Burns at least produced a mass of detail, much of it accurate, which would be difficult to find elsewhere.[3] Yet they aimed to promote the temperance cause, not to write scholarly works of history, and as active members of their movement they had to avoid giving offence to people who were always notoriously thin-skinned and thus extremely susceptible to taking offence.

The predominant source used for the present study consists of primary printed material, such as local newspapers, denominational magazines, temperance journals, temperance tracts, annual reports of temperance bodies, and parliamentary papers. Manuscript sources, particularly manuscript minutes of temperance organizations, are not numerous, but there is valuable material on the drink question in the papers of nineteenth-century Welsh members of parliament, held at the National Library of Wales. The minutes of the national prohibitionist pressure group, the United Kingdom Alliance (established in 1853), exist from 1872 to the end of the period covered by this study, but they are exceedingly stereotyped and fairly uninformative. Comparatively few minute books of local Welsh temperance societies survive, and when they do, they invariably contain substantial gaps. Obviously, it is impossible to get a good idea of the atmosphere and flavour of temperance meetings from printed reports because the individuals involved took their assumptions so much for granted. Consequently, recourse was made to the interviewing of old people who were able to recall their early temperance activities in the late 1880s and 1890s. I am very grateful to Aubrey Davy of Cardiff, Benjamin James of Bangor, and Charles Garrett of Tredegar for providing me, in taped interviews, with such incidental details as could not be obtained elsewhere.

It is both a duty and a pleasure to place on record my debt and my gratitude to many other kind people who have helped me in my work. Professor Ieuan Gwynedd Jones of the University College of Wales, Aberystwyth, supervised my researches at the University College of Swansea, to my very great benefit. Dr. Brian Harrison, the historian of the English temperance movement, was a constant source of enthusiasm and encouragement, and gave generously of his time and expertise in commenting on my findings. My debt to the librarians and staffs of the National Library of Wales and Cardiff Central Library is particularly heavy and my thanks are correspondingly great. I also offer my thanks, for their courtesy and unfailing assistance, to the staffs of the many public libraries and county record offices in Wales who helped me.

I cannot hope that the many temperance reformers who generously assisted me will agree with all my conclusions, but I should like to thank, in particular, Mr. T. Garth Waite of the United Kingdom Alliance and Miss Muriel Daniel of the British Temperance League at Sheffield for their kindness at all times and for providing me with such pleasant working conditions in their libraries.

I must express my warm thanks to the Delegates of Local Examinations, Professor D. K. Fieldhouse, a former Delegate, and to Miss C. G. Hunter, Secretary to the Delegates of Local Examinations, for their valuable encouragement. Mrs. Pamela Cummings and Mrs. Joanne Lovett shared the task of typing my manuscript and I thank them both. At every stage of publication the assistance of Miss Lowri Morgan of the University of Wales Press has been invaluable.

The History and Law Committee of the Board of Celtic Studies, University of Wales, and Dr. Kenneth O. Morgan, publisher and editor, respectively, of the *Welsh History Review,* kindly gave me permission to reproduce material in chapters I and VI which had first appeared in that thriving journal.

In view of such help and kindness from so many quarters it follows that all the mistakes that doubtless remain, both of judgment and presentation, must be my own.

W. R. LAMBERT

University of Oxford Delegacy of Local Examinations
Summertown, Oxford
August 1982

NOTES

[1] J. R. Vincent, *The Formation of the Liberal Party, 1857-1868* (1966), p. 79; see also Brian Harrison 'Drink and Sobriety in England, 1815-1872. A Critical Bibliography', *International Review of Social History,* XII (1967), Part 2, 204.

[2] See, for example, T. J. Morgan, 'Peasant Culture of the Swansea Valley', (ed.), S. Williams, *Glamorgan Historian,* vol. 9 (Cowbridge, n.d.), 106.

[3] See Dawson Burns, *Temperance History. A Consecutive Narrative of the Rise, Development, and Extension of the Temperance Reform* (2 vols., n.d., 1889); *Pen-Pictures of Some Temperance Notables* (1895); P. T. Winskill, *The Temperance Movement and its Workers* (4 vols., 1892). For less useful, hagiographical works, see Samuel Couling, *History of the Temperance Movement in Great Britain and Ireland* (1862); W. Logan, *Early Heroes of the Temperance Reformation* (Glasgow, 1873); Rev. T. Maguire, *Temperance Landmarks. A Narrative of the Work and the Workers.* ('Hand and Heart' publishing office, n.d.).

CONTENTS

TABLES AND FIGURES

ABBREVIATIONS

C.C.L.	Cardiff Central Library.
C.M.G.	*Cardiff and Merthyr Guardian.*
G.R.O.	Glamorgan Record Office.
N.L.W.	National Library of Wales.
P.P.	*Parliamentary Papers.*
P.R.O.	Public Record Office.
S.C.H.C.	Select Committee of the House of Commons.
S.C.H.L.	Select Committee of the House of Lords.
U.C.N.W.	University College of North Wales.
U.K.A.	United Kingdom Alliance.
W.H.R.	*Welsh History Review.*

CHAPTER I

WELSH SOCIETY AND DRINK IN THE NINETEENTH CENTURY

AT the end of the eighteenth century Wales was largely a self-sufficient economic unit. Industry was generally subsidiary to agriculture and in 1800 the great majority of the population was engaged in agriculture. At the apex of society were the owners of large estates, who were largely anglicized squires; below them came the gentleman farmers and clerical landowners, and below these the smaller farmers ranging from yeoman farmers to poorer tenant farmers. The social conditions of the tenant farmers were often quite wretched, usually no better than those of farm labourers. A more comfortable life was lived by village craftsmen and the artisans of the country towns. [1]

Until the last years of the eighteenth century Wales had seemed a static society, but economic and social change proceeded apace from about this time. The coming of industrialisation from the 1780s brought significant social changes, the growth of heavy industry (particularly in the mining areas of Glamorgan and Monmouthshire), and a flood wave of immigration into the south Wales coalfield. One of the Education Commissioners of 1847 could describe the 'gigantic character of the works as a feature not to be passed over which had rendered the ancient divisions of the country a dead letter. The basis of the old parochial terrier was the manor whilst the basis of the new one was the works.' [2] Industrialisation produced new strains also in the rural areas, as it was here that the population explosion first occurred; and until the early years of the twentieth century the migration into the industrial areas of south Wales came largely from the overpopulated rural areas. [3] Of great significance was the growth of the Merthyr Tydfil iron industry in the early-nineteenth century and the development of coal mining in the south Wales valleys from *c.*1850. The industrial areas offered higher wages, shorter hours of work and the attractions of town life, so that there was in many areas a 'deliberate and calculated abandonment of rural labour'. As Dr. D. W. Howell has remarked, the 'pull' of the industrial areas was paralleled by the adverse conditions in the Welsh countryside which helped to 'push' the agricultural labourer to the towns and the 'works'. [4]

Not a great deal is known of the level of population in the eighteenth century, but it has been estimated that the population of Wales rose by 19.6 per cent between 1760 and 1801, largely in Cardiganshire and the counties of north Wales. [5] The rate of population growth throughout Wales during the period 1801-31 was 54 per cent, a feature which reflected the growth of industry, particularly in Monmouthshire, Glamorgan and Caernarfonshire. In the areas of heavy industry—in Monmouthshire and in Merthyr Tydfil—the population increased by about 300 per cent between 1801 and 1831. For the whole of the counties of Monmouthshire and Glamorgan the population increased from 116,465 in 1801 to 389,267 in 1851, and to 968,314 in 1891; between 1860 and 1910 over 320,000 people migrated into the coalfield from the rural areas of Wales.

The consequent urbanization, which was aided by the gradual improvement in communications, led to severe social problems involving the health and working conditions of the labouring population. Yet the distribution of Welsh industry in valleys separated by barren moorlands encouraged the development in the industrial villages and towns of chapels, local newspapers, temperance societies and other voluntary organizations. [6] The importance of this development is that it provided a framework of social stability for the rootless workers of the coalfield. Many immigrants from mid- and west Wales who came into the coalfield during the first half of the nineteenth century brought their religion with them in the form of a letter of recommendation—*llythyr canmoliaeth*—which handed the person over to the care and supervision of another chapel in the district in which he was settling. [7]

Wales's distinctive pattern of cultural life during the nineteenth century was largely a result of the spread of religious nonconformity from the early years of the century. The impulse of the Methodist revival of the late-eighteenth century ensured that the older Dissent in Wales—the Independents and the Baptists—became reinvigorated, and the revival gave rise in 1811 to the foundation of the indigenous, national sect of the Calvinistic Methodists. Under these conditions the Welsh language became the first language in Wales and remained so up to the growth of the public education movement after 1870. [8] Welsh social and political attitudes were expressed and moulded by the growth of a popular Welsh language press in denominational periodicals and newspapers, including, by 1850, fourteen temperance journals.[9] In spite of this development, formal educational provision in Wales was extremely slight, notwithstanding the extension of the circulating schools in the eighteenth century and the establishment of a Works Schools system in which some employers provided elementary schools for their populations in the centres of heavy industries and coalmining.[10] The publication of the notorious *Reports* by the Education Commissioners in 1847, which became known in Wales as the *Treachery of the Blue Books*, 'largely nullified the effect of their report through their mass indictment of the culture, social conditions, religion and morals of the people of Wales';[11] but at least they focused attention on the state of education in the country and had the effect of urging nonconformists to provide undenominational schools to counteract those of the Church, which were spreading rapidly. In time, and not only in the sphere of education, the itinerant methods of the nonconformists proved more suitable than the somewhat static parochial system of the Church in providing for the growing industrial population. This seems to have been particularly true of isolated, single-occupation districts where working-class religious commitment was strong and where a nonconformist denomination could acquire a high degree of identity with the entire community.[12]

Historians of nineteenth-century Wales must acknowledge the pre-eminent position which nonconformity occupied in the life of the country during its industrial evolution. Religion probably exercized a greater influence on the lives of the Welsh people during the last century than was the case in England or in any other Protestant country. Socially and culturally, and often politically, their lives were centred on the chapel; class differences in outlook coincided with religious differences, and this cleavage was intensified by the language barrier.

Mann's religious census of 1851 showed a preponderance of 80 per cent in Wales in attendance at nonconformist chapels on census Sunday, though, significantly, nearly 48 per cent of the population did not attend any religious service.[13] In 1867 it was estimated that there were 3,107 nonconformist chapels available in Wales for a total population of about 1,400,000.[14] Many complaints were made of over-building, and the number of chapels was not a true test of the religious condition of Wales.[15] Many chapels were built under the

influence of sectarian zeal or personal ambition, without due regard
to the heavy debts left upon them.[16] But the chapel—that self-
governing, ecclesiastical republic—was a very important institution
in Welsh communities, for it provided offices of real responsibility
which made status aspiration possible in a society in which status
positions for nonconformists were scarce.[17] For many people, the
chapel became the major centre of cultural activity in their
community. In many chapels five services were held on Sunday, with
further services on three or four week nights. As a writer in the
Calvinistic Methodist *Treasury* in 1881 noted: 'The chapel . . . is the
social centre around which its adherents gather; it is school, lyceum,
club, church, all in one . . . It is round the chapel that not only the
associations common to all forms of Christian faith are wont to
gather, but those which spring from the use of a peculiar and
ancestral tongue.'[18] The writer in *Y Traethodydd* in April 1852 was not
perhaps over-exaggerating when he stated that the Welshman went to
chapel, in part at least, 'to seek for that which the Englishman goes to
the playhouse to look for'.[19]

Chapel influence helped the working population to become more
integrated. It might be suggested that labouring men who drowned
their hardships in drink, who lacked education and possibly a sense of
their individual worth, who might be in turn meek and compliant,
and then desperate and violent, who lacked purpose and vision and
lived almost wholly for the interminable rhythm of their hard labour,
could not expect to rise above the level their birth assigned them.
Nonconformity took hold and shaped some of these men because the
sins it inveighed against were the source of their impotence and the
virtues it extolled were the means of their resurrection. As a
generalization it may be said that a church is likely to be the more
puritanical the closer it is to the masses of uneducated population,
because the need to give some order and discipline to lives which are
not otherwise organized by convention is so great.[20] The inflexibility
of the nonconformist code regarding drinking and nearly all forms of
pleasure may not have offered much scope for personal enjoyment,
but it was the means by which many men found an objective and
secured recognition as well as their self-respect. The chapels produced
many narrow and bigoted people, but what is more important is that
a new standard of personal dignity and self-reliance was presented,
and the rigidity of the discipline had the effect of making men into
more independent and fairly intelligent beings. For, above all,

nonconformity taught the value of the individual soul in the face of his God. The chapel, as a 'moral property', was a very emblem of the community's existence. It attracted men because it gave them something to do; its democratic structure offered scope for the participation and originality of its members; for some, its friendships were the chief source of prosperity in business; it gave the individual duties and obligations and a feeling that he had a share in the consummation of functions. Chapels and Sunday Schools taught the elements of reading and writing and gradually crystallized the canons of moral behaviour. Through the medium of the chapel men learned the art of speaking and organizing. A nonconformist could participate in administering the affairs of his own religious communion; he was, perhaps, able to understand its circumstances, needs and controversies; through its meetings he became acquainted with the conduct of public business; and he was a member of a majority or a minority which tried to make its own opinions prevail. These features helped to make up a political education: the nonconformist was able to look at public affairs with his own eyes; the value of the individual contribution to the collective enterprise was recognized.

* * *

Throughout the nineteenth century the leading spokesmen of Welsh nonconformity contended that Wales in the eighteenth century had been, socially and morally, a land of darkness where ignorance, vice, swearing, gambling, drunkenness and sabbath-breaking prevailed; it was the religious revival of the late-eighteenth and early-nineteenth century which had brought 'pure' religion to the people and sobriety to their conduct.[21] There is a great deal of truth in this contention. Equally true, however, and not necessarily mutually exclusive, is the view which sees the incidence of heavy drinking and drunkenness in Wales shifting from the upper and middle classes to the ever-increasing numbers of the industrial working classes during the first half of the nineteenth century. In the eighteenth century insobriety was distinctly fashionable among the 'middling gentry'.[22] Yet by 1823 one of their number could lament the fact that the 'reign of intoxication is fast drawing to a close. We have no hosts who put the key of the dinner-room in their pockets, no sage philosophers who spend their happiest hours under the table. We are a good-for-nothing set, a crew of pale-blooded milk sops . . . The duty of getting drunk is superseded by the superior duty of the Excise.'[23] He considered that the 'art' of drinking was 'imperative' because it promoted the 'moral healthfulness' of society: 'Without it we are slaves to *ennui*; with it superior intelligences.'[24] Implicit in his comments was a rejection of the view of religious respectability which saw drink and drinking as a matter of popular morality rather than of popular leisure.

The early-nineteenth century was an age when drinking water in Britain was perhaps the most dangerous habit of all.[25] Although untreated water was unsafe to drink, that needed for the manufacture of alcoholic liquor was either boiled in the brewing process or pumped from deep wells. Water was also scarce as well as unsafe. The industrial metropolis of Merthyr Tydfil possessed only three pumps in 1850 when its population was nearly 40,000; the waters of the rivers Taff and Morlais were almost exclusively absorbed by the demands of the ironworks.[26] Up to the late 1850s people at Merthyr had to queue at the local springs for half the night before getting their supply of water, and matters only improved from 1860 when the town launched its system of reservoirs and filter-beds.[27] Milk, too, was almost as dangerous as water during the first half of the century, and the soft drink trade remained in its infancy in Wales up to the 1870s.

An important factor which determined the drinking habits of Welsh people in the early-nineteenth century was that beer was invariably cheaper than tea. In fact tea was a rarity in Wales at this time; De Quincy found the cottagers of Merionethshire still innocent of the habit of tea-drinking in 1802.[28] In north Wales beer cost $1\frac{1}{2}d.$ a pint in 1839 compared with $1d.$ a pint a century earlier.[29] At the end of the French wars in 1815 tea ranged in price in Wales from five shillings to sixteen shillings a pound and quite often very much more: twenty-four shillings a pound for instance in a remote Merioneth village in 1815.[30] The reduction of the duty on tea was proposed as an 'immediate remedy' for drunkenness by the Commons' committee which enquired into the causes of drunkenness among the working classes in 1833-34.[31] Until the growth in popularity and availability of tea and wheaten bread from about the 1840s, the main constituents of meals in rural Wales were buttermilk, taken with potatoes, and oatmeal, with some salted meat and fish when available. Such a bland diet may have produced a listlessness which in its turn created a greater demand for alcoholic stimulant, while it is likely that fish and salt meat made countrymen more thirsty.[32]

Throughout the nineteenth century Wales remained a predominantly beer-drinking country: a comparatively small amount of spirits was consumed. Beer was undoubtedly more widely consumed in the new industrial towns and villages, especially after the repeal of the duty in 1830 brought the price down, than it had formerly been among the scattered peasantry in the Welsh countryside. The public brewer was a comparatively rare figure in Wales until the end of the century and cottage brewing was never very common in the country because so little grain was grown. Home-brewed beer was important, however, in helping to sustain a good relationship between farmers and agricultural labourers on farms in south and mid-Wales. In 1833 130 acres of land were devoted to the cultivation of hops in Wales; of these, 129 acres were found in mid-Wales and only three-quarters of an acre in west Wales.[33] Towards the end of the nineteenth century home-brewed beer declined in importance as a result of the increasing pressure of the company breweries which had been established, albeit very slowly, from mid-century. By the end of the First World War barley production by farmers for the brewing industry had fallen into decline. In 1871 182,000 acres of barley were grown in Wales but by 1891 and 1913 this number had fallen to 124,000 and 92,000 acres respectively.[34] From the 1870s onwards government action decreased the numbers of domestic brewers and special permission or dispensation had to be obtained for home brewing.

Beer fulfilled several important social functions in early-nineteenth century Wales. It was, of course, essentially believed to be a thirst-quencher.[35] It was also thought to impart physical strength and stamina[36]—many recent converts to teetotalism in the 1830s and 1840s expressed surprise that abstention had not weakened them—and, less erroneously, it was thought to kill pain. Beer was an evocative drink which aroused patriotic sentiments in Wales as much as in England during most of the nineteenth century; it connoted the. red-faced John Bull with his foaming tankard, agricultural prosperity and contempt for the wine-drinking Frenchman.[37] At Glynneath in the early years of the century, the 'Lamb and Flag' public house possessed spittoons, the bottoms of which were filled in with portraits of Bonaparte: contempt could not go much further.[38]

Drinking was bound up with the cultural life and tradition of Wales. Rather than being necessarily a personal taste which was the result of conscious choice, the taking of drink, before the temperance movement, constituted a 'system of rule and regulation as to times and occasions' which 'pervades all branches of society in Great Britain—at meals, markets, fairs, baptisms and funerals; and almost every trade and profession has its own code of strict and well-observed laws on this subject. There are numerous occasions when general custom makes the offer and reception of liquor as imperative as the law of the land.'[39] Old drinking customs survived in early-nineteenth century rural Wales as living traditions because of distinctive features present in the life of the countryside. Before the coming of the railway in mid-century there were no serious inroads on the almost self-contained life of country districts, which was based on a high degree of economic subsistence. Above all, drink was associated with the various festivals and days of the calendar, and it also commemorated the chief turning points or 'rites of passage' in the life of a person.

Every Welsh parish had its *gwylmabsant* festival in the eighteenth century and it survived in some areas up to the 1820s. It was the Saint's festival or Saint's day, held on the feast of the patron saint of the parish and it usually marked the beginning and the end of the harvest. The festival usually began on a Saturday and continued until the following Tuesday. The proceedings often included several contests in which the defeated were obliged to supply the victors with beer. Intoxication and fighting seem to have been quite widespread. Some writers have ascribed the later Welsh love of competition in religion, education, literature and music—as enshrined in *eisteddfodau*—to the prominent element of rivalry in the *gwylmabsant*.[40] By the early-nineteenth century this festival had taken on the characteristics of the carnival at the expense of its religious significance. As it became an institution with the sole function of providing recreation it succumbed to the attacks of puritanism. When the strictness of the early-nineteenth century was relaxed the *gwylmabsant* did not revive, yet it is notable that formal recreational activity became once more an adjunct of a religious institution, only this time it was the nonconformist chapel and not the parish church. Many of the characteristics of the *gwylmabsant* were perpetuated in the fair, which was saved from the same fate by the economic service which it provided: that of hiring labour and selling goods. But even so, attendance at the pleasure fair was viewed with disfavour by nonconformists. The Rev. Rhobet Wiliam, a Calvinistic Methodist minister of Llanuwchllyn, 'used to give serious advice before each election and fair for all to behave themselves in a way befitting the gospel of Christ'. [41] When the fair ultimately declined in importance, it was the economic side which suffered most and this was due, not to the opposition of nonconformity, but to the loss of its function of hiring labour and selling livestock. [42]

Warm beer, sometimes mixed with Indian spices, was often consumed in rural Wales at various festivities over the Christmas period—the season for relaxation when the work on the land made least demand on the countryman. In the heart of the winter there were few public assemblies in which the convivial spirit of the season could be released. Hence the numerous house visits for poetic contests or the singing of verses which were maintained for most of the nineteenth century after their religious significance, if any, had been lost. [43] Indeed, Welsh farming communities took advantage of almost every social occasion to prepare quantities of home-brewed beer for domestic requirements. It was customary during the first half of the nineteenth century for beer and cider to be provided for farm labourers at every meal time in Pembrokeshire, south Cardiganshire and west Carmarthenshire, and beer was kept for all informal gatherings as a method of celebrating various tasks accomplished on farms. The hay and corn harvests and the harvest supper were the most important occasions for brewing domestic beer, but much beer was consumed also during the threshing operation and during pig-killing sessions on farms. In Pembrokeshire and west Carmarthenshire a special brew was usually prepared for the day on which pig slaughtering occurred, known as *cwrw bwtshwr,* or beer for the butcher who would be normally a local farmer who specialized in the art of pig-killing. The beer usually consisted of additives like whisky and would be given to the butcher and his assistants before and after the killing. [44]

There were other customs associated with drinking which were restricted to work undertaken by local craftsmen, such as blacksmiths and carpenters. The first, known as *cwrw bando,* was provided by the farmer when the carpenter or wheelwright attended the smithy to complete the task of tireing a wheel. It was an accepted practice that the farmer would supply beer and food for the blacksmith to celebrate the arduous task. The second custom, known as *cwrw cwple,* was celebrated at the final stage of fitting the last trusses on the roof of a building. As a result of temperance influence, the use of beer on such occasions died out towards the end of the nineteenth century, and such celebrations developed into social gatherings, with tea and cakes being provided instead of beer.

The important drinking customs associated with 'rites of passage' originated from the agricultural background and as a result they became natural habits deeply rooted in the everyday life of the inhabitants of rural areas. The consumption of home-brewed beer was an important feature associated with wedding customs, especially the bidding which was almost wholly confined to west Wales. Before a wedding, announcements would be issued soliciting gifts, and informing those who had received such gifts in the past from the parents or relations of the bride or bridegroom that they could now be repaid. The bidding was invariably accompanied by a bid-ale (*cwrw bach*), in which beer would be brewed and sold for considerably more than its market price in order to raise money. Such occasions led to much drunkenness and, more important, facilitated early marriage on an extremely insecure economic basis simply because the money and gifts collected in biddings had to be repaid over the years. In effect, the bidding constituted a primitive form of hire purchase or insurance in which payments were spread over a considerable period of time and the benefits enjoyed at a specific time.[45] A similar collective exercise in self-help consummated by fellowship and drink was the *cwrw bach* or *cwrw gwadd* feast which was held among the poorer members of a community. When any member suffered from a prolonged illness or other misfortune, men and women from the immediate area would organize a feast consisting of beer, bread, cheese and other peasant fare. A charge was made for the food to avoid the possibility of being prosecuted for selling beer, and the money collected was handed over to the family concerned.[46]

Home-brewed beer was also prepared and liberally distributed to mourners and neighbours at funerals; beer was usually given either before the cortège left the house or afterwards, when relations and close friends returned to the house following the service at the chapel or church. This custom died out during the second half of the nineteenth century largely because of the opposition of the temperance movement, but in parts of Cardiganshire beer was still being provided for funerals in the 1880s,[47] while at Llanfechain, Montgomeryshire, spiced beer was distributed at funerals until the middle of the century. Here, an elaborate meal was eaten before the funeral and mourners spent three or four hours smoking shag tobacco and drinking beer in the house before forming the cortège.[48]

Some drinking usages were a result of the exploitation of the intoxicating effects of beer, particularly, of course, on occasions when a person's judgment had to be used. Beer could be used, therefore, as an agent of deceit and persuasion. In north and west Wales during the first half of the nineteenth century a great deal of drinking accompanied sales and auctions, particularly those associated with the letting of tithes.[49] People attending the auction were plied with beer, punch and tobacco, paid for by the local vicar, and when they were sufficiently inebriated, the auctioneer appeared in order to conduct the sale. Each person bidding for a lot was given a glass of beer to drink after each bidding and 'many a one is often surprised on being congratulated the next morning as the taker of one, two or three parcels of tithes'.[50] At Ferryside in Carmarthenshire in the 1860s, the vicar received the tithes of the parish at a public house, and distributed tickets to his parishioners entitling them to so much beer, depending on the amount of tithes paid.[51] By the 1870s, however, this practice was exceptional for with the spread of the influence of the temperance movement drinking customs associated with the church gradually disappeared.

Treating at both contested and uncontested elections was a widespread custom which only finally disappeared after the passage of the Corrupt Practices Bill in 1883. Alcoholic drinks were distributed by candidates and large quantities were often consumed on such occasions. The expenses incurred by a Swansea publican on behalf of Wyndham Lewis, a candidate at the Glamorgan election of 1826, amounted to £65 or 20 per cent of the total election expenses of £362.[52] At the Pembrokeshire elections of 1831 two public houses in Haverfordwest were taken over by the rival candidates as their headquarters.[53] Local publicans sought the patronage of the two sides, and the Whig candidate opened 31 public houses for his supporters. After the elections the publicans submitted their bills. The Whig candidate owed over £15,000, mainly for drink, meal tickets and lodgings. The licensee of his headquarters presented a bill for £1,878, of which £982 was for drink: 42½ barrels of beer, 67 gallons of brandy, 59 gallons of rum, 1,068 bottles of port, and 780 bottles of sherry.[54] At the Caernarfon Borough election of 1832 a huge total of 833 barrels, 7 gallons and 3 pints of beer was consumed, 2,469 gallons, 3 quarts and 1 pint of spirits, and 2,204 bottles of wine.[55] Voters in all constituencies looked forward to elections or visits by their members as opportunities for the heavy drinking they could not afford for themselves at other times. Those who were gathered at Bridgend in 1847 to celebrate the uncontested return of C. R. M. Talbot and Lord Adare, however, were disappointed. 'A considerable sensation' was caused by an announcement, signed by both members, 'who greatly regret that they are disabled from entertaining their friends in the manner heretofore customary', because under the provisions of 5 and 6 Vict., c. 102, 'they could not do so without endangering their return'.[56] But this act applied to parliamentary elections only. At municipal elections, particularly during the period 1850-75, bribery by drink took a more delicate form and voters were plied with drink tickets exchangeable at certain public houses.[57]

Many of these drinking customs and usages gradually came to an end when the shroud of nonconformity descended following the Methodist revival of the late-eighteenth and early-nineteenth centuries. The onset of the Methodist movement led the religious reformers to attack both harmful and harmless recreations indiscriminately. Idle pastimes, it was argued, distracted men from their main task of searching their souls and cultivating their spiritual life in order to work out their salvation; anything which stood in the way of this ideal was condemned as foolish and sinful. Simple-mindedness of purpose in religious matters was now to be regarded as being of overriding importance. Edward Jones, *Bardd y Brenin,* of Merioneth, a collector of traditional Welsh music and poetry, was an extremely hostile witness to this change when he wrote in 1802: 'The sudden decline of the national Minstrelsy and Customs of Wales, is in a great degree to be attributed to the fanatic imposters or illiterate plebeian preachers, who have . . . over-run the country . . . dissuading . . . the common people . . . from their innocent amusements . . . The consequence is, Wales, which was formerly one of the merriest and happiest countries in the World, is now become one of the dullest.'[58]

It has been suggested that the older Dissent in Wales—the Independents and the Baptists—was less antagonistic than the Methodists towards traditional recreations, and that this difference, in part at least, survived the process which infused the older nonconformists with the zeal of the Methodists.[59] Doubtless, old customs and observances for a time were to be found side by side with the newly-founded Methodist 'societies' and the reawakened nonconformist churches of the old Dissent in communities torn between the attractions of two opposing worlds. Later, however, when nonconformity became a majority movement the intense social life of the chapels rather than that of the community as a whole, dominated; people came together more often as members of a chapel than they did as members of the community, and it was the developing secular life of the chapels that ousted the traditional recreations which were alien to the Methodists' outlook on life. [60]

Religious revivalism thus played a major part in helping to smother customs which could be said to foster intemperance. The christening, for instance, became simply a part of a chapel or church service, no longer followed by a drinking bout. The funeral wake succumbed to temperance influences and became a kind of prayer-meeting. Indeed, most of the customs marking the important landmarks in a person's life were gradually shorn of much of their traditional character in response to the influence of social change. Nineteenth-century Welsh Christians came to deplore that recreational complex of behaviour which included drinking, gambling, adultery, cruel sports and sabbath-breaking, all of which had very often taken place together at the drinking place, the 'feast' and the fair. [61]

However, in the new industrial communities, particularly in south Wales, the 'old', eighteenth-century recreations took a longer time to die, and they were indissolubly bound up with the numerous drinking places which were established for the considerable numbers of workmen who flocked to such settlements in the early- and mid-nineteenth century. We find, for instance, that as late as 1843 and 1846, the spring fair at Cefn-coed-y-cymer, near Merthyr Tydfil, was the occasion for people to throng the streets 'reeling, vomiting and quarrelling, in defiance of the distressed state of the times, the restraining of the law, and the precepts of Christianity'. [62] It was not until 1857 that a leading south Wales newspaper felt confident enough to say that the 'brutal and brutalizing pastimes of our ancestors are now gone, never to return; and the Puritanical fanaticism which discountenanced them is now happily relaxing its vigour'. [63]

*   *   *   *

The chapel and the public house constituted the twin foci of most nineteenth-century Welsh communities. Until the 1870s Wales was chronically lacking in recreative counter-attractions to the public house, which thus became the 'people's palace' or a 'masculine republic', providing for many men the only regular, formal opportunity to get out of the house, when they were not at work, and meet each other. For most of the century the public house was, in the words of *Mass Observation* in 1943, 'the only free, non-esoteric, non-exclusive, weather-proof meeting place for the ordinary worker'.[64] With the clientele of most public houses in Wales consisting largely of working men (the better-off having their private cellars and a small number of clubs), some pubs took their names from the predominant occupational group which drank in them. At Merthyr Tydfil, for instance, ironworkers patronised 'The Forge Hammer' and 'The Moulders'; the 'Three Horse Shoes' in Georgetown attracted the smiths (and the Chartists!); the 'Glove and Shears', the farm labourers; and 'The Boot', near the Plymouth works, the cobblers.[65] Obviously, not all drinking in the industrial communities was occupation-specific, but a good deal of it was; and such drinking, it may be argued, was a defence of customary ways of doing things against the forces of religious respectability, which tried to reform the work and leisure of the working man.

Contemporary observers noted with regret the general lack in the new industrial communities of Wales of institutions which might 'elevate' and 'improve' the working man, and the lack of outdoor amenities such as public parks, walks and public baths. Henry Austen Bruce, who was to represent Merthyr Tydfil as a Peelite M.P. from 1852 to 1868 and act as Home Secretary in Gladstone's first Liberal ministry, noted in 1850 that such an important industrial community as Merthyr possessed no gardens, athenaeums and places of recreation, and that the people were left entirely to themselves and their own resources.[66] It is a truism that before any community can obtain adequate social amenities there must be a coherent demand for them on the part of its citizens based on the growth of a collective social conscience or civic pride. The new industrial townships in Wales, up to 1860 at least, had not developed a great sense of community.

The very fact that there were numerous public houses in many towns—more than 200 in the ironworks community of Dowlais alone in 1847—indicated a lack of alternative constructive activity. The *Cardiff and Merthyr Guardian* noted that 'tastes must be created . . . It is not from the mere love of intoxicating liquors that people become drunkards, it is because they have nothing more enjoyable to do than to sit and drink'.[67] Working-class sobriety was to be advocated as a stepping-stone to 'respectability' and as a means of status enhancement: 'As men become more sober the more respectable they become until at length a tone of social opinion is created which does more to root out the evil than all the temperance leagues that ever existed.'[68] Middle-class respectability never tired of suggesting various counter-attractions to the drinking place: a reading society was mooted in Dowlais in the 1830s,[69] working men's allotments in the 1840s and 1850s,[70] and miners' rooms in 1853,[71] but none came to fruition. There were a few Mechanics Institutes in south Wales—only fifteen had been established by 1880—yet the majority of working men sought somewhat easier modes of relaxation than studying such subjects as mathematics, geography and astronomy, which was all the institutes offered.[72] Theatres played a small part in the social life of Welsh people in the nineteenth century; there were none in north Wales up to 1880, and only four in south Wales—at Cardiff, Swansea, Newport and Brecon.[73]

The only institutions which began to flourish in the 1860s and '70s and which provided a recreational rival to the public house were the free libraries with their special newspaper rooms, and the coffee taverns. Twenty-nine Workmen's Libraries were opened in east Glamorgan and Monmouthshire between 1870 and 1895, most of which were financed by voluntary contributions from working men themselves.[74] During the 1870s coffee taverns were established at Newport (1876), and at Swansea (1878) where John Talbot Dillwyn Llewellyn was the main supporter; in the 1880s they spread to Merthyr Tydfil, under the leadership of C. H. James, a Unitarian solicitor, and to Aberdare by 1885.[75] It was hoped that coffee taverns could 'compete with and beat the Publics in cleanliness and comfort' so that 'temperance working men and others would be able to stay in the evenings and recreate themselves for an hour or two; then go to their homes, and be able to rise in the morning with a clear head'.[76] They were regarded as examples of genuine temperance work and the answer to the contemporary exhortation that something more had to be done in the temperance movement than mere pledge-signing and holding meetings to rant and rail against beer and publicans. Moral and mental improvement had to be slowly insinuated rather than rapidly enforced by ceremonial pledge-taking, or by attending lectures on scientific subjects.

With so few competitors the public house was both a popular meeting place for various organizations and an important centre of recreation. Friendly societies were almost dependent on pubs for hospitality. The orders of friendly societies took their origin in areas which felt the earliest impact of the industrial revolution; according to a select committee of the House of Lords in 1831, those counties with ten per cent or over of their population in friendly societies were all of an industrial character.[77] Between 1830 and 1836 111 friendly societies were established in Glamorgan;[78] in 1848 there were 144 friendly societies in Merthyr Tydfil with a total membership of 13,342 or 30 per cent of the population.[79] The great majority of society meetings were held at public houses and invariably the members were expected to pay the publican a 'wet rent'.[80] It was calculated in 1823 that, as a result of friendly society general meetings alone in Britain, £347,039 a year was spent on drink in public houses by working men.[81] The rules of a Glamorgan friendly society provided that 'at the yearly feast 1s. 6d. should be taken from the box for every member, there or not, to be drunk in beer'.[82] During the early 1840s, a Nantyglo friendly society imposed fines on members who refused to drink 'out of the cup'.[83] Generally speaking, however, no accident or illness arising from drinking brought any claims upon the sick funds of the societies.[84]

During the early-nineteenth century in Wales when the temperance movement was in its infancy and when, in some areas, chapels were too expensive to build, religious services were held in public houses. At Rhymney, for instance, services were held in the long room of Rhymney Inn, Protestant services taking place at 9 a.m. and Roman Catholic ones at 11 a.m.[85] Many services of the Wesleyan Methodists were held in public houses in early century through the agency of accommodating publicans. In the late 1830s the Dowlais English Wesleyan Methodist Sunday School met at the Swan Inn;[86] until the erection of a church in 1857 the congregation at Hirwaun worshipped in a public house;[87] the vestry meetings of the parishioners of the parish of Llanfabon between 1865 and 1895 were held at the 'Greyhound Inn', Llanfabon, and the 'Coopers Arms' at Ystrad Mynach.[88] 'The Virgin' public house at Bangor was the early home of nonconformity in the Bangor area; it was here that eight Calvinistic Methodists met in 1802 and held their first 'Seiat'.[89] The Wesleyan Methodists also found refuge at 'The Virgin'; in 1803 when they came to Bangor, the landlady of the pub allowed them to use the horse steps for a pulpit.[90] It is not surprising, therefore, that when the temperance movement appeared, some grateful nonconformist ministers were loath to attack drinking and public houses. [91] In the 1830s and '40s, at Merthyr Tydfil and Rhymney, Father Portal conducted mass in the club rooms of local inns. [92] At Abertillery, where mass was also celebrated in the room of a public house, and where the congregation was recruited from the Irish colliers employed at Cwmtillery, a priest complained that it was 'with the greatest difficulty' that the congregation could be prevented from 'hovering about', though the service had ended, and 'evincing their gratitude' to the landlord when the public house opened, by 'an unlimited consumption' of beer. [93] In 1835 Bishop Baines, the Vicar Apostolic of the Western District, ended the practice of saying mass in public houses in Cardiff as it exposed his flock to what he considered to be the danger of intemperance. [94]

In many different areas of Wales the public house served as the centre of literary and cultural activity. Bangor's first literary society was formed at 'The Eagles' public house in January 1810; in 1813 a branch of the British and Foreign Bible Society was established there. [95] A public house at Nantyglo was the headquarters of *Cymdeithas y Dynolwyr yn Nantyglo* (Nantyglo Humanists' Society), established in 1829. [96] The earliest *eisteddfodau* at Aberdare were held at the Swan Inn in the late 1820s. [97] 'The Stag' Inn at Trecynon nearby was the headquarters of Aberdare Truthseekers Society in 1840. [98] In May 1841 the society held an *eisteddfod* there, and from this dated the *Cymreigyddion y Carw Coch,* under whose auspices the series of *eisteddfodau* of that name was held. The 'Stag' became a notable cultural centre in the Aberdare area and was renowned throughout south Wales as a remarkable intellectual institution. [99] The literary societies in Merthyr Tydfil during the first half of the nineteenth century each held an annual *eisteddfod,* and all were held at local public houses. [100] The pub was also, of course, a centre of amusement and entertainment of a less esoteric nature; harp playing, dancing and singing were popular amusements in Merthyr public houses in the 1840s and '50s, [101] while in some Welsh pubs visiting circus troupes with dwarfs and giants brought in by the publican, provided entertainment. [102]

As meeting places public houses were blamed by middle-class respectability as centres which fostered political disaffection and revolutionary activity. Many believed that revolutionary sentiments developed only in deranged minds and that drink was the most easily accessible deranging influence. Drinking places attracted working people in fairly large numbers and encouraged them to consume a substance which might subvert their customary rational appreciation of the government's power.[103] Many plots were, indeed, hatched in Welsh drinking places whether they were concerned with poaching, Luddism, Scotch Cattle, or Chartist action. The *Cardiff and Merthyr Guardian* was convinced that the beer houses set up after the passing of the Beer Act of 1830 were a major cause of the promotion of Chartist activity in south Wales in the 1830s and early 1840s, as Chartist lodge meetings were often held in such places, which thus became castigated as nurseries for all kinds of evil and wickedness.[104] The newspaper included beer houses with socialists and Chartists as developments the working class should avoid.[105] The Chartist reply was to assert that they usually met in such large numbers that they could not be accommodated in low beer houses; they saw themselves as 'men of considerable influence and they can frequently command the use of rooms connected with large and respectable Inns and licensed Spirit Houses'.[106] Certainly, Chartists frequently met in ordinary public houses simply because a number of publicans were themselves Chartists. The landlord of the 'Three Horse Shoes' in Merthyr was 'a sound Chartist', as were James Horner of the 'Queen Adelaide' in Newport, William Williams, landlord of the 'Prince of Wales', Newbridge and Abraham Evans of 'The Rolling Mill' in Merthyr.[107] In April 1839 the Newport magistrates appealed to the town's publicans 'to allow no meetings of an illegal character to be held in their Houses', and there is sufficient evidence to show that many Chartist meetings were held in both public and beer houses, places which guaranteed good crowds for Chartist orators.[108] The two Merthyr Chartists, Morgan Williams and David John, organized a meeting in March 1842 between Tredegar and Rhymney and arranged to obtain signatures for the Charter at a nearby beer house. Chartist meetings at Merthyr were still being held at the 'Three Horse Shoes' in June 1844.[109]

The temperance reformer's view of the drinking place was that it was a 'hotbed of vice', where crimes were planned, stolen goods received, drunkenness created, and prostitution carried on.[110] The recreational facilities provided by the drinking place were largely ignored; rather, public houses were 'highly mischievous, rearing their aristocratical Fronts in the midst of a humble, industrious and poor population and irradiating forth their devilish attractions to sap the foundations of social. virtue, neatness and comfort'.[111] The newly-established beer houses were even more pernicious, for it was in such houses that 'the youth of our country are corrupted, honesty and virtue are bartered within its precincts, and health and character are drowned in its fatal cup. It is there that . . . deeds subversive of all law and happiness are meditated'.[112] Although many beer houses were well conducted, the very nature of the tenure on which the licences were held was one which had attractions for disreputable members of society. At 'jerries' or *cwrws bach*—beer houses not licensed to sell on the premises but which did nevertheless sell beer—the landlord was at the mercy of his customers, who could inform against him to the Excise, and a heavy fine could be exacted. Such places often became, therefore, favourite resorts for criminals and half-way houses for the disposal of stolen property. There were several such 'receiving houses' for goods stolen in Merthyr Tydfil, north of the town, on the border of Glamorgan and Breconshire.[113]

The proliferation of beer houses in Wales was a direct consequence of the Beer Act of 1830 which was passed as the free traders' remedy for the drink problem. The intention was to make beer accessible and cheap so that once the commodity could be taken for granted, supply would settle down to meet demand and the level of drunkenness would fall. An important factor behind the emancipation of the beer trade was fear of an impending gin age in Britain, for hand in hand with the freeing of the beer trade went an increase in the duties on spirits.[114] The argument of the free traders was that if beer and spirits were sold separately, and if the price of the former was lowered, beer drinkers would be less tempted to switch to spirits. After the Beer Bill had passed its second reading an attempt failed in committee to impose character safeguards for beer sellers. The Act enabled beer houses to be opened by any householder rated to the poor who paid two guineas a year for the licence. The beer could be sold for consumption on or off the premises. Conditions of tenure were similar to those for innkeepers but closing hours in beerhouses were more strictly defined. Any 'respectable' householder could obtain a licence on giving ten days' notice to the collectors and Supervisors of Excise and a sufficient surety of £20, or two of £10. But in practice anyone was enabled to obtain a licence to enable him to sell beer whether the person wishing to do so was a person of respectable character or not. The Sale of Beer Amendment Act of 1834 required the prospective retailer of beer to produce a certificate stating that he was a person of good character and likely to conduct his house in a peaceable and orderly manner. This was to be signed by six resident inhabitants (excluding brewers, publicans and maltsters) rated to the poor at not less than £6 each. The certificate was merely a written statement to the effect that the potential beer seller was a sober and careful person.[115] At Newport in 1838, potential beer retailers surreptitiously filled in the names of working men on blank surety certificates—people who could not be compelled to pay any debts contracted in their name.[116]

The Beer Act increased the facilities for the consumption of beer in an attempt to 'introduce a better beverage into the country for all the subordinate ranks of society', and to put an end to the publicans' practice of adulterating their beer.[117] But it seems unlikely that this particular aim was achieved. The government's policy of taxing the ingredients of beer—malt and hops—but leaving beer, the finished product, free of charge, held out a strong inducement to make beer of anything but malt. Owen Roberts, a Caernarfon surgeon, testified before the Parliamentary Committee on drunkenness in 1834, that the beer sold in Caernarfon was not composed of malt and hops only but that other drugs such as *cocculus indicus* and *nux vomica* were used. This enabled the beer to be made at a cheaper rate, but also made it more intoxicating.[118] By encouraging competition there is little doubt that the Beer Act accentuated the problem of the adulteration of drink. While it is true that consumption of drink is no proof of drunkenness, it is likely that the increased facilities for drinking brought about by the Act of 1830 resulted in an increased level of intoxication, at least during the 1830s. Many beerhouse keepers were guilty of serving highly adulterated brews which were invariably more intoxicating than home-brewed beer. Moreover, with a greater number of drinking places established, the Excise found it increasingly difficult to keep the necessary check on adulteration.

Between 1830 and 1832 the number of persons licensed for the general sale of beer in Wales increased in three of the four Excise Collections as follows:

	1830-31	*1831-32*
East Wales	639	1,116
Middle Wales	156	194
West Wales	158	1,226

The smallest increase occurred in the thinly-populated and predominantly rural mid-Wales area; indeed, in the largely rural

North Wales Collection, the number of persons licensed actually decreased between 1830 and 1832, from 289 to 273, and potential beer-sellers here were slow to take advantage of the new act. The total number of persons licensed in Wales during this three-year period increased from 1,242 to 2,809.[119] Later during the decade each collection witnessed a notable increase. Taking the example of Bangor we find that in 1829 there were 30 public houses in the district, 24 in the town and 6 in the country around the town; in 1836 there were 110 public and beer houses in the area: 95 in the town and 15 in the country.[120] It was argued that the drink trade, being so profitable and so easy to enter, enticed men away from their usual trades.[121] At Aberdare in the autumn of 1830, a number of beer houses were opened by speculators from outside the parish, and in 1831 the Aberdare Vestry unanimously agreed to petition the magistrate acting for the Hundred that henceforth beer house licences should be refused to persons who were not legal parishioners.[122] By the end of January 1831 the number of beer houses licensed under the Act of 1830 at Abergavenny was 240.[123] In 1839 there were 200 beer houses alone in Merthyr Tydfil; at Blackwood in Monmouthshire 124 beer houses catered for a population of 622 in 1842, a ratio of one beer house to every 5 people.[124] In some areas, the increased facilities for obtaining beer led to an increased demand for spirits, which were occasionally illegally introduced into the beer houses. In Newport two regular public houses were compelled to open a spirits shop in order to make up for the diminution in the sale of beer as a consequence of the number of beer houses opened around them.[125] In parts of England, but not in predominantly beer-drinking Wales, the publican's need to compete with beer houses in this manner helped to create the gin palace. Among Merthyr tradesmen it became a general practice to 'add the business of selling intoxicating drink to those respectable branches of trade which they may have formerly carried on. Grocers, shoemakers, and chandlers are smitten with the beer-selling mania.'[126] The ease with which beer could be obtained led many workmen to eat their mid-day meal at a beer house and not at the scene of their labours.[127] According to contemporaries, the overall result of the beer house system in the 1830s and early '40s was a general increase in the incidence of drunkenness.[128]

It must be said, however, that free traders had always *expected* a temporary increase in drunkenness until people had adjusted to the new situation. Gross consumption figures in England and Wales show a modest rise in gross malt consumption which levelled off by about 1840. This might have been a result of a switch from spirits to beer during the 1830s, a development eagerly sought for by the framers of the Beer Act.

The Welsh beer house catered for only the humblest type of labourer. Physically, it resembled a cottage rather than a public house and its owner was recruited from a lower social grade than the publican; in the mining areas of Wales 'butties', or sub-contractors for labour, often took a beer house. Most Welsh opponents of the proliferating beer houses in industrial Wales in the 1830s and early '40s took exception to their recreational facilities rather than increased drink consumption. Clerical opponents of beer houses criticized the sabbath-breaking, cruel sports and gambling which were carried on in such houses. Doubtless, the beer seller's shorter opening hours and, strictly, his inability to sell spirits exposed him to temptations not experienced by publicans. [129]

One of the attractions of opening a beer house was that it was a way of getting on to the electoral register. In order to remedy some of the defects of the beer house system a clause in the Sale of Beer Amendment Act of 1834 stated that no licence for a beer house would be granted after April 1836 for any houses except those rated at £10 a year. An act of 1841 provided that no householder should have a licence for a beer house unless he was rated to the relief of the poor as high as £15 (if the population was above 5,000), the object being to have responsible and respectable householders as beer-house keepers. The property qualification introduced by the Reform Act of 1832 was prohibitive to the majority of working men. In Merthyr Tydfil in 1832, for example, there were only 569 houses of the rateable value of £10 and upwards and these were 'in a very great proportion made up of labourers' cottages, or of small Ale-houses and Beer-shops, or of Retail shops, for supplying the wants of a population in which the higher and middle orders from a very small ingredient'. [130] Because of the fluctuating movement in numbers of the population, responding to variations in the prosperity of the numerous ironworks in the area, the rents of the houses were subject to sudden and great changes. 'A falling off in the labouring population does not indeed make vacant many houses of £10 value, but it converts numerous Houses from being Beer-shops or Retail Shops into mere Dwelling Houses, a change which almost invariably sinks the Houses below the annual value of £10'. [131] That most business premises and middle-class dwellings could readily command a sufficient value to qualify their occupiers to vote is clearly shown by a return of the voters in the borough of Merthyr in 1836 and 1837. The number of voters in both years was 582, and the right to vote was claimed in respect of 223 houses, 104 beer houses, 81 shops, 35 public houses, 35 houses and shops, 35 farms, 26 inns, 17 houses and gardens, 16 houses and land, 3 houses and workshops, while the following each accounted for one vote: a house, shop and beerhouse; a skinner's yard; a warehouse; a brewery; a canal yard; a mill, and a pottery house. Thus the majority of voters in the borough were small traders and publicans and beer-house keepers. [132]

In his reports in the *Morning Chronicle* in 1850, Henry Mayhew's Welsh correspondent stated that Merthyr Tydfil and Dowlais possessed a total of 305 licensed drinking places: 98 public houses and inns and 207 beer houses. [133] He found, on analysing the list of persons entitled to vote in the borough, that of a total of 643 voters, 1 in every $3\frac{1}{2}$ was a publican or beer-house keeper. But he also found that the regulation governing the amount of rating required for keeping a beer house was not strictly adhered to in the town.

> The manner in which the spirit and intention of the Act is violated in this neighbourhood is this. A man living in a row of workmen's houses, whose rent is £7 a year, determines on keeping a beer house. He goes to his neighbours who certify he is a respectable man. He then builds a small shed at the back of his house to give colour to his application to be rated at £15. He now goes to the overseer and calls on him to rate him at that sum, saying he has made additions to the premises. Only too happy to have a contribution to the rate in this increased amount, the overseer rates him as requested; he next applies to the Excise who have nothing to do but grant him a licence, and there is at once another source of temptation created in the neighbourhood. I may add, another voter is also made, who may be easily controlled. I noted in Dowlais the names of two beershops of the same height and size, and of the same roofage as the houses adjoining in the same row, the rents of the neighbouring houses being, as I learnt from the tenants, from £7-£8 a year. If the beer house had been doubled in size, its rental would not have amounted to the statutable requirement, for the population of Dowlais is thrice 5,000. [134]

It was not until November 1870 that the Merthyr Guardians decided to secure the proper assessment of drinking places in the town. [135]

What may be postulated as being the likely causes of drunkenness in industrial Wales in the nineteenth century? Although there was no

unequivocal correlation between increased drinking and drunkenness
and the process of industrialization in the early-nineteenth century,
drink was certainly thought to impart physical stamina and was
closely associated with strenuous trades. [136] The stimulating effects of
drink could temporarily dull the fatigue resulting from long hours
and hard labour. It seems likely, further, that the wretchedness
created by an industrial environment was a major cause of
intemperance. This 'environmentalist' view sees drunkenness as 'the
shortest route out of Manchester' (or indeed, out of Merthyr Tydfil),
a view held by many contemporaries, including Engels who, in his
Condition of the Working Class in England (1844), maintained that a
capitalist society and sobriety were incompatible. [137] In his report on
the sanitary condition of the labouring population in 1842 Edwin
Chadwick showed how the health and conduct of the working classes
were adversely affected and their habits debased by urban
overcrowding and inadequate sanitation. The 'environmentalist'
view was neatly encapsulated by two sociologists writing in 1921:
'When positive increments of happiness are excluded, some
decrement of present misery, by a blunting of the psychic
sensitiveness to the discomfort of environment, is afforded by a
narcotic drug.' [138] Intemperance was a cause of poverty but poverty
was also a cause of intemperance in that the hopelessness of
destitution demanded a short cut to oblivion. Throughout the
nineteenth century the areas of greatest drunkenness in Britain
coincided with the big coalfields where the mode of industrial
employment concentrated drinking at the week-ends. [139]

In what other ways might industrialization make sobriety less
feasible? Dr. B. Harrison has shown how industrialization might
increase the temptations to drink by accentuating cyclical and
technological unemployment; and unexpected idleness was the
gateway to sin. [140] Industrialization created new occupations such as
iron smelting, which exposed workmen to extremes of temperature,
and it facilitated drunkenness by forcing migrant labourers into a
strange environment—as in the industrial centres of Glamorgan and
Monmouthshire—and so weakened traditional sanctions on
conduct. [141] The new industrial regime in Wales led to an increase in
psychological strain together with an increase in the monotony of
work:

> We are caged up like so many birds until night comes, and when we
> are liberated from our tedious engagements, we are let out into the

streets like 'birds of prey', for by the time we finish it is time to go to bed, we must either perambulate the streets or go to the Public Houses, where it is that much amusement can be got in the least possible time, to forget the annoyance of the day. We have a Young Men's Improvement Society and a Mechanics Institute, but we cannot avail ourselves of them. [142]

In some ways, of course, industrialization made sobriety more feasible in that the change in the methods of production produced a social group which had a direct economic interest in curbing drunkenness. Also, the development of the factory meant that some work was carried out indoors away from the elements of the weather.

It seems certain that a period of time elapsed following the attainment of more regular, higher wages, until new customs of expenditure and a new social discipline emerged in response to industrial employment and urban living. This time-lag was as much a question of the delays in the development of opportunities for spending in new ways as in the habits of so doing. A problem of intemperance resulted, for as Professor Mathias has written: 'When men have inherited largely fixed patterns of expenditure and an accustomed style of living, an increment in wages is very likely to be dispersed on leisure and liquor.' [143]

Contemporaries believed that life in industrial Wales was inimical to sobriety. They pointed primarily to degradation caused by severe and heavy labour, overcrowding and insanitation. In the iron industry in particular, the burden of work placed on men was held to be detrimental to health. Work caused degradation and relief was sought in stimulants. 'The man spent with labour and cut off by his condition from higher pleasures', intoned the *Monmouthshire Merlin* in September 1837, 'is impelled to seek a deceitful solace in sensual excess.' [144] In a word, heavy toil made people live for 'the present moment and the body'. [145] Most improvers believed that the answer was to change society so as to prevent an excessive pressure and work-load on the labouring class, and that 'inward spiritual improvement', not legislation, was the answer. [146] Degradation by work caused a lack of self-respect among working men. As wealth was seen by some as an object of worship and the measure of a man's importance, there was a tendency to 'self-contempt' and 'self-abandonment' among those who did not possess it; lack of self-respect meant the lack of a powerful protection against 'low vices'. [147]

Work in industrial south Wales was often highly dangerous as well as onerous. During the years 1841-7 the deaths by industrial accident in Merthyr Tydfil, with its population at this time of between 35,000 and 42,000, averaged 50 a year.[148] The average age of death of firemen in the town during 1847 was 38 years, that of colliers and miners 42 years, both dying largely of pulmonary diseases.[149] Firemen in the ironworks were subjected to extremes of temperature and encountered the danger from blow-backs of the furnaces and overflows of molten metals, while colliers spent almost half their time working in an atmosphere loaded with firedamp and coal dust.[150] The surgeon at the Dowlais Iron Company in 1850 commented on the great number of accidents at the Works among young people, above and below ground, which necessitated amputation.[151] In 1866 a total of 1,760 children between the ages of 10 and 18 years worked for the Dowlais company and, thus, young people were initiated into dangerous working conditions and, possibly, drinking habits early in their lives.[152]

We have seen that the industrialization of south Wales during the first half of the nineteenth century brought great numbers of migrant labourers into the area who were thus freed from the restraints of a settled home and much prone to drunkenness.[153] Most of the migrants came from the surrounding rural counties of Wales and many migrated from valley to valley. They provided the turbulent elements which were a disruptive force in local social life and in industrial relations. They lived together clannishly. Most of them were unmarried, and their lack of responsibility and social interest did not stimulate any movement for improved living and housing conditions, largely because they had no intention of taking up permanent residence; they merely found accommodation in the cheapest possible quarters as lodgers. These elements were too diverse to assimilate into the community rapidly. They frequently lived in overcrowded slum conditions and had little respect for sobriety.

Urban overcrowding was a major factor in driving men to the public house.[154] The unhealthy environment of industrial communities in south Wales in the nineteenth century was a direct consequence both of the sheer lack of housing and also the nature of house construction itself. Settlement patterns tended to take on nucleated characteristics. Houses were built back to back, giving rise to courts and *culs-de-sac*—features of a nucleated congestion rather than the more orthodox elongated type of development. Male migrants invariably lodged with resident families, thus causing a more intensive use of existing houseroom.[155] The housing situation in rural Wales was no better. The movement from a rural to an urban environment was not automatically accompanied by a worsening of housing and social conditions; indeed the condition of the country labourer was deplorable.[156] The people who built town houses in early-nineteenth century Wales were predominantly local craftsmen, who probably used plans which had been common in the Welsh countryside for centuries. The rows of houses, which were frequently without means of sanitation and were badly ventilated, directly resembled their rural counterparts. In most cases they were merely country cottages laid end to end. The ideas which had been used in the construction of dwellings in rural environments were merely implemented in an urban setting, with dire results in home economy and comfort. The workmen who were responsible for the dwellings possessed technical attainments which were based on empiricism and rough-and-ready rule of thumb. They were very little disposed or equipped to consider the housing needs of an urban community.

At least in the early nineteenth century there was a correlation between overcrowding and disease. Typhus and cholera were 'the poor men's diseases'—the products of squalor, overcrowding and insanitation. Great fear was generated during visitations of the cholera and much liquor was consumed as an anaesthetic. John Evans, the manager of the Dowlais Iron Company, informed Lady Charlotte Guest in September 1854: 'The disease is spreading . . . it attacks all the dirty courts and gulleys and the overcrowded houses . . . There is great excitement in the place, and worse than all, the drunkenness is beyond everything, worse than ever, and all from spirits'.[157] Conversely, many temperance advocates believed that drinking caused numerous diseases; that some of those who contracted diseases were in the habit of spending so much of their money on drink, especially at pay time, that they were half-starved during the rest of the week, and thus became easy victims.[158]

The town of Merthyr Tydfil, the *locus classicus* for the growth of industrialization in nineteenth-century Wales and the *raison d'être* of Cardiff, provides a useful case study for a more detailed discussion of the environmental factors behind drinking and drunkenness in industrial Wales in the nineteenth century. Although Merthyr was not 'Wales' in the nineteenth century, the conditions of life in early industrial Wales found their most intense expression in the town.

Merthyr seemed to suffer all the common social ills in excess. This was a result of the peculiar economic circumstances upon which the life of the town was based. Merthyr's whole fortune hinged on the iron and coal industries. What was elsewhere a process of the more or less gradual industrialization of an established community was reversed in Merthyr, so that the industry preceded the town—the town was called into being only by the demands of industry. [159] The industrial revolution in Merthyr Tydfil brought thousands of workers together, but little attention was paid to the problems of man as a social animal and as a worker labouring in co-operative effort with his fellow man. Consequently, many of Merthyr's social and economic problems reflected the human adjustments which had to be undergone in an era of swift industrial change.

Between 1801 and 1851 the population of Merthyr increased by nearly 40,000; the decades of greatest growth were the 1830s and 1840s, which saw an increase of nearly 25,000. [160] Much of the increase in population was caused by migration: 'The youth of Wales directed their footsteps to that El Dorado among the hills . . . It was as if a conscription had called away the strongest and most daring from the families of the poor.' [161] Taking the years between 1831 and 1841, the population figures for Merthyr showed an increased rate of 1,518 a year, two-thirds of which was caused by migration. [162] Between January 1839 and December 1843 the natural rate of increase in Merthyr was 522 a year. [163] T. W. Rammell calculated in 1850 that, of the increase in population in the town of approximately 10,000 between 1841 and 1847, 'about 6,400 must have been caused by migration from other parts'. [164] Migration increased in times of economic prosperity: the Brecon road leading into the town from the north was known as the wages-barometer of Merthyr. [165] Part of the migrating elements, particularly whole families, contributed to the permanent increase in the population of the town, and were integrated into the community. Alternatively, others, mostly unskilled single men constituting mere muscles of industry, formed a group of migrating labourers which formed an unsettled and constantly moving population. The migrants usually consisted of green labour from the Welsh countryside. Many of them were vagrants attracted to Merthyr during the winter months by the cheapness of fuel and, until 1852, by the lack of workhouses in which the labour test could be applied to those seeking food and lodging. [166] The arrival of the Irish in the coalfield, which reached its peak in the late 1840s, exacerbated the problem; in 1851 it was estimated that the Irish immigrants in south Wales in the 1840s numbered 9,700, and in the same year the Irish element in the population of Merthyr amounted to approximately 9 per cent.[167] Their presence caused open dissension and considerable physical violence as the Welsh workmen believed that Irishmen were willing to work for lower wages, and that they imported diseases.[168] Certainly, the Irish usually found their way into the lowest-paid occupations in Merthyr such as patchmen; they were largely employed by sub-contractors and occupied the lowest rented dwellings in the most unhealthy parts of the town.[169]

Merthyr was essentially a working-class town. The most stable element in the community was provided by skilled working men owing to the absence of a developed middle class.[170] There was no growth of any substantial professional section up to 1851, at least, and although Merthyr was better endowed with shopkeepers and small traders than any other towns on the coalfield, there were never enough of them to constitute a third tier between ironmaster and operative.[171] In fact, what could be called a middle-class element amounted to only one per cent of the population in 1851;[172] once having made an appreciable sum of money men tended to leave Merthyr for 'some other more agreeable or more healthy place'.[173]

As T. W. Rammell noted in 1850, one important result of this phenomenon was an 'absence of those civil relations and institutions which exist in more mixed commercial communities'.[174] During the 1830s and '40s it was taken for granted that social conditions should be related to the needs of industry rather than of agriculture, of the town rather than the country. The Municipal Corporations Act of 1835, the health of towns campaign and legislation covering the poor law and education are evidence of the effort to provide the growing towns with public services and amenities specifically planned to meet the requirements of an industrial community. But there was in Merthyr no rapidly-increasing business class with organizing ability; there was a relative lack in the town of individuals who could organize and establish concerns which needed financial resources and administrative ability. Consequently, Merthyr chronically lacked basic public amenities. Until the early 1850s, at least, the town possessed no hospital, no fire engine, no parochial schools, no workhouse, no Board of Health, and no paving and lighting commissioners.[175] A police force was not established until 1841, and the lack of gas lighting in the town proved a great hindrance to the detection of cases of drunkenness and other petty offences.[176] During the first half of the century the pattern of recreation in Merthyr changed from 'invigorating and manly exercises' such as gardening, tennis, fishing and badger-baiting, to 'indoor indulgences' such as drinking and gambling, and to religious services and Sunday School activities, as the public house and the chapel emerged as the major centres of social intercourse in the town.[177]

For the greater part of the century Merthyr constituted a large cottage town of unplanned streets and houses with very few large civic buildings.[178] In 1832, with a population of over 22,000, it consisted of 4,637 houses, only 560 of which possessed an annual value of £10 or more.[179] What factors determined the scope and nature of house building in the town? Apart from the obvious factors of topographical restriction and the increase in population, there were a number of competitors for space whose demands were less tractable than those of labour, and equal in importance, one of the most significant being the industrial waste.[180] Moreover, a large part of the level terrain was used for tramways, and much of the land available for buildings was also very valuable as a source of mineral deposits. Thus, land which was available for housing had to be intensively used. Another important factor was that the quality of the buildings erected varied directly with the capital resources of the builder. The houses built by private speculators, whose interest in the dwellings extended as far as the rental they received, were grossly inadequate compared with the houses built by the iron companies.[181] The former were erected with the sole purpose of maximising a return upon the capital invested; they were built piece-meal, with no consistent pattern or regard for the basic amenities of drainage, space and ventilation. The congested housing of Merthyr constantly increased simply because it was a profitable commercial investment. Courts and alleys existed because they were part of the economy of buildings which had to pay a good percentage to attract loanable funds. It was natural that this should be so. The highest financial return possible was expected from a given area of land. If the houses had been built with a more spacious frontage the capital outlay would have been greater, the dividends of property investment would have fallen and capital would not have been attracted in significant amounts. Dwellings, however deplorable in quality, were in demand; dilapidation, in this context, merely meant lower costs. Thus, in some measure, financial and speculative considerations meant that houses built close together increased, and speculators, receiving substantial dividends out of the congestion, had little incentive to improve. Last, the congested conditions which were profitable to the builders were also, of course, cheaper to the tenants. The majority of migrants who came to Merthyr possessed little industrial skill, and as a consequence, their rates of wages were low. They were also the first to become unemployed in times of depression. This class of low-paid labour was in the majority, and, as such, constituted the main element in the effective demand for house room. Their accommodation was limited to the cheapest dwelling they could rent, and the quality and nature of the building were subordinated to the consideration of cheapness. Even if, in times of full employment and prosperity, they could have afforded a better class of dwelling, they could never have rented it in time of depression. Thus, the income factor had a depressing effect upon quality.

The worst housing conditions were in the 'cellars' of 'China' at Pont Storehouse, that area of the town lying between the High Street and the River Taff, and containing about 1,500 people in 1845, a large proportion being vagrants, prostitutes and criminals.[182] The houses here consisted of two storeys situated in a deep depression so that the houses were often lower than the level of the road. They were mere huts of stone, ill-lit, ill-ventilated and without privies, and they formed a maze of courts and narrow roadways, hardly passable in many places for heaps of house refuse, rubbish and filth, which moved slowly along the lanes.[183] Most houses in Merthyr seem to have been subject to overcrowding; many belonging to the Dowlais Iron Company housed twelve inhabitants.[184] Contemporary opinion was certain that the sheer discomfort of home led many to the drinking place where they sought 'society, change, relaxation or excitement'.[185] The belief was that housing must be improved in order to encourage home drinking because 'men do not get drunk over a pint of beer at dinner or supper'.[186]

In 1847 Merthyr was described as 'the most unhealthy town in Wales';[187] in 1850, as the second most unhealthy town in Britain, after Liverpool.[188] The drainage of the town was sadly deficient. In 1850, with a population of about 50,000, there was no public sewer or drain in the town, even though its topography afforded every facility for sewerage and for cleansing the streets.[189] All rubbish was thrown into open gutters in front of the houses, so that parts of the town were 'complete networks of filth, emitting noxious exhalations'.[190] As has been mentioned, until the early 1860s there was no public supply of water, the reservoirs above the town being utilized for the ironworks only. Water for domestic purposes was obtained from pumps and wells, but most of the latter were fed by surface waters intermingled with house refuse.[191] Water was also obtained from rain-water in casks and butts, and from the canal, which was supplied from the Taff and from the Penydarren fish-pond.[192] This water was, however, impure, being composed largely of diluted mud 'absolutely in motion with living organisms'.[193] Although water for brewing in Merthyr was sifted and boiled in the brewing process, it was taken largely from mountain ponds in which were often found dead animals.[194]

Disease in Merthyr occurred almost entirely amongst working people, due largely to inadequate sanitation.[195] The cholera epidemic of July-October 1849, attacked 3,624 people in the town, of whom 1,524 died, or one death to every 28 of the population.[196] The disease raged with great virulence in Dowlais and Penydarren, districts which were higher and more open than the centre of the town, but which were more neglected and more filthy than the lower parts.[197] One must agree with the comment of a knowledgeable visitor to Merthyr in 1850 that there existed in the industrial areas of south Wales 'some active causes prejudicial to human life' which tended to 'the unhappiness and physical depression of the poor'.[198] To ameliorate such harsh social conditions would have sorely tried the resources of the most stable community, and this the newly-industrialized town of Merthyr Tydfil was not. As the Hammonds wrote: 'Most of the big towns had the administrative equipment of villages', and Merthyr was no exception.[199]

Drunkenness seems to have been widespread in Merthyr throughout the century. Certainly, ample facilities for drink existed. In 1854 Merthyr possessed 506 drinking places excluding unlicensed *cwrws bach*: 298 beer houses and 208 public houses; this was a huge increase of over 200 in the number of drinking places found by Henry Mayhew's correspondent in 1850, and it gave a ratio of one drinking place to every 93 of the population.[200] Accounts of convictions for drunkenness in the local press during the 1830s reveal the almost exclusive incidence of drunkenness amongst the working class: men following the occupations of miner, collier, puddler, blacksmith, patchman, roller, labourer and haulier, are particularly prominent.[201] Illegal drinking places flourished; between

25 October and 1 November, 1833 nine convictions were secured for keeping *cwrws bach* and for beer-house keepers opening their houses during prohibited hours;[202] between 16 and 23 April, 1834 eight convictions were secured;[203] during the first week of December 1837, nine convictions were made.[204] Fifty-two owners of beer houses were summonsed during the period June-September 1846,[205] and in general, throughout the 1840s, beer house offences were four times as numerous as public house offences. Those police statistics of drunkenness that are available (see Table 1) show that during the period from 1842 to 1860 drunkenness in the Merthyr police district ran at an annual average of 58 per cent of the Glamorgan total, and that during the years from 1868 to 1888 the average amount of drunkenness in the Merthyr district declined to 40 per cent of the Glamorgan total.[206] The police returns included those persons summonsed, tried and convicted or discharged, in an area including Merthyr with Dowlais and the surrounding towns and villages of Aberdare, Aberaman, Cwmbach, Hirwaun, Deri, Pontlottyn, Mountain Ash, Penrhiwceiber and Treharris. The police themselves attributed the high incidence of drunkenness in the county of Glamorgan to the demand for labour and consequent migration to the area.[207]

In late-eighteenth century Wales the inseparability of drinking from customary recreations made it difficult to obtain the precise and regular workmanship which was a key requirement of the new industrial system. The frequent complaints about working-class drunkenness in early-nineteenth century Wales were as much indications that the ancient inseparability of work and recreation had become inconvenient as that drunkenness had become more prevalent. Early industrialists needed to create a smooth working rhythm and to induce employees to be accurate and punctual. Some of them, therefore, strove to dissociate work from recreation, and tried to deprive work of its traditional 'play' element.[208]

Thus, the development of an industrial society in Wales entailed a radical restructuring of working habits. Men who were accustomed to work for subsistence, not for maximization of income, had to be made obedient to the cash stimulus. What was needed was regularity and steady intensity in place of irregular spurts of work, and accuracy and standardization in place of individual design.[209] Migrants coming from agricultural or domestic industry did not at first take kindly to the harshness and monotony of the new industrial life; at

TABLE 1. ANNUAL RETURNS OF PERSONS SUMMONSED, TRIED, CONVICTED OR DISCHARGED FOR DRUNKENNESS BY THE GLAMORGAN POLICE, 1842-1860, 1868-1888

Year	Glamorgan Total	Merthyr Total	Merthyr Percentage
1842-43	179	133	74
1843-44	126 (3 quarters only)	78	62.1
1844-45	140	62	44.2
1845-46	130 (3 quarters only)	42	35
1846-47	231	104	47.2
1847-48	318	192	64
1848-49	177 (3 quarters only)	115	65.8
1849-50	147 (3 quarters only)	99	66
1850-51	219	142	64.4
1851-52	234	124	56.4
1852-53	157 (3 quarters only)	96	64
1853-54	118 (2 quarters only)	55	45.9
1854-55	221 (3 quarters only)	110	50
1855-56	316	198	66
1856-57	517	368	83
1857-58	816	588	73.4
1858-59	811	527	66
1859-60	222 (1 quarter only)	153	76.1
1868-69	1,008	382	38
1869-70	244 (1 quarter only)	139	69.1
1871-72	1,208 (3 quarters only)	598	50
1872-73	2,584 (3 quarters only)	1,144	47.4
1873-74	3,551	1,586	45.2
1874-75	2,205 (3 quarters only)	745	37
1875-76	2,437	642	28
1876-77	1,523 (3 quarters only)	428	30.4
1877-78	—	—	—
1878-79	1,947	830	41.1
1879-80	1,636 (3 quarters only)	667	42
1880-81	2,328	965	48
1881-82	2,805	1,107	39.2
1882-83	3,099	992	33
1883-84	2,854	946	34
1884-85	3,277	1,092	36.1
1885-86	2,763	925	37
1886-87	2,790	1,044	37.1
1887-88	3,202	977	30.1

Source: Glamorgan Record Office, Q Em. Box 7, 1/9F, Chief Constable of Glamorgan, Reports and Quarterly Returns, 1842-60, 1868-88. For the care with which police statistics of drunkenness must be handled, see p. 46.

*   *   *   *

least the domestic system had allowed a certain degree of personal liberty and command over a man's time.[210] The employers' most serious problem now was to build up a stable supply of efficient and willing labour, but many workers were described as 'transient, marginal and deviant', or else as 'volatile'.[211] The reasons for the repulsion of factory industry were not all economic. There was a new culture to be absorbed and an old one to be spurned. For many, there was a new environment to face: different relations with employers, new uncertainties of livelihood, new friends and neighbours. Little wonder that the problem was often seen in moral terms.[212]

During the first half of the nineteenth century, the concept of respectability became a powerful force among Welsh workmen, and work discipline was not seen solely as a means of filling the capitalist's pockets. The employers' preoccupation with the morals and manners of their work forces is understandable, for under the conditions of early industrialism the workers were not usually sensitive to the kind of inducements which employers could provide. Workmen did not possess the ambition to work hard so as to command an income higher than that required for subsistence. They had to be made ambitious and 'respectable'. No incentive would be effectual unless workmen wished positively to become 'respectable'. If, in the employers' view, then, most workmen lacked the essential qualities of industry, obedience, sobriety and thrift, they might well be deaf to the exhortations to moral perfection which some employers felt they had to make. The only solution was to indoctrinate the worker with the bourgeois values he lacked.[213] At Dowlais, for example, ironmaster John Guest's urge to make the workers 'respectable' was expressed in the loans for houses granted to privileged workers. Such a move provided much-needed stability for this turbulent community.[214] To attempt such a reformation from above might seem to us today to be an awesomely difficult task. Yet, it was not such a utopian aim if one remembers that not only was there a vital need to inculcate a new discipline into the first few generations of industrial workers, but also that the employer in the period of the Industrial Revolution assumed responsibility for functions which are now provided by public authorities: road-building, education and health.

The basic problem was how to recruit enough skilled and reliable labour and how to overcome the aversion of workers from the unaccustomed rules and discipline in the large industrial enterprises. The Industrial Revolution in Britain was interrupted by major wars with their special demands for labour, and consequently, its problems were exceptionally acute.[215] It is clear that there was not enough free labour available for the new works until the 1820s. Welsh coalowners in the early-nineteenth century were forced to employ numbers of highly disreputable workmen because of the scarcity of any free labour.[216] The iron works at Merthyr Tydfil during this period were reputed to employ runaways and criminals. The shortage of labour meant that furnaces would not be blown out in slack times, for 'the men once lost would be with difficulty regained'.[217] It is not surprising that in such circumstances poaching of labour was quite common in the early decades of the nineteenth century. At Merthyr, at least Bailey, Homfray and Guest, among the ironmasters, were guilty of this malpractice.[218] Drunkenness could be a serious problem among skilled workers who were paid enough to be able to afford it and who were scarce enough not to be dismissed too easily.[219] In eighteenth-century Wales the problem of retaining skilled labour was solved by the extensive use of contracts by which individual workers bound themselves to work for their employers for a stated period of time. But the great iron concerns of south Wales did not continue the practice for very long after the beginning of the nineteenth century. The extent to which they expanded made the continued use of the bond impracticable and the fluctuations in the iron trade made its disappearance an advantage to the ironmaster. However, the masters had a useful instrument available in the form of the truck system, under which debts bound the debtor to the company until they were paid. This was a substantial benefit in view of the workers' migratory tendencies. The truck system was therefore used, in part at least, as a means of keeping the labour force intact.[220]

Most employers realized that the most productive workmen were steady, sober and temperate, and they believed that it was obviously in their interest to have a sober work force. As a group, industrialists maintained that they suffered great losses through the drunken habits of their workmen. Drunkenness prolonged business depression because it made impossible an effective demand for the comforts of life and was destructive of all trades except one. Yet industrialists were precisely concerned with the extension of the home market for consumer goods; and in their attitude to the drinking habits of their work-forces they strove to divert attention from criticism of industrial society to criticism of the individual sinner. The temperance movement received support from industrialists because it induced working people to conserve their own resources; a sober working class would be able to support itself during unemployment, and ratepayers would no longer have to pay out poor relief. [221]

In the decade 1835-45 the productive industry of Britain was computed to be worth an average of £300,000,000 annually; but it was estimated that one day per week was lost through absenteeism as a result of excessive drinking, thus causing a loss to the country of one-sixth of the amount of its productive industry per week. [222] William Menelaus of the Dowlais Iron Company estimated that £500 would be lost if the Dowlais furnaces were stopped on Sundays as a result of Saturday night drinking. [223] The absence of a roller for one shift meant a loss of 8 to 10 tons of iron. [224] At Dowlais in 1846, John Evans, the manager of the works, estimated that several miners and colliers lost, through drinking, either four separate days a month or one week out of four, depending on the system of payment of wages; and this put the company to great inconvenience and expense. [225] Horses were idle when the men could not work, and were overworked towards the end of the month when the men worked fifteen to sixteen hours a day to make up for their lost time. The company incurred losses in being forced to store the coal at great expense. Offers of 1*d*. and 3*d*. per ton extra to induce the men to work regularly did not succeed. [226] Samuel Homfray, director of the Tredegar Iron and Coal Company in the 1840s, maintained that since an increase in wages in 1845, his men had been working irregularly, particularly during the first and second weeks of the month when the company's iron production, for want of coal, was one-third less than it was in the second half of the month. [227] At the Pentwyn and Golyros Company Works, drunken workmen were blamed for the loss of iron caused by leaving it a few minutes too long in the furnace so that it melted and ran to cinder. The workmen were so unreliable that the company kept an additional number of labourers and horses to do the extra work towards the end of the month. [228] At Blaina, too, it was found that the weekends following monthly pays were given over to drunkenness. The output of coal at a local colliery testifies to this. The colliery produced 523 tons of coal in the first week of October 1840, and 872 tons in the last; 290 tons in the first three days of December 1840 and 531 tons in the last three days. The effort to swell wages at the end of the month led to excessive, exhausting and harmful labour, and to a high rate of accidents. [229] Benjamin Whitworth, M.P., who possessed considerable industrial interests in the Tredegar-Rhymney area of Monmouthshire, estimated in July 1882, three months before the Welsh Sunday Closing Act of 1881 became operational, that the result of Sunday drinking at one of his works, which seldom commenced full-time work on Mondays, was a loss of £35,000 a year, a sum equal to 4 per cent on the capital employed.[230] The inconvenience to the employer caused by week-end drinking was almost as serious a disadvantage as financial loss, particularly before the Sunday Closing Act came into force. The manager of a Swansea copper works maintained that, 'Before the passing of the Sunday Closing Bill, it often happened that men (who were to come on duty on Sunday night) were found unfit to work through being intoxicated. This meant a great deal of trouble and annoyance—the night watchman having to seek for sober men who grumbled to 'come on' out of turn. It has sometimes happened that the work has had to be 'patched up', one man doing duty for two. Several of the Monday morning turn were often found drowsy and more fit for bed than work.'[231]

Welsh industrialists varied in their attitudes towards the drinking habits of their employees. Some tried to remedy them; others were indifferent to them, or condoned, of they did not encourage, them by entering for their personal profit into agreements with publicans; while some believed that thriftless workmen would be too engrossed in drink to interest themselves in such subjects as politics and unions. Conversely, others believed that public houses were the places where the workmen fell in with agitators, who often encouraged strikes.[232]

A major problem that had to be faced was the selling of beer by contractors, sub-contractors, butties or gaffers at the local works or, in the majority of cases, by an influential friend of the contractor.[233] In fact, selling beer was considered the easiest method of making money quickly. In 1854 at Merthyr, 158 of the 298 beer house keepers in the town were employed in the iron works, most of them as petty agents.[234] In May 1867, a month after the iron works at Blaina had ceased working and with little hope of their restarting, there were seventeen applications for new licences at the local licensing sessions.[235]

In March 1796, John Harford, the Ebbw Vale industrialist, decided that all his employees were to abstain from selling drink in any form. Workmen were employed only if they undertook to be 'constantly sober' and not to sell any liquor. If the promise was broken the stick was taken up and the workman fined a guinea for each offence. The concern of the Harfords for sobriety was adhered to strictly, except on those occasions when it was thought that allowances of drink should be used as incentives to finish important tasks. For instance, Harford, in his anxiety to get a new boiler finished for his furnace, agreed on 22 April 1796 that Jenkin Griffith should rebuild the boiler front for two guineas and '2s 6d to drink if he makes a good job of it'.[236] With the exception of this peccadillo, the company was hostile to drink, and licensed houses were not allowed on its land, despite offers of profitable rents.

The Dowlais Iron Company laid particular stress on the sobriety of its workmen and preferred to employ teetotallers.[237] John Griffiths was dismissed in 1798 for being found drunk at his work.[238] Yet in the late-1820s allowances of beer were given to the company's workmen on certain occasions.[239] In 1831, however, Josiah John Guest, considering the rapid multiplication of beer houses in Merthyr and Dowlais, ordered that 'no person employed in our Service must have anything to do with keeping a Public House or Beer Shop and if any person now does so he must be warned to leave one of the two'.[240] It should be noted that the reasons for this stern injunction were not merely the sobriety and industry of the work-force, but also the prevention of truck. Similar rules were laid down at Hill's Plymouth Works and at the Pontypool Ironworks in 1865.[241] John Evans and his brother, Thomas, the manager and agent respectively of the Dowlais Company in 1840, resorted to the carrot in an attempt to secure efficiency · by rewarding those workmen who became teetotallers with new hats valued at 24s.[242] Similarly, at a temperance meeting at Blaina in July 1855, Thomas Brown, the local ironmaster, attempted to check drunkenness by offering £25 to any of his workmen who, wishing to build themselves houses, would save £25 towards that purpose.[243] In 1848 John Morgan, a puddler of Mountain Hare, was dismissed by the Dowlais Company for keeping a beer house; Guest maintained that he would tempt his fellow workers to drink at his house after work.[244] In 1852 Guest succeeded in his efforts to close the 'Walnut' public house, 'which was considered the greatest nuisance', situated as it was near the gates of the Ivor Works.[245] During the 1860s the Dowlais Company engaged solicitors to oppose at licensing sessions all applications for public houses near the iron works, a policy which proved highly successful.[246] Excessive drinking interferred so much with work during the difficult years of transition from iron manufacture to coal production that the manager of the Nantyglo and Blaina Company announced at the licensing sessions in 1874 that any workman convicted of drunkenness, or of selling beer and spirits illegally, would have to leave his house if it were the property of the company. [247]

Many employers in south Wales realized the advantages of using the truck system to encourage sobriety. In the nineteenth century the truck system consisted mainly of compulsion to deal with the employer's grocery shop at risk of reprimand or discharge. In certain instances, this compulsion was a general condition of employment in the company, although more frequently it was exercised only on workmen who made irregular anticipations of wages accrued, but not yet due to be paid. [248] In his evidence before the Select Committee of the Commons on the Payment of Wages Bill in 1854, Hugh Seymour Tremenheere, a factory inspector and formerly the first inspector of mines and collieries, stated that twelve of the seventeen principal iron works in south Wales paid wages in truck goods. [249] The system bound men to masters by contraction of debts, and it was said to reduce real wages by 10 per cent. [250] However, in some isolated areas remote from market towns, the truck system was a positive advantage. The system compensated for lack of coin; in Monmouthshire in 1827 only half the legal currency needed was in circulation, and the truck system was reverted to in many works in order to relieve employers of periodic liquid embarrassments. [251] Many ironmasters convinced their workmen that the profits of the truck shops made possible low tenders for contracts and so ensured more regular employment. Some truck shops were established at the request of the work force; the shop attached to the Dowlais Iron Company was closed in 1823 but re-opened in 1828 at the wishes of the workmen. [252]

The truck system was described by its defenders as a system of regulated relief in which the wife handled the money: the less the husband received of his wages, the better off was his family, for truck was bound up with the frequency of pay days and 'draws', the payment of wages in public houses, and drunkenness. At most of the industrial concerns in south Wales, wage settlements were at least monthly, or more generally, at longer intervals, and the combination of long pay periods with compulsion to spend irregular advances at the company shop was a sumptuary device in two ways. First, long pay periods reduced absenteeism due to drunkenness, which was widely reported on Mondays following weekly pay-days.[253] Frederick Levick, acting partner in Blaina Ironworks, stated before the Payment of Wages Committee in 1854 that 'the extent to which men go to public houses is one of my greatest troubles in managing works, and I would keep a truck shop or take any other possible means to prevent them'.[254] Secondly, compulsion to deal at the company shop prevented an employee from drawing in his accrued wages at his discretion to spend in riotous living at a public house.[255] Thus, the truck system was used, in part, to control drunkenness. Indeed, employer control of drink consumption was likely to be highly effective on account of the geographical isolation of many of the industrial enterprises.[256]

The long pay originated in the truck system, the object being to compel workmen, by means of few payments at long intervals, to depend upon the company shop for the supply of the necessities of life.[257] There were two pays only at Blaina in the quarter ending June 1870—'an experiment to see if lengthening pays decreased drunkenness', explained the shopkeeper.[258] At Cwmbwrla tinplate works in 1871, the employers agreed to revert to the short pay and to pay the men fortnightly and not monthly, laying down the condition that every workman who absented himself through drunkenness should be fined £1. But, as a result of drunkenness and absenteeism by a minority of the workers, the short pay system was soon abandoned and recourse made to monthly pays.[259] The widely-held view was that the more infrequently the men were paid, the less drunkenness there would be.[260] The Rhymney Iron Company argued that when the pays were short the loss of time from drinking at the pay made it difficult to keep the works going for lack of coal.[261] At Dowlais in 1859 even the four to five week pay was found to be too short, and a ten to twelve week pay was introduced in June.[262]

The truck system subjected large numbers of workmen who had no intention of spending their earnings on drink to a sumptuary control for the restraint of a minority of drunkards. As far as the employer was concerned, the system was not foolproof. Since the goods sold by truck shops were widely consumed, workmen had little difficulty in converting them into cash at local grocery shops or public houses. A considerable part of the business of local retailers in the vicinity of the Ebbw Vale Company's works was buying and re-selling goods from the truck shops.[263] In fact, the truck system did not prevent a man drinking, for beer was obtainable in exchange for truck goods.

Tobacco was the most attractive commodity in the truck shop to purchase for resale or exchange because it was packaged, it was not highly perishable, it was widely consumed and it was dealt in by publicans.[264] Truck goods were exchanged for beer at public houses at a loss, and often reverted again to the truck shop, where they were re-purchased at some 15 to 20 per cent below the wholesale price.[265] At Merthyr in 1842, 'if a man wants a quart of beer, he cannot get his 6d. to pay for it, but he goes to the shop and gets tobacco or sugar, for which he has to pay 8d., and then the publican gives him his quart of beer for that article'.[266] A Tredegar publican testified in 1854 that he gave two quarts of beer worth one shilling for a quarter of tobacco worth 1s. 4d.[267] In 1870, at Blaina and Nantyglo, for a quarter of tobacco costing 1s. 9d. publicans gave their regular customers three quarts of beer (value 1s. 6d.) and five pints (1s. 3d.) to others.[268] An Ebbw Vale publican received 15s. worth of tobacco in one week in 1870, and stated that occasionally he took tobacco back to the company shop and this was 'paid' to the workmen again so that the tobacco became a 'circulating medium'.[269] Those goods received by the publican and not sold back to the company shop often found their way back to the workmen at a cheaper rate than that offered by the company shop,[270] or else they were bartered to local shopkeepers in return for groceries and draperies. Between April and October 1851, a Nantyglo grocer bought goods to the value of £50.10s. from local publicans.[271]

The truck system was not the most perfect instrument to check drunkenness and absenteeism. It might be argued that had ready cash been paid to the workmen they would have been less likely to part with it recklessly than when they were forced to do business without it. The more frequently and regularly their wages were paid to them in cash, the less likely would they be to contract debt by obtaining credit.

There was a barely concealed element of truck in the practice of paying wages in public houses owned by works' officials. Public houses were needed as a source of change. At Dowlais in 1840, one collier deputed by a group to draw its weekly wages might take £20 or £30, most of it in £5 notes, from the cashier.[272] In the public house the gaffers usually deducted about 3d. from each man for 'getting change', and each workman was more or less bound to pay 6d. for a quart of beer, it being an 'understood thing that the men must throw back 6d.'.[273] The system was declared illegal in 1842 (5 and 6 Vic.

c. 99), but most workmen, whether through ignorance, fear or tact, seem to have been unaware of the fact that having once been paid in a public house, they could in law compel the repayment of the amount. The possibility of social and moral evils arising out of the payment of wages in public houses was voiced by the rector of Llanhilleth in 1846:

> This state of things actually prevents the operative from being sober and thrifty, and holds out a reward for the drunkard, it being the interest of the employer as agent to have such men as will spend their all at his house: nor is he slow in intimating to such as are not in the habit of frequenting his house, that their services are not acceptable, and thus the more sober a man is, the more he is exposed to petty annoyance from his employer.[274]

The employers did not gain much if they employed gaffers between them and the work force: the fruits went to the gaffers. Obviously, the employers were losers, too, when workmen spent a considerable proportion of their wages at the public house during pay time and were absentees from their work the following day.

The Dowlais management was very anxious to repress the practice. In 1841 the company made arrangements for a sufficient supply of gold, silver and copper coins for the payment of each worker separately, and issued a notice to the effect that there was no need to make any charge for change at public houses. In other words, the men were to be paid individually through the office instead of through the contractors. In 1848, gaffers and contractors were ordered by Guest to either relinquish their public houses or give up their jobs.[275] However, a further attempt in 1852 was necessary before this reform became operational.[276] The Crawshays at Cyfarthfa also debarred their contractors from owning public houses in 1848 and subsequently started to pay their men direct. Robert Crawshay informed his father, William Crawshay, in 1859 that 'we now pay all the men, colliers and miners, separately, so it takes more hands to do it, and it pays well '.[277] At several works in south Wales, however, the system persisted on the basis of the unwritten understanding between the gaffer and publican, which defeated the good intentions of the employer. At Rhymney and Blaenavon the practice continued into the 1870s.[278]

The wage payment itself was used as a tool of discipline. Faced with irregularities of work, employers could use the mercantilist device of holding down wages in an effort to prevent idleness.[279] The rate of

drunkenness varied directly with the rate of wage paid: insobriety
increased when wages rose and declined when wages fell.[280] The
mineral and land steward of Sir Watkin Williams Wynn wrote to
Guest in 1835: 'I never yet knew high wages obtainable but
drunkenness, idleness and loss of time were sure to be the
consequences, as young men whose wages exceed their reasonable
wants of food, lodging and clothing, generally spend the surplus in
the Ale Houses, thus breaking the *Pit set* to which they belong, and in
the end causing others to be as idle and dissolute as themselves, and
that less work is done by the many than the few'.[281] Robert
Crawshay estimated in January 1873 that his production of rails and
bars had fallen by a hundred tons a week as a result of a recent
increase in wages, which caused widespread intoxication and
absenteeism amongst the employees.[282] The waste caused by
excessive drinking during times of prosperity was heavily stressed by
industrialists and temperance reformers during trade depressions in
an effort to bring home to the working man the consequences of his
'immense folly' in not working hard when times were good and
saving money for bad times.[283] Moralists and example-setters, who
believed that spiritual progress in Wales depended upon material
hardship, lamented that to the workman more work and more pay
meant more beer and more play.[284] During the depression of 1843 in
the south Wales coalfield, the first miners and colliers to be
discharged were invariably 'the most drunken and disorderly'.[285] At
Dowlais, John Evans saw no reason why the company should increase
the wages of the colliers who struck for an increase in June 1855,
maintaining that the men and the company were better off with
reduced rates: 'They work more regularly and earn as much money
as before'.[286]

   Although the majority of employers in south Wales saw it as their
duty to encourage sobriety in their labour forces, other employers, in
the interests of industrial harmony, were reluctant to withdraw access
to drink. Some collieries and iron works operated tap rooms in
connection with the works. They were established mainly to provide
beer as drink in the pits and about the furnaces, but they had a
sumptuary effect in so far as they permitted the employers' agents to
observe the off-duty drinking habits of the men. The Rhymney Iron
Company, established in 1837, erected its own brewery two years
later 'for the supply of beer to all persons employed in the works'.[287]
The brewery was only a quarter of a mile from the company shop,

and the men received beer notes from the latter and redeemed them at the former. [288] A timekeeper with the company during the closing years of the century testified to the absenteeism and 'broken time' caused by excessive drinking, but stated that at least 'the company could console itself with the reflection that what they lost on the swings as employers they gained on the roundabouts as brewers'. [289] Similarly, the Pentyrch and Melingriffith Company gave its employees notes for beer allowances—usually three to four quarts—which could be used at any public house in the vicinity. The publicans sent in the notes to the company at monthly intervals in order to redeem the money. [290] At Nantyglo, Crawshay Bailey did not encourage any counter-attractions to the public houses. When it was suggested to him that he should close the Bush Inn, he retorted that he could not run his works without it: many of his agents and officials drank there. Moreover, a neighbouring public house was used as a school for workers' children. [291] At the Bush Inn on the wedding day of Crawshay Bailey Jnr. in 1863, 6,000 quarts of beer were distributed, a quart free of charge to everyone over twelve years of age employed at the works. [292]

*   *   *   *

Beer has accumulated a mass of statistical information because it has for so long been subject to governmental regulation and taxation. Consequently, it is a straightforward matter to discover from official returns the production of non-home brewed beer for sale in England and Wales (Wales being rarely separated statistically from England), the numbers of licensed brewers and publicans, the imports and exports of beer or the annual product of the malt, hops and beer duties, for any date over the last two centuries or more. These sources provide invaluable material for the statistician, economist and economic historian, but for the purpose of social history they are far from satisfactory. There are, for example, no official figures of total or *per capita* consumption, and the question is barely touched upon in all the scores of volumes of parliamentary papers and annual returns on the drink trade which proliferated in the nineteenth century. Even if such figures existed, they would not take us nearly far enough. The social historian wants to know not merely how much beer was drunk per head, but by whom, at what times, and at what cost. What part

has drink played in the nation's life and diet over the last two
centuries? What proportion of the national and domestic budget has
been spent on it? What factors have affected its consumption in the
long and short terms? How far have changing habits of consumption
been related to changing social values, standards of living and
patterns of expenditure?

Drunkenness was the offence which most occupied the attention of
the police. During the first six months of 1852, for example, 80 per
cent of the proceedings at Cardiff Borough Police Court were the
result of drunkenness.[293] But statistics of drunkenness in the
nineteenth century are sometimes misleading, largely because of
varying police enforcement.[294] In some areas, first offenders were
discharged with a caution, while in others it became the practice of
the police not to take any person into custody for drunkenness alone
unless it was accompanied by disorderly conduct.[295] With the passing
of the Local Government Act in 1888 the responsibilities of the
Quarter Sessions in many Welsh counties were transferred to
Standing Joint Committees composed equally of justices and county
councillors. In Caernarfonshire, for example, over half the members
of the committee were county councillors, most of whom were
nonconformists and strongly opposed to the drink trade. There was
henceforth a more determined attempt on the part of the police to
deal with drunkenness and they were specifically charged to be
diligent in enforcing the licensing laws. In 1890, the young alderman,
David Lloyd George, suggested the appointment of a plain clothes
detective at a salary of £100 a year to supervise the operation of the
licensing laws in the county; although his suggestion was not taken up
at the time, a very similar plan was adopted in Caernarfonshire in
1900.[296] In 1892 the Caernarfonshire Standing Joint Committee
decided that whenever the police prosecuted for drunknness they
should make every effort to discover the public house at which the
defendants were last supplied; a copy of this resolution was circulated
by this active nonconformist committee to every licensee in the
county as a warning.[297]

Fines for drunkenness did not vary a great deal throughout the
century. In 1822 the bailiffs of Cardiff imposed a fine of 5 shillings on
each person found drunk, and the same amount was exacted in the
late 1850s.[298] At Newport in 1842, drunkards were discharged with
an admonition upon promising to join a temperance society.[299] In
general, police supervision during the greater part of the first half of

the century seems to have been inadequate and lax, largely because of a shortage of manpower. In 1841 the Merthyr Tydfil police force consisted of twelve constables only, or one constable to every 2,900 people. [300] During the late 1830s, the police force at Bridgend consisted of a shoemaker over 60 years of age and a younger tailor, both of whom were themselves often found in a state of intoxication; [301] a Caernarfonshire constable who applied for promotion in 1865 could only state in support of his application that he had been a teetotaller for over twenty years. [302]

The commissioners of inquiry into the state of education in Wales in 1847 reported widespread drunkenness mainly among the unskilled working class, a conclusion based largely upon the evidence of Anglicans who imputed this state of affairs to the dominance of nonconformity in the country. [303] Drink and drinking places were considered to be the great hindrance to moral and religious improvement. Although the education report was prejudiced against nonconformity and the Welsh language, the social criticism it contained was probably nearer the mark. The efforts of men like the Rev. Evan Jones ("Ieuan Gwynedd"), Independent minister of Tredegar, to vindicate the character of his countrymen, were called for and well meant, but they should not blind us to the fact that the country as a whole was very largely uncultured and untaught, and, if ignorance is the mother of vice, immoral as well. Articles on the immorality and ignorance of the people appeared with great regularity in the denominational press, particlarly *Y Dysgedydd*, in which the Independent minister, the Rev. Evan Davies ("Eta Delta") of Llanerchymedd, had sufficient courage to acknowledge, in May 1848, that much of the 1847 report was true. [304]

Such statistics as are available, however, point to the period between the late 1860s and the early 1880s as being the high-water mark for apprehensions and convictions for drunkenness in Wales. [305] Within this period, drunkenness seems to have greatly increased during the early 1870s. At Swansea drunkenness almost trebled between 1869 and 1873, and between 1871 and 1873 a proportion of one person in every 74 was convicted of drunkenness. [306] In north-west Wales convictions for drunkenness at Pwllheli more than trebled between 1869 and 1870, and the average number of convictions for each year of the 1870s was twice that of every year of the 1860s. [307] At Wrexham the statistics for apprehensions for drunkenness nearly trebled between 1869 and 1876 as the table below shows. [308]

TABLE 2. DRUNKENNESS IN WREXHAM, 1869, 1873, 1876

Year	Number of drinking places			Population	Apprehensions for drunkenness	Population for each case of drunkenness	Population to each drinking place
1869	Public Houses	65	} 84	8,361	46	181	99
	Beer Houses	19					
1873	Public Houses	64	} 85	8,794	116	75	103
	Beer Houses	21					
1876	Public Houses	64	} 85	9,680	128	75	113
	Beer Houses	21					

But Wrexham was not a particularly drunken place at this time. Statistics reveal that, in 1877, the greatest number of apprehensions for drunkenness was made in Caernarfonshire (100 per 10,000 head of population) closely followed by Glamorgan (94 per 10,000) and Flintshire (84), [309] and that in 1881 in south Wales the most drunken places were Pontypridd, with a proportion of 9.1 convictions for drunkenness per 1,000 population, and Cardiff with 8.9 per 1,000. [310] During the 1870s and '80s drunkenness was much less marked in rural mid-Wales. At Barmouth between 1875 and 1895, only 107 people were apprehended for drunkenness, most of them being farm labourers; [311] at Towyn during the same period only 43 people were apprehended. [312] By the end of the period covered by this study, the highest number of apprehensions for drunkenness in Wales were in Glamorgan, Monmouthshire and Pembrokeshire; the fewest in Merionethshire, Radnorshire and Anglesey. [313]

It is most difficult to obtain precise information about the social class of drunkard arrested or to identify habitual drunkards, except when they were notorious local characters. We know that Ellen Sweeney of Swansea, for example, received her 156th conviction for drunkenness in December 1880. [314] Occasionally, however, Head Constables' reports to the licensing magistrates were published in the local press and from them it is possible to gain some idea of the social class of the people arrested. Unfortunately, the only such report found for Wales is that for Newport in 1885-6 and it reveals that a clear majority of the 436 persons proceeded against for drunkenness and disorderly conduct for the year ending 31 August 1886 were unskilled working men; interestingly, over 25 per cent of the total was female.[315]

TABLE 3. NUMBERS AND OCCUPATIONS OF THOSE PROCEEDED AGAINST FOR DRUNKENNESS AND DISORDERLY CONDUCT IN NEWPORT, 1 SEPTEMBER 1885 TO 31 AUGUST 1886

Labourers	136	Seamen	54	Firemen	22
Hawkers	12	Hauliers	9	Butchers	8
Colliers	7	Masons	6	Tin-workers	6
Moulders	5	Clerks	4	Donkey-men	4
Engineers	4	Shoe blacks	4	Boiler-makers	3
Cab drivers	3	Carpenters	3	Drapers	3
Porters	3	Farmers	2	Glass-blowers	2
Hucksters	3	Painters	2	Puddlers	2
Tailors	2				

and one each of baker, baller, beer house keeper, brass fitter, chair mender, clockmaker, dairyman, drover, grocer, hairdresser, herbalist, horse dealer, miller, plasterer, ropemaker, shoemaker, soldier and traveller.

Married women 49;   prostitutes 37;   widows 13;   spinsters 10.

*   *   *   *

Apart from the emphasis on the consumption of beer, rather than spirits, Wales does not seem to have possessed its own drinking identity for most of the nineteenth century. Certainly, the amount of drinking and drunkenness in Wales per capita did not differ markedly from that in England and Scotland. What was distinctive about the country's drinking habits, however, was the nature of Welsh rural drinking usages before the coming of the nonconformist religious revival with its dominant world-rejecting ethic. What came to be widely regarded as a Welsh drink problem was not caused, but was greatly exacerbated, by the factors which made for a squalid environment in parts of Wales. Yet it is obviously rash to assume that reforming movements spring up at a time when the evil they attack is at its worst. The temperance movement did not appear solely 'in reaction to' the conditions brought about by the process of industrialization. If religious revivalism, was also a strong motivating force so was the economic self-interest of industrialists and manufacturers, and the growth of religious respectability among the middle and upper working classes. Before the Beer Act of 1830 the level of drunkenness in Wales may well have been declining, but its

increasing incidence among larger numbers of working men from the
1830s, particularly in the raw industrial communities, helped to focus
the attempts of nonconformity to push for working-class
'improvement', a necessary corollary of which was the destruction of
the old popular culture with its drinking customs and brutal
recreations.

NOTES

[1] For this background see W. Davies, *The Agricultural and Domestic Economy of North Wales* (1811);
The Agriculture and Domestic Economy of South Wales, 2 vols. (1815); A. D. Rees, *Life in a Welsh
Countryside* (Cardiff, 1950); A. H. John, *The Industrial Development of South Wales, 1750-1850* (Cardiff,
1950); A. H. Dodd, *The Industrial Revolution in North Wales* (Cardiff, 2nd edn., 1951); D. Williams,
The Rebecca Riots (Cardiff, 1955); D. J. V. Jones, *Before Rebecca. Popular protests in Wales,
1793-1835* (1973); Henry Richard, *Letters on the Social and Political Condition of Wales* (1867); and
idem., *Letters and Essays on Wales* (1884).

[2] *Reports of the Commissioners of Inquiry into the State of Education in Wales, P.P.*, 1847, XXVII (870),
Part I, p. 12.

[3] See B. Thomas, 'The Migration of Labour into the Glamorgan Coalfield, 1861-1911',
Economica, 1930.

[4] See *Report on the decline in Agricultural Population of Great Britain, 1881-1906, P.P.*, XCVI (1906),
p. 15: quoted in D. W. Howell, *Land and People in Nineteenth-Century Wales* (1978), pp. 96-7.

[5] See D. Thomas, *Agriculture in Wales during the Napoleonic Wars* (Cardiff, 1963), p. 10.

[6] See K. O. Morgan, *Wales in British Politics, 1868-1922* (Cardiff, 3rd edn., 1980), p. 11.

[7] *Y Diwygiwr*, 1852, p. 117.

[8] See K. O. Morgan, op. cit., p. 8.

[9] See Ifano Jones, *Printing and Printers in Wales and Monmouthshire* (Cardiff, 1925); C. Evans, The
Rise and Progress of the Periodical Press in Wales up to 1860 (unpublished University of Wales
M.A. thesis, 1926); W. R. Lambert, Drink and Sobriety in Wales, 1835-95 (unpublished
University of Wales Ph.D. thesis, 1970), Appendix 8, pp. 466-82.

[10] See L. W. Evans, *Education in Industrial Wales, 1700-1900* (Cardiff, 1971), pp. 15 ff.

[11] Morgan, op. cit., p. 3.

[12] This general point is made in H. M. Pelling, *Popular Politics and Society in Late Victorian Britain*
(2nd edn., 1979), p. 20.

[13] *Census of Great Britain, 1851. Religious Worship, England and Wales. Report and Tables* (1853),
pp. 122-5.

[14] Henry Richard, *Letters on the Social and Political Condition of Wales*, p. 19.

[15] For example, see *Y Diwygiwr*, January 1852, p. 13; *Y Drysorfa*, October 1852, p. 353.

[16] See *Church Quarterly Review*, vol. 15, no. 29, October 1882, p. 68. For example, 73 of the 997
Independent chapels in Wales in 1875 had been established between 1839 and 1842. Most of them
were 'Chartist churches', having been established by members of already existing Independent
chapels, who disagreed with their fellow worshippers on the question of the Charter. See Thomas
Rees and John Thomas, *Hanes Eglwysi Annibynnol Cymru* (Liverpool, 1875), vol. I, pp. 21, 118, 189;
vol. 2, pp. 15, 88, 184-5.

[17] On this see Thomas Darlington, 'The Church in Wales an alien Church', *Contemporary Review*,
LXIII, June 1893, p. 819; C. C. Harris, 'Church, Chapel and the Welsh', *New Society*, no. 21, 21
February 1963, p. 18.

[18] The Treasury, 18, 1881, p. 239.

[19] *Y Traethodydd*, April 1852, p. 454.

[20] See D. Jenkins, *Congregationalism: a restatement* (n.d.), p. 113.

[21] See, for example, NLW MS 12,059 C (D. D. Williams 7), Rev. D. D. Williams, The
Influence of the Methodist Movement on Social Life in Wales, p. 82.

[22] *A Gentleman's Tour in North Wales* (1794), p. 108.

[23] W. F. Deacon, *The Innkeepers' Album* (1823), p. 196.

[24] Ibid., p. 192.

[25] P. Mathias, 'The Brewing Industry, Temperance and Politics', *Historical Journal*, I, 1958,
no. 2, p. 106.

[26] *Morning Chronicle*, 4 March 1850.

[27] C. Wilkins, *History of Merthyr Tydfil* (Merthyr Tydfil, 1908), pp. 434-6.

[28] Thomas de Quincy, *Confessions of an Opium Eater* (Everyman edn., 1969), p. 131.

[29] A. H. Dodd, op. cit., p. 350.

[30] *Bye-Gones*, 1880-1, pp. 154-60.

[31] *Report of the Select Committee of the House of Commons on the causes and consequences of the prevailing vice of intoxication among the labouring classes*, *P.P.*, 1834, VIII (559), pp. 322-3.

[32] A point made for the seventeenth century in K. Thomas, *Religion and the Decline of Magic* (paperback edn., 1980), p. 22.

[33] E. Scourfield, *Farmhouse Brewing* (Cardiff, n.d., *c.* 1977), p. 3.

[34] Ibid., p. 5.

[35] See B. Harrison, 'The Power of Drink', *The Listener*, 13 February 1969, 204.

[36] See *Report of the Royal Commission on Land in Wales and Monmouthshire*, *P.P.*, vol. 5 (C.8221), 1896, XXXIV, QQ. 3,649-51, 3,727, 5,347-8, 7,304-7, 49,841-5.

[37] Harrison, op. cit., 204.

[38] C. Wilkins, *The History of the Iron, Steel, Tinplate and other trades of Wales* (Merthyr Tydfil, 1903), p. 280.

[39] J. Dunlop, *Philosophy of Artificial and Compulsory Drinking Usage in Great Britain and Ireland* (6th edn., 1839), p. 3.

[40] See T. Gwyn Jones, *Welsh Folklore and Folk Custom* (1930); Edward Lhuyd, *Parochialia*, Part 3 (1911), p. 49.

[41] *Rhobet Wiliam, Wern Ddu, Atgofion amdano* (Bala, 1889), p. 64 (transl.), quoted in E. Davies and A. D. Rees (eds.), *Welsh Rural Communities* (Cardiff, 1960), pp. 216-7.

[42] See Howell, op. cit., p. 99.

[43] See T. M. Owen, *Welsh Folk Customs* (Cardiff, 1978 edn.), p. 69.

[44] See Scourfield, op. cit., p. 9.

[45] See Owen, op. cit., pp. 161-2; D. Williams, *Rebecca Riots*, pp. 94-5.

[46] See NLW MS 16,157 B, Material for a history of Nantyglo and Blaina, parish of Aberystruth, Mon. by Edward Ifor Williams; *Western Mail*, 29 May 1884; R. M. Evans. 'Folklore and Customs in Cardiganshire', *Transactions of Cardiganshire Antiquarian Society*, 12, 1937, 55.

[47] Scourfield, op. cit., p. 9.

[48] W. M. Williams, 'A Slight Historical and Topographical Sketch of the parish of Llanfechain', *Montgomeryshire Collections*, V, pp. 255-6.

[49] *P.P.*, 1834, VIII (559), p. 134.

[50] Ibid., QQ. 1,862, 1,871, evidence of Owen Roberts, Caernarfon surgeon.

[51] Henry Ladd, *The Vital Question of the Day, or How to Suppress Drunkenness from a Publican's Point of View* (Carmarthen, 1877), p. 6.

[52] Royal Institution of South Wales MS, Glamorgan Election, 1826.

[53] David Williams, 'The Pembrokeshire Elections of 1831', *Welsh History Review*, No. 1, 1960, 50.

[54] Ibid., 58.

[55] University College of North Wales, Plas Newydd Correspondence, Series IV, No. 5,997, cited in E. Gwynne Jones, 'Borough Politics and Electioneering, 1826-52', *Transactions of Caernarvonahire Historical Society*, 17, 1956, 81-2.

[56] *Swansea and Glamorgan Herald*, 4 August 1847; R. D. Rees, 'The Parliamentary Representation of South Wales, 1790-1830' (unpublished University of Reading Ph.D. thesis, 1962), p. 581.

[57] See *Cambrian*, 5 November 1858; 23 November 1866; 17 September 1875; T. Ridd, 'The Development of Municipal Government in Swansea in the Nineteenth Century' (unpublished University of Wales M.A. thesis, 1955), 415-6.

[58] E. Jones, *The Bardic Museum* (1802), p. xvi, quoted in Owen, op. cit., p. 25.

[59] See R. T. Jenkins, *Bardd a'i Gefndir* (1948), p. 7.

[60] See Owen, op, cit., pp. 23-4.

[61] See ibid., pp. 142-4; Howell, op. cit., p. 99; Wirt Sikes, *Rambles and Studies in Old South Wales* (1881), pp. 194-201.

[62] *Cardiff and Merthyr Guardian*, 22 April 1843, 18 April 1846 (henceforth cited as *C.M.G.*).

[63] Ibid., 6 June 1857.

[64] Mass Observation, *The Pub and the People. A Worktown Study* (1943), p. 165. For 'masculine republic', see H. W. J. Edwards, *The Good Patch. A Study of the Rhondda Valley* (1938), p. 158.

[65] Charles Wilkins, op. cit., p. 272.

[66] H. A. Bruce, *On Amusements* (1850), p. 15, and *Merthyr in 1852* (1852), p. 17. For the lack of outdoor amenities see *Monmouthshire Merlin*, 15 September 1838; *C.M.G.*, 31 August 1839; *Report of the Health of Towns Commission into the Sanitary Condition of the Labouring Population of Britain*, *P.P.*, 1845, XVIII, p. 324.

[67] *C.M.G.*, 10 November 1845.

[68] Ibid.

[69] *Silurian*, 10 December 1836.

[70] G[lamorgan] R[ecord] O[ffice], Dowlais Iron Company MSS, H. J. Hooper to G. T. Clark, 18 May 1855, ff. 388-9; *C.M.G.*, 30 October 1841.

[71] G.R.O., Dowlais MSS., Thomas Sopwith to Lady Charlotte Guest, 13 February 1853, ff. 686-88.

[72] NLW MS 14,696 D, D. T. Eaton, 'The Mechanics Institutes of South Wales' (1946). A typescript.

[73] See Wirt Sikes, op. cit., p. 277; for portable theatres see Cecil Price, 'Portable Theatres in Wales, 1843-1914', *National Library of Wales Journal*, 9, 1955-6, 65-92.

[74] Evan Owen, *Workmen's Libraries in Glamorgan and Monmouthshire* (Cardiff, 1895), pp. 7-14. See also J. H. Phillips, *An Essay on the Advantages of Free Libraries* (Cardiff, 1867), pp. 8-9; R. R. Davies, *First Prize Essay on the desirability and advantages of recreation grounds for the working classes and poor children of Swansea* (Swansea, 1875), pp. 35-7.

[75] See *Report of the Royal Commissioners appointed to enquire into the operation of the Sunday Closing (Wales) Act., 1881, P.P.*, 1890, XL, Q. 6,597; *Aberdare Banner of Faith*, 2 June 1885, p. cxli; *Monmouthshire Merlin*, 28 September 1888.

[76] *Aberdare Banner of Faith*, 2 June 1885, p. cxli; *Monmouthshire Merlin*, 28 September 1888.

[77] See P. H. J. H. Gosden, *The Friendly Societies in England, 1815-1875* (1963), p. 23.

[78] C[ardiff] C[entral] L[ibrary], MS.4.762, A list of all Friendly Societies in the county of Glamorgan established under the powers of 10 Geo. 4, *c.* 56, up to 5 April 1836.

[79] *C.M.G.*, 9 December 1848.

[80] P.R.O. FS 1/909/91, FS 1/917/296, FS 1/917/298; *Cambrian Temperance Chronicle*, 1, no. 1, 1 June 1891, pp. 5-6.

[81] J. H. Clapham, *An Economic History of Modern Britain* (Cambridge, 1926), i. p. 298, quoted in Gwyn A. Williams 'Friendly Societies in Glamorgan, 1793-1832', *Bulletin of the Board of Celtic Studies*, part 3, November 1959, 278.

[82] B. H. Malkin, *Society for the Improvement of the Working Population in Glamorgan. Tract No. 5. On the Advantages of Friendly Societies* (Cardiff. n.d. *c.* 1830), p. 4.

[83] NLW. MS 16,157 B, loc cit.

[84] See *C.M.G.*, 9 April 1836; Rev. Thomas Page, *An Earnest Appeal to the Nation at Large on the mischievous effects of beer houses* (1845), p. 47.

[85] Thomas Jones, *Rhymney Memories* (Newtown, 1938), p. 17.

[86] *C.M.G.*, 5 January 1839.

[87] W. D. Wills, 'Ecclesiastical Reorganization and Church Extension in the Diocese of Llandaff, 1830-70' (unpublished University of Wales M.A. thesis, 1965), p. 284.

[88] C.C.L. MS. 3,674, Parish of Llanfabon, Churchwardens' Minute Book, 1866-95, passim; see also *Gelligaer. Transactions of Gelligaer Historical Society*, 3, 1966, 14; 4, 1967, 26.

[89] John Ingman, 'Notes on some old Bangor Inns', *Transactions of Caernarvonshire Historical Society*, 10, 1949, 45.

[90] Ibid.

[91] A. H. Williams, *Welsh Wesleyan Methodism, 1800-1858* (Bangor, 1935), pp. 112, 118, 286-7.

[92] D. Attwater, *The Catholic Church in Modern Wales* (1935), p. 71.

[93] *Franciscan Missions among the Colliers and Ironworkers of Monmouthshire* (1876), p. 61, see also pp. 26, 35; Raphael Samuel, 'The Catholic Church and the Irish Poor', paper before the *Past and Present* conference on Popular Religion, 1966, 46. I am most grateful to Mr. Samuel of Ruskin College, Oxford for kindly lending me a copy of this paper.

[94] G.R.O., D/DX ha 5/2, Notes on Catholicism in Cardiff and Glamorgan.

[95] Ingman, op. cit., 39.

[96] NLW MS 16,157 B, loc. cit.

[97] NLW MS 3,463 E, Notes on some Old Aberdare Eisteddfodau by D. M. Richards (1903), quoted in A. C. Davies, 'Aberdare, 1750-1850. A Study in the growth of an Industrial Community' (unpublished University of Wales M.A. thesis, 1963), 316.

[98] Ibid., 315.

[99] Ibid., 316.

[100] David Morgans, *Music and Musicians of Merthyr and District* (Merthyr Tydfil, 1922), p. 206.

[101] *Report of the Select Committee of the House of Commons on Public Houses, P.P.*, 1854, XIV (231), Q. 2,964.

[102] For example, see *The Universe*, 1, no. 30, 31 July 1846, p. 6. For further general information on the public house as a recreational centre see J. Kay, *The Social Condition and Education of the People in England and Europe* (1850), i. p. 604; C. Holdenby, *Folk of the Furrow* (1913), p. 82.

[103] See Brian Harrison, 'Pubs', H. J. Dyos and M. Wolffe (eds.), *The Victorian City*, vol. 1 (1973), pp. 178-9.

[104] See *C.M.G.*, 7 December 1838, 28 December 1838; Evan Jenkins, *Chartism Unmasked* (Merthyr Tydfil, 1840), p. 22.

[105] *C.M.G.*, 11 December 1841.

[106] *Western Vindicator*, no. 18, 22 June 1839.

[107] A. V. John, 'The Chartist Endurance: Industrial South Wales, 1840-68', *Morgannwg*, XV, 1971, p. 28.

[108] NLW. Tredegar Collections, Samuel Homfray to Octavious Morgan, M.P., 40/55, cited in W. T. Morgan, 'Chartism and Industrial Unrest in South Wales in 1842', *National Library of Wales Journal*, 10, 1957-8, 9.

[109] G.R.O., QE, Box 7, 1/9F, Chief Constable's Report for Glamorgan, 1844.

[110] See ibid., 1842; P.R.O. HO 73/8, Returns from Poor Law Guardians, 1837 (Gladestry Parish, Radnorshire); *Monmouthshire Merlin*, 10 March 1832, 6 February 1836; Rev. Richard Jones, *The Claims of the Temperance Movement on Christian Ministers* (Manchester, 1860), pp. 5-6.

[111] NLW MS 8,391 B, The Diary of Eben Fardd.

[112] *The Teetotal Times and Essayist*, no. 14, February 1849, p. 15.

[113] G.R.O., QE, Box 7, 1/9 F, Chief Constable's Report, 28 June 1842; see also K. Strange, 'In search of the Celestial Empire: Crime in Merthyr Tydfil, 1830-60', *Llafur*, vol. 3, no. 1 (Spring 1980), p. 66.

[114] See Brian Harrison, *Drink and the Victorians, The Temperance Question in England, 1815-1872* (1971), Chapter 3, passim.

[115] For example, see University College of North Wales, Porth-yr-Aur MSS, f.4,442.

[116] *Monmouthshire Merlin*, 17 March 1838.

[117] Rev. Thomas Page, op. cit., pp. 90-1.

[118] *P.P.* 1834 (559), VIII, QQ. 1,849, 1,891.

[119] *Account of the number of brewers, licensed victuallers and persons licensed under the Act 'to permit the general sale of beer by retail in the U.K.'*, *P.P.*, 1831 (60), XVII, pp. 73-4; ibid., *P.P.*, 1831 (223), 1831-32, XXXIV, pp. 27-9.

[120] *Y Dirwestydd*, no. 12, June 1837, pp. 96-8.

[121] Ibid.

[122] G.R.O., Aberdare Vestry Minutes, *sub* 29 August 1831; A. C. Davies, op. cit., 256-7.

[123] *Monmouthshire Merlin*, 19 February 1831.

[124] *Report of the Royal Commission on the Employment of Children in Mines*, *P.P.*, 1842, XVII, p. 489.

[125] See Page, op. cit., 20-1.

[126] *C.M.G.*, 9 October 1847.

[127] For example, see Page, op. cit., 21-2.

[128] See *Monmouthshire Merlin*, 9 April 1831; *C.M.G.*, 6 April 1833, 10 August 1833, 3 May 1834, 9 February 1839, 25 January 1840; *P.P.*, 1847, XXVII, 366.

[129] *Report of the Select Committee of the House of Lords to consider the operation of the Acts for the Sale of Beer*, *P.P.*, 1850 (398), X, QQ. 26, 63, 323, 505.

[130] See *Morning Chronicle*, 8 April 1850.

[131] *Report of the Boundaries Commissioners*, 1832, vol. 4, part ii, p. 101: cited in I. G. Jones, 'The General Election of 1868 in Merthyr Tydfil', unpublished typescript, 1953, pp. 7-8; see also *Monmouthshire Merlin*, 10 March 1832.

[132] *P.P.*, 1837-8 (329), XLIV, p. 616.

[133] *Morning Chronicle*, 8 April 1850.

[134] Ibid. Cf. the evidence of Henry Wren, Superintendent of police at Merthyr Tydfil to the Select Committee of the House of Commons on Public Houses. *P.P.*, 1854, XIV (231), QQ. 2,916-21.

[135] *Merthyr Telegraph*, 26 November 1870; *Alliance News*, 10 December 1870.

[136] See Thomas Jones, op. cit., p. 101.

[137] F. Engels, *The Condition of the Working Class in England* (1958 edn.), translated and edited by W. O. Henderson and W. H. Chaloner, p. 116.

[138] E. L. Collis and M. Greenwood, *The Health of the Industrial Worker* (1921), p. 278. For a similar view see NLW MS 1,025 C (Ieuan Gwynedd 1), Essay on the Elevation of the Working Classes, n.d., *c.* 1851; J. C. Campbell, *A Lecture on the Social State of the Mineral Districts* (Cardiff, 1850), p. 7; *C.M.G.*, 29 December 1849.

[139] Collis and Greenwood, op. cit., 276; *Western Mail*, 30 January 1889; [David Davies], *The Welsh Sunday Closing Act* (Cardiff, 1889), pp. 79-80; W. C. Sullivan, *Alcoholism: A Chapter in Social Pathology* (1906), p. 106: P. E. H. Hair, The Social History of British Coalminers, 1800-1845 (unpublished University of Oxford, D.Phil. thesis, 1955), p. 251.

[140] Harrison, *Drink and the Victorians*, p. 40.

[141] See J. H. Morris and L. J. Williams, *The South Wales Coal Industry, 1841-1875* (Cardiff, 1958), pp. 234-9; A. H. John, op. cit., pp. 63-6. For fewer sanctions on conduct see R. G. McCarthy, *Drinking and Intoxication* (New Haven, 1959), p. 108; N. Smelser, *Social Change in the Industrial Revolution* (1959), p. 278; D. J. Pittman and C. R. Snyder (eds.), *Society, Culture and Drinking Patterns* (New York, 1962), pp. 49, 58.

[142] A letter to the press (*c.* 1863) quoted in NLW MS 14,696 D, D. T. Eaton, op. cit.

[143] P. Mathias, op. cit., 109-10.

[144] *Monmouthshire Merlin*, 16 September 1837.

[145] Ibid. See also Edward Miall, *The British Churches in Relation to the British People* (1849), pp. 327, 353-4.

[146] *Monmouthshire Merlin*, 16 September 1837; see also C.C.L. MS 3. 386, 'Aurelius', The Dignity of Labour. Prize Essay at the Aberdare National Eisteddfod, 1885, p. 9.

[147] *Monmouthshire Merlin*, 16 September 1837.

[148] *Morning Chronicle*, 21 March 1850.

[149] Ibid., 27 March 1850; see also C. H. James, *A Lecture on Wages delivered before the Total Abstainers of Merthyr Tydfil* (Merthyr Tydfil, 1851), p. 8.

[150] *Morning Chronicle*, 27 March 1850.

[151] *Morning Chronicle*, 8 April 1850.

[152] G.R.O., D/DG. Section C, Box 5, William Menelaus: Memorandum on the Employment of Women and Children in the Iron Works of South Wales.

[153] See B. H. Malkin, *The Scenery, Antiquities and Biography of South Wales* (1807), i, p. 273; G. S. Kenrick, *The Population of Pontypool and the Parish of Trevethin, situated in the so-called 'Disturbed Districts'* (1840), p. 24; *P.P.*, 1842, XVII, p. 516; Thomas Rees, *Miscellaneous Papers on Subjects Relating to Wales* (1867), p. 91.

[154] For example, see C.C.L. MS 2.329, 'A Cambrian Literary Gentleman', The Social, Industrial and Literary State of the Cambrian Nation (1880), pp. 134-5; *C.M.G.*, 8 January 1853; *Report of the Select Committee of the House of Lords on Intemperance, P.P.*, 1877, XI (271), pp. 573-5.

[155] See K. T. Weetch, 'The Dowlais Ironworks and its Industrial Community, 1760-1850' (unpublished London School of Economics M.Sc. (Econ.) thesis, 1963), p. 142.

[156] I. C. Peate, *The Traditional Welsh House* (Liverpool, 1946), p. 134; David Williams, *Rebecca Riots*, pp. 98, 109.

[157] G.R.O., Dowlais MSS, J. Evans to Charlotte Guest, 25 September 1854, f. 479; see also M. Elsas (ed.), *Iron in the Making. Dowlais Iron Company Letters, 1782-1860* (1960), pp. 73-4.

[158] For example, see G. Bird, *Observations on Cholera* (Swansea, 1849), p. 59; *C.M.G.*, 2 October 1852; *Merthyr Telegraph*, 26 November 1870; A. Emrys-Jones, *Diseases produced by Drink.* (1888), passim.

[159] See *C.M.G.*, 17 November 1832; 29 December 1832.

[160] U.K. Census, 1851, Division X, p. 23.

[161] *Western Mail*, 14 February 1889.

[162] *Report of the Health of Towns Commission into the Sanitary Condition of the Labouring Population of Britain by Sir Henry de la Bêche, P.P.*, 1845, XVIII, 148 (henceforth cited as the *de la Bêche Report*).

[163] Ibid.

[164] *Report to the General Board of Health on a Preliminary Inquiry into the Sewerage, Drainage and Supply of Water, and the Sanitary Condition of the Inhabitants of Merthyr Tydfil, P.P.*, 1850, XI, 14 (henceforth cited as the *Rammell Report*).

[165] C. H. James, op. cit., p. 12. For immigration and emigration and the state of the market in Merthyr, see Elsas, op. cit., p. 47; *C.M.G.*, 11 May, 26 October, 23 November 1833; 10 and 24 December 1836; 5 and 19 February, 16 April, 21 May, 4 June, 20 August 1842; 25 March, 24 June, and 1 July 1843; 24 February, 1 June and 7 December 1844; *Cambrian*, 30 June and 25 December 1857; 29 January, 5 and 19 March 1858.

[166] H. A. Bruce, *Merthyr in 1852*, p. 7 'He was sorry to say, all the ragamuffins of the immense population made Merthyr their headquarters. As decomposed elements in refuse water, all gravitated to the bottom of the basin, so all the dregs of the vast population found their way to Merthyr—all the gypsies, thieves, rag-and-bobtail of those 200,000, all the way from Pontypool, were sure to be found at Merthyr. They lived in unity by themselves, and were in perfect peace among themselves, but at war with all the rest of the world.' *C.M.G.*, 7 April 1866. Speech of John Griffith, rector of Merthyr, at the annual general meeting of the Llandaff Diocesan Society.

[167] U.K. Census, 1851, p. 893.

[168] *Morning Chronicle*, 15 April 1850; *C.M.G.*, 13 July 1850.

[169] H. A. Bruce, *The Present Position and Future Prospects of the Working Classes in the Manufacturing Districts of South Wales* (1851), p. 4.

[170] It is difficult to gain a precise statistical idea of the proportion of skilled to unskilled workmen in the Merthyr ironworks, but a partial indication can be given by examining the numbers and

occupations of men employed at several furnaces.

Grades Of Workmen Employed

Denomination	Numbers	Percentage
Furnace and Millmen	70	25
Miners and Colliers	100	35.7
Artisans	40	14.3
Labourers	35	12.5
Boys, women, inferior workmen and old aged	35	12.5

Report on the State of Elementary Education in the Mining Districts of South Wales, P.P. 1840, XL. pp. 207-8. This information was derived from 'several ironmasters' in the area and probably conformed to an average blast furnace and rolling mill in Merthyr. The categories of men in the table who could have been classed as skilled were the furnace and millmen, some of the colliers and the artisans (carpenters, masons, etc.). The proportion of all skilled men to unskilled was approximately 40 : 50 per cent. These skilled men were recruited, for the most part, in the immediate vicinity of the works. (See *Report of the Select Committee of the House of Commons on the Payment of Wages Bill, P.P.* 1854, XVI, Q. 6,085.)

[171] *C.M.G.,* 9 November 1833, 24 September 1836; H. A. Bruce, *On Amusements,* pp. 10-11.

[172] For evidence of the small middle-class element in the population of Merthyr in the nineteenth century, see U.K. Census, 1851, Division XI, p. 826; *Morning Chronicle,* 4 March 1850; *Rammell Report,* pp. 11-12, 22, 24; *P.P.,* 1854, XIV (231), Q. 2,863; William Kay, *Report on the Sanitary Condition of Merthyr Tydfil* (Merthyr Tydfil, 1854), p. 4; *Contemporary Review,* April 1882, p. 659.

[173] *Rammell Report,* p. 11.

[174] Ibid.

[175] See *C.M.G.,* 11 February 1837, 6 January 1838; J. L. and B. Hammond, *The Town Labourer, 1760-1832* (1917), p. 81; S. Williams (ed.), *Glamorgan Historian,* vol. 4 (Cowbridge, 1967), pp. 32-4.

[176] *C.M.G.,* 12 November 1842; *Morning Chronicle,* 4 March 1850.

[177] C.C.L. MS 4,683, Henry Murton, *Recollections of Dowlais, 1808-1812,* p. 35.

[178] This paragraph leans heavily on Weetch, op. cit., pp. 135-55.

[179] *Monmouthshire Merlin,* 10 March 1832.

[180] See *Rammell Report,* pp. 24-30.

[181] See *C.M.G.,* 27 October 1848.

[182] *de la Bêche Report,* p. 322.

[183] *Morning Chronicle,* 29 April 1850.

[184] G.R.O., Dowlais MSS, Thomas Thompson to Lady Charlotte Guest, 20 September 1854, 1,243.

[185] *Merthyr Express,* 25 May 1867.

[186] Ibid.

[187] *C.M.G.,* 17 July 1847.

[188] Ibid., 3 May 1850.

[189] *Morning Chronicle,* 4 March 1850.

[190] *de la Bêche Report,* p. 318; see also *Education Report, P.P.,* 1847, XVII, pp. 303-5.

[191] *de la Bêche Report,* pp. 320-1, 328.

[192] *Rammell Report,* p. 36.

[193] C.C.L. MS 4. 683, pp. 22-3.

[194] *Rammell Report,* p. 40.

[195] See G.R.O., Dowlais MSS, John Evans to Lady Charlotte Guest, October 1854, ff. 833-6.

[196] *Morning Chronicle,* 4 March 1850.

[197] Ibid., 15 April 1850.

[198] Ibid., 4 March 1850.

[199] J. L. & B. Hammond, op. cit., p. 81.

[200] *P.P.,* 1854, XIV (231), QQ. 2,869-70.

[201] For example, see *C.M.G.,* 15 and 29 October, 1833; 5, 12 September; 3, 10, 17 October 1835; 23 January, 27 February, 26 April, 14 and 31 May, 7, 14 and 21 June 1836.

[202] Ibid., 2 November 1833.

[203] Ibid., 26 April 1834.

[204] Ibid., 9 December 1837.

[205] Ibid., June-September 1846.

[206] G.R.O., Q Em, Box 7, 1/9F, Chief Constable of Glamorgan, Reports and Quarterly Returns, 1842-60, 1868-88. The remainder of the Glamorgan Police District comprised Newbridge (Pontypridd), Ogmore and Swansea.

[207] Ibid., *sub* 15 September 1846.

[208] For this, see Harrison, *Drink and the Victorians*, p. 40.

[209] See R. Bendix, *Work and Authority in Industry* (1934), pp. 203-4; Sidney Pollard, *The Genesis of Modern Management* (paperback edn., 1968), p. 213.

[210] For a useful summary of the advantages of domestic industry see P. Mantoux, *The Industrial Revolution in the Eighteenth Century* (revised edn., 1961), p. 409. For freedom in Welsh slate quarries see D. Pritchard, 'The Slate Industry of North Wales' (unpublished University of Wales M.A. thesis, 1935), p. 71.

[211] S. Pollard, op. cit., p. 190; A. Ure, *The Philosophy of Manufactures* (1835), p. 15.

[212] Ibid., p. 191; M. I. Thomis, *The Town Labourer and the Industrial Revolution* (1974), ch. 6.

[213] For 'respectability', see Pollard, op. cit., pp. 229, 231.

[214] See Weetch, op. cit., pp. 53-4, 144.

[215] T. S. Ashton, *Economic Fluctuations in England, 1700-1800* (1959), pp. 173-4.

[216] See Charles Wilkins, op. cit., p. 52.

[217] N.L.W. Cyfarthfa MSS., William Crawshay to Crawshay jun., 19 January 1814; G.R.O., Dowlais MSS, T. Bridge to W. Taitt, 2 June 1815. See also J. P. Addis, *The Crawshay Dynasty* (Cardiff, 1957), pp. 60, 73, 125.

[218] For specific examples, see Elsas, op. cit., pp. 64-70.

[219] See Pollard, op. cit., p. 227.

[220] See E. W. Evans, *The Miners of South Wales* (Cardiff, 1961), pp. 11-12.

[221] See P. T. Winskill, op. cit., vol. 1, p. 70; B. Harrison, 'The British Prohibitionists, 1853-1872. A Biographical Analysis', *International Review of Social History,* XV (1970), part 3, p. 390.

[222] See *P.P.,* 1834, VIII, 319.

[223] G.R.O., Dowlais MSS, D/DG, Section C, Box 5, Menelaus Memorandum, n.d.

[224] *Merthyr Express,* 2 September 1865.

[225] *Report of H. Seymour Tremenheere on the State of the Population in the Mining Districts, P.P.,* 1846, XXIV, 418-9.

[226] Ibid.

[227] Ibid.

[228] Ibid.

[229] N.L.W., MS 16,157 B, op. cit.

[230] *Monmouthshire Merlin,* 7 July 1882.

[231] G.R.O., D/D, GV/35, Sunday Closing Act, Correspondence, 1889: W. J. Bray to Pendarves Vivian, 14 June 1889.

[232] See W. E. Kochs, *A Short Treatise on Labour, Strikes, Liberty, Religious, Political and General Public Questions* (Cardiff, 1892), p. 17.

[233] See *C.M.G.,* 18 January 1840; *Report on the State of the Population in the Mining Districts, P.P.,* 1847, XVI, 403; *The Reformer and South Wales Times,* 11 October 1861.

[234] *C.M.G.,* 23 June 1854.

[235] N.L.W., MS 16, 157 B, op. cit.

[236] Monmouthshire Record Office, John Harford's Memorandum Book, *sub* 22 April 1796, quoted in A. G. Jones, 'The Economic, Industrial and Social History of Ebbw Vale, 1775-1927' (unpublished University of Wales M.A. thesis, 1929), pp. 37-8.

[237] See, for example, G.R.O., Dowlais MSS, Robert Napier to William Gardener, 27 April 1827; Elsas, op. cit., p. 25.

[238] Ibid., p. 35, John Griffiths to William Taitt, 8 February 1799.

[239] Ibid., p. 79, John Wareteg (pseud.) to Josiah John Guest, 3 April 1829.

[240] Ibid., J. J. Guest to E. J. Hutchins, 28 February 1831.

[241] *de la Bêche Report,* p. 324; Monmouthshire Record Office, Bythway MSS, f. 0067, quoted in Morris and Williams, op. cit., p. 213.

[242] *The British Temperance Advocate,* 15 February 1840.

[243] *Star of Gwent,* 14 July 1855.

[244] G.R.O., Dowlais MSS, John Guest to John Evans, 15 August 1848, f. 987.

[245] Ibid., 28 April 1852, f. 158.

[246] See *Merthyr Express,* 2 September 1865.

[247] *Newport Evening Telegram,* 7 September 1874, quoted in N.L.W., MS 16, 157 B, op. cit.

[248] See G. W. Hilton, *The Truck System* (Cambridge, 1960), p. 1. For details of the truck system in south Wales, see E. W. Evans, op. cit., pp. 9-14, 73-8.

[249] *P.P.,* 1854, XVI, 821.

[250] William Crawshay the younger estimated in 1860 that the truck system gave his rivals an illegal advantage of 10 per cent in wages. N.L.W., Cyfarthfa MSS, William Crawshay to Robert Crawshay, 26 March 1860, quoted in J. P. Addis, op. cit., p. 118.

[251] P.R.O. HO 40/22, 24 May 1827.

[252] *Report of the Select Committee of the House of Commons on the Payment of Wages in Goods*, *P.P.*, 1842, IX (471), Q. 1,405.

[253] See *P.P.*, 1854, XVI, Q. 6,408; *Report of the Commissioners appointed to enquire into the Truck System*, *P.P.*, 1871, XXXVI, p. xxiii, QQ 3,266-76, 4,099-102, 4,182, 27,538, 35,478.

[254] *P.P.*, 1854, XVI, Q. 6,363.

[255] *P.P.*, 1871, XXXVI, p. vi. See also *Report on the State of the Population in the Mining Districts*, *P.P.*, 1852, XXXI, p. 8. At Blaina in April 1864 it was alleged that trade union leaders from England had been brought into the town by shopkeepers and publicans to agitate against the company shops; see *Monmouthshire Merlin*, 2 April 1864. Guest's company shop at Dowlais was closed when Guest became a Member of Parliament in 1832; he had obviously to make himself popular with those publicans and shopkeepers who possessed the vote. See *P.P.*, 1854, XVI, QQ. 6,038, 6,437.

[256] See *Monmouthshire Merlin*, 11 June 1842; 'Ignotus', *The Last Thirty Years in a Mining District* (1867), pp. 41-3; Morris and Williams, op. cit., pp. 227-8.

[257] See the interesting article on truck and long pay by one of Henry Mayhew's Welsh correspondents, in *Morning Chronicle*, 8 April 1850.

[258] *P.P.*, 1871, XXXVI, Q. 22,839.

[259] *The Ferret or South Wales Ratepayer*, 15 February 1871.

[260] For example, see *P.P.*, 1871, XXXVI, QQ. 27,713-14, 27,554, 26,658-63, 23,691-702, 29,555, 31,659, 43,602-13.

[261] Thomas Jones, op. cit., pp. 114-5. Yet, long pays could cause problems. A thirteen weeks' pay at Rhymney in October 1882 brought drunkenness and rioting. 'People seemed almost mad . . . nothing would satisfy them but fighting.' *Merthyr Express*, 14 October 1882.

[262] *Cambrian*, 10 June 1859.

[263] *P.P.*, 1871, XXXVI, Q. 19,351.

[264] See Hilton, op. cit., p. 30.

[265] *The Reformer and South Wales Times*, 13 September 1861.

[266] *P.P.*, 1842, IX, Q. 1,816.

[267] *P.P.*, 1854, XVI, QQ. 4,461, 4,498-9, 4,622, 4,628, 4,791; cf. *P.P.*, 1871, XXXVI, QQ. 19,360-63.

[268] N.L.W., MS 16, 157 B; *P.P.*, 1871, XXXVI, QQ. 19,487, 19,545.

[269] Ibid., QQ. 19,399, 19,406-8, 19,469.

[270] For example, see ibid., Q. 18,720.

[271] *P.P.*, 1854, XVI, Q. 5,657.

[272] *P.P.*, 1842, IX, Q. 2,001; *P.P.*, 1,846, XXIV, p. 412.

[273] *Morning Chronicle*, 27 March 1850.

[274] *P.P.*, 1847, XXVII, 299. For similar criticism of the system see *C.M.G.*, 18 January 1840, 8 February 1840, 29 February 1840; *Monmouthshire Merlin*, 1 November 1844.

[275] *C.M.G.*, 27 May 1848.

[276] See *P.P.*, 1846, XXIV, p. 37; *P.P.*, 1854, XVI, p. 383.

[277] N.L.W., Cyfarthfa MSS, Box 4, Bundle 13, R. Crawshay to W. Crawshay, 16 April 1859, quoted in Williams and Morris, op. cit., p. 231.

[278] For example, see *Morning Chronicle*, 27 March 1850.

[279] On this, see E. P. Thompson, 'Time, Work-discipline and Industrial Capitalism', *Past and Present*, no. 38 (December 1967), p. 81.

[280] For example, see *C.M.G.*, 19 December 1835, 24 May 1845; *P.P.*, 1846, XXIV, pp. 414, 418; *Merthyr Telegraph*, 23 April 1870; *South Wales Daily News*, 1 April 1873.

[281] G.R.O., Dowlais MSS, Exuperius Pickering to J. J. Guest, 6 March 1835; Elsas, op. cit., p. 68.

[282] *South Wales Daily News*, 14 January 1873.

[283] For example, see *C.M.G.*, 10 September 1842.

[284] See *Alliance News*, 6 August 1870.

[285] *C.M.G.*, 8 July 1843.

[286] G.R.O., Dowlais MSS. John Evans to Charlotte Guest, 13 July 1855; Elsas, op. cit., p. 57.

[287] G.R.O., D/D. Rh 224; *A Hundred Years of Brewing: Andrew Buchan's Breweries, 1839-1939* (1939), p. 5. See also *P.P.*, 1842, IX. Q. 1,800; Proceedings of the World's Temperance Convention (1846), p. 93; *P.P.*, 1854, XVI, QQ. 859-67.

[288] *Merthyr Express*, 16 May 1885.

[289] Thomas Jones, op. cit., pp. 138-9.

[290] *P.P.*, 1871, XXXVI. QQ. 20,463, 20,469-70.

[291] *Star of Gwent*, 5 January 1856.

[292] *C.M.G.*, 2 October 1863.

[293] *Silurian*, 31 July 1852.

[294] See pp. 227, 232.

[295] For example, see G.R.O., 1/9F, Chief Constable of Glamorgan Report, 1842.

[296] Caernarfon Record Office, Caernarvonshire Police Records, Standing Joint Committee Minutes, *sub.* 3 April 1900; J. O. Jones, *The History of the Caernarvonshire Constabulary, 1856-1950* (Caernarfon, 1963), p. 55.

[297] Ibid., p. 56.

[298] See, for example, *Cardiff Reporter*, 23 September 1822; *Cambrian*, 1 April 1859.

[299] *C.M.G.*, 1 October 1842.

[300] G.R.O., 1/9F, op. cit.

[301] *C.M.G.*, 27 July 1839. For drunkenness amongst Merthyr police in the 1830s and 1840s, see C.C.L. MS 2.1294, C. H. James, 'What I remember about myself and Old Merthyr', 1892, p. 21.

[302] J. O. Jones, 'The History of the Caernarvonshire Police Force, 1856-1900' (unpublished University of Wales M.A. thesis, 1956), p. 125.

[303] See *P.P.*, 1847, XVII, pp. 286, 351, 478-85.

[304] *Y Dysgedydd*, May 1848, pp. 147-8.

[305] For example, see L. Levi, 'The limits of legislative interference with the sale of fermented liquors,' *Journal of the Statistical Society*, 35, 1872, 54-5.

[306] W. W. Hunt, *'To guard my people.' An account of the origin and history of the Swansea Police* (Swansea, 1957), p. 67.

[307] J. O. Jones, *The History of the Caernarvonshire Constabulary*, op. cit., p. 88.

[308] *Report of the Select Committee of the House of Lords on Intemperance, P.P.*, 1877, XI, p. 757.

[309] Ibid., XIV, pp. 586-9.

[310] *South Wales Daily News*, 16 November 1881.

[311] Merionethshire Record Office, Merionethshire Constabulary, QA/P, Register of Charges, 1875-1939, 2 vols.

[312] Ibid.

[313] J. Rowntree and A. Sherwell, *The Temperance Problem and Social Reform* (1899), p. 88.

[314] *Cambrian*, 31 December 1880.

[315] *Monmouthshire Merlin*, 17 September 1886.

CHAPTER II

THE GROWTH OF THE TEMPERANCE MOVEMENT IN WALES: MODERATIONISTS VERSUS TEETOTALLERS, 1831-53

The temperance movement originated in America in the mid-1820s and found its way to Wales after successful progress through Ireland, Scotland and the north of England. At first, the 'temperance movement' was an anti-spirits movement only, advocating total abstinence from spirits and moderation in the use of beer and wine. The British and Foreign Temperance Society (B.F.T.S.) was founded in London in 1831 as the national moderation organisation. In 1834, however, the doctrine of total abstinence or teetotalism appeared in Lancashire, and it seemed to offer a more certain and uncompromising solution to the drink problem. By 1838 teetotalism had almost completely usurped moderation as the most likely and the most popular solution to the drink problem in Britain. [1]

The temperance movement in Wales aimed to bring men to a higher level of moral perfection. The heart of the doctrine of temperance lay in the manner in which it coupled economic and social success with moral virtue: the theme of uplifting the underdog through temperance reform and through stressing both self-help and middle-class example-setting, was a major one in nineteenth-century Welsh temperance literature and oratory.

The first Welsh temperance societies were established not in Wales but amongst the Welsh populations of Manchester and Liverpool. At Manchester on 7 October 1831, the Rev. Humphrey Jones, a Wesleyan Methodist minister, presided over the inaugural meeting. [2] On 17 February 1832, a society was established at a Welsh chapel in Pall Mall, in Liverpool, and others were soon formed in connection with the various Welsh congregations in Liverpool and district. [3] It is not surprising that this should have been so. The north-west was the first and the strongest home of the temperance movement in England, and Liverpool and Manchester had attracted immigrants from north and mid-Wales for some years. The Welsh communities in the two towns obviously shared strong cultural affinities with those from which the immigrants came and reproduced many of their religious and national characteristics. To people newly uprooted from Welsh rural life the mere size of Liverpool and Manchester must have been daunting, and identification with some familiar group such as that of chapel or church a matter of necessity. Often the only source of help for the newcomer, who by virtue of his 'foreigness' was not eligible for help from local sources, was the friendship and charity of his fellow nationals, organized through their various religious bodies which thus provided a kind of 'moral and physical chaperonage'. [4] Social life centred on the chapel or church, which was for many years the only socialising influence at work on the immigrants. It is thus possible to see the Welsh temperance societies in Liverpool and Manchester as 'friendly societies' for Welshmen cast adrift among Englishmen.

Social anthropologists inform us that modern Africans moving from country to town often form new types of voluntary association: small private societies which unite the like-minded, replace the community ties which gave structure to rural life, and assign prestige through elections to petty offices. [5] The Welsh temperance societies in Liverpool and Manchester were institutions of this sort. Like its great rival, the public house, the temperance society could ensure that the newcomer to the towns received recognition, education, employment, friends and support; it could encourage him to resist the temptations of urban life; and it could provide a framework for daily conduct. Like the urban chapels to which they were so often physically attached in Liverpool and Manchester, Welsh temperance societies were 'havens of refuge in an utterly strange and alien landscape. Here, and here only, could the old links with home be maintained, the familiar forms of worship be recovered.' [6]

The first temperance society to be established in Wales itself was at Holywell in March 1832, [7] and this was followed by auxiliary societies of the B.F.T.S. at Pembroke (June 1832), Swansea (June 1833), Wrexham (August 1833), Cardiff, Neath and Newport (December 1833), Ruabon (January 1834), Abergavenny, Pontypool and Merthyr Tydfil (February 1834), Newtown (April 1834), Denbigh (May 1834), Ebbw Vale (August 1834), Carmarthen, Haverfordwest and Narberth (October 1834), Crickhowell (May 1835), Brecon and Glasbury (July 1835), Aberystwyth, Builth Wells, Cardigan, Fishguard and Llanidloes (October 1835). [8] All such moderation societies allowed members to drink beer, porter and wine. For example, as its name implies, the Ebbw Vale Two Pints a Day

Society allowed each member to drink in a public or beer house, two pints of beer every day in the week except Sunday, on which day members were not allowed to visit any drinking place. As a disciplinary measure, any member who transgressed this rule was fined 2s.6d. Local publicans became so alarmed that they tried to put pressure on their potential customers by refusing to sell any refreshment to members of the society.[9]

On 8 March 1835 the first Welsh total abstinence or teetotal society was formed at Rose Place, off Scotland Road, Liverpool.[10] The first public meeting in Wales for the advocacy of teetotalism was held at Tabernacle Chapel, Bangor, on 5 May 1835, the chief speaker being Robert Williams, ('Corfanydd'), of Liverpool.[11] During the early and mid-1830s, the leading advocate of teetotalism in Wales was the Rev. Evan Davies, ('Eta Delta'), of Llanerchymedd, who wrote frequently on the subject in Y Dysgedydd. Most of his articles were based almost wholly on Irish and American temperance tracts, and in some cases they were straight translations of them into Welsh. On 13 May 1835 a teetotal section was established as a branch of the Llanerchymedd Temperance Society, and Evan Davies and his wife were the first people to sign the teetotal pledge. On 4 November 1835 Davies lectured on teetotalism at Llanfechell in Anglesey. Over twenty people signed the pledge, and there thus came into existence the first bona fide teetotal society in Wales.[12]

Under the impulse of religious revivalism the cause of moderation, and later, of teetotalism, made rapid progress in Wales in the 1830s. In the south-west, for example, the membership of Pembroke Temperance Society increased more than six-fold during the first year of the Society's existence.[13] By February 1834 membership of B.F.T.S. auxiliary societies in Wales stood at 1,291, while by October of the same year the number had increased to 1,600.[14] The following is a typical account of the formation of a B.F.T.S. auxiliary society in Wales:[15]

> 2 January 1834: a meeting was held at the Boys National School Room, Dowlais, the Rev. Evan Jenkins in the Chair, for the purpose of forming a Temperance Society. The meeting was addressed by Owen Clarke, agent of the parent society at London, who moved a resolution that it was expedient to establish a Temperance Society at Merthyr, as an Auxiliary to the British and Foreign Temperance Society. The resolution was seconded by Thomas Revel Guest and carried. A resolution was also carried for forming the officers and Committee of the Society. On 3 January a meeting favourable to the object took

place, for the purpose of taking the steps requisite for bringing the Society into a state of operation. At this meeting several ministers of Merthyr and Dowlais subscribed their names as members of the Society and a Committee was formed to carry the objects of it into effect.

The functions of a B.F.T.S. auxiliary were to distribute weekly tracts, to collect subscriptions and generally to promote the aims of the Society. The great advantage of the tract was that it provided an excuse for visiting people's homes; and since temperance reformers had to call back to collect it, a second visit would follow. In this way, the barriers between one individual and another were broken down. At Pembroke, for example, the B.F.T.S. divided the town into seventeen districts each of about thirty houses, and one member of the local society was allocated to each district.[16]

During the mid-1830s however the growth in the number of teetotallers rapidly overtook that in the number of moderationists. The number of people who had taken the teetotal pledge in north Wales and amongst the Welsh population of Liverpool up to 15 December 1836 was estimated to be 29,058.[17] The strongest areas of support were Bethesda (2,804 teetotallers), Ruabon and Rhos (1,200), Denbigh (1,150), Newtown (950), Llanrwst (900), Liverpool (870), Llanidloes (800), Ruthin (750), Caernarfon (736), Holywell (700), Treffynnon (700), Bangor (605), Wrexham (600), Adwy'r Clawdd (554), and Trefriw (553).[18] Particularly noticeable is the remarkable rate of growth of Welsh teetotal societies between 1836 and 1838. Llangollen Total Abstinence Society increased from two members in September 1836 to 260 members in October.[19] The Liverpool Welsh Total Abstinence Society grew in numerical strength from 122 members in March 1836 to 1,272 members in March 1837; Betws Gwerful Goch Society increased from 18 to 538 members between December 1836 and December 1837. The forty-six teetotal societies of Anglesey, whose patron was W. O. Stanley M.P., and whose treasurer was the future M.P., Richard Davies, reported a membership of 24,780 in August 1838, a gain in one year of 13,955 members.[20] By April 1838 it was claimed that there were 70,000 teetotallers in north Wales, including 20,000 in Anglesey, 7,000 in the Vale of Clwyd, and 1,300 in Machynlleth, a town with an estimated population of 1,750.[21] At Bangor, twenty-six beer-house keepers gave up their houses, largely through lack of custom, and nine of them joined Bangor Teetotal Society.[22]

Such striking growth was partly facilitated by itinerant lecturers and by the circulation of temperance magazines in the Welsh language. *Y Dirwestydd*, for example, which first appeared in August 1836, edited by John Jones of Llansantffraid, claimed to have a total circulation of 75,000 in January 1838;[23] by April 1838, 4,000 copies of the magazine were printed each month.[24]

The opinion of the itinerant Preston temperance advocate, James Teare, in September 1836 had been that 'Wales is in a dreadful state'.[25] During 1836 and 1837 he undertook several tours of Wales lecturing on teetotalism, urging the formation of teetotal societies and the conversion of existing temperance societies into teetotal societies. His visit to Wrexham in April 1836—'something like the visits of Paul to Athens'—resulted in 400 people signing the teetotal pledge.[26] From several parts of Wales, local correspondents of the *Preston Temperance Advocate* were witnesses to the fact that moderation had proved a failure and that teetotalism was proving to be a permanent solution to drunkenness. A Denbigh correspondent noted: 'Every Sunday night we have a teetotal prayer meeting after all the sermons are ended.'[27] From Conwy a correspondent wrote: 'We hold teetotal meetings in every chapel of every denomination, and many drunkards are wonderfully reformed. This is the Lord's doing.'[28] The most powerful indigenous teetotal spokesmen in north Wales in the 1830s were the Revs. John Elias, Christmas Evans, William Williams of Wern, David Charles of Bala, grandson of Thomas Charles, Robert Parry (*Robyn Ddu Eryri*), Henry Griffith, rector of Llandrygarn, and the industrialist and future M.P. for Merionethshire, Samuel Holland.

The progress of both moderation and teetotalism was slower in south Wales than in the north, and the Rev. Dr. John Thomas of Liverpool gave as a reason for this that drinking was more general in the larger private houses of south Wales than in those of the north, and that, as a consequence, the natural leaders of the move-ment—respectable middle-class example-setters—were slow to advocate the temperance movement in the south. Certainly, a much larger proportion of country estates in south Wales at this time employed maltsters. Malt houses were a common architectural feature of such estates and were built for the purpose of preparing barley malt, not only for the immediate household, but for the estate tenants as well.[29] Of greater significance, however, is the fact that in north Wales the leading nonconformist denomination was that of the

Calvinistic Methodists, which, under the strong moral leadership of the Rev. John Elias, constituted the most enthusiastic support of temperance. The leading denominations of the south—the Independents and the Baptists—did not, in general, lag very far behind in their support of temperance, but for most of the 1830s they seemed to lack the vigorous temperance missionary impulse manifested in north Wales by the Calvinistic Methodists.[30] Teetotalism made its first appearance in south Wales in October 1836 when the Cardiff Total Abstinence Society was established, strongly supported by John Cory, a local ship owner and Wesleyan Methodist.[31] The second teetotal society formed in the south was at Carmarthen on 20 December 1836 when the Rev. John Davies, a Wesleyan Methodist minister, signed the pledge.[32] The movement was strongly supported by the Carmarthen Presbyterian College. Two lectures by Joseph Livesey of Preston, the founder of teetotalism, *The Great Delusion* and *Twelve Reasons*, were translated into Welsh and published by the Carmarthen society.[33] However, the dissemination of teetotalism in south Wales was not as spectacular as that in the north. In August 1837 the Revs. Owen Thomas of Bangor and R. P. Griffith of Llanberis were deputed by the North Wales Temperance Association to visit south Wales to lecture on teetotalism. Sceptics suggested they would remain alive until they reached Merthyr Tydfil.[34] They visited the Quarterly Association of Calvinistic Methodists of South Wales at Haverfordwest on 24-25 October, where they were well received and promised support by the south Wales Methodists. The effect of this was to throw open the Calvinistic Methodist chapels of south Wales to Thomas and Griffith for use as lecture halls.[35] In all they visited 119 places in five months and accepted 1,195 members into the temperance fold.[36]

At first, relatively few ministers of religion in south Wales were willing to support the teetotal movement which until early 1839 relied upon periodic injections of enthusiasm from north Wales and occasionally from Lancashire. In February 1838 Robert Parry travelled through south Wales lecturing on temperance,[37] and in February 1839 the Rev. D. Griffiths of Bethesda undertook a temperance missionary tour of south Wales during which he recruited 9,000 people as members of local teetotal societies.[38] However, there was one south Wales minister whose support of temperance was very important for the growth of the movement in the area: the Rev. David Rees, Independent, of Llanelli. His publications, *Y Dirwestydd*

Deheuol (1838) and *Y Dirwestwr Deheuol* (1840) were the first teetotal magazines to be published in south Wales, and he was instrumental in the establishment of the Llanelli Total Abstinence Society in April 1837. Of the ministers of religion in the Llanelli area in 1837 only Rees publicly supported temperance. In its first few months of existence the Llanelli society failed to find a single chapel prepared to open its doors for teetotal meetings. Indeed, recourse had to be made to the long room of the 'Wheat Sheaf', a local public house, where meetings were addressed by Rees and by north Wales ministers. In July 1837, however, the influence of David Rees enabled the Independent chapels in Llanelli to be thrown open to the society. [39]

Temperance reformers of the 1830s quickly came to embrace teetotalism, maintaining that moderation failed to get to the root of the drink problem. Wales was essentially a beer-drinking country and the anti-spirits pledge therefore, was almost superfluous in its attempts to bring a greater degree of sobriety to the country. [40] Backsliders from the moderation pledge were numerous. A member of Denbigh Moderation Society maintained in November 1836 that the society had failed to reclaim, permanently, a single drunkard; [41] at Swansea too, moderation had been 'an utter failure'. [42] A Merthyr Tydfil temperance reformer maintained in the late-1830s that 'the moderation societies could do no more to stem the current of intemperance than could a tissue-paper screen divert the Niagara'. [43] It became apparent to many that forbidding alcohol under one name and allowing its use under another name, was not an effectual way either to reclaim the drunkard or to prevent the moderate drinker from becoming intemperate. A Flintshire teetotaller noted in 1846 that 'the failure [of moderation] has illustrated the futility of conselling against effects while we supply the causes. [44]

For contemporaries, the advantages of teetotalism were that it seemed to be a safe and a very simple remedy for insobriety. Teetotalism was more precise in its aims than moderation, and more resolute and combative in its methods. Teetotallers were more confident that a really dramatic change in national habits could be speedily secured; teetotalism offered the attraction of a sudden social transformation. The move against the 'mere' moderation of the B.F.T.S. was led by a nonconformist dislike for its aristocratic and Anglican support and structure. The B.F.T.S. appealed only to the respectable and did little to reclaim the drunkard. It encouraged example-setting from above rather than generating self-help from below; it sought to confirm the sober in their sobriety rather than to reclaim the intemperate.[45]

The Rev. William Jones of Bangor preferred teetotalism to 'mere temperance', because teetotalism was 'perfectly safe—herein you will be in no danger'.[46] Whereas many people found the moderate use of drink very difficult, teetotalism they found comparatively easy.[47] The real case for the extreme view of teetotalism was that since temperance propaganda consisted essentially of personal persuasion, one could not persuade another man to go along a certain road unless one were going along it oneself. But for some it was a very difficult journey. 'Eben Fardd', the bard of Clynnog, considered that 'hard teetotalism' did 'great violence' to his temper.[48] There were, assuredly, many teetotallers who, as the *Cardiff and Merthyr Guardian* put it, were 'longing for a lark' but who did not wish to break their pledge immediately.[49]

It was claimed that teetotalism was a cause which appealed to the 'higher principles of man's moral nature', and as such it was destined to seize a firm hold upon the 'influential' and 'thinking portion of society'.[50] Throughout the century, arguments of self-interest were used by temperance reformers to win middle-class support.[51] For instance, it was estimated in 1881 that the public house cost the ratepayers $2s.6d.$ in the pound in the shape of poor rates, police rates and gaol rates.[52] Thus ratepayers were urged to encourage working-class sobriety. So, by definition, temperance advocates were usually the polite, the respectable and the law-abiding.

In order to justify the appearance, and to facilitate the progress of teetotalism, drink and drunkenness were portrayed as being at the root of a multitude of social ills: the public house led to pawnshop, pauperism, poorhouse, policeman and prison. 'Drunkenness is a sure sin, very repugnant and atrocious: it opens the door to every sin and filth . . . to every lie and treachery. It destroys every earthly comfort . . . Drunkenness is a sin . . . thus it is ungodly'.[53] Drunkenness was described as the chief destructive agent in the human family: it brought disease and premature death.[54] Drink destroyed the whole of man's higher nature; it caused his fall, and consequently temperance reformers must have a moral compulsion to 'save'.[55] In the light of these views, moderation seemed 'shameful nonsense'.[56] 'Only the sober walk with God', warned *Yr Eurgrawn* in February 1836.[57]

The arguments of the moderate drinker, that man must trust his reason in not drinking excessively, and that man needed release from his inhibitions were foreign to the doctrine of teetotalism. As teetotallers believed that 'impulse renunciation' and the control of desire and spontaneity were the keys to moral conduct, drinking became a great threat because it could engulf the drinker in demands which he could not control. Anything less than perfect regulation of behaviour, anything less than command, was a concession to nature and a sin of great magnitude. Sobriety ensured self-command. In nineteenth-century Wales there was much fear that if the restrictions on impulsive action were even slightly lowered, the individual would go to the extremes of evil and moral and social ruin. Teetotal propaganda often gave detailed accounts of excessive impulsive actions brought about by that one fatal drink.

Generally speaking, the transition from moderation to teetotalism in the Welsh temperance movement was not attended by a great deal of opposition from the mass of the people. However, there were some influential individuals in Welsh life who came out strongly against teetotalism, notably, the Rev. William Williams ('Caledfryn'), of Caernarfon, the Rev. Benjamin Jones ('P.A.Môn'), and 'Eben Fardd' of Clynnog. Caledfryn and P.A.Môn believed that having to take an official, ceremonial pledge of total abstinence was an admission of man's weakness and a gross violation of his potentialities for self-control. This view, though not seeming to be widespread, did find expression elsewhere in Wales. At Cardiff Cymreigyddion Society in April 1839, for instance, Ebenezer Thomas of Caerffili won first prize for the best song 'ridiculing teetotallers and teetotalism, imputing it to their weakness and ignorance; and showing particularly the benefits, privileges and comforts that arise from drinking beer and wine in moderation'.[58]

Caledfryn publicly supported moderation and opposed teetotalism, a stand which required great courage as teetotalism was widely regarded as a highly religious activity, and anyone opposed to it was increasingly regarded as being of the Devil.[59] In a pamphlet published in 1836 Caledfryn admitted that the sins of drunkenness and intemperance were destructive of men and the family, and that drunkenness was almost certainly at the root of 'lying, stealing, whoring and murder'. The only remedy for the hopeless drunkard maintained Caledfryn, was teetotalism.[60] But he held that it was a pity that one felt obliged to use compulsion in order to compel some people to give up drink altogether and to compel others to be temperate. Food and drink existed to maintain life, and for pleasure, and eating and drinking in moderation for pleasure were not denied to man by law or by the Gospel. But not all kinds of food and drink agreed with all men because of differences of appetite and custom. Was it reasonable for one man to condemn the other? asked Caledfryn. Are alcoholic drinks, taken in moderation, destructive of nature in general? As some people demanded a universal teetotalism it was necessary to prove that the drinks from which one should totally abstain contained bad things. But *all* alcoholic drinks were judged by teetotallers to be injurious without distinction, as if they were bad for everyone. Teetotallers argued that alcohol was poisonous, but if this was so, did it follow that it should not be used with other things? One could use the same logic with the air we breathe, argued Caledfryn, as some elements in the air, if taken alone, would destroy man's constitution.

Caledfryn's major principle was that all men should judge for themselves and moderationists should not be compelled to abstain from things other men abused. Temperance in all things was necessary for the full development of the Christian character but teetotal societies, which were not mentioned in the Bible, held that it was an obligation on every Christian to be a teetotaller. Caledfryn objected strongly to the linking of temperance with religion.[61] He maintained that the teetotal position depended almost wholly on Paul's reference to sitting down to eat in the temple of idols—'Wherefore if my food is a hindrance to my brother I shall not eat meat ever lest I offend my brother' (1 Corinthians 8). But this verse proved nothing in favour of Christian temperance, agrued Caledfryn, for it was eating in temples that was objected to by Paul but drinking that was objected to by teetotallers. Furthermore, teetotallers put teetotalism in place of the Gospel. Some of them had maintained that they were succeeding in reclaiming drunkards where the Gospel had failed. If ever there was a 'perfect deism', said Caledfryn, this was it, and Paine and Voltaire and the citizens of Paris had not gone further when they dispatched the Bible out of that city, and chose Voltaire's writings instead to moralise the world. Caledfryn noted that there was abundant proof in the New Testament to show that Christ ate and drank in moderation. Did the teetotallers of Wales believe that their example would affect the world more than the example of Christ?

Teetotallers scorned Caledfryn's views.[62] They asserted that he was not a true Christian, that he had no right to be a minister and that his pamphlet on the matter had been 'broadcast in some areas secretly as if it were the work of Voltaire or Tom Paine'.[63] Early in January 1837 Morris Hughes of Port Dinorwic published a reply to Caledfryn which teetotallers came to regard as the perfect answer.[64] Hughes maintained that Caledfryn argued against the worst aspects of teetotalism and that he was totally inconsistent with his profession as a minister of the Gospel because he was an enemy to an institution—the teetotal society—that was intended chiefly to oppose the corruption of the age. Caledfryn was wrong when he said that teetotalism could not be equated with men's freedom to judge for themselves. If laying down a rule for members of a society to abstain from alcoholic drinks was contrary to the principles of freedom then every society was guilty of this fault, for every society had its particular rules. Moreover, teetotal societies were not forcing men to abstain: members voluntarily accepted the teetotal vow.[65] To Caledfryn's charge that teetotalism had taken the place of the Gospel, teetotallers argued repeatedly, that teetotalism was ordained and commanded in the Bible, and that it was the purpose of teetotal societies to teach this truth to the *gwerin*.[66]

Caledfryn's answer appeared in the same month. In *Ystyriaethau Ychwanegol am Lwyrymwrthodiad* (*'Further Considerations on Total Abstinence'*), he maintained that he did not object to men becoming teetotallers, but he did object to the compulsion and ferocity that was customarily directed against men who differed from teetotallers. But the most amazing thing was that 'Men who were a moral disgrace to humanity a few months ago, are the leading advocates of the total abstainers at present, and those are the ones who consider character and the circumstances of men who have lived unstained lives all their life'.[67] According to Caledfryn, the duty of the church was to give an example of virtue and goodness to the world. There was no proof in the Scriptures to show that it was the church's task to discipline the world: it should only urge sinners to repent and believe in Christ. Or, in other words, the church had no right to discipline anyone except its own members, for only God judged unbelievers. But Caledfryn asserted that teetotal societies had grasped the whip of discipline from the church, and had put it into the hands of unrepentant drunkards. Increasingly, teetotalism was becoming the most important consideration when church members were accepted; personal failings and weaknesses were hidden or neglected.

Caledfryn declared himself convinced that the Bible sanctioned moderate drinking. Wine held an important place in the Bible and it was foolish to say, as teetotallers did, that the wine of the east was non-intoxicating. He claimed that some teetotallers even denied the miracle of turning the water into wine by telling their listeners that the wine was a non-alcoholic variety, because it had not had time to ferment. Wine was used as a sacrificial drink and it was offered with most meat offerings. If wine was a sinful drink and a poison, as teetotallers asserted, would God commend it as an offering on his altar? Moreover, God gave the Israelites detailed instructions on how to treat and keep wines, and one of the greatest judgments that threatened Israel was the taking of their wine from them. In the face of these facts, argued Caledfryn, it was clear that wine was 'a providential preparation for Israel'. The Israelites drank it without worry, and the only thing that was condemned in the Bible was excess. If there was alcohol in the wine of the east, and if the Scriptures allowed men to drink it in moderation, it did not appear that the Bible condemned the moderate use of alcoholic drink in Wales either.

Caledfryn charged teetotallers with gross deceit; it was quite clear, he alleged, that the force of the teetotal pledge and the shame of breaking it were the only considerations that kept them from being drunk and from turning like 'the dog towards its own vomit, and the sow washed in the wallow of the dunghill'. The truth was, said Caledfryn, that man could never change his faults without changing his principles. A tempest could prune the twigs of an oak, but the oak remained. Teetotallers were deluding themselves when they maintained that their example would make drunkards sober. 'After all the noise and the hubbub and the tumult, it is seen quite clearly again, that when the zeal and the hot-headedness cools, the Gospel has to be reverted to in order to make drunkards sober; and it seems that the force that the pledge makes, only prunes a little on the tips of the branches of the bad tree, which will readily be prepared to grow once more.' Teetotalism touched a man's emotions and not his principles, judgment or reason. Caledfryn also criticised the 'guile' in the teetotal movement; it was fairly easy, he asserted, for a cunning man to gain popularity in it, because a host of uneducated *gwerinwyr* had joined the movement. For Caledfryn, the greatest fault of teetotalism, however, was its wild denunciation, which led to slander, libel and persecution.

This re-statement of his views again aroused vigorous opposition to

Caledfryn. All teetotallers were urged to refuse to attend services held by ministers who were opposed to teetotalism.[68] For his part, Caledfryn admitted in September 1837, that he had been 'a teetotaller for weeks', and that he had never argued against men being teetotallers, but 'there is no obligation on the moral and temperate man to join anything but that he chooses to do so'.[69] Early in 1838 a meeting of Caernarfon Temperance (Moderation) Society was held 'to consider the merits of the Teetotallers Society and what appropriate action should be taken towards it by men who are already devoted towards the service of virtue and decency, together with the happiness of the world'. The meeting decided that teetotal societies were 'to be opposed as *something more than one sin*', because they opposed 'every true and holy principle', and because they were teaching the *gwerin* 'disgraceful religious sins' by their example.[70] It was decided to establish a monthly publication at Caernarfon opposed to the compulsion and irrationality of teetotalism. *Yr Adolygydd* was first published at Caernarfon in March 1838 and Caledfryn became editor. He laid down the policy of the new magazine in a pointed address in the first number. The aim of the magazine was not to oppose teetotalism as such but 'those things which we oppose will be those unashamed and impudent assertions that the teetotal society is based on religion—that it is a Godly society—that it is better than the Gospel—that it saves men—that it is the forerunner of the millenium—that it is a divine revelation—that there is no means of being a Christian without being teetotal —that it gives life to the sinner . . . All its foolishness, together with the malicious attacks made on worthy men's characters who are not fools enough to follow them, that is what we oppose steadfastly'.[71]

After the Cymanfa of the Independent Union or Connexion of Caernarfonshire at Conwy in June 1838 the debate took a new turn. At the Cymanfa, Robert Parry ('Robyn Ddu Eryri'), one of the teetotallers' most influential spokesmen, was declared an 'irregular preacher' by the Connexion. The teetotallers believed—and not unnaturally, as the Connexion was the concept of Caledfryn—that the Connexion was attacking them. The conflict was ostensibly about temperance, a continuation of the teetotalism-moderation debate, but in reality it was a conflict concerning the government and organisation of the church. The individual Independent chapels were jealous of their rights and freedom, but Caledfryn believed that there was need for more unity among Independents in order to face problems caused by the various changes of the age and the weight of chapel debts.[72] The rapid growth of Calvinistic Methodism showed the Independents that unity and cooperation were essential ingredients for success and growth. Efforts to reduce Independent chapel debts were largely successful; by 1836 they had been reduced by £24,000.[73] However, the Rev. Arthur Jones of Ebenezer chapel, Bangor, and Caledfryn's old teacher, was alienated because Bangor chapels, which had contributed nothing to the common treasury, were excluded from the share-out. Jones soon became isolated from Caernarfonshire Independency. For many years he had been attacked by some of his fellow Independent ministers in the county for preaching unorthodox doctrines.[74] His method of accepting and expelling members, and his method of raising preachers, was contrary to accepted Independent practice, for he never asked the opinion of his church, and sent preachers into the world without having proof of their character, saintly living and qualifications. He kept everything in his own hands: he alone supervised the church collections, and he alone accepted pew fees and kept all the business books of the church.[75]

Although Jones kept clear of his denomination's meetings he was very active in Bangor Teetotal Society.[76] He believed that temperance and religion were indivisible, and as such, he welcomed reformed drunkards into the church. One of these was Robert Parry. For some years Parry had been a member of the Calvinistic Methodists, but he soon became disillusioned with them for reasons that are not clear, and joined the Wesleyan Methodists. Expelled from the latter, he joined the Established Church and harboured pretensions for the priesthood. But by becoming a drunkard he was judged to be 'totally unsuitable for such an honourable and responsible post'.[77] However, quite suddenly in 1836, Parry decided to give up drinking and signed the teetotal pledge at Bethesda.[78] His sudden conversion to teetotalism was seized upon by teetotallers and he agreed to lecture on teetotalism in north Wales. In January 1837 he was accepted as a full member of Ebenezer chapel, Bangor;[79] in February 1838 the Rev. Arthur Jones invited him to preach.[80]

Caledfryn and Parry were rival bards, and the personal animosity between them had been exacerbated in 1832 when Caledfryn won the Chair at the Beaumaris eisteddfod.[81] Caledfryn did not approve of what he regarded as the immoral ways of Parry, and he disapproved of Arthur Jones for inviting such a disreputable man to preach for the denomination in 1838. Soon after Parry's conversion to teetotalism, attacks upon him began to appear in the periodical press. The conflict became crystallised as one between Parry, Jones and teetotalism on the one side, and Caledfryn and moderation on the other.[82] In April 1838 Parry accused Samuel Evans, editor of *Seren Gomer* and a close friend of Caledfryn, of saying in a public meeting, that drunkenness was not a sin and that Christ himself had been drunk. Evans retaliated by saying that Parry, as the 'authoritative missionary of the Total Abstainers and the great supporter of morality', was a liar who was guilty of totally denying Christ's miracles.[83]

In spite of the attacks on Parry as a teetotaller, it was his work in preaching the Gospel that roused the storm against him. After the annual Cymanfa of the Independents at Conwy in June 1838 had decided that Parry did not belong to the Caernarfonshire Union of Independents and that he was not, therefore, a regular preacher,[84] it asked Arthur Jones to justify his method of running his church and to join the Union; but he desisted, seeing in the Union a Presbyterian attempt to fetter the churches and bring them under the authority of conferences and committees. He continued to defend Parry.[85] A hard core of Caernarfonshire teetotallers believed that it was they that Caledfryn and the Conwy Cymanfa attacked, and they began to win over as many of the ministers who attended the Cymanfa as they could, reproaching them for attacking such 'an upright and innocent brother'. At a Cymanfa at Llanrwst in August 1838, presided over by Arthur Jones, eight ministers who had agreed with the decisions of the Conwy Cymanfa and who were all teetotallers, joined ranks with Jones and Parry.[86]

The debate had a prominent place in temperance periodicals, and it seemed to contemporaries to be a debate wholly concerned with temperance. Accordingly, it rapidly assumed the character of a fairground argument. Caledfryn and the Conwy ministers were all liars, claimed Gweirydd ap Rhys.[87] Libellous pamphlets were published on the *Anti-Teetotal Madness* in order to blacken Caledfryn and whitewash Parry.[88]

Caledfryn tried to bring the debate back to its roots by reminding people that it was concerned with uniformity and church order, not with a continuation of the quarrel between teetotallers and moderationists.[89] He maintained that the ministers of Caernarfonshire had nothing to do with Parry's character as a teetotaller, and that teetotal societies had no right to say that Parry was a regular preacher

in the Independent Union. But the emphasis on temperance in the
quarrel continued. Gweirydd ap Rhys asserted that the ministers at
the Conwy Cymanfa had cooperated with Caledfryn, 'that Public
Bacchannalian', in an attempt to close the doors of the monthly
magazines— Y Dirwestydd, Cronicl yr Oes and Y Dysgedydd—to the
teetotallers.[90] However, although Parry continued to complain in Y
Dirwestydd that someone from Caernarfon was attaching libellous
posters about him to chapel doors, Caledfryn was getting tired of the
temperance aspect of the debate.[91] In February 1838 he stopped
publishing Yr Adolygydd because 'the silliness and pomp of the
teetotals is ceasing'.[92]

However, in October 1839, Caledfryn, on a visit to south Wales,
further aroused the antagonism of teetotallers by repeating his view
that Parry was not a regular preacher. James Williams, the secretary
of Merthyr Tydfil Total Abstinence Society, challenged Caledfryn to
prove his charges to Parry's face at a public meeting.[93] Instead,
Caledfryn replied to the challenge in a pamphlet published at
Merthyr in October 1839, in which he doubted the sincerity of
Parry's reformation and alleged that Independent chapels in
Caernarfonshire were shutting their doors against Parry.[94] The Rev.
David Rees of Llanelli expressed his concern that the subject of
Parry's regularity as a preacher should be solved, and as a first step in
this direction, Rees' magazine, Y Diwygiwr, printed Caledfryn's
pamphlet in reply to James Williams.[95] Before Rees could publish
Parry's reply, two important developments occurred in north Wales.
First, the Independent ministers of Denbigh and Flint decided at a
quarterly meeting held at Ruthin in December 1839, that Parry
should be considered a regular preacher.[96] Second, at a meeting at
Bontnewydd, Caernarfonshire, in the same month, the ministers of
the Caernarfonshire Union decided to adhere to their view that Parry
was an irregular preacher.[97] In January 1840, a defence of Parry was
published in Y Diwygiwr, signed by nineteen Independent ministers
from Montgomery and Merioneth.[98] In March 1840 Rees came out,
formally, on the side of Parry, maintaining that he was a regular
preacher.[99] But suddenly, in early 1841, and with great concern to
teetotallers in Wales, news came from London that Parry had fallen
from grace: he had been drinking heavily and associating with
prostitutes;[100] a great blow had been dealt to temperance and
religion.[101]

The complex debate has an important place in the growth of

Independency in Wales. In was the first battle fought between the supporters of the 'Old Composition' and the 'New Composition'.[102] Arthur Jones represented the old order, Caledfryn the new. Robert Parry was the symbol of the inefficiency of the old order, but he was also a symbol of what Caledfryn abominated: the fruit of mixing religion with temperance.

Like Caledfryn, Eben Fardd's main objections to teetotalism were that it was too extreme a doctrine, and that it conflicted with Biblical teaching. He criticized temperance reformers for not admitting that the evils of intemperance resulted from the abuse of alcoholic liquors and not from their moderate use. Simple abstaining from what was only, through abuse, the occasion of sin, was not the complete answer. Eben Fardd believed that 'extreme views' had 'beyond dispute, operated most mischievously, and to a wide extent among intelligent Christian men, and above all, among Christian ministers. Much has been spoken on this point, and not a little at *utter variance* with the most distinct *declarations of scripture*—much that *impeaches* at once the *inspiration* and *authority* of its decision, and the *morality of the Son of God!* Against these extreme views we enter our *emphatic protest*, and they will ever find in us most *uncompromising adversaries*; we espouse those views only which are according to *truth and soberness*. To our minds it is clearly made out that the *great bulk of the benefits* which have accrued to society have arisen from the labours of men holding *extreme views*, but we ascribe their success to their truth, not to their *error*'.[103] Writing to Caledfryn in March 1837, refusing to allow his views to be published in an anti-teetotal pamphlet that Caledfryn was preparing for the press, Eben Fardd said: 'I have a strong aversion to engage publicly in the Teetotal controversy, because the advocates of the system (if system it be) are characterised with such a peculiar degree of extravagance and fanaticism in the zeal for the upholding of their favourite hobby, that no deliberate and impartial enquiry can ever be made, so as to bring the controverted point to a satisfactory issue.'[104] He admitted that in the early years of the temperance movement it was important that advocates be zealous and 'powerful'; but what was wanted now, he argued, was 'an increase in another class of advocates' who were capable of proselytizing the middle and upper classes of society—'someone with a knowledge of medicine and a knowledge of man, a clear logic, a persuasive eloquence, polished manners and a gainful presence'.[105] He declared himself to be on the side of those publicans who were 'railed at' by teetotallers.

'Teetotallers should bring all their artillery not against these public dispensers of what their customers demand, but against the corrupt tastes and habits, the mischievous customs, the mistaken opinions and the foolish notions of the community at large. Publicans are . . . a respectable, neat, beneficial and highly serviceable department.'[106] Eben Fardd maintained that to win large-scale support, the temperance movement had to be placed on its *'proper ground'*, that of *'expediency'*, and argued not in a *'dogmatical'* but in a *'deferential'* spirit.[107]

Eben Fardd said he preferred moderation 'for scriptural reasons as well as general propriety and utility'.[108] For him, teetotalism seemed to be an unattainable and unobtainable perfection which was far too extreme, too impractical and too faddist. He firmly believed that the moderate drinking of alcoholic liquors was sanctioned by the Bible and that the wine referred to therein was of an intoxicating nature. He advanced several reasons for this view. First, there was no proof in the Bible that wine of an unfermented nature was used, except by the literal translation of metronymical passages. Secondly, even if an unfermented wine was proved, divine sanction could be produced upon the temperate use of the fermented wine. Thirdly, the intoxicating nature of Hebrew wines could be proved from the etymology of their names and derivatives. Fourthly, condemnation of wine was never found in the Bible unless it was used in connexion with intemperance and excess. Fifth, as meats and drinks were so often treated of in the Bible one might reasonably expect to find alcoholic liquors specially condemned if their use in any and every degree was sinful. But in the Bible there was no reference to a particular wine that was unlawful; on the contrary, the same original terms were employed to describe it as both the blessing of God and the occasion of drunkenness. Last, if teetotalism was the doctrine of Scripture if would have been found long before the nineteenth century. Mere physical or scientific truth may linger undiscovered; new views of doctrine may also continually arise, but no entire doctrine itself could have been hidden in God's Word until the nineteenth century.[109] Eben Fardd believed that teetotalism was 'only another batch of fig leaves, which man has invented to hide the wickedness of these evil days . . . It is man's remedy and not God's remedy for sin'.[110] He concluded that teetotalism 'is a good thing, but it is dearly purchased by the disruption of our Churches, the undermining of Revelation, the disparagement of the Gospel and the kindling of bigotry and intolerance through the length and breadth of the land, especially as truth, charity and the Bible unite to point out a more excellent way'.[111]

Vigorous opposition to teetotalism came also from certain economic interests in Wales during the early years of the movement. In 1836 the publicans of Carmarthen established a Society for the Protection of Trade and Commerce, one of the aims of which was to prevent dealing with teetotallers,[112] but generally speaking, there are very few recorded instances of opposition of the drink trade towards temperance in the 1830s and 1840s. Naturally, farmers were alarmed at the early progress of the temperance movement, as they feared that the demand for barley used in the malting process would decline. The colliery proprietors at Sweeney New Colliery, just inside the Welsh border near Oswestry, issued a handbill in February 1838 expressing their determination 'not to employ any teetotallers, therefore none need apply'; this, they said, 'is a duty we owe to the agricultural interests of the country, as well as to the welfare of the public in general'.[113] Nearby at Meifod, near Llansantffraid, a violent incident occurred which is interesting as it reveals the 'Tory' attitude of the local gentry to a movement which posed a threat to its livelihood.[114] Teetotalism had been introduced into the Llansantffraid area in November 1836 and immediately ran into opposition from local farmers who boycotted tradesmen who had signed the pledge, dismissed teetotal workmen and evicted teetotal tenants.[115] On 30 March 1838 the teetotallers were met by three gentlemen-farmers, Thomas Henry Humffreys of Llanfyllin, John Bill Pryse and Robert Perrott, both of Llansantffraid, who were returning in various states of inebriation from a hunting dinner party, on a road outside Meifod. The farmers verbally abused the teetotallers, running their horse and carriage through the teetotal ranks a few times. Lawsuits ensued, and although the teetotallers were successful in two instances, the costs to the Meifod Teetotal Society totalled £1,000. A committee was established to raise subscriptions in order to defray the costs. The chairman of the committee was a former maltster and publican who had converted his public house into a Temperance Hotel. He was so successful in his new business that local publicans did their utmost to disrupt his trade by laying large stones outside the hotel. A commissioner for roads, who was alleged to be in league with the publicans, laid complaints before the magistrates that wagonners using the hotel were obstructing the highway.[116]

Thus temperance and teetotalism aroused strong feeling and controversy in Wales in the 1830s and 1840s. Many critics of teetotalism saw it as a creed which was exclusive and intolerant, particularly towards those who chose to stand outside its circle. As the temperance question was essentially one of agitation, it taught denunciation which many adherents abused. A Wrexham teetotaller complained in 1836: 'The moderation men are our greatest enemies. We meet with opposition from every class except the drunkard. Several ministers have preached against us. We have been represented as mad-men, fit for strait-jackets, perverters of the Scriptures, destitute of human feelings and destroyers of the comfort of the working people.'[117] At Narberth in Pembrokeshire in 1839, opposition to teetotalism was so strong that a room could not be obtained for meetings, and the local society had to resort to the yard of a public house.[118] In 1841, following the Caledfryn-Parry controversy, the Rev. David Rees of Llanelli refused to publish temperance news in his Y Diwygiwr on the grounds that the subject had become too contentious.[119] Within a few years, however, Rees relented and devoted considerable space in the magazine to the temperance issue. Very often during the first few decades of the temperance movement, the doctrine of teetotalism seemed to lack respectability; at Merthyr Tydfil, in January 1850, a Ladies Temperance Association was established 'to combine total abstinence with charity, and to give respectability to the temperance cause by allying it to a Dorcas Society'.[120]

*   *   *   *   *

During the early decades of the temperance movement in Wales, the issue of sobriety was used—in part out of self-interest—by some moral-force Chartists in their struggle against the aristocracy, while during the early 1840s the temperance movement cooperated with the Anti-Corn Law League's agitation for the abolition of the bread tax.

Teetotal Chartism was not particularly strong in Wales but the majority of those moral-force Chartists who supported the temperance movement did so because they realised that no working-class movement could flourish without encouraging regular habits.[121] Working-class sobriety might win middle-class support as it might make the working class respectable and trustworthy in the eyes of the middle class: 'Make the people sober, and none but rogues will object to their being invested with political power.'[122] The general feeling was that no state of freedom could improve the man who was the slave of his own vices. The declared purpose of the Newport Chartist Working Men's Association, established in 1838, was 'to probe our social evils to their source and apply effective remedies'.[123] All drunken and immoral men were specifically excluded from membership of the Association. Drinking and smoking were strictly forbidden at meetings of the Association because such profligacy made working men the slaves of unprincipled political leaders;[124] many Chartists shared the radicals' belief that drunkenness drugged potential supporters into political timidity.[125]

An important factor behind Chartist support of the temperance movement was that such support might embarrass the government by contributing towards the reduction of the excise.[126] 'Our aim,' said John Frost, the Newport Chartist, in July 1839, 'should be to cripple the revenue.'[127] This was part of the Chartist system of exclusive dealing whereby Chartists were urged to deal only with those shopkeepers and tradesmen who were in favour of the Charter. Frost maintained that the trade of the maltster and brewer depended almost entirely on working men: 'The power of the industrious classes is certain, if properly exercised . . . let them tell the landlords that if they buy malt of the enemies of the people, that no Chartist will buy the beer brewed from it.' In this way it was hoped to make middle-class shopkeepers 'as noisy agitators as they were in 1832'.[128]

The leading Teetotal Chartist in Wales at this time was Henry Vincent, a political missionary, popular in the west of England and south Wales, and in many ways a 'Welsh' figure. A keen advocate of self-improvement and sobriety, he believed that a tyrannical aristocracy governed only through the vices of the poor and that Chartists must, therefore, become teetotallers.[129] No early Victorian argument against franchise extension was used more frequently than the accusation that drunkenness was widespread among the lowest grades of voter. Vincent believed that working people should prove themselves to the middle class; they should 'forsake the gin palace, and so show the aristocracy that they were a people worthy to be entrusted with the power they claimed'.[130] He claimed to believe that the Frost rising at Newport had begun as a demonstration, and had become a rebellion only because government spies urged the Chartists to drink. 'No riot was intended', wrote Vincent in January

1842, 'until some drunken men madly and wickedly fired upon the Westgate Inn.'[131]

The religious basis of support for Chartism in south Wales was not as marked as that in Scotland and the north of England. Comparatively few nonconformist ministers were Chartists; the Calvinistic Methodists, in particular, were antagonistic towards Chartism. [132] In fact some nonconformist temperance reformers often took publicans to task for letting their rooms out to Chartist meetings. Those temperance advocates who deprecated physical force were quick to point out that Zephaniah Williams had been a publican in the parish of Aberystruth in 1838. [133] William Williams, landlord of the 'Prince of Wales' beer house in Pontypridd, took the chair at many meetings of Pontypridd Chartists in 1840, while at Swansea, in May 1839, suspicions that a local publican had harboured in his house physical-force Chartists led to a police enquiry. [134] A common claim was that the organisation of Chartism in Monmouthshire and east Glamorgan was in the hands of publicans and beer house keepers because the movement brought a great deal of custom to their houses. [135] Thus, where Chartism was strong in south Wales, most publicans and shopkeepers claimed to be in favour of it, for it was a question of using the movement for personal gain or possibly risking having to close businesses. 'We were not Chartists', declared Sarah Edwards of 'The Greyhound', Pontllanfraith, 'but we were afraid to say so to the colliers.'[136] Not a single publican appears to have accompanied Zephaniah Williams on the march to Newport. Richard Williams, landlord of the Navigation Inn, Crumlin, a Chartist lodge in Zephaniah's district, heard of the intended rising on 2 November and next day he found sanctuary at Penderyn. [137] Neither of Zephaniah's relations, beer-house keeper John Williams and publican Llewellyn Williams (Zephaniah's son), are known to have joined the marchers. [138]

There were strong links, too, between Welsh supporters of the Anti-Corn Law League and the temperance movement during the 1840s. The Leaguers who recommended teetotalism did so, not for its own sake, but because, like the moral-force Chartists, they felt it would enhance the dignity of their supporters, and, by implication, discredit their opponents. Many Leaguers believed that free trade could bring prosperity only to a temperate people; they recognised that reducing the demand for alcoholic drink would have the same effect on corn prices as extending overseas grain supply. [139]

Walter Griffith, the Anti-Corn Law League's Welsh lecturer, received important assistance from Welsh teetotallers, whom he described in 1840 as 'our excellent allies'.[140] 'I can assure you that teetotallers are the best friends of repeal', wrote Griffiths from Brecon in November 1840, 'and good reasons why, as many of them have told me: "Our society brings the people to drink water, and yours brings them plenty of bread with it . . . the visitors of the pot-houses are the greatest enemies of our cause. There the council of our foes used to meet".'[141] Griffith's attendance at temperance meetings gave him the opportunity of expounding free trade principles and distributing League tracts. The practice of the temperance society at Bagillt in 1840 was to hold anti-corn law meetings immediately after temperance meetings.[142] At a league meeting at Newport in February 1844, John Jenkins, the League's representative in south Wales, allowed a teetotaller to give an address on teetotalism at the completion of his lecture.[143]

Temperance reformers in Wales were able to help the League's agitation by securing many lecture rooms for its meetings. In return the League often provided teetotal drinks at its banquets for those who preferred them. In south Wales, the League complained that the public halls in most places were under the management of county magistrates who were, in general, 'tithe parsons' and 'landowners' implacably opposed to any League discussion on the bread tax. Similarly, publicans were unwilling to let any rooms to free traders because publicans 'depended on the landed interest, and by letting their rooms for Anti-Corn Law meetings they would lose their custom'.[144]

*　　　*　　　*　　　*　　　*

The temperance revival in Wales lasted until the early 1840s when enthusiasm waned and feelings of millenarian expectancy declined. The progress of the temperance movement in Wales throughout the rest of the nineteenth century was marked by sudden enthusiasms, followed by equally sudden periods of cooling off. It thus confirms E. J. Hobsbawm's point about social movements with a 'millenarian atmosphere' which 'expand in jerks'; the history of such movements, as the itinerant temperance lecture tours in nineteenth-century Wales testify, contains periods of 'abnormally, often fantastically rapid and easy mobilization of hitherto untouched masses', almost as rapidly followed by extensive backsliding and a falling away from the ideal.[145] At times of religious revival, the Welsh temperance cause was greatly resuscitated and received fresh injections of enthusiasm and vigour which enabled it to exist. The essence of millenarianism is the hope of a complete or radical change in the world which will be reflected in the millenium—a world rid of all its present deficiencies. For many Welshmen, this was precisely the hope they nurtured when they took the teetotal pledge.

NOTES

[1] The term 'teetotalism' under the Welsh form 'titotaliaeth' was used at first to denote the movement, but it was soon superseded by the word 'dirwest' which was used in the Welsh New Testament not only for 'temperance' but also for 'abstinence'. At a meeting to promote teetotalism in Flintshire in 1836, consultation between the Revs. William Morris, Rhuddlan, Owen Jones, Llandudno, and Griffith Hughes, Holywell, resulted in the term 'dirwest' being selected as a designation of the movement. It came to be generally used.

[2] Rev. John Thomas, D.D., *Jubili y Diwygiad Dirwestol yng Nghymru* (Merthyr Tydfil, 1885), p. 39.

[3] P. T. Winskill and Joseph Thomas, *History of the Temperance Movement in Liverpool and District, 1829-1887* (Liverpool, 1887), p. 10.

[4] See M. B. Simey, *Charitable Effort in Liverpool in the Nineteenth Century* (Liverpool, 1951), p. 16.

[5] See H. Kuper (ed.), *Urbanization and Migration in West Africa* (University of California Press, 1965), pp. 102-6; G. Breese, *Urbanization in newly-developing Countries* (New Jersey, 1966), pp. 87-8, 98, cited in B. Harrison, 'Pubs', p. 184.

[6] I. G. Jones, 'The Merthyr of Henry Richard', Glanmor Williams (ed.), *Merthyr Politics* (Cardiff, 1966), p. 52.

[7] John Thomas, op. cit., p. 40.

[8] See *The British and Foreign Temperance Herald*, vols. 1-4, 1832-5; *C.M.G.*, 4 January 1834, 4 October 1834; *Monmouthshire Merlin*, 27 September 1834; *Caernarvon and Denbigh Herald*, 4 June 1836.

[9] *C.M.G.*, 3 February 1838.

[10] Winskill, op. cit., vol. 1, p. 212; John Thomas, op. cit., p. 45.

[11] Winskill, op. cit., p. 212.

[12] *Y Dirwestydd*, no. 2, September 1836, p. 9; John Thomas, op. cit., p. 55.

[13] *The British and Foreign Temperance Herald*, 1, no. 6, June 1832, p. 65; 2, no. 2, August 1833, p. 108.

[14] See ibid., 3, no. 26, February 1834, p. 13; no. 34, October 1834, p. 109.

[15] *C.M.G.*, 4 January 1834.

[16] *The British and Foreign Temperance Herald*, 4 July 1835, p. 77. For temperance tracts, see Brian Harrison, 'Drunkards and Reformers. Early Victorian Temperance Tracts', *History Today*, 13, no. 3 (March, 1963).

[17] *Y Dirwestydd*, January 1837, p. 59.

[18] Ibid. See also *London Temperance Intelligencer*, 1, no. 10, 21 January 1837, p. 77; Dawson Burns, *Temperance History*, op. cit., vol. 1, p. 111.

[19] *Y Dirwestydd*, December 1836, p. 34.

[20] For these instances of growth, see ibid., April 1837, pp. 80-1; February 1838, p. 162; August 1838, p. 209.

[21] *The Temperance Advocate and Herald*, April 1838, p. 24; *The Friend. Religious, Moral and Political Intelligencer for Shropshire and North Wales*, January 1838, p. 4; The New British and Foreign Society for the Suppression of Intemperance, *First Annual Report*, 1837, p. 34.

[22] *Y Dirwestydd*, January 1838, p. 151.

[23] Ibid., p. 149.

[24] Ibid., April 1838, p. 174.

[25] *Preston Temperance Advocate*, September 1836, p. 67.

[26] Ibid., June 1836, p. 46; P. T. Winskill, op. cit., p. 212.

[27] *Preston Temperance Advocate*, January 1837, p. 5.

[28] Ibid., p. 14.

[29] See Scourfield, op. cit., p. 4.

[30] See pp. 137-40.

[31] Dawson Burns, op. cit., p. 111.

[32] Winskill, op. cit., p. 213.

[33] Ibid.

[34] *Y Dirwestydd*, March 1838, p. 165; *Y Diwygiwr*, 2, 1837, pp. 47-50.

[35] Ibid., p. 92.

[36] *Y Dirwestydd*, March 1838, p. 165.

[37] Ibid., pp. 169-70.

[38] Ibid., March 1839, p. 17.

[39] Ibid., December 1837, p. 145.

[40] For example, see ibid., August 1836, p. 2.

[41] *Preston Temperance Advocate*, November 1836, p. 84.

[42] Ibid., January 1837, p. 5.

[43] *Merthyr Express*, 8 May 1939 ('Merthyr's Place in the Temperance Movement').

[44] *The Universe*, 9 June 1846, p. 4.

[45] Harrison, *Drink and the Victorians*, op. cit., 113, 115.

[46] *London Temperance Intelligencer*, 1, no. 6, 17 December 1836, p. 48.

[47] For example, see Rev. Richard Jones, *The Claims of the Temperance Movement on Christian Ministers* (Manchester, 1860), p. 11.

[48] N.L.W., MS 8,392 B, Diary of Eben Fardd, n.d.

[49] *C.M.G.*, 7 November 1840.

[50] Ibid., 29 May 1847; see also *The National Temperance Chronicle and Recorder*, 3, no. 33, September 1848, p. 342.

[51] For example, see *C.M.G.*, 10 August 1844; *Alliance News*, 25 January 1868, p. 30, 3 September 1870, p. 281; *The Ferret or South Wales Ratepayer*, 2, 27 January 1872, p. 4; 3, 4, January 1873, p. 7; *Merthyr Express*, 27 November 1886.

[52] *South Wales Daily News*, 28 September 1881.

[53] *Seren Gomer*, 17 August 1834, pp. 231-3.

[54] See N.L.W., MS 16, 735 B, At Eglwys yr Annibynwyr Cymreig cynulledig yn Nghapel y Graig, Machynlleth, n.d. See also *Y Diwygiwr*, 2, 1837, p. 274.

[55] N.L.W., MS 16,735 B, op. cit., See also Morris Hughes, *Traethawd ar Annghymedroldeb* (Wyddgrug, 1844), p. 9.

[56] *Yr Eurgrawn*, February 1837, p. 111.

[57] Ibid., February 1836, p. 45.

[58] *C.M.G.*, 6 April 1839.

[59] For Caledfryn, see G. R. Hughes, 'Bywyd Caledfryn a'i weithgarwch fel Gŵr Cyhoeddus' (unpublished University of Wales M.A. thesis, 1958), especially pp. 77-131.

[60] William Williams, *Cymedroldeb a Llwyrymataliad. Sylwadau ar y ddwy eguyddor* (Caernarfon, 1836), p. 2. See also Benjamin Jones ('P.A.Môn'), *Temperance versus Teetotalism. Cymedroldeb. The Total Overthrow of Teetotalism. Llwyr-Ddymchweliad Titotaliedyddiaeth* (Llanrwst, 1838), p. 77.

[61] See William Williams, op. cit., p. 3. See also 'P.A.Môn', op. cit., pp. 43-5, 108-9, 118-9. Jones argued here that the teetotal movement attacked God as the creator, for if teetotallers attacked alcohol they also, of necessity, attacked God, because He created it.

[62] For example, see Joseph Davies, *Epistol at y Llwyrymatalwyr yn Cynnwys Adolygiad ar Draethawd y Parch William Williams, Caernarfon* (Denbigh, 1836).

[63] *Y Dirwestydd*, January 1837, p. 52.

[64] M. Hughes, *Traethawd ar Llwyrymwrthodiad: yn cynnwys Adolygiad ar Draethawd y Parch William Williams, Caernarfon* (Caernarfon, 1837).

[65] Ibid., p. 7.

[66] For example, see ibid., p. 31.

[67] William Williams, *Ystyriaethau Ychwanegol ar Lwyrymwrthodiad* (Caernarfon, 1837), pp. 1-16.

[68] *Yr Athraw, sef cyhoeddiad Llenyddol, Crefyddol, Dirwestol*, March 1837, p. 40; *Y Dirwestydd*, April 1837, p. 80; Hugh Jones, *Ffrwyn i Asyn: yn cynnwys yr Achosion a'r Rhesymau fod William Williams o Gaernarfon, yn gwrthwynebu y Llwyrymwrthodwyr* (Caernarfon, 1837).

[69] N.L.W., MS 15,405A, William Williams to Robert Williams, 15 September 1837.

[70] *Y Dirwestydd*, May 1838, p. 181.

[71] *Yr Adolygydd,* March 1838, p. 1.

[72] *Y Diwygiwr,* January 1840, p. 6.

[73] G. R. Hughes, op. cit., p. 99.

[74] Ibid., pp. 101-2.

[75] William Williams, *Robyn Ddu Eto. Sylwadau ar gopi o lythyr Diaconiaid y Taihirion* (Caernarfon, 1840), pp. 4-5, 7-8.

[76] John Thomas, op. cit., p. 66; see also *Seren Gomer,* May 1838, p. 159.

[77] G. R. Hughes, op. cit., 102.

[78] Robert Parry, *Teithiau a Barddoniaeth Robyn Ddu Eryri* (Caernarfon, 1857), pp. 52-3; see also *Seren Gomer,* November 1838, p. 332.

[79] *Y Diwygiwr,* January 1840, p. 19; March 1840, p. 80.

[80] *Seren Gomer,* November 1838, p. 332.

[81] G. R. Hughes, op. cit., 104.

[82] *Yr Athraw,* March 1838, p. 69.

[83] *Seren Gomer,* April 1838, p. 108.

[84] Ibid., August 1838, 247.

[85] *Yr Athraw,* September 1838, pp. 204-5.

[86] *Y Dirwestydd,* September 1838, p. 214; *Seren Gomer,* November 1838, p. 332.

[87] *Y Dirwestydd,* September 1838, p. 214.

[88] Sianco'r Criws Bach, *The Anti-Teetotal Madness: containing the attestations and decisions of Wil Dalcen Prês (Brasshead) and Huwcyn Bentarw (Bullhead) against Temperance and Abstainers* (Merthyr Tydfil, 1838), p. 2. The Rev. Hugh Jones ('Cromwell o Went') was Huwcyn and Caledfryn was Brasshead. Ianto Smala o Lletty'r Brandi, *The Conference of Wil of the North and Huwcyn of the South in relation to Temperance and Abstainers. To this is added the History of the Religious Carousal of the little Sunday night crew, together with many another secret thing, amusing and funny* (1838).

[89] William Williams, *Crynodeb o'r Pynciau Sylfaenol ac Ymarferol a Ddelir gan yr Annibynwyr* (Caernarfon, 1838), passim. See also *Seren Gomer,* November 1838, p. 336.

[90] U.C.N.W., Bangor MSS, 4,870, no. 48.

[91] *Y Dirwestydd,* February 1839, p. 48.

[92] *Yr Adolygydd,* February 1839, p. 48.

[93] William Williams, *Robyn Ddu: Copi o lythyr a ddanfonwyd gan James Williams* (Merthyr Tydfil, 1839), p. 2.

[94] Ibid., p. 8.

[95] *Y Diwygiwr,* December 1839, p. 354.

[96] Ibid., February 1840, p. 48.

[97] William Williams, *Robyn Ddu Eto,* p. 9.

[98] *Y Diwygiwr,* January 1840, p. 18.

[99] Ibid., March 1840, p. 81.

[100] *Seren Gomer,* February 1841, p. 58.

[101] *Y Diwygiwr,* March 1841, p. 85; *Yr Haul,* May 1841, pp. 151-3.

[102] G. R. Hughes, op. cit., p. 131.

[103] N.L.W. Cwrt Mawr MSS, 481 B, ff. 121-23: Notes for a letter written by Eben Fardd and published in *The Christian Witness,* November 1846, 221.

[104] *Y Traethodydd,* April 1885, p. 184 (a letter of 11 March 1837).

[105] N.L.W., Cwrt Mawr MSS, 481 B, 121-3.

[106] N.L.W., MS 8,392 B, *Diaries and Letters of Eben Fardd.*

[107] N.L.W., Cwrt Mawr MSS, 481 B, 124-5. See also the Rev. William Jones, *The Character of the Welsh as a Nation.* Prize essay. Liverpool Eisteddfod (1841), p. 124.

[108] N.L.W., MS 8.392 B, op. cit.

[109] N.L.W., Cwrt Mawr MSS, 481 B, 124-5; *The Christian Witness,* December 1845, p. 253.

[110] N.L.W., Cwrt Mawr MSS, 73 C.

[111] Ibid., 481 B, 124-5.

[112] The New British and Foreign Society for the Suppression of Intemperance, *First Annual Report, 1837,* p. 45.

[113] John Thomas, op. cit., 185-6; Samuel Couling, op. cit., p. 135; P. T. Winskill, *The Comprehensive History of the Rise and Progress of the Temperance Reformation to 1881* (Warrington, 1881), p. 151.

[114] On this, see N.L.W. MS 8,371 D, Cyfarchiad oddiwrth Gyfeisteddiad Cymdeithasau Dirwestol parthau isaf swydd Drefaldwyn, at y Cymdeithasau Dirwestol Cymreig yn gyffredinol, 27 Tachwedd 1838; U.C.N.W., Bangor MSS, 737 (139); *Y Dirwestydd,* September 1838, 217-8; January 1839, 4-5; *The British Temperance Advocate and Journal,* 1, no. 7, July 1839, pp. 73, 76.

[115] See David Jones, *A Tee-Totaller's Defence in an Address to the inhabitants of the parish of Llansaintffraid* (Oswestry, 1837), pp. 4, 6; *Y Dirwestydd,* June 1837, pp. 105-7; *London Temperance Intelligencer,* no. 31, June 1837, pp. 256-7.

[116] *Journal of the New British and Foreign Temperance Society,* 2, no. 37, September 1840, p. 303; no. 47, November 1840, pp. 379-80.

[117] *The Preston Temperance Advocate,* no. 8, August 1836, p. 62.

[118] *The British Temperance Advocate and Journal,* 1, no. 4, April 1839, p. 45.

[119] N.L.W., MS 10,276 E (Solva 2), Llythyrau at Hugh Jones. David Rees to Rev. Hugh Jones, Tredegar, 11 August 1841, f.170.

[120] *C.M.G.,* 19 January 1850.

[121] B. Harrison, 'Teetotal Chartism', *History,* 58, 1973, p. 196.

[122] *The English Chartist Circular and Temperance Record for England and Wales,* 1, no. 2, 1841, p. 16.

[123] *Address and Rules of the Newport Working Mens Association for benefitting politically, socially and morally the Useful Classes* (Newport, n.d., *c.* 1838), p. 2; David Williams, *John Frost: a Study in Chartism* (Cardiff, 1939), pp. 109-110.

[124] *Address and Rules,* op. cit., p. 3.

[125] B. Harrison, 'Teetotal Chartism', p. 200.

[126] See B. Harrison, 'Religion and Recreation in Nineteenth-Century England', *Papers Presented to the Past and Present Conference on Popular Religion,* July 1966, p. 36, (typescript).

[127] *Western Vindicator,* 20 July 1839; see also ibid., 10 August, 17 August, 28 September 1839.

[128] Ibid., 29 June 1839.

[129] Harrison, 'Teetotal Chartism', p. 198.

[130] *Northern Star,* 6 March 1841, p. 8, quoted in B. Harrison, 'Teetotal Chartism', p. 203.

[131] *National Vindicator,* 8 January 1842, p. 4, quoted in Harrison, 'Teetotal Chartism', p. 201.

[132] See C.C.L., Bute MS, XX, 7, for two examples of nonconformist ministers at Llanfabon who were Chartist sympathisers.

[133] N.L.W., MS 16,157 B, op. cit.

[134] Glanmor Williams, 'Chartists, "Rebecca", and the Swansea Police', *Gower,* 12, 1959, 22-5.

[135] See G.R.O., Chief Constable's Report (Glamorgan), 1/9 F, June 1844; *Western Vindicator,* 22 June 1839; *C.M.G.,* 17 December 1839, 18 January 1840; *The Two Colliers or a Dialogue Between Two Colliers of Gloucester and Blackwood, Mon.* (Monmouth, 1840), p 6.

[136] N.L.W., MS 16, 157 B, op. cit.

[137] C.C.L., Bute MSS, XX, 72.

[138] N.L.W., MS 16, 157 B, op. cit.

[139] Harrison, *Drink and the Victorians,* p. 177; N. McCord, *The Anti-Corn Law League* (1958), p. 205.

[140] *Anti-Corn Law Circular,* no. 47, 19 November 1840, p. 7.

[141] Ibid.

[142] Manchester Public Library, Anti-Corn Law League correspondence, Walter Griffith to the Secretary of the League, 12 June 1840. Letter book 4, 4.640. See also I. G. Jones, 'The Anti-Corn Law Letters of Walter Griffith', *Bulletin of the Board of Celtic Studies,* XXVIII, Part 1, November 1978, 95-128.

[143] *Monmouthshire Merlin,* 10 February 1844.

[144] *Anti-Corn Law Circular,* no 54, 28 February 1841; *Anti-Bread Tax Circular,* 3 November 1842, p. 7.

[145] E. J. Hobsbawm, *Primitive Rebels* (paperback edn., 1963), p. 105. For nineteenth-century millenarianism in general see J. F. C. Harrison, *The Second Coming. Popular Millenarianism, 1780-1850* (1979), and E. Royle, *Radical Politics, 1790-1900. Religion and Unbelief* (1971).

CHAPTER III

THE TEMPERANCE SOCIETY

THE basic aim of the temperance society was to reclaim drunkards to sobriety by restoring their self-respect.[1] This was regarded as the 'cornerstone' of the 'moral reformation' for which temperance societies, as 'organizations of evangelical principles', were striving.[2]

How could Wales be delivered from the bondage of strong drink? asked Samuel Roberts ('S.R.') of Llanbrynmair in 1837.

> I believe that it is to be delivered . . . by the voluntary use of moral means, by the instrumentality of such means as the discussions and arguments, and appeals of such meetings as these, by such agencies as those of these Temperance Societies: I regard the total Abstinence Society as an important branch of that system of moral means that must be used for the reformation of the world . . . The Society uses no compulsion. It violates no conscience. It inflicts no pains or penalties.[3]

'S.R.' maintained that membership of a temperance society and the upholding of its principles made for independence and self-sufficiency, in short, the making of the 'Independent Gentleman—a man that has plenty to *eat,* plenty to *wear,* and plenty to *do'.*[4] However, the temperance society aimed at much more than the reclamation of the casualties of drink, and temperance reformers attacked much more than mere drunkenness. Most societies pledged themselves to 'the removal of the causes which lead to intemperance by moral, social and legislative action', and this involved the societies and their members in an attack upon all the social evils of the nineteenth century. Temperance reformers saw temperance as influencing all human activity; they should declare war against all influences 'obstructive of the course of progress, and be found the first and foremost advocates of everything tending to the elevation of human character'.[5] The object of the temperance movement, claimed the *Merthyr Express* in October 1877, was 'to refine the taste, to improve the mind and to elevate the social status of the people'.[6]

Reclamation of the reprobate remained a constant aim of the temperance society in nineteenth-century Wales, and although political aims came to the forefront in 1853 with the formation of the prohibitionist United Kingdom Alliance at Manchester, the local

society continued to perform its functions of inculcating ideas of
moral improvement and providing recreation. Indeed, many of the
early temperance societies of the 1830s and '40s expressly forbade the
introduction of any topic of a political nature in any meeting.[7]
Political aims, notably the election of temperance men at local and
national levels, were usually undertaken by larger regional
bodies—temperance associations and temperance unions—to which
local societies were usually affiliated.

To obtain membership of a temperance society the aspirant first
had to take the pledge. As in England, a considerable controversy
developed in Wales during the 1830s and '40s over the nature of the
teetotal pledge to be taken.[8] Should the pledge be 'short', affirming
personal total abstinence only, or should it be 'long', adding to
personal abstinence an obligation to refrain from selling, giving or
offering intoxicants to others? Eben Fardd offered a social
interpretation:

> To the *Labouring Classes* the adoption of the *Long Pledge* involves but
> little hardship, it is much otherwise with the *Middle* and *Upper Classes* of
> Society, it would frequently place *Heads* of *Houses* in circumstances
> exceedingly painful and perplexing; at once to carry it out, would
> often be to break up *friendly circles,* and *hazard the peace* of *family
> connections. Abstractly* considered our own personal preferences are for
> the *Long Pledge, but when all this would prove serious hardship,* and an *obstacle*
> to *signing at all,* we will cheerfully take the *Short One.* On this point, some
> *Outrageous things* have been said. In this way, it is vehemently asserted
> that the Short Pledge is no Pledge at all, nay, it is even worse than
> moderate drinking. Now this is surely worse than foolish, it is *absurdly
> false* and *exceedingly monstrous, hugely mischievous!* To take the Short Pledge
> is a great step, to many a man it is, on various grounds, a very serious
> matter. He who takes the Short may one day find himself at liberty to
> take the Long Pledge—Nay, were the *Short Pledge* to become universal,
> it would render the *Long* One wholly unnecessary. It would cut up our
> Drinking Customs by the roots. Let our motto then be, Instruction,
> Forbearance, Patience, Perseverance.[9]

The more thorough-going long pledge was ultimately adopted
almost everywhere in Wales. That for the Carmarthen Temperance
Society (established in December 1836) ran as follows:

> I voluntarily engage while a member of this Society to abstain from
> Distilled Spirits, Wine, Ale, Porter, Cider and all other intoxicating
> liquors except for medicinal purposes or in a religious ordinance, and
> to discountenance the causes and practice of intemperance.[10]

Although this particular pledge was in widespread use throughout Wales in the late 1830s and '40s, local variations existed; at Port Dinorwic methylated spirits was specifically included as an intoxicant to avoid[11]; and the Good Templars, a pseudo-Masonic organization of extreme temperance zealots, which spread quickly in Wales in the early 1870s, had a four-fold pledge: against alcohol, tobacco, gambling and obscene language.[12]

Great importance was attached to the taking of the pledge. By signing the pledge a person rejected one set of values—one system of recreation—for another. When the Wesleyan Methodist and colliery proprietor, Lewis Davies of Ferndale, took the pledge at Bryndderwen in 1856, Lewis Williams of Cardiff, who was present, described it as 'a most solemn and important means of grace'.[13] A year earlier, Davies had asked for Williams' help on the matter but 'he decided to think out the question for himself, and not take any public action for twelve months'. In north Wales where, in the 1830s, teetotalism was almost exclusively confined to the nonconformist denominations, the teetotal pledge was considered to be almost a religious test.[14]

For a leading middle-class, example-setter like John Griffith, Rector of Neath in 1865, taking the pledge involved 'a condescension to the simple reasonings of men of low estate'.[15] He maintained that what made him sign the pledge was 'a solemn conviction that these drinking customs (innocent perhaps in themselves, but not so in their effects on the general welfare of the people) fostered a habit which struck at the root of national advancement, desolated their homes, hindered among them the progress of all good, tied the wheels of the Gospel chariot . . . and produced in fact a physical incapacity for the reception of religious truth, kept men fools and made thousands brutes,—led me some years ago to set my face against them, and to believe that by doing so I was discharging a public duty, and listening to the call of philanthropy, patriotism and religion . . . The task of yielding was not easy; there were hindrances in the way: my health had to be thought of, my social position, the opinion of others whom I respected, and whom I knew were opposed to the principles of total abstinence. But my most important work under heaven was to win souls to Christ and to prepare them for another world.'[16]

A person often had to struggle hard to sign the pledge and still more to adhere to it. Drink was one of the many weaknesses of Eben Fardd and between 1836 and 1846 he made nine recorded attempts—mostly personal vows—to give up drinking.[17] On 1 November 1836 he vowed not to take more than half a pint of beer or two glasses of porter in any period not exceeding six hours, and in December 1836 he joined the moderation society of Zion chapel in Clynnog.[18] At this time he scorned teetotalism and, when his daughter signed the teetotal pledge without his knowledge, he called it a 'childish act'.[19] On 11 January 1838 he vowed 'by the aid of God to avoid strong drink' but also added that he hoped he would not 'in future wantonly squander more money than will be apparently necessary for the same'.[20] Two days later he was drinking beer and rum 'mixed'.[21] In desperation, on 6 March 1838, he subscribed his name to a teetotal pledge 'to expire only when the paper on which it is written shall be either lost or destroyed'. He added proudly, 'Now I am a TEETOTALLER'.[22] But it was not to be, for under his diary entry for 8 March, Eben Fardd wrote: 'Found that "secret teetotalism" would not answer and destroyed my paper'.[23] On 30 March he experienced a severe hangover as a result of the bacchanalia associated with the previous day's election of guardians, and he decided to 'make a pledge to be perpetually in force—O! heavens;'[24] on 9 January 1839 he 'gave up all intoxicating liquors whatever';[25] on 10 March 1839, after lapsing yet again, he resolved to 'abstain rigorously' from beer 'for a long time';[26] on 8 May 1840 he maintained that 'teetotalism is a most excellent thing', but on the following day he wrote: 'As yet I do not know *when* I shall totally abstain, but I hope it will be before long'.[27] On 27 December 1845, in the last entry in his diary concerning drink, he maintained that he was finding teetotalism 'loveliness all but',[28] but it seems to be a matter of great doubt as to whether Eben Fardd remained in this moral state for very long.

Once the pledge was taken, many members of temperance societies found it impossible to keep themselves inviolate. The first week following the signing of the pledge was the period of greatest trial to the teetotaller as withdrawal symptoms took their toll.

> The palate longs for the beverage to which it has been habituated . . . And the stomach, accustomed to unnatural distension by the quantity of fluid forced into it, craves for the old supplies; but let the teetotaller persevere in the use of moderate quantities of nourishing diet and good spring water, and those cravings and the sinking sensations which sometimes accompany them, will shortly subside, and then will be experienced the benefits of teetotalism in the increased activity of the body and the improved elasticity of the mind.[29]

Backsliders from the teetotal pledge were quite numerous. Caernarfon Teetotal Society reported in 1838 that 134 members out of a total of 2,433 had broken their pledges during the two years of the society's existence.[30] Over 140 members are reported as having transgressed the rules of Aberystwyth Auxiliary Temperance Society between 1846 and 1855, but there is no record of them having been expelled.[31] This society kept 'a strict watch' on those members who were advised by their doctors to drink porter.[32]

On 16 May 1842 a member of a Rechabite Tent at Aberystwyth was expelled for drinking peppermint.[33] But the Independent Order of Rechabites, a temperance friendly society, was hardly affected by large-scale backsliding. Rechabites maintained that the death rate among their members was only 8 per 1,000, compared with 11 per 1,000 in non-temperance friendly societies, and also that whereas other temperance societies lost on average, 40 per cent of their pledges in one year, the Rechabites lost only 1 per cent.[34] The Rechabites then had the power to retain their members to a greater degree than other temperance organizations because the benefit paid by members led to vested interest.[35] Rule 41 of the Rechabites provided that any member who broke the pledge must re-sign it and be fined 2s. 6d. for the first offence, 5s. for the second, 10s. for the third and £1 for the fourth. 'Brothers so offending will be suspended from all benefit and privileges till such fine be paid, and till such Brother has also re-signed the pledge according to Rule 1.'[36]

Several other temperance societies based on the Rechabite system were established in Wales in the 1870s. In 1871 the Rev. J. R. Hughes of Anglesey began to form Temperance and Provident Associations in north Wales. Self-help was encouraged by inducing members to make periodical payments to the associations, such sums being forfeited by those who broke the pledge but which fructified for those who kept it.[37] The same principle lay behind the Machynlleth Temperance Club established in 1875. Each member promised 'not to make, buy, sell, use, furnish or cause to be furnished to others, as a beverage, any spirituous or malt liquors, wine or cider'.[38] Any member found guilty of breaking his obligation was fined 2s. 6d. for the first offence, 5s. for the second and was expelled from the Club for the third. Each subscription to the Club had to be over 6d. If the subscription fell three weeks behind the member was expelled and lost all claim to his money. All subscriptions were paid into a bank and were repaid to members plus any interest that might accrue, on each anniversary of the Club. [39]

Nevertheless, the membership of most temperance societies fluctuated constantly throughout the nineteenth century. A Tredegar nonconformist minister told H. Seymour Tremenheere in 1846 that 'for every twenty whom I induced to join it [the local temperance society] a few years ago, I have not now five who have remained'. [40] As Owen Hughes, Superintendent of the Merionethshire Police Force, testified to the Welsh Sunday Closing Commission in 1889, temperance societies 'are very active at times, and at other times there is a lull, as it were. Fits and starts?—Yes.' [41] The Band of Hope attached to the Cefn Coed English Wesleyan Sunday School collapsed and revived four times between 1889 and 1895. [42] Temperance societies in Wales received accretions of numerical strength after the visits of famous temperance orators such as Jabez Inwards and John Bartholomew Gough, after temperance missions and during the millenarianism and emotional ecstasy generated by frequent religious revivals. [43] But many such members did not remain members for very long.

There is a considerable body of evidence to show that during the period 1835-40 the backbone of temperance support in the industrial areas of south Wales was provided by working men. Looking back in 1865, John Griffith, Rector of Neath, wrote:

> In the early days, teetotalism in Wales was a popular institution. It was to the people that it mainly commended itself, and it was by the people themselves that its work was chiefly done. [44]

We know that the formation of the Crickhowell Temperance Society in April 1835 was a direct result of a requisition addressed to the vicar, signed by the working men of the village. [45] Similarly, working men formed the basis of the temperance cause at Merthyr: 'We have very few of the higher tradesmen and wealthier classes to assist us in agitating, and bearing the expenses', complained Rhys Lewis in 1842. [46] But middle-class support was needed to lend the temperance movement in Wales organizational flair, respectability and long-term stability. Such support was seriously lacking up to mid-century; during the 1840s and '50s, teetotalism in Wales, according to John Griffith, 'suffered and became weak . . . because it had not the support of that class in society whose position, experience and power, had they been found on its side, would have given it stability and strength. The recognised leaders of the public mind withheld their sympathy from it; the men, who, standing between the two great divisions—the upper and lower classes—in society, possess an influence that no other men have, did not think it worth their while to secure for the movement what they had the power of doing, viz. the kind consideration of those who governed; while they themselves refused to lend it that organization which was essential to its maintenance, and which those who had hitherto worked for it had not the leisure or wisdom to supply'.[47] However, with the spread of the prohibitionist movement in the 1860s and the recourse to legislative action on the drink problem, many Welsh temperance organizations came to be led by middle-class Gladstonian Liberals, who were also militant nonconformists and leading figures in their communities.

Many registers of Welsh temperance societies have survived, and in most instances, they record the occupations of many of those who joined them. Such registers do not tell us how long these people remained members but they are useful because they show the type of person attracted to membership of a temperance society and the class basis of support for the temperance movement. The extant registers, most of which cover the small towns of rural north Cardiganshire and Merionethshire, reveal strong support for temperance among the skilled working class.[48]

TABLE 4. OCCUPATIONS OF THOSE WHO SIGNED THE MODERATION PLEDGE OF ABERYSTWYTH AUXILIARY TEMPERANCE SOCIETY, AUGUST 1835 TO FEBRUARY 1836

Shoemaker	37	Cabinet maker	3
Mason	21	Sawyer	3
Draper	18	Labourer	3
Mariner	14	Currier	3
Joiner	14	Glazier	3
Tailor	13	Printer	3
Carpenter	10	Tanner	2
Servant	9	Miller	2
Farmer	7	Maltster	2
Butcher	5	Painter	2
Carrier	5	Plasterer	2
Calvinistic Methodist Minister	5	Shipbuilder	2
Mercer	4	Druggist	2
Smith	4	Excise Officer	2
Schoolmaster	3	Wesleyan Methodist Minister	2
Clerk	3	Baptist Minister	2

and one each of nailor, land surveyor, grocer, hatter, tinman, ironmonger, dressmaker, brickmaker, bellman, hairdresser, watchmaker, and shipwright.

Aberystwyth Auxiliary Temperance Society was established on 31 August 1835 as an ancillary of the national moderation body, the B.F.T.S. The pledge of the society declared that members were 'to abstain from the use of distilled spirits except for medicinal purposes, to use other liquors only in moderation, and to discountenance the causes and practices of intemperance. We also agree not to frequent Public Houses and Beer Shops, and on every occasion to observe due moderation'.[49] The Aberystwyth society soon experienced difficulty with members who transgressed the rules of the society, as correspondence with the parent society concerning the mode of discipline that should be employed testifies.[50] During the first six months of the society's existence, August 1835 to February 1836, 507 persons signed the moderation pledge, of whom only 51 are recorded as having gone on later to sign the teetotal pledge. Occupations are given in the register for 226 of these 507 converts.[51]

A separate register of the society is preserved which gives an account of those who took the teetotal pledge between 1836 and 1855. In all, 3,025 names are recorded but for only 958 are occupations given. Generally speaking, the pattern of the early support for the society—mostly from skilled, manual workers—was continued.[52]

It is noteworthy that several persons following the same occupation joined the Aberystwyth Society on the same day, thus suggesting a well-developed sense of occupational solidarity. The percentage of those who transferred from the moderation to the teetotal register was 90 per cent. The total number of members who transgressed the rules of the society in the period 1836-55 was 147, and, not surprisingly, over 80 per cent of these had been members of the moderation society. The percentage of women who joined the society in this period was 44 per cent.[53]

The affairs of the society were managed by the officers or the committee, which was composed of 20-30 members. A rule of the society stated that all the clergymen, nonconformist ministers and medical practitioners who joined the society were to become members of the committee.[54] With this exception, it appears that no particular occupation was favoured in the selection of the committee. That for 1850-51 included a druggist, a cabinet maker, a schoolmaster, a plasterer, two grocers, a watchmaker, a tailor, a clerk, and a smith.[55] In all, 26 people served on this committee in 1850 but occupations are given for only ten of them. The remaining sixteen, we can be sure, included ministers of religion, and perhaps, some doctors of

TABLE 5. OCCUPATIONS OF THOSE WHO SIGNED THE TEETOTAL PLEDGE OF ABERYSTWYTH AUXILIARY TEMPERANCE SOCIETY, 1836-1855

Shoemaker	176	Calvinistic Methodist Minister	5
Mariner	87	Quarryman	5
Labourer	63	Cooper	4
Tailor	60	Ironmonger	4
Carpenter	48	Weaver	4
Mason	48	Hawker	3
Draper	42	Clerk	3
Joiner	38	Maltster	3
Cabinetmaker	34	Coachman	3
Blacksmith	25	Glover	3
Servant	22	Builder	3
Butcher	20	'Commerce'	3
Painter	19	Glazier	3
Water carrier	15	Schoolmaster	2
Sawyer	13	Umbrella mender	2
Flour Miller	11	Baptist Minister	2
Plasterer	10	Land surveyor	2
Watchmaker	10	Excise officer	2
Hairdresser	9	Auctioneer	2
Grocer	9	Bailiff	2
Tanner	9	Nurse	2
Hatter	8	China and glasswareman	2
Tinman	8	Baker	2
Ropemaker	8	Laundress	2
Ostler	7	Inn Keeper	2
Barber	7	Police officer	2
Saddler	7	Bookbinder	2
Farmer	7	Shipbuilder	2
Druggist	5	Speculator	2

One each of washerwoman, banker, chandler, chainmaker, hosier, wheelwright, coal merchant, plumber, skinner, milliner, turner, shopkeeper, Independent Minister, Wesleyan Methodist Minister, pedlar, blockmaker, lawyer, dyer, and relieving officer.

medicine. The committee for 1855-56 was composed of two druggists, a bookseller, two schoolmasters, two drapers, a shoemaker, a cabinet maker, two captains, a printer, a currier, a land surveyor, a plasterer, a foundryman, a master mariner, a watchmaker and all ministers of religion who were members of the society.[56]

As occupations are given for less than a third of the members who joined the society, it is not possible to determine exactly the percentage of support given by those following the same occupation, but from those whose occupations are given a definite trend emerges; it is that, again, the bulk of support was coming from the shoemaker, the tailor, the draper—the manually skilled, self-employed tradesmen.

Registers also survive for temperance activity at Dolgellau but they give very little information about the social-class basis of support for temperance in the locality. The register of *Cymdeithas Dirwestol yr Ieuanctyd Dolgellau,* a society established in October 1857, gives the occupations of only 41 people out of the total number on the register of 238 which joined the society between October 1857 and November 1858. [57] The members included 10 drapers, 4 printers, 4 shoemakers, 3 saddlers, 2 tailors, 2 plasterers, 2 druggists, 2 tinmen, a mason, a sawyer, a miner, a nailor, a barber, a butcher, a smith, a weaver, a currier, a carpenter, a joiner and a potter. [58] Again, only 15 out of 122 members of the society in the period 1875-7 had their occupations recorded. These comprised 4 printers, 2 tailors and one each of plasterer, flour dealer, draper, farmer, schoolmaster, butcher, shopkeeper, sailor and joiner. [59]

At Carmarthen the total number of members on the register of Carmarthen Temperance Society between 1841 and 1859 was 367.

TABLE 6.   OCCUPATION OF MEMBERS OF CARMARTHEN
TEMPERANCE SOCIETY, 1841-1859

Tailor	22	Preacher	3
Shoemaker	17	Carpenter	3
Tinman	9	Saddler	3
Labourer	9	Servant	3
Weaver	9	Tanner	3
Student	7	Coffee House Keeper	3
Shop Assistant	7	Merchant	3
Draper	6	Toymaker	2
Mariner	6	Painter	2
Printer	5	Confectioner	2
Cabinet Maker	5	Hatter	2
Sailor	4	Ropemaker	2
Carrier	4	Cooper	2
Druggist	4	Cropper	2
Butcher	4	Milliner	2
Mason	4	Policeman	2
Fathers (Poor House)	4	Glover	2

And one each of smith, joiner, brazier, soldier, flour merchant, governor of gaol, slate merchant, farmer, baker, barber, teacher, shopkeeper, gardener, tinplate worker, attorney's clerk and hairdresser.

Of these, occupations are given for 183. There were 70 women among the number of 184 for whom occupations are not given, and 19 children.[60] As in Aberystwyth, several people of the same occupation signed the pledge together.

Sources other than membership registers of temperance societies assist in shedding light on the class basis of support for temperance in the nineteenth century. For example, petitions from temperance societies in the slate-quarrying districts of Caernarfonshire to the magistrates of the borough of Caernarfon asking for the operation of the minimum hours of opening as embodied in H. A. Bruce's Licensing Act of 1872, reveal the strength of working-class support for temperance in the area at that time.[61] Although these petitions were devised by local temperance societies, many of the signatories were not members of societies but merely sympathetic residents living in the communities in which the societies functioned. At Llanddeiniolen, occupations were given for all 216 of the signatories and the three dominant occupations are quarryworkers (163), labourers (20) and farmers (17). Similarly, at Brynyrodyn the most numerous occupational groupings are quarryworkers (95), labourers (22) and farmers (17). Here, occupations were given for a half of those who signed: 162 out of 321. The petition from Caernarfon borough itself was signed by 3,303 people; the table below shows those occupations which were given among the first thousand signatories.[62]

TABLE 7.   OCCUPATIONS OF SIGNATORIES IN FAVOUR OF MINIMUM HOURS OF OPENING OF PUBLIC HOUSES IN CAERNARFON BOROUGH, 1872

Drapers' assistants	34	Carriers	9
Master Mariners	23	Printers	8
Sailors	22	Milliners	8
Servants	18	Flour dealers	7
Labourers	18	Clerks	7
Shoemakers	16	Milliners' assistants	6
Dressmakers	14	Ironmongers' assistants	6
Carpenters	13	Millers	5
Grocers	12	Bakers	5
Smiths	11	Porters	5
Drapers	11	Chemists	5
Painters	10	Confectioners	5
Joiners	10	Quarrymen	5
Butchers	9	Cabinetmakers	5

Charwomen	4	Watchmakers	2
Tailors	4	Bricklayers	2
Farmers	4	Fishermen	2
Slate splitters	4	Fitters	2
Ironmongers	4	Laundresses	2
Fishmongers	3	Surgeons	2
Ropemakers	3	Sail makers	2
Engineers	3	Coal merchants	2
Plasterers	3	Schoolmasters	2
Moulders	3	Bakers' assistants	2
Booksellers	3	Washerwomen	2
Coach proprietors	3	Slateframers	2
Weavers	2	Compositors	2

And one each of barber, auctioneer, shipowner, clergyman, Calvinistic Methodist minister, tool merchant, builder, slater, journalist, pilot, teacher, chimney sweep, lathe-splitter, stoker, fireman, nailor, ostler, book-keeper, grinder, bookseller, and tin-plate worker.

Unfortunately, no registers of temperance societies seem to have survived for industrial south Wales. The only direct evidence is the trust deed of 1867 for Merthyr Tydfil Welsh Temperance Society which was established in 1852. According to this the occupations of the trustees in 1867 were: chemists (2), grocers (2), tailors (2), a stationer, a glazier, a butcher, a tea dealer, an accountant, a printer, a shoemaker, and a clerk at the county court.[63] In addition, we know that the President of the Church of England Temperance Society at Rhymney in the early 1880s was an analytical chemist with Rhymney Iron Company.[64] In place of such direct evidence it is possible, if subscription lists in the annual reports of local societies can be found, to discover the social complexion of support for temperance, by using original census returns and trade directories. However, in south Wales, only the annual reports of Newport Temperance Society have been found to exist. Newport was not a characteristically 'Welsh' town and the reports are available for certain years only in the 1880s.[65] The major occupations of the members for 1882 and 1885 are given opposite.

In each of the two years one-third of the total amount of money subscribed came from one subscriber, Henry Phillips, a J.P. and an English Baptist, who on each occasion gave £25. However, the society did not list subscriptions under 2s. 6d., and so the mass membership of the movement in Newport, which possibly gave nothing at all, remains obscure.

TABLE 8. OCCUPATIONS OF MEMBERS OF NEWPORT
TEMPERANCE SOCIETY, 1882 and 1885

	1882	1885
Ministers of religion	11	14
Grocers	9	14
Drapers	5	8
Temperance Hoteliers	2	3
Boot and shoemakers	3	8
Tailors	5	6
Physicians	2	4
Shopkeepers	2	6
Printers	4	6
Coal merchants	2	3
Hairdressers	2	2
Watchmakers	2	2
Monumental Masons	2	3
Chemists	2	2
Ironmongers	4	4
Building Contractors	2	2
Ship brokers	1	1

Obviously, the main financial support of any temperance society
was a large subscribing membership. Membership fees usually varied
between 1s. and 2s. 6d., such a payment usually carrying with it the
right to speak and vote at the annual meeting. Subscribers of 2s. 6d.
per annum and upwards were usually eligible for election as officers
of the society. [66] At the head of the hierarchy of officers was the
president who should be 'a man of sterling worth and goodness, not
necessarily a man of position or money, not necessarily a minister,
but a man of principle, judgement and honour who possesses the
confidence and respect of all who know him'. [67] Of greater practical
importance, however, was the secretary, who should be 'a fanatic,
that is, a person affected by excessive enthusiasm—he will have to do
with plenty who are indifferent, cynical and suspicious, but he must
allow nothing to damp his ardour—he must be at it and always at
it'. [68] The secretary must further the cause of temperance by keeping
up a good correspondence in the local press, and particularly by
making sure that the press reported deaths caused by alcohol:
'Hundreds will read a newspaper who will never come to a
temperance meeting'. [69] Great importance, too, was attached to the
agency of the lecturer. At a time when many were unable to read, the
lecturer was important as 'the living voice', as the 'department of

popular illustration'.[70] Most temperance lecturers worked
strenuously for the cause. Between 1886 and 1889 the Rev. Morris
Morgan of Morriston addressed, on average, 160 temperance
meetings every year for the South Wales and Monmouthshire
Temperance Association.[71]

Enthusiasm was the fundamental principle of the teetotal faith and
it found graphic expression in Welsh teetotal oratory. Teetotal
speeches were generally very lively and animated. Was it a mere
coincidence when, on 18 January 1860, the morning after the
American temperance orator, J. B. Gough, had delivered one of his
thrilling temperance addresses at the Temperance Hall, Merthyr
Tydfil, Richard Crawshay, the chairman of the meeting, was struck
with total paralysis of the aural nerves?[72] Teetotal addresses were also
shrill, exceedingly repetitious, heavy, and dripping with self-
righteousness. Most successful temperance reformers possessed what
Walter Bagehot called 'the first great essential of an agitator—the
faculty of an easy anger'. With this went a certain extremism, and
Welsh teetotallers suffered badly from violence of the tongue.
Teetotal speeches, maintained the *Cardiff and Merthyr Guardian* in
1854, were more remarkable 'for their fiery and riotous declamation
than for the force or closeness of their reasoning . . . teetotalism is a
thing of feeling not of reasoning'.[73] The Rev. John Elias thundered
at a temperance meeting in Bangor in 1832:

> Drunkards tremble! You sin against heaven, and wrong your own
> souls; you hate wisdom and love death. . . . It is in your power to do
> much good that some of you do not. Therefore to him that knoweth to
> do good and doeth it not, to him it is sin. Cursed be the man that
> buildeth the city Jericho; shall I say cursed be the man that buildeth a
> fortress for drunkenness in Wales. No, I dare not say, Be the man
> cursed, but I venture to say that cursed he will be.[74]

The Rev. William Rees, who was an Independent minister at
Llechryd, Cardiganshire until his teetotal views forced the diaconate
to get rid of him, held uncompromising views on temperance. In
1888 he condemned a local doctor:

> Dr. —— is a dutiful son of the public house —— and has become a
> beer barrel —— and such a big belly. Such sots are insane in spiritual
> things, fools in polemics, and idiots in morals, boars and wild beasts
> that devastate and desolate the churches. The approach of energetic
> angels will prove stifling to them everywhere—thieves and robbers and
> liars.[75]

The vast majority of teetotal speeches consisted only of denunciations of the vice and evil of drunkenness, but such denunciation only served to increase the miseries of habitual drunkards, and made it more likely that their drunkenness would degenerate into chronic alcoholism.[76] 'As soon as society makes drunkenness disgraceful the drunkard has to withdraw from society.'[77] Newport Temperance Society hailed the day when 'the inveterate drunkard would stand alone, an object of scorn and contempt, no longer countenanced by Society as a good fellow, nor tolerated on the score of conviviality, but would pass his life of vice without friendship, pointed at as a thing to be avoided and despised, staggering with vomiting idiocy into a premature grave, unpitied and unwept'.[78]

During the late 1850s, with the rise to prominence of the prohibitionist United Kingdom Alliance, the first aim of the temperance movement was directed not so much against drink itself, but against the traffic in drink. Consequently, Welsh teetotallers, rather than attempt rationally to convince publicans and brewers of the evils of the drinking customs of society, went on verbally to abuse members of the drink trade on account of their vocation. Publicans and brewers were 'wholesale and retail manufacturers of drunkards'.[79] All publicans were bad, for they 'make a trade out of men's degraded appetites'. Everyone who was not a friend was an enemy. In March 1878 the teetotallers of Tredegar took the vicar of the town severely to task for attending and speaking at the Bedwellty Licensed Victuallers Association. 'Teetotal advocacy', commented the *Merthyr Express* with more than a hint of genuine regret, 'consists largely in personal abuse.'[80] In 1883 the Chief Constable of the Caernarfonshire Constabulary had to face a particularly scurrilous and virulent attack on his administration of the police force by a local temperance society led by the Rev. J. Eiddon Jones of Llanrug, who claimed that the Chief Constable was not doing all he could to suppress drunkenness in Caernarfonshire.[81] So intense was the furore that the magistrates were forced to hold a public inquiry, during the course of which the Chief Constable was specifically charged with not having taken proceedings against publicans reported to him as having broken the licensing laws. He was, however, completely exonerated by the Court of Inquiry. *Yr Herald Cymraeg* deplored the action of the temperance society and severely criticized Jones for not minding his own business instead of 'bringing people to trouble by his search for a mare's nest'.[82]

Many of the more moderate temperance advocates were not slow to criticize such extremism as they saw how much it damaged the temperance cause, particularly in the eyes of potential supporters. Henry Richard, writing in 1884, maintained that early temperance reformers 'dwelt with no doubt somewhat exaggerated emphasis' on the extent of the evil of drunkenness.[83] In particular, the nonconformist press had denounced the 'sin' of drunkenness in language of 'great vigour and vehemence, and with an unguarded latitude of expression which was then the besetting sin of our worthy teetotal friends'.[84] Yet still, in 1889, the periodical *Cymru Fydd* asserted that 'teetotallers are guilty of uttering in speech and print an enormous quantity of rubbish that will not stand the test of facts'; but it also maintained that such were the evils of drink 'that men justly became hot-headed about them'.[85] At Neath in March 1859, a temperance meeting, during the course of which some teetotallers were said to have resorted to 'low personalities' and 'Billingsgate abuse', was the occasion for an anti-temperance demonstration, during which the Vale of Neath Brewery Band played outside the meeting hall surrounded by 2,000 sympathisers, and during which the effigy of a teetotaller was carried through the town several times and afterwards hung publicly on a tree.[86]

Members of temperance societies were bound together as much by form as by content,[87] and indeed, in Wales, during the second half of the century, the ceremonial, recreative functions of temperance societies increasingly usurped the purely practical function of temperance teaching. The temperance movement called for the giving up of something which many working men valued as a compensation for the dullness of their everyday lives. The campaign for free associations of working men, for a humane poor law and for better working conditions, were all influences which added to the freedom of the oppressed labouring population. But the temperance movement seemed to take it away. To get the intended beneficiaries to come over to the temperance side was therefore a far more difficult, lengthy and necessary business than fighting the publicans and brewers. Sobriety had to be made as attractive as possible, and accordingly, 'an alluring mode of proceeding' was adopted. Temperance societies organized themselves as special 'orders', and the use of the word 'order', as in 'Independent Order of Rechabites' and 'International Order of Good Templars', showed a keen understanding of human psychology, particularly of young people.

The members were witnesses to a special vocation to which they were called and which they invited others to accept. They were offered not only fellowship in a cause but the thrill and excitement of a campaign. The use of uniforms, regalia, banners and badges, music and songs, grades of initiation and attractive titles, such as the High Chief Ruler of a Rechabite Tent, brought colour into their propaganda and made membership appear at once attractive and exclusive.[88] As Thomas Jones of Rhymney wrote:

> I was myself a member of a children's lodge of the Rechabites. We too had our official positions and titles, and very wonderful they were. I stood and called the meeting to order with a tap of a mallet, like the President of a World Conference. We also had splendid regalia and banners. Napoleon said you could manage men if you gave them toys and decorations to play with. Certainly, Thomas Williams managed us easily in the vestry of Tabernacle Chapel and with permanent results for I have never quite rid myself of a prejudice against alcohol or ceased to feel secretly censorious when seeing others consuming it, despite strenuous efforts to be broad-minded.[89]

The use of temperance ritual and regalia extended to weddings and funerals, occasions which were often characterized by a great deal of drinking. A teetotal wedding took place at Ruthin in 1836, under the auspices of the Ruthin Temperance Society, the groom being a reformed drunkard.[90] Many temperance societies buried their own dead. On October 16, 1836 a teetotal burial occurred at Rhosllannerchrugog, when *dirwestwr* Mary Jones was laid to rest. Behind the hearse marched 52 members of Rhos Temperance Society, carrying mourning banners.[91] At a teetotal funeral at Llandwrog in Caernarfonshire in March 1838, the coffin was decorated with temperance banners, four placed at each corner, similar to the position of the four candles at a Catholic burial, and four banners placed around the grave at the interment.[92] The use of regalia by temperance reformers aroused the ire of some nonconformists. Rosser Beynon, conductor of the temperance choir at Zoar Independent Chapel in Merthyr Tydfil, was asked to leave the chapel in 1838 because the diaconate objected to the wearing of 'vain' medals at temperance concerts and demonstrations.[93]

Ornate ceremonial was best developed in the Independent Order of Good Templars, introduced into Wales in 1871. Good Templary was described as being 'a cross between a Christian Church and Freemasonry'.[94] It was essentially a Church Militant and it featured grips, passwords, and rites of its own, performed in the secrecy of lodge meetings. The shape of the Templar regalia suggested unity for it was 'of one piece, round, encircling the neck as a token of affectionate brotherhood or sisterhood. It is a kind of yoke, but graceful, elegant, and easy, how much better than the dreadful yoke of intemperate habits. It is so formed that it covers the emotional parts. That gaudy collar palpitating above the breast of yonder brother covers a heart beating with love for the brotherhood . . . or when rising and falling upon the bosoms of the fair sisterhood tells only of generous pity and loving acts of mercy . . . We live in an age of advertising and what more resplendent and dazzling advertisement could we have than our gaudy collars?'[95]

The struggle against drink took the form of a military campaign.

> Come with us into the battlefield, and let us as Christians, display our indomitable courage in seeking to pull down the strongholds of Satan, and build up the walls of the Heavenly Jerusalem. . . .
>> Come and join our noble Army,
>> Be ye soldiers brave and hardy,
>> Then we can exclaim with joy,
>> King Alcohol we will destroy.[96]

There were ample precedents in the Old and New Testaments for the use of military imagery in Christian endeavour. The name of the Blue Ribbon Gospel Temperance movement of the 1880s was taken from Numbers, Chapter 15, and it soon came to be known as the Blue Ribbon Army. At a Blue Ribbon meeting at Newport in April 1882, Samuel Harse, a leading temperance reformer in the town, maintained that during the previous year there had been 'an advance along the whole line', [97] and he then recited a poem on the Battle of Naseby.[98] On New year's Day, 1838, the organization of Harlech Temperance Society's procession to Dolgellau was put in charge of a former soldier.[99] Such temperance hymns as *Hold the Fort* and Ieuan Gwynedd's *Byddin Dirwest* were very popular throughout Wales, while in literature one of the most widely read books was the Rev. Joseph Evans' *Arrows from a Temperance Quiver*, published at Carmarthen in 1864.[100]

'J.B.', a correspondent from Carmarthen, wrote to *The Working Man's Teetotal Journal* in 1844:

> It is quite a mistaken notion if we imagine that our work is done when we get men to sign the pledge, for it is only then commenced. Our

> labours are lost unless we can get men away from their old associations, and introduce them into new; give them new recreations and a more intellectual bent of mind. [101]

It was vital that the new convert to temperance be persuaded to take up entirely different leisure habits; he should be provided with 'other and more permanent sources of interest, amusement and instruction than the mere repetition of temperance arguments and speeches'. [102] Contemporaries correctly believed that it was not so much a craving for drink which took the vast majority of drinkers to the public house as a desire for company and recreation after the day's work. [103] Consequently, the temperance society itself had to become a counter-attraction to the public house, offering its own particular type of 'harmless', 'rational' recreation. This was a very necessary development for, as we have seen, the Wales of the first half of the nineteenth century was seriously lacking in counter-attractions to the public house. [104]

However, the recreation provided by Welsh temperance societies took the form of amusements which could be enjoyed only by the members of these societies. Here, we must distinguish between members of temperance societies and sympathetic adherents of the temperance cause who campaigned for general 'improvement'. The latter believed that full-blown temperance reformers should extend their influence from within the narrow confines of the temperance society and help to establish those practical counter-attractions and aids to sobriety, and improvment such as coffee taverns with newspapers, literary and debating societies, workmens' libraries, allotments, and mechanics institutes. Such establishments would do more to reduce drunkenness than 'all the homilies ever delivered or the tracts ever printed. . . . Men are sociable . . . and it is the neglect of providing for the exercise of the social instinct in men which has made Temperance Societies comparative failures in checking drunkenness and its attendant crimes. Man must be improved as he is, and not after some ideal standard which he has not attained.' [105] Any recreation the temperance society offered was invariably anti-drink orientated and in the majority of cases catered for a group of people already saved from the ravages of strong drink.

Some form of entertainment was essential if temperance societies were to retain the bulk of their rank and file members. At Merthyr Tydfil, a series of temperance *eisteddfodau* was held every year during the period from 1848 to 1879 under the auspices of *Y Cymmrodorion*

Dirwestol or the 'Temperate Cambro-Brethren'.[106] All the festivals were held on Christmas Day, and all in local chapels, in contrast to the previously existing practice of holding them in public houses. The singing of temperance hymns and songs was a particularly prominent feature of such occasions. Musical composition was introduced at the first temperance *eisteddfod* in 1848, and choral singing was introduced in 1849: both were innovations in any Merthyr *eisteddfod*. Special temperance singing classes had begun at Merthyr in 1843, composed of the most accomplished singers of the different chapel congregations in the town, who met twice a week in a 'Temperance room' set aside for the purpose.[107] The various competitions at such *eisteddfodau* consisted of such subjects as essays on 'Universal Brotherhood', songs on 'Family Happinesss' and 'How Sweet the Redemption', poems on 'My Mother' and 'Water', six *englynion* on the visit of temperance lecturer G. E. Lomax to Merthyr and a translation of Aikin's 'Hill of Science'.

In 1854, a larger association, the *Gymanfa Gerddorol Ddirwestol Gwent a Morgannwg* was established at Merthyr, its declared objectives being to promote temperance, congregational singing and choral music. The annual festival of the association was customarily given over to a whole day of temperance music, at which the choirs sang 'glees, anthems and choruses singly, and congregational tunes and anthems unitedly'.[108] In north Wales the *Undeb Cerddorol Dirwestwyr Ardudwy* was formed in 1867.[109] It met annually in Harlech Castle, during which one meeting would be given over to secular music and one to sacred music.[110]

Plays and mock trials of 'Sir John Barleycorn' were popular forms of entertainment with most temperance societies. Characters such as Robin Quicktipple, Mr Sensual, Abraham Drinkwater and Lord Chief Justice Farsight were played by members of the society and, invariably, Sir John Barleycorn would be brought from the bar of a public house to the bar of justice and thereafter remain a reformed character.[111] The reading of extracts from parliamentary blue books on the drink question and from novels such as *Uncle Tom's Cabin* was also popular.[112]

A most important means of both recreation and propaganda for any temperance society was the annual festival when members gathered together and marched in procession through their town or village. The forms of procession varied very little from place to place.[113] That at Merthyr Tydfil which took place on Easter

Monday, 1838 is not untypical. At 8 a.m. 850 teetotallers met on
Swansea Road, about one-and-a-half miles from the town centre.
The procession passed down through Cefn, up alongside
Penydarren Iron Works to the New Market House at Dowlais (lent
by Josiah John Guest, M.P., for the day). Here, a large group of
Monmouthshire teetotallers joined the festival and a public meeting
was held. A religious service took place first and the meeting was then
addressed by the chairman, George Smith Kenrick of Varteg Iron
Works, who emphasised the benefits of teetotalism. Addresses then
followed by several nonconformist ministers, and at 2 p.m. a 3,000
strong procession formed, including among its numbers six reformed
drunkards who carried large banners inscribed: 'Sobriety and
Happiness', 'Our Weapons are Prayer, Reason and Scripture',
'Sobriety and Virtue', and *'Dirwest, cred a gweddi'*. The procession
moved through the town singing temperance hymns and finally
dispersed to Zoar and Pontmorlais chapels for further worship.
Pledges were taken throughout the day.[114]

Very similar in many respects to the annual festival was the
temperance demonstration, which, in most cases, was an event of
organized amusement and recreation which had little connection with
serious temperance work. A large Good Templar demonstration took
place at Beaufort in August 1869.[115]

> This place was 'en fete' on Monday last. The friends of Temperance
> and Templarism, in particular, had decided to get up a grand
> demonstration, the lodges of late having been augmented by the
> enrolment of a number of active and influential members. The
> weather, which had been unsettled during the morning, cleared up
> about mid-day to the great relief of all concerned. At 2.30 a procession
> was formed, starting from the lodge-room in the following order:
> Charter of adult lodge, followed by a choir composed of the whole of
> the senior lodge, under the leadership of Mr. W. Davies, stationer;
> then came the juvenile charter and lodge followed by a number of
> Good Templar visitors, bringing to a close the procession numbering
> nearly 300 persons. The route of march extended from the Brynmawr
> toll-gate, at the east end, to Carmel Chapel at the west end of the place,
> the choir singing suitable temperance selections all along the route.
> The whole proceedings were under the superintendence of Mr. W.
> Pritchard (Gwilym Risiart), D.M. of the Monmouth and East
> Breconshire district. A tea was provided at the lodge-room, Beaufort
> Hill, when about 400 partook of the good things provided by Mr.
> Samuel Davies, confectioner, Ebbw Vale, admission being by ticket.
> After tea, young and old repaired to the hill-top where innocent games
> were indulged in until about 8 o'clock, when a general rush was made

towards the Board schoolroom, Beaufort Hill, where an open lodge entertainment was given, the Rev. J. Morris, Ebbw Vale, presiding. The following programme had been prepared: Selection, choir; recitation, Richard Davies; part song, juvenile choir; address, Miss Thomas (Salvation Army); recitation, 'An Appeal', L. G. Davies; duet, 'The Swiss Toy Girl', H. Harris and M. Morgan; recitation, Alice Morgan; recitation, David Charles; recitation, Polly Edmunds; duet, 'The Old Black Cat', E. and W. Pembrey; recitation, 'I am only a boy', T. Greenland Davies; recitation, 'The Deed of Horror' (by request), Mr. E. C. Pugh, secretary of the Monmouthshire Temperance Association; part song, juvenile choir; recitation, Sarah A. Davies; song, 'Father's a drunkard', E. Pembrey; duet, 'Hard Times', Messrs. T. Thomas and J. Churchill; recitation, Messrs. W. Pritchard, W. Davies, J. Churchill and T. Thomas. Owing to the lateness of the hour at which the proceedings commenced, a part of the programme had to be omitted. Much of the entertainment was quite inaudible to that part of the audience in the farthest end of the room, owing to the noise prevailing throughout the evening, more especially during the last recitation on the programme. A vote of thanks to the members of the Llangattock School Board, for the use of the room was proposed by Mr. Hoddin, stationmaster. The usual vote of thanks to the chairman was proposed by Mr. E. C. Pugh and carried unanimously, and the proceedings terminated.

Recreation played an increasingly important rôle in the activities of temperance societies in Wales during the last few decades of the century. In the 1880s St. John's Parochial Branch of the Church of England Temperance Society in Cardiff met weekly for 'a little social intercourse. . . . We spend our time very pleasantly in listening to songs, readings and recitations, with a little earnest temperance talk put in between by one or another as padding.'[116] At the annual festival of the Llanmartin branch of the same society in 1881 the Rev. R. Valpy French reminded the gathering that there was a danger that temperance festivals might deteriorate into 'mere holiday outings', whilst the 'real and serious object' of temperance might be 'lost sight of'.[117] But the die seems to have been cast. At the annual meeting of Swansea Gospel Temperance Union in January 1890 it was stated that during the greater part of the year it had been intended to conduct the meetings on 'the old lines', confining them almost entirely to the advocacy of teetotalism. But it was impossible to provide two or three fresh, effective and popular speakers on a well-worn theme every week. The audience began to thin, the interest languish, while the expenses went on at the same rate. They found that the people they most needed were not with them, so they began to make their meetings more attractive. The character of the new departure was a 'combination of innocent recreation with instruction'.[118]

It would be erroneous to assert that temperance societies existed for entertainment purposes only. But it is true, nevertheless, that the only practical work of social improvement undertaken by temperance bodies in Wales during the second half of the century was carried out, not so much by the small individual societies, but by district lodges of the Good Templars and by larger temperance unions and associations to which, of course, some of the local societies were affiliated. At Merthyr Tydfil in 1872, the Good Templars bought the 'White Lion' public house and converted it into a British Workmen's Public House.[119] The Aberystwyth Templars did the same in 1873, leasing a local pub at a rental of £60 a year.[120] The Templars of East Glamorgan organized a relief fund in February 1873 in order to relieve distress caused by the strike in that area.[121] In October 1888 the Merionethshire Temperance Conference became the first temperance organization in Britain to support the British Medical Association's plan for making compulsory the permissive Kerr—B.M.A. Habitual Drunkards Amendment Act of 1888 which had been hailed as the 'first permanent legislation in the interests of the inebriates in the United Kingdom'.[122] In 1892 the Gwynedd Temperance Association appointed commissioners to enquire into the condition of the agricultural labourers of Caernarfonshire and Anglesey. But while the report stated that opportunities for self-help amongst them were limited as the labourers worked a fourteen hour day, no action was taken.[123] The North Wales Women's Temperance Union, established at Blaenau Ffestiniog in September 1892, took 'temperance' in its broadest sense and aimed at the promotion of 'social purity'.[124] The union erected a Shelter for Young Girls at Wrexham, and corresponded individually with many girls in order to keep them on the straight way, and make them feel that 'an interest is being taken especially in each of them.'[125]

*   *   *   *

There is little doubt that the temperance society provided colour, interest and amusement in what was, to many of its members, a fairly drab life. The influence of 'temperance' in nineteenth-century Wales was ubiquitous. There existed a temperance way of life with its own temperance drinks, temperance funerals, temperance weddings and temperance benefit societies. [126] In Cardiff, in the 1850s there arose Temperance Town, a drink-free suburban utopia so called because the owner of the land—market-gardener Jacob Scott Matthews—was a teetotaller and made it a condition that no public house should be erected there. [127] The temperance movement in Britain has been compared with the denomination. This seems to have been true of the Welsh movement with its status-conferring positions in an official hierarchy, its prayers and hymn-singing, its temperance sermons and special Temperance Sundays, its voluntary contributions and its temperance halls, so similar, architecturally, to chapels. [128]

NOTES

[1] See N.L.W., MS. 11,614 E (D. Morgan Lewis 1), 'A Brief View of the Operations and Principles of Temperance Societies'; see also *C.M.G.*, 17 April 1841.

[2] *The British and Foreign Temperance Herald,* vol. 4, June 1835, pp. 70-1 (letter from Crickhowell).

[3] *Pleadings for Reforms. Published Fifty Years Ago by Samuel Roberts of Llanbrynmair* (Conway, n.d.), pp. 118-9.

[4] Ibid., p. 119.

[5] *C.M.G.*, 2 October 1859.

[6] *Merthyr Express,* 20 October 1877.

[7] See Carmarthenshire Record Office, Museum Collection, 326 Register of Carmarthen Temperance Society with the names of those who signed the 'pledge' and additional memoranda, 1841-59. See also *Y Dirwestydd,* no. 13, July 1837, p. 98.

[8] See Henry Carter, *The English Temperance Movement. A Study In Objectives* (1933), pp. 36-8, 252-3.

[9] N.L.W., Cwrt Mawr MS, 481, p. 122; E. G. Millward (ed.), *Detholion o Ddyddiadur Eben Fardd* (Cardiff, 1968), p. 199 (Eben Fardd's italics).

[10] Carmarthenshire Record Office, Museum Collection, 326.

[11] *Y Dirwestydd,* no. 19, January 1838, p. 152.

[12] *Merthyr Express,* 20 September 1879. For a brief history of the Good Templars in Wales see *Good Templary in Wales. Diamond Jubilee, 1874-1934* (Gowerton, 1934).

[13] Rev. David Young, *A Noble Life. Incidents in the career of Lewis Davies of Ferndale* (1913), pp. 181-2.

[14] P.R.O. HO 45/454, Part 1, 'Organization of Teetotallers in Wales' by Thomas Yates, incorporated in Edwin Chadwick, Memorandum on Disturbances in Wales, 11 July 1843.

[15] John Griffith, "Clerical Experiences, Personal and Parochial. No. 1 of a series of papers by the abstaining clergy." *Church of England Temperance Magazine,* 1 January 1875, p. 28.

[16] Ibid., pp. 27, 29.

[17] N.L.W., MS. 8,392, Diary and Letters of Eben Fardd. See also *Wales* (ed. O. M. Edwards), 1894-5.

[18] N.L.W., MS. 8,392, op. cit., *Wales,* vol. 1, October 1894, p. 271; Millward, op. cit., p. 45.

[19] N.L.W., MS. 8,392, op. cit.

[20] Ibid.

[21] Ibid.

[22] Millward, op. cit., p. 67.

[23] Ibid.

[24] Ibid., p. 71.

[25] Ibid., p. 102.

[26] Ibid., p. 103.

[27] Ibid., p. 129. In 1846 Eben Fardd wrote: 'I damn the whole Department of Intoxication, but conscientiously make private use of a small quantity at home and at other private houses. I do not hereby unqualifiedly condemn but subject these to the jealous and strict surveillance of the conscience, the understanding, the judgement, the reason and christian influence . . . The Pledge. First, it should be so worded as not to implicate the occasionally offending teetotaller in the sin of perjury.' N.L.W. MS. 8,392.

[28] Millward, op. cit., p. 173.

[29] *Monmouthshire Merlin,* 7 September 1839.

[30] *Caernarvon and Denbigh Herald,* 29 September 1838.

[31] N.L.W., MS. 8,324 D (Edward Mathews 4), A roll of 3,226 persons from Aberystwyth and district who signed the Total Abstinence pledge between 21 October 1836 and 13 August 1855, with their addresses and occupations.

[32] Ibid.

[33] N.L.W., MS. 19,911 B (Padarn Davies 2), Minute Book of Pabell Padarn, Independent Order of Rechabites, March 1842-October 1846: meeting of 16 May 1842.

[34] *Alliance News,* 14 August 1891.

[35] See *Cambrian Temperance Chronicle,* vol. 1, no. 2, July 1891, p. 25.

[36] *Annual Directory and Rechabite Reference Book, 1892-93* (Manchester, 1893), p. 34.

[37] *Caernarvon and Denbigh Herald,* 15 July 1871; *Alliance News,* 22 July 1871.

[38] N.L.W., MS. 16,735 B (Bontdolgadfan 9), Temperance Miscellanea 1858-78.

[39] Ibid.

[40] *P.P.,* 1846 (XXIV), op. cit., p. 418.

[41] *Report of the Royal Commissioners appointed to enquire into the operation of the Sunday Closing (Wales) Act, 1881* (C.5994), H.C. (1890), XL. 1, Qq. 11,599-600.

[42] C.C.L., MS. 3,492, Minute Book of Cefn Coed English Wesleyan Sunday School, 1889-1910, *passim.*

[43] See Abercarn Teetotal Association, *Annual Report 1877-78,* p. 5; J. S. Bushnan, *Religious Revivals in relation to nervous and mental diseases* (1860); D. J. Thomas, *The Temperance Movement in Newport (Mon.)* (Newport, 1937), p. 51.

[44] *Church of England Temperance Magazine,* 1 January 1865, p. 26.

[45] *Crickhowell Temperance Advocate,* no. 1, May 1836, p. 34.

[46] *The National Temperance Advocate and Herald,* vol. 1, no. 2, 15 February 1842, p. 18.

[47] *Church of England Temperance Magazine,* 1 January 1865, p. 26.

[48] 'Working class' includes 'men who work daily at their handicraft trade without a master, and even sometimes employ a journeyman or apprentice, provided that they derive their chief support from their own labour, and not from the labour of others, or the profits arising from capital or the supply of materials.' Letter to Overseers from the Poor Law Board, 2 January 1866, *P.P.,* 1866 (3616), p. 161.

[49] N.L.W., MS. 8,323 B (Matthews 3), Minute Book of the Aberystwyth Auxiliary Temperance Society, 1835-7; 1855-6. Meeting of 31 August 1835.

[50] Ibid., 18 February 1836.

[51] N.L.W., MS. 8,322 B (Matthews 2), A Roll of members of the Aberystwyth Auxiliary Temperance Society.

[52] N.L.W., MS. 8,324 D (Matthews 4), Roll of 3,226 persons from Aberystwyth and District who signed . . . the pledge between 1836 and 1855.

[53] Ibid.

[54] N.L.W., MS. 8,323 B, Minutes, 31 August 1835.

[55] N.L.W., MS. 8,324 D.

[56] N.L.W., MS. 8,323 B. Minutes, 31 December 1855, 1 January 1856.

[57] N.L.W., MS. 2,741 B (Edward Griffith 51), Register of Cymdeithas Dirwestol Ieuangctyd Dolgellau.

[58] Ibid.

[59] Merionethshire Record Office, M/1/238, Register of Dolgellau Temperance Society, 1875-77.

[60] Carmarthen Record Office, Museum Collection, 326, op. cit.

[61] Caernarvonshire Record Office, Licensing, 1872: Petitions for early closing of public houses.

[62] Ibid. Other registers of temperance societies in mid and north Wales held at the National Library of Wales but which do not give the occupations of members are as follows: N.L.W., MS. 11,489 B (part of this is in the hand of Samuel Roberts, Llanbrynmair); N.L.W., MS. 16,734 B (Bontdolgadfan 8); N.L.W., MS. 12,072 A; N.L.W. MS. 16,146 B (E. C. Powell); N.L.W. Roll, Bay 31, Shelf 3.

[63] G.R.O., D/D. Vau, Merthyr Tydfil Welsh Temperance Society, Trust Deed 1867.

[64] *Merthyr Express,* 2 April 1881.

[65] Newport Total Abstinence Society and Gospel Temperance Union, *Annual Reports, 1882, 1885-89; Owen's Directory for Glamorgan, Monmouth, Shropshire, Hereford and Radnor* (1878); *Kelley's Directory* (1884), pp. 84-96. In 1882, the total number of subscribers was 122. Of this number, the occupations of 95 have been found. For 1885 the total number of subscribers was 170, of which the occupations of 145 have been traced.

[66] See, for example, Newport Temperance Society, *Annual Reports, 1882, 1885-88.*

[67] Livesey-Clegg House, Sheffield, British National Temperance League MS. 'A Homely Talk with Total Abstainers with a few suggestions for the successful working of a Temperance Society.'

[68] Ibid.

[69] Rev. Evan Jones, 'The Possibilities and Probabilities of Teetotalism', *The Teetotal Times and Essayist,* no. 1 new series, January 1848, p. 2.

[70] Ibid.

[71] 'Rev. Morris Morgan'. A manuscript account of his life and work in the offices of the South Wales and Monmouthshire Temperance Association, Cardiff.

[72] *Merthyr Express,* 17 May 1879.

[73] *C.M.G.,* 1 December 1854.

[74] *National Temperance League Annual, 1882* (1882), pp. 45-6.

[75] N.L.W., MS. 12,863 F, Journal of William Rees, Llechryd, *sub* 3 October 1888. See also *Western Mail,* 13 March 1968.

[76] Cf. G. J. Holyoake, *The Social Means of Promoting Temperance* (1859), p. 9: 'He [the teetotaller] paints alcohol in all the alluring language of seductiveness. He calls it the irresistible drink, the everlasting syren, who always bewitches you. . . . If the licensed victuallers were wise they would keep in their pay several well-known teetotal lecturers.'

[77] B. Harrison 'The Temperance Question in England, 1829-1869' (University of Oxford D.Phil. thesis, 1965), p. 563.

[78] D. J. Thomas, op. cit., p. 19.

[79] For example, see *The Reformer and South Wales Times,* 13 September 1861.

[80] *Merthyr Express,* 6 April 1878.

[81] *North Wales Chronicle,* 24 February 1883.

[82] *Yr Herald Cymraeg,* 1 March 1883, quoted in J. O. Jones, *The History of the Caernarvonshire Constabulary,* op. cit., p. 52.

[83] Henry Richard, *Letters and Essays on Wales* (2nd ed., 1884), p. 202.

[84] Ibid.

[85] *Cymru Fydd,* vol. 2., no. 4, April 1889, pp. 211-12; see also N.L.W., MS. 18,342 C, 'An essay on the effects of alcoholic drinks on the human system', National Eisteddfod, 1875.

[86] *Cambrian,* 4 and 25 March 1859, 8 April 1859. Evan Evans, the head of the Vale of Neath Brewery, disseminated posters claiming he knew nothing of the Band's activity.

[87] See Hobsbawm, *Primitive Rebels,* p. 150.

[88] See Rev. William Jones, *The Character of the Welsh as a Nation. Prize Essay. Royal Gordovigion Eisteddfod, 1840* (1841), p. 124; A. V. Murray, *The Ethics and Techniques of Persuasion* (Cardiff, 1953), pp. 11-15. Cf. *Alliance News* 6 July 1872, p. 495: 'The Templar Order . . . is based on the principle of fascinating the young and middle-aged by rank, show and title.'

[89] Thomas Jones, op. cit., pp. 133-4.

[90] *Y Dirwestydd,* no. 4, Tachwedd 1836, p. 27.

[91] Ibid., no. 6, Rhagfyr 1836, p. 45.

[92] Ibid., no. 21, Mawrth 1838, p. 171.

[93] David Morgans, op. cit., pp. 41, 47.

[94] *The Good Templars Advocate of Wrexham,* vol. 1, no. 9, 26 April 1873.

[95] *The Templar of Wales,* vol. 1, no. 15, 6 September 1873, p. 3.

[96] *The Treasury,* vol. 1, 1864, p. 118.

[97] Newport Temperance Society, *Annual Report, 1882,* p. 1.

[98] *Monmouthshire Merlin,* 7 April 1882.

[99] *Y Dirwestydd,* no. 20, Chwefror 1838, p. 163.

[100] *Y Caniedydd* (Swansea, 1960), p. 357.

[101] *The Working Man's Teetotal Journal,* 1884, p. 228.

[102] *C.M.G.,* 19 February 1848.

[103] Ibid., 10 November 1865; *Western Mail,* 21 January 1874.

[104] See Chapter 1, pp. 14-15. See also G.R.O., Dowlais MSS, 1755, f. 388-9; *Silurian,* 10 December 1836; *C.M.G.,* 24 December 1836, 31 August 1839, 11 March 1864; *Monmouthshire Merlin,* 18 June 1836, 15 September 1838; H. A. Bruce, *Merthyr in 1851,* p. 17; J. H. Phillips, op. cit., pp. 8-9; R. R. Davies, op. cit., pp. 35-7; Evan Owen, op. cit., pp. 7-14; *Y Dyngarwr,* vol. 1, no. 2, Chwefror 1879, pp. 18-19; Wirt Sikes, op. cit., pp. 227, 295-6; *The Aberdare Banner of Faith,* vol. 2, June 1885, p. cxli.

[105] *South Wales Daily News*, 15 July 1874.

[106] See *C.M.G.*, 23 December 1845, 30 December 1848. For temperance *eisteddfodau* at Merthyr see David Morgans, op. cit., pp. 42, 214-28.

[107] *C.M.G.*, 23 September 1843.

[108] *Report of the Royal Commission on the Church of England and other religious bodies in Wales and Monmouthshire, 1911*, C. 5438, vol. 7 appendix 27, p. 121.

[109] *Caernarvon and Denbigh Herald*, 8 July 1871.

[110] See N.L.W., MS. 7,995A, Minute Book of *Undeb Cerddorol Dirwestwyr Ardudwy*, 1870-77.

[111] See, for example, *Cambrian*, 25 March 1859; *Monmouthshire Merlin*, 27 February 1885.

[112] Ibid.

[113] *Y Dirwestydd*, no. 21, Mawrth 1838, p. 172.

[114] *C.M.G.*, 21 April 1838. For other examples of processions see *Y Dirwestydd*, no. 2, Medi 1836, p. 14; no. 19, Ionawr 1838, p. 151; *Merthyr Star*, 7 November 1860; E. G. Millward, op. cit., pp. 55, 57, 62; Gwyn A. Williams, 'The Merthyr of Dic Penderyn', in G. Williams (ed.), *Merthyr Politics*, p. 16.

[115] *Merthyr Express*, 2 August 1879.

[116] *St. John the Baptist Parish Magazine*, January 1884, p. 5.

[117] *Monmouthshire Merlin*, 13 May 1881. See *Merthyr Express*, 5 November 1887, for a similar warning from Mountain Ash.

[118] *South Wales Daily News*, 2 January 1890.

[119] *Merthyr Express*, 31 August 1872.

[120] *The Western Good Templar*, vol. 2, no. 9, May 1873, p. 131.

[121] Ibid., vol. 2, no. 7, March 1873, p. 108.

[122] *British Medical Journal*, 2, 1888, pp. 729, 896, quoted in R. M. Macleod, 'The Edge of Hope. Social Policy and Chronic Alcoholism, 1870-1900', *Journal of the History of Medicine and Allied Sciences*, vol. 22, no. 3, July 1967, p. 231.

[123] *Welsh Weekly: an independent journal of Religious and Social Life in Wales*, vol. 1, no. 2, 15 January 1892, p. 14.

[124] N.L.W., Deposited MS 637-8 A, Minute Books of the North Wales Womens' Temperance Union, 1892-95: meeting of 22 September 1892.

[125] Ibid., 23 February 1894.

[126] For temperance drinks, see *Yr Athraw sef cylchgrawn llenyddol a dirwestol*, vol. 1, no. 12, December 1836, p. 169; Evan Evans, *A Duoglott Guide for making Temperance Drinks* (Cowbridge, 1838), passim.

[127] Thomas Jones, 'The Place Names of Cardiff', *South Wales and Monmouth Record Society*, 1950, no. 2, p. 61; see also 'Two Former Curates', *Father Jones of Cardiff. A Memoir* (1907), p. 66.

[128] For temperance hymns, see *Y Caniedydd Dirwestol, sef casgliad o hymnau addas i'w canu mewn cyfarfodydd a gwyliau dirwestol* (Llanidloes, 1838); see also *Y Dirwestydd*, no. 27, Medi 1838, p. 220.

CHAPTER IV

TEMPERANCE AND RELIGION

IN 1894 T. E. Ellis, Liberal M.P. for Merionethshire and Chief Whip, maintained that the first outcome of the eighteenth-century revival in Wales was religious education and 'culture', and that the second was temperance, which he defined as 'religion influencing social life'. [1] The temperance movement in Wales, like the anti-slavery movement in Wales, and to a lesser degree, like the anti-Corn Law and peace movements in Wales, assumed the characteristics of a moral and religious crusade, which throughout the century, was predominantly nonconformist in character. [2] Invariably, the best and most able writers on the political and social topics of the time were ministers and clergy and this made agitations for social betterment into religious crusades. [3] What made the temperance movement in Wales an intensely religious phenomenon was the literal interpretation of the verse in Corinthians which stressed that 'No drunkard . . . shall inherit the Kingdom of God' (I *Cor.* VI, 10). Great stress was laid on the after life and on keeping oneself 'good' and 'pure' for it, so much so that temperance was conceived of in an 'other-worldly' sense, as a matter of spiritual and religious conscience, almost totally divorced from the more practical human and social aspects of the drink problem.

Many meetings of the early temperance societies in Wales were held in nonconformist chapels and, in return, collections were often taken, where necessary, for the defrayment of the expense of liquidating chapel debts. [4] Such meetings were almost indistinguishable from ordinary chapel services; at Amlwch in 1836, for instance, meetings of the Amlwch Temperance Society were opened by reading a portion of the Scriptures, and by hymn-singing and prayer. [5] Members of temperance societies often held their own public temperance prayer meetings and private meetings—'meetings of the members'—which were similar to church meetings, and at which members were received and expelled. [6] The general attitude to religion and society shared by many evangelicals and nonconformists in the nineteenth century was that of evangelical pietism, the essential characteristic of which was the setting up of a barrier of customs and prohibitions, of things done and not done, between the withdrawn, socially-isolated religious group and society in general. [7]

It is a commonplace, of course, that in its religious adherence nineteenth-century Wales was predominantly nonconformist with, broadly speaking, Calvinistic Methodism holding sway in north Wales and Independency and the Baptists predominating in south Wales. [8] The strength of nonconformity was revealed statistically in 1851: two in every three of the people who had attended religious services on census Sunday were nonconformists; over half of the population of Wales attended a place of worship compared with only a third in England. [9] Of the working population which attended, 22 per cent are said to have attended the services of the Established Church and 78 per cent are said to have attended nonconformist chapels. By 1866 it was claimed with justice that 'in Wales, nonconformity is—speaking broadly—the national creed and the national practice'. [10]

However, the disabilities of nonconformity disqualified many people from becoming effective members of the social order long after the repeal of the Test and Corporation Acts. Little wonder that a Merthyr nonconformist could write in 1885 that 'the history of Nonconformity is that of one long continuous fight of right against might and of the oppressed against the oppressor'. [11] The sense of deprivation was caught in some of the hymns of the period: *Alone on the raft, Throw out the lifeline, Hold the fort, The Heavy Cross.* Voluntary introversion played a part. The Rev. J. Idrisyn Jones of Brecon maintained in 1881 that it was the interpretation of the New Testament that separated nonconformists from churchmen, and this 'led the earlier Nonconformists to endure their terrible persecutions and sufferings, and leads modern Nonconformists to incur the loss of social prestige, and often times the frown of their neighbours and losses in business'. [12] As Professor Gwyn Williams has remarked: 'A religion of manners and morals characterized this socially-isolated group whose exclusion from power and prestige served only to emphasise its ingrown and inward-looking satisfaction with itself and its values.' [13] Involvement in the temperance crusade required its supporters to endure personal self-sacrifice and even persecution, and this naturally attracted religious groups with a recent tradition of suffering for their beliefs.

Dr. Kent has argued that for Britain as a whole deprivation amongst nonconformists bred social aggression and that, beneath the

surface, the 'nonconformist conscience' was chiefly a way of fighting
for social objectives—'a form of social aggression rather than of
outraged morality'. He sees the nonconformity of the second half of
the nineteenth century as having been engaged in an attempt to
impose its own standards on the rest of British society, and explains
this as a reaction to the fact that although it was strong and self-
confident it nevertheless felt itself to be socially rejected.[14] But 'social
aggression' was not the only motivation, for many nonconformists
took account of the seriousness of the social problems which they
sought to mitigate by crusading zeal and by legislation.

The other-worldly nature of the temperance movement in Wales
may be explained largely by the powerful influence of Calvinistic
teaching which dominated Welsh nonconformist theology in the
nineteenth century. The major tenets of such teaching included the
doctrine of predestination, original sin and a belief in the inherent
depravity of mankind, particular redemption, free justification
through the imputed righteousness of Christ, effectual grace in
regeneration, the everlasting happiness of the righteous, and the
endless punishment of the wicked. A man was called of God for a
particular duty and therefore any activity outside the limits of his
allotted task was a revolt against the purpose of God. This theory
resulted in an attitude which took obedience to the Will of God as
implying complete satisfaction with, and acceptance of, things as they
were. Belief in a Providence of moral purpose could easily be
maintained as an authority for existing conditions, regardless of their
moral justification. If abuses in the system of industrialization, and
wretched social conditions, were part of an over-ruling purpose,
decreed from eternity, what could mere human effort avail to remove
them? In practice, religion became an apologia for social inequalities
instead of a criticism with a new standard of values to impose upon
the life of men. This type of attitude towards life would make all
human efforts at improvement, material or spiritual, individual or
social, futile and unnecessary. If it was original sin that caused abuses
to exist, what steps could man, the sinner, take to remove them?[15]

The Calvinistic Methodists introduced to Wales the mystical
doctrine of salvation by personal experience. They taught that the
only way to be 'saved' was to experience an awareness of having
sinned, to repent, and to experience, directly, forgiveness from God.
The insistence on direct personal experience led to the development
of a strong individualism in Welsh nonconformity and tended to

make religion highly emotional. The passion for personal salvation tended to produce the self-reliant person who had little interest in social reform. The fact that the value and integrity of the human soul and the responsibility for salvation lay with the individual raised the personality to the supreme level and gave it the obligations for its own resurrection. This emphasis carried with it certain difficulties. Place responsibility on the individual and seek to correct human and social ills by direct appeals to personal conscience, and one loses sight of the power of social conditioning. Many nineteenth-century preachers spoke vaguely of certain fundamental principles which must permeate society, and which, if followed, would automatically solve all problems. They found security behind such abstractions as 'love', 'justice', 'honesty' and 'soul'—vague terms which possessed a mystical fascination, and which were not sufficient in themselves to supply guidance to human conduct. Generally speaking, nineteenth-century Welsh nonconformity was unable to define its 'principles' in terms of attitudes towards wider social change because it believed that 'conditions do not make men, only a revolution in the individual spirit toward God will transform the man and the world he lives in'.[16]

The strongest Christian opponents of social reform were those who believed most completely that body and soul were antithetical, and that it was the duty of a Christian to reject 'this' world.[17] Nonconformists were organized through the 'societies' into communities of believers standing over and against the 'world'. Some of the hymns of the nineteenth century encapsulated this belief. 'Zion' was often used to designate those who had crossed Jordan to their eternal home, as well as the faithful on earth, so associating them in one 'community'.[18] The religion of Christ, maintained a Baptist Circular Letter in 1875, was no compromise, nor did it, under any circumstances, admit of compromise with the world: 'The Gospel rule for the regulation of the practical conduct of believers is clearly defined and rigid, demanding a stern nonconformity to the principles, practices, and aims of the worldlings and godless. A Christian is one who has been *"called out of the world"*. He is to *live in* the world, where labour, provision and recreation are necessary conditions, but he is no longer OF IT. There is to be a sacred visible separateness or distinction between him, and those who are *of it,* though sometimes the nature and character of their toils and pursuits and pleasures may be identical. The followers of Christ are to be to men noble examples of *self-denying abstinence from all excesses* in business and pleasure, in eating and drinking and in dressing; *moderate* and *reserved* in *all things* pertaining merely to this life, that they may give proof of their heavenly citizenship, and their loyalty to a higher order than earth makes them superior to all external influences.'[19]

The social conservatism of Welsh nonconformity expressed itself in an attempt to distinguish between the social aspect of the temperance question and its religious aspect. The Calvinistic Methodist *Treasury* declared in 1870 that 'in the light of religion, the stakes are far more important than they are in the light of mere social science [because] . . . it is distinctly told us that the drunkard shall not inherit the Kingdom of God'.[20] The drunkard would be cast away from the presence of God and this was 'a more lamentable feature of the evil effects of the drinking customs of our country than anything relating to this life'.[21] But in 'this' world, drink 'despoils our Churches of members', and for these reasons earnest-minded Christians were exhorted to make great efforts to fight the evil. 'Upon social grounds alone, the drinking habits of our country should be combated earnestly; but how much more so upon religious grounds! Especially by those who profess that they have at heart the eternal welfare of immortal souls and the success of Christ's kingdom in the world.'[22]

The same theme was repeated throughout the century: the man who has been addicted to drinking to excess will never bear the fruits of divine grace unless he abstains totally from drink. What were prayers, tears, morality, almsgiving, or any number of good deeds and sacrifices to save a soul from death? 'Works' were all important but 'let them come in their proper order and be received not as a *means* of salvation, but as the result. Instead of working *for* life, we should work *from* life.'[23] Although many Christian spokesmen stressed also that if the salvation of man could not be attained because of drunkenness then 'it is a great thing, in our belief, to lessen the temporal ills of men and to improve their social happiness', the dominant view was that the evils done by drink to religion and to the spiritual welfare of men were more serious than the 'social ills' which men suffered through their drinking habits because the latter were limited to 'this' life alone.[24] A Calvinistic Methodist, writing in 1890, recognized that 'the temptations to drink are entwined too much with the habits and customs of society', but he still condemned drunkenness as a question, or a failing, of personal morality.[25]

One can only emphasize that during the nineteenth century in Wales the general attitude of the churches towards the drink problem

was stern and moralistic and that morality was conceived of in too
negative and individualistic a fashion. Drunkenness was seen as a
delinquency not as a disease. The Welsh denominational magazine
was more likely to give its space over to barren theological polemics
rather than to social questions. It is a statement, not a criticism, that
the whole conception of religion was individualistic, sabbatarian,
bibliolatrical and other-worldly. A national temperance organization
complained in 1895 that the churches had been so much concerned
with men's souls that in too many cases they had forgotten their
bodies. [26]

*   *   *   *

'4 August 1633. Item paid for 1 quart of claret wine and 1 quart of
sack for Mr. Henry Thomas, preacher of God's Word . . . 18d.' [27]
Long before the temperance movement began, many ministers of the
gospel were as much disciples of John Barleycorn as of John the
Baptist; and many remained so during and after the zenith of the
temperance movement in Wales. In some places public houses were
associated with certain chapels, as at Pontypool in 1837, where the
'Three Cranes' was kept by a Calvinistic Methodist elder. [28] Itinerant
preachers in Wales were supplied with beer kept in a barrel under the
pulpit, and this was later replaced by peppermint when the
temperance movement gathered momentum. [29] A minister's account
for food and drink at Tredegar between 1829 and 1839 reveals that
preachers of the gospel often drank beer with their meal before going
to chapel. [30] All the ministers named in the account—up to 1835 at
least—took beer with their lunch, dinner and supper. Each minister
paid on average 3s. 3d. for his day's food, and of this, an average of
9d. was paid for beer. The consumption of beer declined very slightly
during 1835-7 as teetotalism made progress, but during the years
1837-9 the number of ministers taking alcohol decreased markedly. [31]
    The drinking usages of the church were not confined to ministers.
At Blaina and Nantyglo it was the custom to give beer at vestry
meetings—informal gatherings at the local public house—as a reward
for unpaid service. The beer was paid for by the parish of
Aberystruth, and the practice continued there until mid-century.
Moreover, paid or unpaid workmen, employed in or about the
church customarily received beer; until the 1840s there were regular
occasions for free beer such as decorating the church on Christmas
morning. [32] A common habit among the London Welsh in the 1860s

was to go straight from the chapel to the public house on Sunday evenings.[33] According to a local publican, the vicar in the Ferryside area of Carmarthenshire in the 1870s received the tithes of the parish at a public house, and at the same time distributed tickets amongst his parishioners which would entitle them to so much beer or spirits depending on the amount of tithe paid.[34] In some areas special local circumstances determined the attitude of church members. At Rhymney, for instance, Thomas Jones testified that teetotalism was one subject on which Rhymney churches gave forth 'an uncertain sound', as many church members were employed at the Rhymney brewery.[35] Throughout Wales during the nineteenth century there may well have been many 'back-door people' of the type described by the wife of a publican to a sociologist in a Monmouthshire valley town in 1940: her best customers were 'chapel folk who come round by the back so they can't be seen, bolt a quick one and run off'.[36]

The dominant theme in the advocacy of temperance by the respectable religious community in Wales was that of example-setting: evangelicals preferred encouraging example-setting from above to generating self-help from below.[37] Great stress was laid upon the character of the minister: his office was held to be a sacred piece of public property. It connected the minister with both worlds: he had to be righteous before God, and blameless before men. He must, by example, be a teetaller, and support everything that tended to benefit man physically, morally and spiritually.[38] Many ministers argued 'for teetotalism as a principle of self-denial and self-sacrifice for the good of others, and, paternalistically, the removal of temptation from the path of those who were either in danger of being ensnared or who had already fallen.[39] Indeed, temperance was regarded as an excellent way of converting 'the carnal . . . sensual man who wishes to have his religion without the cross'.[40]

In an individual church or chapel it is difficult to ascertain, generally, whether the congregation influenced the minister to support temperance or *vice versa*. We know that the Rev. Thomas Davies of Merthyr was induced to become a teetaller by the members of his own chapel 'who often invited him, for the sake of others, to give temperance the influence of his advocacy and example'.[41] Some nonconformist ministers may well have been obliged to hold back their advocacy of temperance to a hostile congregation because of the voluntary principle;[42] on the other hand, critics of nonconformity and of temperance claimed that ministers

supported temperance to serve their own selfish end: to obtain from
the people money that otherwise might have been spent on drink.[43]

Dawson Burns, the historian of temperance, estimated that in 1837
the total number of ministerial advocates of teetotalism from all
denominations in Britain totalled 311, of whom 180 were Welsh.[44]
The early temperance movement in Wales was almost wholly in the
hands of nonconformity, with the notable triumvirate of William
Williams of Wern (Independent), Christmas Evans (Baptist) and
John Elias (Calvinistic Methodist) playing a leading rôle.[45] At
Swansea the temperance movement was promoted by a group of
Quakers led by Joseph Rutter, a ship's chandler.[46] At Ystradgynlais
temperance principles were supported almost wholly by Independents
and Calvinistic Methodists.[47] Many observers testified to the fact
that nonconformity remained the mainstay of the temperance
movement in Wales throughout the nineteenth century.[48]

Ministers who took the pledge up to 1838 in Anglesey,
Caernarfonshire, Denbighshire and Flintshire belonged to the
following denominations:[49]

	Calvinistic Methodists	Independents	Baptists	Wesleyan Methodists	Wesleyan Reformers	Church of England
Anglesey	27	14	10	10	3	—
Caernarfonshire	48	41	7	18	5	2
Denbigh-Flintshire	57	41	16	47	2	—

It was estimated in January 1838 that throughout the whole of
north Wales 600 ministers had signed the pledge, including nearly all
the Calvinistic Methodists.[50] The same general trend of
denominational support manifested itself at a Manchester conference
to promote the 'Temperance Reformation' in April 1848; the Welsh
ministers present comprised 11 Calvinistic Methodists, 6
Independents, 2 Baptists, 1 Primitive Methodist and 1 Anglican.[51]
Unfortunately it is not possible to discover how many ministers did
not take the pledge. What does seem likely however is that the
temperance movement, particularly in south Wales, drove a wedge
between the older and younger generation of ministers, especially in
Glamorgan, Monmouthshire and Carmarthenshire, the older
ministers believing that the younger were going too far in their
protest against drunkenness.[52]

Welsh teetotallers argued that the Bible at no point praised
intoxicating drink. Tortuous explanations were used by many
teetotallers to explain away those passages of the Bible—the marriage

feast in Cana of Galilee and Paul's advice to Timothy—which seemed to sanction the taking of drink. Nearly every article published on temperance in the 1830s and 1840s consisted of arguments based on Biblical quotations, and little else; teetotallers avidly engaged in Bible criticism in order to defend their position. [53] A popular temperance claim was that the Bible sanctioned the use of unfermented wine for the communion. By November 1841, 28 chapels in Cardiganshire had abandoned the use of fermented wine. [54] After the passing of the Welsh Sunday Closing Act in 1881 it seemed highly inconsistent to have Sunday closing and yet provide intoxicating liquor in chapels on Sunday, and, consequently, many chapels reverted to the use of unfermented wine. [55]

At the celebration of the jubilee of the temperance movement in Wales at Merthyr Tydfil in 1885, the Rev. Thomas Levi, Calvinistic Methodist minister of Aberystwyth, said that one of the first things he remembered of the temperance movement was the holding of temperance demonstrations at Cefn-coed-y-cymmer; he thought the millennium had arrived. [56] Temperance was regarded as a necessary prerequisite to the millennium, that period of one thousand years when Christ would reign on earth, and the Kingdom given to the Saints. The two leading features of the millennium were said to be the great reduction in numbers and lessening in intensity of all evils, both of sin and suffering, throughout the whole world, and the vast increase of good, holiness and happiness. [57] During the millennium men would be temperate, sober, chaste and 'regular in all things': drunkenness, gluttony and licentiousness would disappear. [58] Many sincerely believed that influences were at work which would eventually subjugate the world to the faith of Christ, and that the temperance movement, as one of these influences, was concurring with other influences which had been called forth to usher in the millennial era. [59]

Although teetotalism found ready support from the religious community in Wales, there were some religious people who strongly opposed it. As we have seen, Caledfryn claimed that teetotalism was an impudent denial of man's self-control. Eben Fardd, the poet of Clynnog, believed temperance to be an absurd and extreme doctrine and maintained that it was 'only another batch of fig leaves, which man has invented to hide the wickedness of these evil days. . . . It is man's remedy and not God's remedy for sin'. [60] He cautioned those

ministers who exaggerated the extent of drunkenness, and when he
found himself tired and depressed after abstaining from drink for a
few weeks in 1840 he declared himself 'fully persuaded that Jesus
Christ, the divine founder of the religion I profess, never
contemplated that his disciples should thus deprive themselves of the
comforts of life because the world at large may abuse such comforts.
What grievous burdens are added to the simple religion of Jesus by
the enthusiasts of the present day!'[61]

The reasons for opposition to teetotalism by some Christians in the
1830s and '40s have been analysed by Dr. Harrison.[62] First, as with
Eben Fardd, the temperance belief that man's health could be
brought under man's control conflicted with religious conviction that
disease was divinely ordained and could not be evaded by man's
effort. The temperance view, which was shared by the secularist, was
that man's health was governed by natural laws which every
individual could perceive for himself. Secondly, teetotalism was
linked to an optimistic view of human capacities scarcely compatible
with doctrines of original sin. Third, to those who did not accept that
the Bible recommended teetotalism, teetotallers seemed to be
declaring Gospel morality inadequate. Total abstinence elevated
works over faith and turned away from the emphasis on doctrine
towards an emphasis on moral reform.

In the 1830s and '40s some Christians in Wales complained that
teetotalism was regarded as the 'counsel of perfection', and as such
was being elevated above religious observance.[63] In this view,
teetotalism was an unwarrantable interference with the province of
the Gospel, which was the only remedy for moral evil. Teetotalism
affected the habits and conduct only, and not the heart, and was
therefore inimical to, if not subversive of, the principles of the
Gospel. To this charge, temperance reformers consistently
maintained that to make a drunkard sober would be to place him in a
better position to receive the grace of God. 'We do not make total
abstinence a substitute for the Gospel. We do not propose to *convert*
and *sanctify* by total abstinence but to *reclaim* and *preserve.*' The Rev.
Evan Jones of Tredegar (Ieuan Gwynedd) maintained in 1847 that
teetotalism in Wales was exclusively under the guidance of religious
men and was considered to be allied to religion;[64] most temperance
meetings were held in chapels and were seldom concluded without
reminding the members that although teetotalism was an excellent
system for the social improvement of the world, sinners must come to

Christ and to Him alone.[65] It was argued that intemperance possessed a two-fold character: it was a sin against God, and it was a great social evil, and that in so far as it was a sin, the grace of God was the only remedy for it. Nevertheless, far from being set up as a system in place of the Gospel, teetotalism set up nothing, but attempted to remove an element inimical to the social well-being of society. 'So teetotalism is not intellectual cultivation, sanitary improvement, or Gospel ministry—it only drains the social soil of an injurious element; and thus ensures to the schoolmaster, the social reformer, and, we trust, to the Christian minister, a more abundant return for the labours they bestow.'[66]

A valid criticism made by contemporaries was that the church deliberately used temperance as an instrument of proselytism; temperance offered a way by which the churches could proselytise without going into the world. The recreational aspect of those temperance societies attached to individual churches acted as a bait to attract non-church goers. With the public house and the chapel as the twin foci of social life, the temple of Bacchus—the People's Palace—became of necessity the deadliest competitor of the house of God. The public house was seen as being anti-God. Thomas Revel Guest, brother of Sir John Guest, the Dowlais ironmaster, attacked unionism in 1831 partly because it 'brings you into those places where as men fearing God you should not be found, the Public House is not the usual place of resort for the Disciples of Christ, that is not the place where prayer is wont to be made. . . . Are the frequenters of the Public House the most suitable companions for those that fear God and are you not then in danger in such Society of being drawn aside?'[67] Many ministers believed that temperance made their hearers more ready to receive the Word; they maintained that the temperance movement was of divine origin.[68] The Rev. Thomas Daniel of Swansea was convinced that teetotalism was an auxiliary to the process of spiritual conversion. Teetotalism would not only help to suppress intemperance but also 'pave the way for the dawn of millennial glory'.[69] The Rev. Richard Williams, a Calvinistic Methodist minister at Towyn, in giving evidence before the Royal Commission on the Church of England and Nonconformist bodies in Wales in 1908, considered that the people of Wales were generally temperate not because of the ordinary spiritual provision but because temperance was advocated in order to spiritualise them, and in this sense temperance was a spiritual provision of the church.[70] In 1868 it had been argued that the test of teetotalism should be used as a step towards bringing the habitual drunkard into a condition to receive the grace of God.[71]

In order to win religious support, therefore, temperance advocates had to stress that temperance was a powerful and effective agent of proselytism. An excellent example of temperance claims was contained in the declaration of the principles and objectives of the Abergavenny Total Abstinence Society in 1840.

> They are well aware that the temperance reformation falls far short of that change of heart which the scriptures assert to be indispensable for salvation; consequently they are anxious to impress on the minds of all who join their society the necessity of seeking religious instruction in the use of the appointed means, namely, the reading and the hearing of the word of God with sincere and humble prayer. Although their society is not strictly speaking a religious society, yet they consider that its bearing on the interests of religion is highly important, and on this ground they invite the cooperation of their christian friends of all denominations. Their aim is to suppress the vice of drunkenness, and they humbly conceive that it will be generally admitted that this vice is one of the most obstinate antagonists with which religion has to cope; intemperance is the most fruitful source of religious declension and apostasy. Fearful tales may be related of the disgrace which this dire evil has brought upon Christian professors, and of the misbelief it has wrought among Christian societies. Threequarters of the cases requiring church exercises arise out of the common use of intoxicating beverages, and were these baneful draughts universally renounced and discountenanced by religious persons, punitive discipline would be less frequently called into exercise. Intemperance prevents thousands from hearing the gospel, and hinders the edification of many who attend in many of our different places of worship. On the contrary, whenever teetotalism extensively prevails, religious congregations are greatly increased, and in numerous instances still happier results appear in large additions of hopeful converts to the church of Christ. Temperance societies may be regarded as performing the service of pioneers for religion, removing the obstacles which impede its progress, and preparing the way for its holy principles. In this view they deserve and demand the cordial and active support of all who desire the diffusion of vital Christianity, and who pray as the Saviour instructed his disciples, 'Thy Kingdom come'.[72]

Teetotalism then was seen as a handmaid to the Gospel. Indeed, as Dr. Harrison has noted, there were many parallels with early Christianity: the miraculous conversion, the itinerant apostle, the group of supporters distinguished from ordinary men by their elevated conduct, and the success of a new cause among lower social groups far from the centres of power.[73] Adherents to teetotalism claimed that it did not seek to do the Gospel's work of saving souls; it had no atonement to give for sin and it had no power to reconcile man with God. But it did seek to remove the influence exerted by drink, an influence which was held to be a great hindrance to the Gospel.[74] The Rev. Joseph Evans of Carmarthen was sanguine that teetotalism would enable many working men to clothe themselves decently, and so bring them to a place of worship more frequently.[75] Many individual churches and chapels in Wales took up the temperance cause with a great deal of enthusiasm, and it seems safe to assume that proselytism was a major factor which lay behind such action.[76] It is not surprising that of all the various manifestations of temperance sentiment it was the Band of Hope that proliferated to the greatest extent amongst the chapels of Wales. It was believed that drunkenness robbed Sunday School teachers of their 'choicest fruit'.[77] A vigorous band of hope connected to a chapel invariably tended to increase the number of attendants at the Sunday School belonging to that chapel. The band of hope was regarded as the feeder of the Sunday School. The pledge was not onerous to children, most of whom had not experienced temptation. The Rev. John Williams, a Baptist minister at Pontypool, believed that the prevention of drunkenness 'begins with the children, when their minds are receptive, when their hearts are tender, when their wills are pliant, and before alcohol has laid its cruel hand upon them. . . . You are cultivating virgin soil comparatively free of weeds and rubbish, which generally yields a hundred fold in return for your labours'.[78] In 1892 a writer classed temperance societies in general and bands of hope in particular among 'the religious societies for the promotion of Christianity'.[79]

'Those that were worshippers of Bacchus, and enemies to God, are now coming and weeping towards Zion and exclaiming, "What shall we do to be saved?" '[80] Many converts were won over to the churches and to the temperance cause during religious revivals. The growth of nonconformity in nineteenth-century Wales was most marked during the revival of 1837-43; henceforth, the growth of nonconformity was a continual process, inspired by national revivals at the end of almost every decade and by occasional local revivals. Observers noted that the Revival of 1841-43 had been preceded by a temperance movement; indeed, it was believed at the time that the chapels which supported the temperance movement benefited most from revivals. [81] The temperance view was that the revivals were the consequence of the overthrow of drunkenness in Wales. [82] In five parishes in the Bala district in 1841, over 5,000 of the total population of approximately 6,000 were teetotallers. The Rev. David Charles considered that the great religiosity of the area was attributable to God's blessing upon the operation of teetotal societies which had prepared the minds of the people for the reception of the Gospel and had led them to seek for more than the immediate benefits of teetotalism, 'even the salvation of their undying souls'. [83]

Revivals were most powerful where teetotalism was strongest. [84] John Jones of Rhyl wrote in November 1840:

> There are a multitude of revivals in our congregations, 28 joined our church lately, 40 another church, not far from us, 60 another, and this is the general talk in several parts of Cambria's hills and vales, that none hardly enter the churches, without being teetotallers. Yea, some churches refuse all but such, and have they not lawful ground to stand upon for doing so. Why? Because hundreds have been misled by these cursed drinks from their profession, and have backslided across the alcoholic half pints, and have been cast like Jonah, into the sea of intemperance, but, teetotalism, like the whale, swallows them, and casts them on dry ground; blessed be God for such a glorious cause. Hallelujah! [85]

Churches in Flintshire which opposed 'this blessed temperance reformation' were said to be 'withering'. [86]

As a method of recruitment, revivalism was largely confined in its operation to the lower socio-economic groups which alone could readily give untheological, unintellectual and uninhibited public response, and which were uncritical of the devices used by some to arouse emotional response. As was only to be expected with a 'church of the poor' and the 'dispossessed', understanding was largely inspirational in character. [87] Especially was this so during 'cholera revivals'. Cholera struck south Wales in 1831-2, 1849 and 1866. The prevalence of the disease generated great fear and religious meetings were of frequent occurrence; the alarm produced by sudden deaths and quick burials was directly calculated to bring people to a decision on the great subject of the soul's eternal destiny. [88] At Merthyr in 1849 the numbers seeking religious consolation were so great that special meetings were held in most chapels; [89] it was estimated that as a result of the revival the number of communicants in churches and

chapels in the area increased three-fold.[90] At Sirhowy, Carmel
Baptist chapel received 309 new members.[91] During the cholera
outbreak of 1866, which was mainly confined to north
Monmouthshire, Zoar Independent chapel at Tredegar held services
every evening for six months.[92] Hundreds walked in procession
through the streets singing hymns: 'It must have sounded almost like
the Trumpet of Judgment in the various public houses, and some of
the reckless tipplers would actually come out, as if by instinct, to join
the procession. . . . It was also specially observed how willing the
"young converts" were to *give* up or *take* up anything required of
them as followers of Jesus Christ. They would generally sign the
temperance pledge with scarcely any hesitation.'[93] Accession of
numerical support to the church and to temperance during 'cholera
revivals' however was invariably short-lived. Inevitable reaction
brought with it backsliding and the 'increasing hardness of the
hearers'.

During the years immediately preceding the great 1859 revival a
great apathy and indifference prevailed in the Welsh churches.
According to the Rev. William Edwards of Aberdare this was a time
of spiritual bankruptcy and stagnation, a lukewarmness and
desolation which were symptomatic of an almost apostate church.[94]
Unlike some previous revivals, that of 1859 was not confined to one
denomination, but manifested itself amongst all denominations and
produced a high degree of ecumenism.[95] Most ministers found it
difficult to trace the causes of the revival. It was not the result of
anything external such as an epidemic, and it was attended with
much less excitement than some former revivals.[96] The major
preoccupation in south Wales during the revival was with social
improvement; great efforts were made to provide for the leisure time
of the working classes, a result of general slackness in industry.

The Rev. Owen Jones of Manchester claimed that the 1859 revival
brought 12,000 new teetotallers into the Welsh temperance
movement.[97] Ministers from all parts of Wales testified that the
revival had, in their localities, transformed drunkards and
blasphemers into 'sober and praying people'.[98] At Bala the revival
was regarded almost as a 'Temperance Revival'.[99] At Aberystwyth,
400 new recruits were added to the Calvinistic Methodist chapels,
and eight publicans became teetotallers.[100] A brewer poured the
contents of his casks into the Teifi.[101] At Abergwili in
Carmarthenshire, 'some of the public houses are gasping for breath,

as though they were in the *last struggle*.[102] Twelve pubs were forced to close in the Bethesda district, and four in Morriston.[103] Many former chapel members attributed their backsliding to drink, and when a person was made a member of a church, teetotalism was strongly recommended to him as a safeguard to himself and as an example to others.

A particularly powerful temperance revival occurred at Tredegar in 1859, when an itinerant cutler, Richard Reese, gave a series of temperance lectures. Within a few weeks, nearly 7,000 people signed the pledge. Local tradesmen supported the movement because they obviously saw it as a potentially profitable venture; on the other hand, the receipts of Rhymney Brewery plummeted by £500 per month during the summer.[104] Reese personally supervised the collection, by subscription, of £2,000 for the erection of a Temperance Hall in Tredegar.[105] But traditional modes of recreation were hard to break and the fervour did not last: 'When the first intoxication of teetotalism was over . . . the working class, who after most seriously alarming the publican, returned to their *cwrw* and degraded habits.'[106]

After 1859 no great revivalistic upsurge occurred until 1904-5. The period 1859-95, however, was marked by several local revivals. In 1871, a period of intense prayer preceded a revival in the south Wales coalfield as a result of a recent evangelistic mission in the area supported by the Cory brothers, the Cardiff industrialists.[107] A revival affected north Monmouthshire between 1875 and 1877.[108] 'Enthusiasm is power', noted the Monmouthshire Particular Baptist Association, 'A church or denomination is weak without it, but invincible with it. The power of the gospel cannot gain expression through lukewarm hearts. The great want of our time is fervency of spirit. The denomination who has it, moves forward with irresistible power.'[109] Revivals promoted by the Salvation Army shook Tredegar in 1878 and the Rhondda valley in 1879.[110] Later revivals were restricted to particular chapels, such as those at Caersalem Baptist chapel, Dowlais in 1890 and at the Baptist chapel at Pontnewydd in 1892.[111]

The popularity and strength of the temperance cause in Wales are explained partly by the relations between Established Church and nonconformity. Participation in the war against drink required its supporters to endure self-sacrifice and possibly even persecution, and this obviously attracted religious groups with a recent history of suffering for their beliefs. Anglican persecution seemed very much alive to nineteenth-century nonconformists who refused to pay church rates and saw the Established Church taking their property.[112] Teetotalism flourished among nonconformists because, in general, they wished publicly to demonstrate their moral superiority to the Established Church.[113] From 1847, nonconformists in Wales, aggrieved at the vilification they had received from the education commissioners in their report of that year, felt that they had to maintain that, from the seventeenth century, Dissent had rescued Wales from moral laxity, drunkenness and religious infidelity, evils about which the Church in Wales had done very little.[114] As a Cardiganshire Tory confessed in 1891: 'I say this of the Nonconformist: he has taught and preached and given us of his best, he has changed frivolous, pleasure-loving people, into a serious and earnest nation. He has made a drunken people sober. It is right that this work should be recognised. It is just. He has done what the Clergy has neglected; he has built his Hebrons and Bethels where the clergy would not go.'[115] It was believed that the Calvinistic Methodists, in particular, had brought spiritual religion to Wales, and in so doing had moralized the land, taught the people to observe the Sabbath and to 'pray in their families'.[116] To the assertion of the Bishop of Llandaff in 1857 that nonconformity was 'nearly worn out' in south Wales,[117] the Rev. Thomas Rees of Beaufort pointed out that in the diocese of Llandaff itself, nonconformity had attracted multitudes from public houses, wakes, dances, Sunday sports and other sinful, irreligious amusements, but not from the parish churches, for such people were not to be found there. Nonconformity, Rees argued, had been the means of making thousands of colliers, miners, mechanics and labourers of the mining and agricultural areas of south Wales, decent and moral human beings.[118] As Rees saw it, the failure of the church to evangelise Wales during a whole century—1660-1760—when it had the country entirely to itself, without nonconformist teachers to attract the people from its clergy, meant that if it had not been for nonconformity, Wales by the mid-nineteenth century, would have been a dark, unenlightened land.[119] Wales' relative freedom from serious crime was the subject of a common nonconformist boast, and was assigned to the moral effects of Welsh nonconformity.[120]

A vigorous attack on the moral influence of nonconformity in Wales was made by a writer in the *Church Quarterly Review* in October

1882. The author asserted that drunkenness and prostitution in Wales were the 'revelations of the influence and inner workings of Dissent'.[121] The claim aroused the opposition of Henry Richard, who maintained that, on the contrary, nonconformity was the chief upholder of temperance and morality in the country: 'The most remarkable thing in connection with the Temperance cause in Wales, and it goes far to explain its extraordinary success, was the admirable readiness with which the ministers of the Gospel and the leading men in the different religious denominations took it up and laboured for it . . .; The clergymen of the Church of England generally looked upon the thing with a good deal of contempt.'[122] Richard maintained that only one churchman, the Rev. Henry Griffith of Llandrygarn, supported the temperance movement in its early years, but he conveniently forgot the strong advocacy of Dean Cotton of Bangor, Canon Evan Jenkins of Dowlais, the Rev. E. O. Hughes of Llanbadrig and the Rev. Richard Pritchard, who preached a temperance sermon in Llandaff cathedral as early as 1839.[123] Yet Richard's conclusion that nonconformity was left to struggle alone 'in this holy war while the authorised teachers of the people stood aside', is largely true.[124]

As W. D. Wills has shown, the Established Church in south Wales in the 1830s was an institution organized for commercial, economic and political ends, in which the spiritual and religious function was apparently lost.[125] Whereas nonconformity was able to expand through the subscriptions, donations and offerings of the working class, the church was completely dependent upon rich benefactors and grants from the London societies, The *Cardiff and Merthyr Guardian,* no nonconformist organ, maintained that during the 1830s the church was unable to stem the progress of 'Dissent, of Immorality, of practical Infidelity'; in particular, it was failing to provide for the moral and religious culture of the young.[126] However, following the Chartist decade the church in south Wales became more concerned with the social and moral instruction of the masses. This was probably an exercise in social conditioning and social control, as the church's belief was that where spiritual destitution prevailed, so also would vice, demoralization and 'political excesses and public turbulence'.[127] Alfred Ollivant, the bishop of Llandaff, believed that men who did not have any 'spiritual existence' formed the 'element of future mischief, the raw material of every social danger'.[128] But throughout the century the church was unfortunate to have to deal with a region which presented such a combination of adverse conditions: a large area, a large population, diminutive endowments, and two languages.[129]

During the controversy aroused by the report by the education commissioners in 1847, a significant literary warfare occurred between John Griffith, rector of Aberdare, and the Rev. Evan Jones (Ieuan Gwynedd) of Tredegar. Griffith published a series of spiky letters in the *Cardiff and Merthyr Guardian* under the pseudonym of 'Cambro Sacerdos' and in *John Bull* as 'Ordovicis', alleging that nonconformity was responsible for drunkenness and vice in Wales, in much the same way as he had done before the education commissioners. His charges were refuted by Evan Jones in a series of articles which appeared in the *Monmouthshire Merlin*.[130] He maintained that drunkenness had been rife under clerical patronage before nonconformity appeared.[131] After repeating the customary claim that clergymen were very slow to support the temperance movement, Jones asserted that the working men of south Wales drank, not because of the influence of nonconformity and the Welsh language, but because of the facilities for drink provided by the companies which provided and profited by public houses, and which practised the iniquitous truck system.[132]

The verbal conflict between church and nonconformity over the 'morality' of Wales was not dominated by the latter. The bad feelings between the church and nonconformity often degenerated into slanging matches, during the course of which nonconformist ministers became 'swarms of self-constituted illiterate priests who have a great influence over the people's minds in Wales'; such influence 'has never been surpassed in any age of the world, considering the character of the men who are mere personifications of cant and whose elysium is vested in tobacco and *cwrw*'.[133] The church criticized nonconformity for interpreting morality as a spiritual witchcraft which converted all that it touched into a sin.[134] Ollivant, preaching at the consecration of All Saints Church, Cwmavon, in 1853 maintained that although nonconformity had covered the land with chapels, it had not taught the mass of the people morality and religion.[135] In 1867 temperance was criticized as being one of the 'semi-religious novelties' which were 'constantly resorted to in order to sustain the Dissenting cause'.[136] But twenty years later, the Rev. J. R. Buckley, Vicar of Llandaff, told his fellow temperance workers that no parish in the diocese should be without its temperance association 'because it was an enormous help to Church defence seeing that it attracted masses of people to the church'. [137] By 1889, a district organizer for temperance work—the Rev. J. L. Meredith—was active in the diocese of Llandaff. He believed that political activity had taken the place of religious devotion in Welsh nonconformity, [138] and that that was the church's opportunity to put into action diocesan agencies of a spiritual character: temperance associations and missions. [139] At a Church Defence meeting at Barmouth in February 1892, the Rev. Thomas Edwards (Twm Gwynedd) charged vigorously that the Baptists in Wales gave little support to temperance. [140] Dr. Rowland Williams immediately called Edwards to account, but the quarrel quickly lapsed. [141]

If the temperance question helped to exacerbate the feelings between Anglican and nonconformist, it helped also to draw them together. Evangelicalism inculcated religious enthusiasm, and Victorian evangelicalism was a social rather than a spiritual religion concerned with the wider aspects of religion, with moral and social needs, rather than spiritual reinvigoration or the promotion of any specific theological doctrine. Evangelicalism was not exclusively either Anglican or nonconformist: its spirit was broad and almost ecumenical in character, particularly during the period 1850-65.

The annual festivals of the early Welsh temperance societies in the 1830s provided occasions for a certain degree of co-operation between the various nonconformist denominations themselves, and between nonconformity and the church. Thus at Liverpool in 1837, the second annual festival of the Welsh teetotal societies in that city was held at the Pall Mall chapel, and addresses were delivered by ministers of each Welsh nonconformist denomination in the town, and by a local curate. [142] Swansea Total Abstinence Society was established in June 1836 largely by a group of Quakers, assisted by a minister of each denomination in the town and the vicar of St. John's church, the Rev. Herbert Crowther. [143] At Pen Nebo in north Wales, the Rev. Hugh Williams, a Baptist, delivered occasional temperance sermons at the Calvinistic Methodist chapel. [144] Amlwch Temperance Society regularly met at Salem Baptist chapel and in March 1835, a large temperance gathering there was attended by a Calvinistic Methodist minister, an Independent minister and the Rev. Henry Griffith of Llandrygarn. [145] In 1837 a correspondent at Barmouth wrote of the 'unanimity and brotherly love' that the advocacy of temperance had caused to exist amongst the denominations there. [146] When the Gwent and Morgannwg Temperance Association was established at

Merthyr in July 1845, the Rev. Richard Pritchard, vicar of Llandaff, became its first president and the Rev. Thomas Levi, Calvinistic Methodist of Morriston, its first secretary and itinerant lecturer. [147]

The 1840s, however, witnessed little co-operation between the Church and nonconformity in Wales. In south Wales there were deep suspicions among Anglicans about the presumed connection between nonconformity and the disturbances in the coalfield. In 1839 it was reputed that certain chapels had been involved in Chartism. [148] On the other hand, some nonconformists, notably the Rev. Dr. Thomas Thomas, of Pontypool Baptist College, charged that the majority of the physical-force Chartists were members of the established Church. [149] Relationships remained embittered until the 1850s. The social policies of the denominations during the 1850s and '60s sprang from the series of calamities which Wales experienced in those years: cholera, religious revival, and years of crisis, unemployment and economic depression following the end of the Crimean War and the end of the coal and iron boom. [150]

Both Anglicans and nonconformists saw that the depression was due to natural causes and that its solution was social retrenchment, not social protest. Their answer was an organized temperance campaign, which was greatly aided by two vigorous campaigns by the great American temperance orator, John Bartholomew Gough, in south Wales, the first in 1854 and the second in 1860. Between 1850 and 1855 Anglicans and nonconformists had competed in building places of worship but during the late '50s they co-operated over the building of Temperance Halls and Reading Rooms. A leading light in this movement was John Griffith, rector of Merthyr. In a sermon at St. David's church, Merthyr in May 1860, at the height of the depression, he pointed out the beneficial and instructive value of the economic hardship: 'It was a rough lesson and he trusted the lesson would not escape them. The worst times he remembered at Aberdare were, religiously speaking, the best times the workmen ever had. He turned the tide of his prosperity, not into the good of his soul, but into the ruin of his soul and his body. The good times God gave him became the devil's own time; he it was who reaped a good harvest from them. Oh! who does not remember when wages poured into the workmen's lap like a stream flowing from the horn of plenty, the drinking, the debauchery, the spending there was. . . . It is only by tethering us with affliction and trials that He prevents us from straying.' [151]

At Taibach, near Aberavon, a temperance society was formed in
May 1858 at meetings held in Independent and Calvinistic Methodist
chapels, attended by John Griffiths, rector of Neath, and the vicar of
Aberavon.[152] The Temperance Hall at Aberdare was opened in July
1858 by John Griffith, rector of Merthyr, and H. A. Bruce,
supported by David Davies, Wesleyan Methodist and coal-owner of
Blaengwawr, John Coke Fowler, the Rev. Dr. Thomas Thomas of
Pontypool and other leading nonconformist ministers.[153] At
Cwmavon, the clergymen of Michaelston took the initiative in
forming a temperance society in December 1858, assisted by the Rev.
John Roberts and his congregation of Calvinistic Methodists; the
society held meetings in Baptist, Independent and Calvinistic
Methodist chapels.[154] At Neath the temperance cause was revived in
the spring of 1859 under the leadership of Griffiths, the rector, and
James Kenway, the mayor of Neath, and nonconformist
businessman, two men who had earlier quarrelled bitterly over the
issue of church rates.[155] Bishop Ollivant, in an address in 1859 to the
working men of Newport Temperance Society, referred in friendly
terms to the Baptist periodical *Seren Gomer* as an example of efforts
being made by all denominations, not only in Newport, but
throughout south Wales, to improve society and to encourage self-
restraint.[156] At Pentyrch, near Cardiff, temperance meetings at
nonconformist chapels were presided over by the vicar, H. J.
Thomas.[157] In north Monmouthshire, the temperance revivalist,
Richard Reese, brought together nonconformist and Anglican 'with
true catholicity of feeling'.[158] At Tredegar the temperance movement
was strongly supported by Reese, the vicar, and the Baptist chapels,
and encouraged, during the economic recession, by industrialists
Samuel Homfray, R. P. Davies and Richard Fothergill.[159] At
Dowlais the leadership was provided by the rector, Canon Evan
Jenkins, whose co-operation with nonconformists, and with Father
Millea, a Catholic priest, was very close.[160] In December 1859, in a
lecture at Cardiff on the prohibition law operating in the American
state of Maine, Jenkins publicly acknowledged the co-operation and
efforts of the nonconformists at Dowlais, particularly the Calvinistic
Methodists, in the campaign for the prohibition of drink.[161] At
Cardiff, Canon Leigh Morgan, vicar of St. Mary's, recommended
teetotalism to the Anglicans of Cardiff from his pulpit;[162] in
September 1860 he chaired a public meeting called by Anglicans and
nonconformists in Cardiff to petition the magistrates not to grant

licences for any new public house in the city.[163]

The spirit of co-operation did not last long, for with the reinvigoration of the Liberation Society in 1861-2 nonconformity became more assertive, abrasive and dynamic. The apparent disintegration of the denominations in the immediate post-Crimean War period, the failure to establish a distinct image and the general sense of decline were reversed.[164] The basic reasons were probably the religious revival of 1859, which gave the chapels added numerical strength and a greater degree of confidence, and the division in the Established Church over ritualism.[165] Later, most spokesmen of the Established Church became convinced that nonconformity was more of a political than a religious organization, and that the result of this was the almost universal prevalence of Liberalism in Wales.

'The only rivalry there should be between the various denominations', maintained the rector of Llanfwrog at Ruthin in 1866, 'should be to provoke each other to the love of good works'.[166] But, apart from the unanimity of the Church and nonconformity in Wales over the issue of Welsh Sunday closing,[167] the temperance question did not play an important rôle in bringing both together after 1860.

*   *   *   *

Of the nonconformist denominations, the Calvinistic Methodists were by far the strongest advocates of temperance in the nineteenth century. In 1811, when the Calvinistic Methodists broke away from the Established Church, their Rules of Discipline of 1801 were unanimously sanctioned by the whole Connexion. The rules enjoined: 'That we judge it proper that the elder preacher of the Connexion be first chosen to the work who have given satisfactory proofs of faithfulness, sobriety, sincerity, piety, and suitableness to the work of the administration of the ordinances.'[168] Great emphasis was placed upon the necessity of personal religion. Calvinistic Methodist sermons in the 1830s and '40s invariably stressed the difficulty of restraining the desires, appetites, and passions which tended to destroy the 'intellectual and moral nature'. The Christian was warned that he would have his battles to fight with the love of self and the love of a sinful world, and he was implored not to let his resolution fade or his spirit rest, until the throne of God and the ascendancy of holy principles were established within him.[169] The necessity of a total and immediate change of character—as might be embodied in a teetotal pledge—was urged upon all. The terrors of an offended God were portrayed in vigorous language, and the certainty of everlasting condemnation was announced against all who did not awake from their vain trust in any acquired goodness of their own.[170]

The promotion of teetotalism flourished within this theological framework. The annual association of Calvinistic Methodists in south Wales which met at Llandeilo in July 1835, expressed its wholehearted approval of the principles and objectives of the British and Foreign Temperance Society.[171] The resolution, signed by Thomas Richards, Moderator, and Ebenezer Richard, the Secretary, of Tregaron, supported the B.F.T.S. in wishing to suppress intemperance 'as well by prevention as by reformation. . . . We strongly recommend the members of our churches and congregations to promote its blessed objects with all their might; to assist in forming societies, and enter themselves as members; to abstain from spirits and be moderate in other liquors.'[172] The North Wales Association, meeting at Denbigh in March 1837, called the attention of the churches to the importance of getting 'the best and most spiritual among our people' on the side of temperance reform;[173] in October 1838, at the Association at Ruthin, it was resolved to urge all members of the denomination who were connected with the drink trade, either as brewers or as publicans, to sever their connection with it as soon as possible, and to urge all office-holders in the churches to be faithful to the temperance cause.[174] Mandatory measures quickly followed; a further meeting at Bangor on 1 November 1838 ruled that no member of the denomination was to be permitted to become engaged in the drink trade,[175] and at Llanfair Caereinion in April 1840 it was decided that no one was to be elected an office-holder in the church or teacher in the Sunday School unless he was a teetotaller.[176] Thus, temperance restrictions on church officers and members began to be applied by the Calvinistic Methodists in 1838. However, individual churches had previously seen fit to expel members for constant drunkenness. Lewis Edwards of Bala informed Henry Richard in January 1879 that the Calvinistic Methodists acting as an Association before the first ordination in 1811, had, in 1807, expelled one of their most eminent clergymen, Nathaniel Rowland, son of Daniel Rowland, the eighteenth-century evangelist, for habitual drunkenness.[177] We know also that Ann Williams was expelled from Morriah Calvinistic Methodist chapel, Caernarfon, in June 1837 because she had been found drunk a third time.[178]

By the early 1840s, the Calvinistic Methodists constituted the largest nonconformist denomination in Wales. The government of the church was presbyterian, the power of discipline being in the hands of the preachers and elders. The system of ecclesiastical organization of the Calvinistic Methodists made it possible and almost inevitable that the denomination should be guided and controlled by one man, especially by powerful personalities like Thomas Charles or John Elias of Llangefni. From 1820 to 1835 Elias's influence was unquestioned: the voice of John Elias was the voice of Welsh Methodism. As a correspondent complained in *Y Dysgedydd* in 1833, as the Fron was the Seraglio, so Llangefni was the Ottoman Porte of the Welsh Calvinistic Methodists.[179] The denomination was well known for its very strict rules of discipline and many contemporaries observed that, of the denominations in Wales, the Calvinistic Methodists were the most zealous supporters of teetotalism.[180] The various individual churches were regarded as branches of the one body and this gave the Methodists the power for concerted action.[181] All the members participated in the affairs of the church: they elected all the officers and selected their minister. The deacons or elders possessed almost as much authority as the minister—some thought too much authority.[182] The 'society' which preceded the sacrament Sunday was generally considered to be a preparatory meeting at which the authorities inquired about the morals of the members, and exercised disciplinary measures against those who had done wrong.

Throughout the early years of the temperance movement in Wales, the Calvinistic Methodists gave their support to it where other denominations at first refused to co-operate. This was the case at Tredegar;[183] at Merthyr, where in 1839 only the Calvinistic Methodists opened their chapels for temperance meetings;[184] at Llangollen, where a temperance society was established in a Calvinistic Methodist chapel in September 1836;[185] and at Ebbw Vale, where a teetotal society was organized at Penuel chapel in 1839.[186] In north Wales, the temperance movement received strong support from the advocacy of the Rev. David Charles of Aberdovey and John Elias. In the 1830s it was claimed that Elias had effected a 'moral revolution' in Anglesey.[187] Elias himself said that he had turned from moderation to teetotalism for the purpose of reclaiming drunkards and bringing them to God.[188] He testified that the advocacy of teetotalism gave ministers great power over 'the masses of society'.[189] Such ministers believed that teetotalism, while not being the Gospel, was a necessary forerunner of it; God sent teetotalism to cast out the unclean spirit—drunkenness—and then He sent the Gospel to save the man's soul.[190]

The rules of discipline relating to drinking and drunkenness were relaxed in 1850, as a result of inability to enforce strict rules and great disappointment over inevitable backsliding. Calvinistic Methodists were now charged to be 'willing and determined . . . to forsake every evil way . . . to abstain from all corrupt practices, such as card playing, going to plays and assemblies for dancing; from intemperate feasting, rioting and drunkenness, and to behave themselves as becometh Christians. . . . That every member be temperate and sober in eating and drinking, neither a glutton nor a drunkard. Surfeiting and drunkenness overcharge the heart, unfit us for God's service and prove our state to be such as will at last prevent our entrance into the Kingdom of Heaven. *Luke,* 21, 34. I *Corinthians,* 6, 10'. The eighth Rule of Discipline, 'That they be not covenant breakers but conscientiously fulfil all their lawful engagements to the utmost of their power', extended to the temperance pledge.[191] The North Wales Association passed a resolution in September 1871 calling the attention of the Monthly Meetings of the churches to the importance of strictness of discipline on the temperance question, and stressing that none should be allowed to remain in the church who were given to *excessive* drinking.[192] Indeed, some members of the Calvinistic Methodist church were allowed to keep public houses in the 1860s and '70s; in April 1873 the Carmarthenshire Monthly Meeting recommended that all members of the Connexion who kept public houses should be requested to take the six days' licence and close their houses on the Sabbath.[193] The suggestion that teetotalism be made an absolute condition of membership, much canvassed during the period 1830-50, now became a distinct improbability.

Almost inevitably, as the strict ideal of teetotalism faded, temperance organization in the Calvinistic Methodist church became more sophisticated.[194] In 1878 a General Standing Temperance Committee under the Rev. David Phillips of Maesteg was appointed by the South Wales Association in accordance with a request made by the General Assembly;[195] a committee for north Wales was established in 1881. Both committees consisted of one representative each from each monthly meeting of the presbytery and six members appointed by the Association itself. [196] The monthly meetings of individual presbyteries were asked to appoint local temperance committees to correspond with the general temperance committees. [197] Invariably, public temperance meetings were held in connection with the Quarterly Association. [198] As a result of resolutions passed at the Quarterly Association of North Wales in 1881, a Temperance Union, composed of both moderationists and teetotallers, was formed for the South Wales Association. Moreover, every church was urged to keep a pledge book and to form a temperance committee, the functions of which were to prepare petitions and to urge education authorities to introduce temperance readers in day schools. [199]

It is generally accepted that the Calvinistic Methodists of nineteenth-century Wales were not politically minded. Walter Griffith, the Anti-Corn Law League's lecturer in Wales, complained in 1840 that 'the Wesleyan and Calvinistic Methodists will give no help . . . and speak in many places against our cause; but they have always been the same in the principality in all struggles for reform'. [200] As Professor I. G. Jones has shown, however, although the Calvinistic Methodists were not politically motivated, in the sense that they accepted the political system as God-given and outside the scope of their activities, they took a keen interest in political questions, especially those which affected their religious activities. [201] They were always ready, for example, to support the policy of political and legislative action against the existence of the liquor traffic which was championed by the United Kingdom Alliance, the national prohibitionist body, from the mid 1850s. Calvinistic Methodists particularly approved of the Alliance plan of giving the ratepayers of a district a voice in the granting of public house licences, and congregations were requested to support Alliance policy by petition whenever called upon. [202] Electoral activity on the drink question was enthusiastically supported. At the Quarterly Association of North Wales at Pwllheli in August 1885 the Rev. Dr. Owen Thomas carried a resolution urging Calvinistic Methodists to vote only for those candidates who had promised to support temperance legislation. [203]

Teetotalism was a leading feature of the Forward Movement, an evangelistic crusade which began at Cardiff in May 1891, under the auspices of the General Assembly of the Calvinistic Methodists. The movement was largely financed by David Davies of Llandinam,[204] but the inspiration behind the Movement was provided by the Rev. John Pugh of Pontypridd, who had founded the South Wales Temperance Association at Swansea in 1885. Principal Prys of the Theological College at Aberystwyth became the first President of the Movement.[205] The objectives of the Movement were 'to reach non-Church goers, to rescue poor neglected children, and to get all to abstain from the use of strong drinks'.[206] The organ of the Movement announced that 'We are not aiming to form a Temperance Society within the Church, but rather, to impress upon all that the church is itself a Temperance organization'.[207] Pugh was concerned with the indifference of the working man, who, he believed, was kept away from the church by the latter's ultra-respectability.[208] The Forward Movement took on the aspect of an aggressive crusade and the gospel, with temperance as its handmaid, was taken to the people. Higher Criticism was thrown aside, and cottage prayer meetings, house to house visitation and open-air preaching by the evangelist, Seth Joshua, brought many back to the church.

The attitude of the Calvinistic Methodists to the temperance question was insular and narrow. A complex social problem was reduced to a question of the personal morality of those who had already been 'saved' from the world. In 1870 *The Treasury* exhorted every Calvinistic Methodist to 'observe the magnitude of the social evils caused by drinking'.[209] But this seemed to be as far as the denomination wished to go; it acted as a great example-setting body and little else.[210] Not untypically, Calvinistic Methodists suggested in 1877 that drink could be fought by three methods: first came prayer, then preaching, and lastly, 'organized action', that is, 'the setting up of temperance societies'.[211] All three methods seemed to be increasingly unrealistic as the nineteenth century progressed.

Strong support of the temperance movement in nineteenth-century Wales came also from the Wesleyan Methodists. The Welsh Wesleyans were never great in number in the nineteenth century, their membership in south Wales in 1882 being 4,431. Unlike the Calvinistic Methodists they did not constitute an indigenous Welsh denomination; they had to fight an uphill struggle in a religious community whose theology was high Calvinism.[212] But the Wesleyan Methodists exercised an influence out of all proportion to their numbers. Speaking to an assembly of Wesleyans at Aberystwyth in 1891, Principal Thomas Charles Edwards said: 'You did not found

Welsh Methodism. You did not originate our spiritual societies. But you have softened the asperity of our Calvinism. You have made it more human, more genial, and today we are not ashamed of it.'[213] A commentator remarked in 1895 that the Welsh Wesleyans 'have, as a rule, held aloof from the mere political Dissenters'.[214]

The Welsh Wesleyans had held their first annual conference in 1744 and although there is no account of a strictly Welsh Wesleyan Conference until late in the nineteenth century, it would be rash to assume that the relationship between English and Welsh Wesleyans was so close that the decrees of Conferences held in England were representative of the Welsh Wesleyans.[215] For instance, the Wesleyan Conference of 1841 resolved that no Wesleyan chapels should be used for temperance meetings and that no unfermented wines should be used in the administration of the Sacrament.[216] Yet, despite this official attitude, large numbers of Wesleyan Methodists in Wales took up the temperance cause. In Aberystwyth the leading temperance advocate among the Wesleyan Methodists was the Rev. James Jenkins, a local preacher.[217] In 1847 the Quarterly Meeting of the Aberystwyth circuit unanimously decided that every leader and preacher in the circuit should advise and even warn members against celebrating a wedding at which intoxicating liquor would be provided.[218] In July 1839 Lot Hughes, a prominent Wesleyan Methodist of Anglesey, was presented with a silver medal in the Calvinistic Methodist chapel at Beaumaris, for his work for temperance.[219] In 1842 *Yr Eurgrawn Wesleyaidd* held up Walter Watkins, a London Welshman, as a model for other members: he had handed over to the Missionary Society the sum of five guineas, the 'profit' he had made from drinking water.[220] During the late 1870s the Wesleyan Conference set apart one Sunday in the year—Temperance Sunday—for the special advocacy of teetotal principles in the denomination.[221]

It is very difficult to find the official opinion of Welsh Independency on a given subject before 1872 when the Union of Welsh Independents was formed. The Independents in England had formed a union in 1831, and in Wales the Indpendents had held a *Gymanfa* as far back as 1778.[222] But these *Cymanfaoedd* were little more than preaching festivals.

During the nineteenth century there is strong evidence to suggest that the Independents in Wales took a keen interest in social and political issues. It was their religious humanitarianism that led them

to agitate for the abolition of slavery, the passage of factory legislation
and the repeal of the corn laws. Up to 1840-1 the strongest
denominational supporters of the Anti-Corn Law League's agitation
in Wales were the Independents. Their ministers supported Walter
Griffith in lecturing, and the use of many of their chapels was freely
granted. The case for free trade advanced by the Independents
possessed a strong religious flavour for it was made on religious and
moral grounds as well as on those of political expediency. [223] Of the
twenty-seven Welsh ministers who attended the League's conference
of ministers of religion in Manchester in August 1841, seventeen
were Independents. [224] Up to 1872 the Independents were
independent of all committees and assemblies and this made it
possible for their members in general and their ministers in particular
to turn immediately from activities within their own churches to
active participation in the life and problems of society.

Between 1815 and 1890, as Canon E. T. Davies has shown, the
aristocratic and middle-class elements in the ranks of Welsh
nonconformity slowly diminished. [225] This was particularly true of
Independency, and during the nineteenth century it was largely the
miner, the labourer and quarryman, who filled the ranks of the
denomination. [226] Independency's strongest resources and its greatest
leaders came from the working class. Williams of Wern was the son of
a cottager, Hiraethog was called from the plough, and Thomas
Aubrey came from the furnaces of Merthyr and north
Monmouthshire. The Indpendents seemed to be convinced of the
value of the worker and his importance in society. An early article in
Y Gwerinwr emphasized the dignity of every honest calling in life. [227]
In 1859 Y Diwygiwr severely criticized the custom of some middle-
class people of despising working men. [228] But there were socially
conservative elements in Welsh Independency also. Although in 1852
Hiraethog admitted that the Welsh nonconformists as a whole had
been too long silent on matters of general interest, and urged that the
pulpit should teach the people their social responsibilities as citizens of
a free country, as well as their duties as sinners and as Christians, it
should be remembered that there were a number of instances of
complaints from Independents against the movement towards social
and political reform that was slowly permeating the churches. [229] As
far back as 1831 the letter issued from the Cymanfa at Panteg had
urged the churches to pay more attention to the condition of the
soul. [230] In 1837, the Rev. Evan Davies (Eta Delta) of

Llanerchymedd, complained in *Y Dysgedydd* that the best brains of the denomination were being dedicated to worldly affairs.[231] The *Cymanfa* at Talybont in 1850 feared that the new zeal for co-operative action would prove disadvantageous to personal religion: 'We mean that excessive emphasis is being placed upon public remedies and social efforts. The public and social spirit of the age has operated to harmful excess in the Church as well as in the world.'[232]

The leading individual supporters of teetotalism among the Independents before 1850 were Eta Delta, Williams of Wern, the Rev. William Edwards, Aberdare, the Rev. David Rees, Llanelli and the Rev. Evan Jones (Ieuan Gwynedd), of Tredegar. In his memoirs Williams argued the case for temperance by making it clear that he supported teetotalism in order to set an example:

> I saw that the most pious persons among ministers and laymen were becoming teetotallers and I thought that all those of whose piety I entertained a high opinion would soon attach themselves to this movement, and I feared that if I did not speedily join the society I should be a stumbling block in the way, and should wound their feelings—a thing I would not do for all the world. So I resolved to follow those who had gone before me, and to anticipate others as quickly as I could; and I already perceive that things have turned out just as I had expected, and I would not under any consideration be an anti-teetotaller today if it were upon no other ground than regard to the feelings of others. We entreat our friends to join us for the sake of our feelings—you deeply wound our minds, not only when opposing us, but when you allow us to remain in the field unassisted by your presence, counsel and cooperation. To *use* intoxicating drinks cannot be a matter of conscience with you; to abstain from them *is* a matter of conscience with us. You can give them up out of respect to our feelings without wounding your conscience; we cannot give abstinence up without wounding and defiling our consciences. But our opponent says that is your weakness. Granted; And will you 'offend the weak brother for whom Christ dies'? And in sinning against the weak brethren and wounding their consciences, you sin against Christ. Ah! To offend and wound the weak conscience of a weak brother is what some of us would not do for much gain—to say nothing of sinning against Christ.[233]

In south Carmarthenshire David Rees led Independency's support of temperance; as we have seen, he was instrumental in making available Independent chapels in the Llanelli area for temperance meetings after the Independent Temperance *Gymanfa* of Carmarthenshire, Pembrokeshire and Cardiganshire was forced to meet in the long room of the 'Wheat Sheaf' public house in Llanelli in June 1837.[234] Rees was a profound believer in what he regarded as

the 'self-denying, philanthropic and evangelical principles of Total
Abstinence'.[235]

The most prolific writer among the Independents on the
temperance question in Wales in the nineteenth century was Evan
Jones of Tredegar.[236] He set out his views in *The Teetotal Essayist* in
1847.[237] He held that the manufacture, sale and use of intoxicating
drinks was morally wrong. The moral quality of an action belonged
to the intention; he defined a moral action as the voluntary action of
an intelligent agent who was capable of distinguishing between right
and wrong or of distinguishing what he ought to do from what he
ought not to do.[238] The followers of Christ were those who preferred
to act as Christ Himself would have done had He been on earth. As
all men ought to have been His disciples it had to be considered if it
was morally right or wrong for any person to manufacture, sell or use
liquor.[239] The word of God, Jones argued, binds men to oppose
drunkenness, and a lawful and effective means of doing so is
teetotalism. Men are under a moral obligation to promote the public
good, and the public good is not at variance with what is right. That
which is right is a duty and all men are under a moral obligation to
discharge all their duties towards God and their fellow men. Moral
duties are of universal obligation, independent of all enactment
because they are right. In morals, as in law, there is no wrong without
a remedy.

Jones admitted that teetotalism was not explicitly prescribed by the
Bible, but maintained that it was demanded by the universal law of
God's universe, under which men were bound to promote the glory
of God and to abstain from everything that might detract from that
glory; men were bound not to do what might be inimical to the public
good. In order to promote the general good men were bound not to
expose others to danger by self-indulgence, especially with regard to
actions which were of doubtful authority; men were bound to abstain
from things, lawful in themselves, if they were offensive to others;
and men were bound to use all lawful means to promote the
happiness of each other: 'the Church must either crush drunkenness,
or drunkenness will crush the Church'. The financial resources of
religious societies were crippled, not by the economic vicissitudes of
the time, but by the revenue which was paid into the coffers of
Bacchus. 'Christian liberality has dried up, Christian influence is
paralysed and Christian victories are lost.' Thus, drunkenness
detracts from the glory of God; Christians are bound to promote the

glory of God; therefore Christians are bound to oppose drunkenness. Teetotalism was the most effective means to oppose drunkenness because if a man did not drink he would not get drunk; Christians were bound to oppose drunkenness in the most effectual way; therefore Christians were bound to oppose drunkenness by means of teetotalism. To support any traffic that tended to detract from the glory of God would be morally wrong; the traffic in intoxicating drinks tended to detract from the glory of God; therefore the support of that traffic was morally wrong.

For Jones, moderate drinking was no way to avoid drunkenness and consequently it was not the best means to promote the glory of God and the well-being of man. For a Christian to drink was a dangerous and sinful compliance with a custom of the world which ought to be avoided by men who were sworn nonconformists. What Jones called 'respectable, moderate, social drinking', constituted in his view the greatest obstacle to the success of the temperance reformation. Drunkenness was 'an unnatural habit created by natural causes'. It obtained mastery over the moral nature of man by means of the complete subjection into which it brought his animal faculties. This unnatural habit was created not by solitary but by social drinking, not by immoderate but by respectable, moderate drinking. The example to drink was always provided by the moderate drinker as men would never become drinkers by following the example of drunkards.

Jones blamed the 'higher orders' of society, including ministers of religion, who had set a bad example to the 'lower orders'. Many 'respectable' and 'moderate' drinkers were governed by motives which were lacking in the class by which their example was imitated. The influence of education, superior intellect, self-control, 'official connexions' and 'domestic endearments', operated as powerful checks on the minds of a vast majority of moderate drinkers. If all the influential, respectable segments of society could set their faces against drinking, drunkenness would disappear because the prestige of drinking would vanish. The effect would best be avoided by refraining from the cause. The moral quality of the action rested in the preliminary moderate drinking: · drunkenness was only the physical quality and 'not the evil we have to deplore, but the antecedent state of mind which induced it'. Jones stressed the view that men are responsible for others: 'God has constituted us our brother's keepers. God will hold us responsible for the moral tendency of our actions.' What may be not only harmless, but even lawful, must be abstained from if it should be injurious to others. Jones supported this argument with Biblical quotations: 'All things are lawful but all things are not expedient' (*Cor.* X.23); 'It is good neither to eat flesh, not to drink wine, nor anything whereby thy brother stumbleth, or is offended or is made weak' (*Romans,* XIV, 21); 'But take heed lest by any means this liberty of yours become a stumbling block to them that are weak—and through thy knowledge shall the weak brother perish for whom Christ died?' (I *Cor.* VIII, 9).[240] Jones ended his argument by exhorting ministers of religion to think more of 'moral obligation' than respectability—to fear the frown of God more than the frown of the world. If ministers wish to maintain their 'already waning influence' on the minds of the lower orders, they must lead them on to self-improvement and moral elevation.[241]

The impact of such ideas on certain religious communities was quite often dramatic and showed itself in schism between—in the vast majority of cases—a radical, teetotal minister and his conservative congregation. We have an outstanding example among the Welsh Independents of such dissension caused by temperance in the ranks of an individual congregation. This occurred at Llechryd, Cardiganshire, where, in February 1880, the Rev. William Rees was locked out of the Independent chapel with some of his congregation. The basic causes were Rees's extreme views on temperance and his adherence to the teaching of Emanuel Swedenborg.[242] The affair involved a religiously radical minister coming into conflict with a middle-class diaconate, composed chiefly of wealthy barley-growing farmers.

Rees was introduced to Swedenborgian doctrines through reading Swedenborg's *The Apocalypse Revealed* in 1877. The Swedenborgians regarded themselves as being members of a 'New Church', and they believed that the scriptures should be interpreted in both a natural and a spiritual sense. The natural sense was that which had been understood by other Christian churches, whilst the spiritual sense was only made known for the first time by Swedenborg, the Apostle of Stockholm, to whom the privilege had been given to converse with angels and spirits. The rites of the New Church differed little from those practised in other Protestant sects and chapels, but Swedenborgians took greater interest in matters concerning the mysteries of a future life. Man was to pass after death into an intermediate state where he who was good would receive a fuller dose of truth which would prepare him for Heaven, and he who was inwardly wicked would finally reject all enlightenment, and would thus go down for ever among the reprobate.[243] According to Rees, the preparations for such a 'New Age' began in the theosophy of Jacob Behman and in the 'deep thinking' of Morgan Llwyd of Llanrwst.[244] Rees believed that the great curse of society was that of making religion and human action two distinct things.[245] For him, the signs of the New Age were to be seen in the moral awakening of mankind, in the endeavour to bring love and good works to the front, and in the longing for a Christian union on a finer and higher ground than sects and creeds.[246] Temperance was a vital part of the New Age: 'Drunkenness is the product of the Old Church and temperance the product of the New Church. The New Church cannot tolerate us to indulge a passion, nor habit, unfit for the shining place we desire to enter into when the last breath is gone out.'

Rees's account of the conflict at Llechryd, published in 1888 as *The Devil's Keys. Cloi Dirwest o dŷ Dduw*, was justly described by contemporary reviewers as 'a most awful book, and the fullest of electric fire in the Welsh language . . . his short sentences . . . burn like fire'.[247] Rees claimed that when he came to Llechryd in December 1874, drunkenness was sanctioned there by the precept and example of the religious portion of the community.[248] 'The pot-houses were consecrated by the deep drinking of the pastors of the flock, who had led the sheep astray from beside the calm waters to the turbid pools of Bacchus, the boiling whirlpools of Hell, spouting forth the spray of woe, loading the air with plagues and the whistling wind with groans . . . our Pulpit and Churches crawl like adders licking the dust at the feet of Bacchus and Mammon.'[249] The trouble between Rees and the chapel deacons began when Rees preached a sermon on 'The Spiritual Evils of Intemperance' in the summer of 1877, the same year that he was converted to Swedenborgianism.[250] In September 1878 Rees delivered a sermon on 'The Divine Beauty of Teetotalism' and refused to use fermented wine in the Sacrament.[251] When, in January 1879, he strongly urged that a petition be raised in favour of Sunday closing in Wales, one of the deacons objected vigorously and shouted out: 'This House is for the preaching of the Gospel: it is contrary to the conditions of the lease to speak here against the public house.'[252] But Rees continued to warn the deacons of drinking and drunkenness, and finally, in February 1879, the 'guilty' ones were named from the pulpit.[253]

But 'as the preacher denounced the sins of which the lords of the pulpit seat were guilty, the purse was soon closed'. In April 1880, Rees and his supporters—the majority of his congregation—were locked out of the chapel by the deacons, who served notice on Rees that: 'According to the information and resolution of a general meeting of the Independent Church of the Lower Chapel held after public notice, on Thursday, February 26, 1880, we inform you and give you notice that you are not to perform any service as the Minister of the Church henceforth. It was also resolved that the quarterly collection towards the Ministry, due April 11, is to be paid to you, in order to help you to look out for another field of labour.'[254]

Rees maintained that the general meeting was not a proper meeting of the church and that the notice was an 'outrage upon all the principles of Independency'. At first, he and his supporters worshipped in a private house, but ultimately, to the chagrin of their opponents, they built a new chapel called Tabernacle at a cost of £900, opened free of debt on land leased by Mrs. Finch, a local widow, who, ironically, was a local innkeeper.[255] The persecution Rees had suffered strengthened his extreme views; after the lock-out he wrote that 'the divine purity of Temperance shone in upon my mind as the original and final estate of man'.[256] Most Independent chapels in south Wales closed their doors against him, but he was welcomed by the Ynysmeudwy Society of the New Church, founded in 1885 under the leadership of John Mainwaring. This was the first Welsh New Jerusalem Church to be established and it followed the expulsion of the treasurer and 66 other members from the Independent chapel at Ynysmeudwy in the early 1880s. Rees claimed that the expelled had been excommunicated at a small meeting of 37 members, held without previous notice, out of a church membership of over 120, and that the excommunicators were closely connected with Pontardawe brewery.[257] Similarly, at Llandovery, in the 1870s, two deacons who were also maltsters, succeeded in prohibiting the preaching of temperance at one of the town's Independent chapels, and the temperance members left the chapel.[258] Temperance divided a congregation at Tredegar also, for, in 1866, at the English Baptist chapel in the town, a group of members unsympathetic to temperance informed the minister that they would not worship with the group of teetotallers in the chapel. The anti-temperance members finally left the chapel after refusing to pay their contributions.[259]

At a Church Defence meeting at Barmouth in February 1892 the

Rev. Thomas Edwards stated that the reason why David Lloyd George should speak so strongly in favour of temperance was that he belonged to a 'wet sect'.[260] Whether or not this sweeping comment from a besieged Welsh Anglican was true, the Baptists in Wales were certainly less ardent in their support of temperance than most other denominations. Thomas Jones of Rhymney maintained that it was the Baptists in the town who lagged behind in denominational support of temperance.[261] When William Morris was inducted as pastor of his Baptist chapel at Treorchy in May 1869, he was the only teetotaller in his church, 'a distinction he held for several years'.[262] It is also true that very little space was allocated to the temperance issue in the Baptist magazines. There is, for example, very little on the matter in *Y Bedyddiwr* before 1852-3, in which year a series of six articles appeared on the possibilities of the legislative suppression of the liquor traffic. It was not until August 1879 that the Baptist Union Temperance Association was formed.

But many leading individual Baptist ministers supported the temperance cause throughout the century; for example, Christmas Evans, Isaac Jones (Staylittle), Joseph Daniels (Denbigh), John Pritchard (Llangollen), and the poet Dewi Wyn o Eifion in the 1830s; Dr. Thomas Thomas (Pontypool), Robert Jones (Llanllyfni), H. Morgan (Dolgellau), Nathaniel Thomas (Cardiff), John Jones, 'Mathetes' (Swansea and Rhymney), W. Roberts, 'Nefydd', and R. Ellis, 'Cynddelw' (Sirhowy) in the 1840s.[263] Some of these ministers exercised great · personal influence. In the late 1840s Mathetes persuaded the publicans of Porthyrhyd to close their houses on Sunday.[264] It was claimed that the influence of Thomas Thomas of Pontypool was largely responsible for ensuring that greater support was given to temperance in Monmouthshire by the Baptists rather than by the Calvinistic Methodists and Independents.[265] Thomas considered temperance essential for the process of 'advancing the glory of God and the good of society', and he suggested that temperance and moral economy would secure the vote for the labouring classes.[266]

Because of the prevailing congregational polity, in most cases each Baptist chapel was allowed to go its own way, and any discipline needed for wayward members was never as harsh as that meted out to their own members by the Calvinistic Methodists. For instance, if any officers of the Baptist chapel at Sirhowy were found drunk, the procedure was that they be called to account before a meeting; but in practice such cases were invariably dropped.[267] Certain Baptist chapels provided fermented wine for their communion services until late in the century. The account book of Caersalem Welsh Baptist chapel, Dowlais, for 1864-8, reveals that two gallons of such wine were bought for the sacrament during that period from a church member, Mrs. Davies, of the 'Owain Glyndŵr' public house.[268] The aims of Baptist associations in Wales were to aid the formation of Baptist churches in the 'destitute' parts of the country, to promote missions and to contribute generally to the extension of religion *'provided always* that there be no interference with the complete and separate independent and individual action of the several churches' within those associations.[269] The several stock resolutions in favour of temperance issuing from the associations were thus by no means necessarily the views of the individual churches, and were certainly not binding upon them.

The Baptists seem to have had a more radical and realistic attitude towards the affairs of the world than did the Methodists and even the Independents. The Baptist emphasis on personal decision and commitment gave the individual a heightened sense of responsibility which found an outlet in politics, and this probably militated against a widespread support of temperance which was invariably regarded by nonconformity as 'spiritual' and 'other worldly'.[270] Nevertheless, at times during the century, various 'English' sections of the Baptist Church emphasized social and and moral duties; the 'Welsh' Baptists seem to have remained noticeably quiescent on such matters. The Glamorgan and Carmarthenshire English Baptist Association maintained in 1866 that too much stress was laid upon belief, and too little on conduct: 'Dogmas and creeds are often preached when spiritual life is allowed sadly to decline. Let us not have faith in that religion which sternly rebukes 'heterodoxy' in belief, but winks at immorality in conduct. In the sight of God, dishonesty, drunkenness, untruthfulness, sensuality, meanness and crooked policy are much more 'heterodox' than the rejection of all the theological systems ever composed by Divines.'[271] In 1890 James Owen asserted that the Baptist Church should take an interest in all that concerned the material and spiritual welfare of humanity, 'in the home, in the workshop, in the factory, in the coal-mine, in the school', and should demonstrate that 'man everywhere is precious, that although his nature may be debased by poverty and brutalised by drink, and crippled by crime, yet that he may be saved, liberated, dignified by the grace of God and the indwelling of the Holy Spirit'.[272] But Baptist associations could only 'urge' the churches to support temperance and 'hope' that temperance societies would be established in each church.[273]

In 1838 there were approximately 6,250 Roman Catholics in Wales—most of them Irish immigrants—of whom over one-half lived in Monmouthshire. In that year they were distributed in the main centres of population as follows: Newport, 1800; Merthyr Tydfil, 940; Cardiff, 900; Pontypool, 600; and Swansea, 400.[274] These numbers increased greatly throughout the nineteenth century; at Merthyr in 1860, for example, the Catholic community numbered 4,180.[275] Several missions were taken to the Irish Catholics in south Wales in the nineteenth century, but a serious obstacle to their success was the general lack of facilities. At Dowlais, throughout the period from 1836 to 1847, Father James Carroll was forced to hold a mass every Sunday in a public house, and at Merthyr in a loft above the town's slaughterhouse.[276] Very few churches, mission halls or mission funds were set up. There were, of course, economic reasons for this, but also of great significance was the hostility of the indigenous Welsh and non-Irish population to the fact that Irish Catholics—invariably 'labourers of the poorest class'—were willing to work for lower wages than themselves. At Merthyr it was not an unusual occurrence for Father Carroll to be spat upon by the less elevated of the Welsh population.[277]

Drunkenness stems from cultural tradition and social organization, and drink and religion formed the opium of these socially unassimilable communities of *emigré* Catholics in nineteenth-century Wales. Welsh imitators of Father Mathew, the great Irish temperance advocate, began Catholic temperance activity in south Wales in the 1850s; because of the vital question of the sacrament, such activity was moderationist rather than teetotal. In 1853 Father Millea of Dowlais gave a series of temperance lectures to the English Temperance Society of Merthyr.[278] In December 1857 Father Richardson established the Roman Catholic Association for the Suppression of Drunkenness in connection with St. Mary's Church, Stow Hill, Newport, 'for the suppression of drunkenness among the lower orders of Irish'.[279] The Association embodied a conscious attempt to use temperance in order to increase the social status of the Irish Catholic: to make him more respectable and more self-sufficient, and to enable him to attain 'higher office'.[280]

The Association was one of the first of its type amongst exiled Irish Catholics in Britain, and similar associations were established in early 1858 at Cardiff, Swansea and Treforest, near Pontypridd. [281] The Newport association possessed its own characteristic ritual. At each meeting Richardson called for three cheers for Daniel O'Connell. One important endeavour was 'to encourage the members by raising them each year to a higher dignity until after a few years they became 'veterans' and to distinguish them by a different insignia each year . . . for the third year, a bar like the military medals with these words—"By the help of Mary Immaculate." ' [282] At Cardiff, the St. Patrick Temperance Society, founded in 1861 by the Rev. Joseph Costa, made great use of flags and banners, one of which showed the Virgin Mary trampling the 'Drink Demon' under her feet. Significantly, every meeting of this society ended with a vote of thanks to the Protestant teetotallers 'for the marked respect they had shown to them'. [283]

The Newport association divided the town into districts under a number of stewards who were fined 2s. 6d. for every case of drunkenness they failed to report. The strength of the association was that it was not teetotal: its leading members constantly stressed that, in contrast to the prohibitionists, their enemy was not the trade in drink but drunkenness. [284] To encourage thrift and to ensure a loyal membership, a special Penny Bank and a funeral society were established. In May 1863 the Society of St. Joseph, a 'cadet corps to the Association', was set up in order to indoctrinate children against drink. [285] Recreational needs were provided for, as Richardson's aim was to show that it was possible to enjoy 'healthy and invigorating' amusement and recreation without gross intoxication. [286] However, the removal of Richardson to London in the early 1870s dealt a virtual death blow to the Association in Newport, and it was eventually merged with the national League of the Holy Cross, founded by Cardinal Manning in 1873.

As Welsh issues, temperance and teetotalism were closely identified with Welsh nonconformity and were seen in an 'other worldly' light. The attitude of Welsh nonconformity to the drink question was almost exclusively based on ideas of personal salvation and personal morality, so that temperance was seen as a moral issue, not as one of social amelioration in 'this' world. [287] Drunkenness was seen as an all-explaining evil which led to a multitude of other sins

rather than as the possible outcome or manifestation of social
conditions. The problem of drink was thus approached in blinkers; it
tended to be viewed in isolation from all the other social evils of the
environment. For the Welsh-speaking, evangelical nonconformist,
the good life for most of the nineteenth and much of the twentieth
century, was largely interpreted in such negative terms as teetotalism
and Sunday observance. Welsh nonconformist theology was hardly
affected at all by the movements in English theology represented by
Maurice who sought to stress the social implications of the Christian
faith. Canon E. T. Davies found, for example, that whereas during
the period from 1832 to 1900, the Monmouthshire English Baptist
Association occasionally expressed sympathy with hungry families in
industrial Monmouthshire, the Monmouthshire Welsh Baptist
Association did not once discuss the social conditions in the county,
except, characteristically, for some other-worldly pronouncements
about temperance and Sunday closing.[288] Indeed, Welsh
nonconformity in industrial Wales was in general more conservative
in social matters than both the English nonconformist chapels in the
same area and Welsh nonconformity in rural Wales. Davies ascribes
this difference in outlook—given Welsh nonconformists' belief that
little could be done about social conditions and problems—to the fact
that in the industrial areas Welsh nonconformity possessed social and
political power because there was no resistance; it inherited largely
virgin territory and formed a new society in its own image in an area
where the Established Church, Toryism and landlordism had not
really mattered. There was nothing in the new society, as there was in
the old rural society, to put Welsh nonconformity on its mettle and
little resistance was offered to it.[289]

Welsh nonconformists everlastingly bemoaned drink, drinking and
drunkenness, but for the most part they were never willing to step
into the 'world' and ask themselves whether anything was needed in
the way of 'harmless', 'rational' amusement to combat the evil.[290]
With the exception of prayer meetings, Bible meetings and Bands of
Hope, all of which had a strong recreational content, little recreation
was offered by chapels and churches in the last quarter of the century.
A working man pleaded in September 1892: 'I want somewhere to go
in the evening, a place that's comfortable and warm and where I can
find suitable company. I don't care for street corners, and, after all,
you know, I am a total abstainer. Let it be a mutual improvement
class, a debating class, or any class, and only a limited number of

hymns.'[291] A Rhondda man suggested that the 'palatial-looking chapels', which were practically closed for six days a week and the cost of which was paid by the mass of ordinary people, should be opened on week days for working men to spend their leisure time there. He advocated setting up chess and billiard rooms with newspapers which could be attached to the chapels and would act as a counter-attraction to the public house.[292] His suggestion was regarded as being of particular importance if the eight-hour day was ever achieved in practice, a development which would give men more time to attend the pub.[293] But such appeals fell largely on deaf ears. The connection of the temperance movement with the kill-joy prejudices of Welsh nonconformity meant that excessive drinking was treated as a sin, not as a psychosomatic disorder and still less as a disease.

NOTES

[1] *The Cardiff Review and Monthly Record of Christian Work*, vol. 1, no. 1, March 1894, p. 10; N.L.W., Ellis Papers, f. 3,022, n.d.

[2] See G. E. Owen, 'Welsh Anti-Slavery Sentiments, 1790-1865. A Survey of Public Opinion' (unpublished University of Wales M.A. thesis, 1964), *passim*; T. H. Williams, 'Wales and the Corn Laws, 1815-46' (unpublished University of Wales M.A. thesis, 1952), *passim*; Goronwy Jones, *Wales and the Quest for Peace* (Cardiff, 1969), *passim*.

[3] See T. Evans, *The Background of Modern Welsh Politics* (Cardiff, 1936), p. 225.

[4] For example, see *Caernarvon and Denbigh Herald*, 11 March 1837; 18 March 1837; *C.M.G.*, 7 January 1843.

[5] *Caernarvon and Denbigh Herald*, 9 April 1836.

[6] *The Universe*, vol. 1, no. 23, 9 June 1846, p. 6. Letter from Machynlleth.

[7] See G. V. Bennett and J. D. Walsh (eds.), *Essays in Modern Church History in Memory of Norman Sykes* (1966), p. 185.

[8] See *Minutes of the Committee of Council on Education, 1839-40*, 174, 176-7; Childrens Employment Commission, Part I, p. 449; C.C.L., MS. 2.329, A Cambrian Literary Gentleman, The Social, Industrial and Literary State of the Cambrian Nation, 1880, pp. 5-7. For this pattern in Glamorgan in the 1830s, see C.C.L., MS. 5.153, Return of Nonconformists in Glamorgan in 1836.

[9] For useful criticism of the census see E. T. Davies, *Religion in the Industrial Revolution in South Wales* (Cardiff, 1965), pp. 32-42.

[10] *Welsh Nonconformity and Welsh Representation* (1866), p. 1; see also *Y Goleuad*, 17 August 1884; *Western Mail*, 23 August 1884

[11] *Merthyr Express*, 20 June 1885.

[12] Rev. J. Idrisyn Jones, *Why are we Nonconformists?* (Newport, 1881), p. 6.

[13] G. A. Williams, 'Hugh Owen (1804-1881)', *Pioneers of Welsh Education* (Swansea, n.d.), p. 59.

[14] Bennett and Walsh (eds.), op. cit., p. 191.

[15] On the general background to this paragraph, see R. L. Hugh, 'The Theological Background of Nonconformist Social Influence in Wales, 1800-1850' (unpublished University of London Ph.D. thesis, 1951); G. Richards, 'A Study of Theological Developments among the Nonconformists of Wales in the Nineteenth Century' (unpublished University of Oxford B.Litt. thesis, 1956).

[16] On this, see E. T. Davies, op. cit., chapter 2, *passim*; K. Inglis, 'English Nonconformity and Social reform, 1880-1900', *Past and Present*, 13, 1958, 83; Mark Rutherford (pseud. W. H. White), *The Revolution in Tanner's Lane* (4th ed., n.d.), p. 336; C. R. Williams, 'The Welsh Religious Revival of 1904-5', *British Journal of Sociology*, 3, 1953, 243.

[17] Thomas Jones recollected: 'Nor did we dare to hope for an economic millenium on the earth. Our Utopia was elsewhere. For us, the judgement of this world was not a remote contingency but an impending doom. In my first Welsh reading book I was forbidden to love the world or ought that is within it. "Hold the fort for I am coming" was the most popular children's hymn.' *Rhymney Memories*, p. 159.

[18] E. Davies and Alwyn D. Rees (eds.), *Welsh Rural Communities* (Cardiff, 1960), p. 47.

[19] *Circular Letter of Glamorgan and Carmarthenshire English Baptist Association, 1875* (Swansea, 1875), pp. 5-6. For the same sentiment, see Rev. Thomas Thomas, *A Course of Lectures on the Present Duties Devolving on Christian Professors as members of a Civil Community. First Lecture* (Newport, 1847), pp. 3, 6-7.

[20] *The Treasury*, 7, 1870, p. 119.

[21] Ibid.

[22] Ibid., p. 121. Similarly, Alfred Ollivant, Bishop of Llandaff, maintained that the main aim of temperance societies was to fit people for the life to come, *C.M.G.*, 21 May 1859.

[23] John Thomas, *Sunshine on the 'Hills', being a narrative of the Lord's Work at Tredegar during a visitation of the cholera in 1866* (1868), pp. 33-4.

[24] Rev. Joseph Evans. *Arrows from a Temperance Quiver* (Carmarthen, 1864), pp. 12, 16.

[25] *Monthly Tidings: A Repertory of Christian Thought and a Record of Christian Work among the Calvinistic Methodists of Wales*, vol. 6, no. 1, January 1890, p. 4.

[26] *National Temperance League Annual, 1843* (1844), p. 39.

[27] Caernarfonshire Record Office, The Town Accounts of Caernarvon, 1632-33.

[28] E. T. Davies, op. cit., p. 62.

[29] John Thomas, op. cit., p. 36.

[30] N.L.W., MS. 10,291 B (Solva 17), Miscellaneous Account of Ministers at Tredegar for food and beer, 1829-39.

[31] Ibid.

[32] N.L.W., MS. 16,157 B, op. cit.

[33] Rev. John Williams, *Notes and Narratives of Thirty Years' missionary and ministerial labours in England and Wales* (Machynlleth, 1885), p. 102.

[34] Henry Ladd, op. cit., p. 6.

[35] Thomas Jones, op. cit., p. 138.

[36] G. H. Armbruster, 'The Social Determination of Ideologies' (unpublished University of London Ph.D. thesis, 1940), p. 127.

[37] Brian Harrison, *Drink and the Victorians*, p. 115.

[38] See *The Teetotal Essayist*, I, no. 5, 15 May 1847, pp. 33-4; *C.M.G.*, 16 June 1849.

[39] Rev. John Lewis, *A Memoir of the Rev. William Griffith, Holyhead* (Liverpool, n.d.), p. 120; *The Treasury*, 10, 1873, pp. 76-8; *Monmouthshire Merlin*, 27 January 1882.

[40] *The Millenial Harbinger or Voluntary Church Advocate*, 2, no. 15, May 1836, p. 325 (letter concerning north Wales Baptists).

[41] *C.M.G.*, 18 October 1856.

[42] *National Temperance Chronicle and Recorder*, I, no. 11, November 1846, p. 255; no. 14, February 1847, p. 29; *Merthyr Express*, 18 December 1869.

[43] See *Merthyr Express*, 4 October 1884.

[44] Dawson Burns, *Temperance History*, vol. 1, p. 127.

[45] See U.C.N.W. MS. 5,757, Papurau ap Vychan, f. 37; P.R.O. HO 45/454, Part I, Memorandum on teetotalism by Thomas Yates; J. N. Stearns (ed.), *Temperance in all Nations* (New York, 1893), vol. 1, pp. 435-9; W. H. Howse, *Radnorshire* (Hereford, 1949), p. 156.

[46] *Preston Temperance Advocate*, July 1836, p. 72; *High Moveable Conference of Rechabites* (Swansea, 1903), pp. 43-5.

[47] *The Principality*, 20 April 1849.

[48] For example, see *Proceedings of National Temperance Congress at Chester, 1895* (1895), p. 166.

[49] Data taken from *Y Dirwestydd*, January-October 1838; *London Temperance Intelligencer*, 28 October 1837; 6 December 1837; 16 December 1837; *The New British and Foreign Temperance Intelligencer*, 7 July 1838; 14 July 1838.

[50] *The Friend. Religious, Moral and Political Intelligencer for Shropshire and North Wales*, no. 1, 10 January 1838, p. 3.

[51] *Teetotal Times and Essayist*, 1848, pp. 65-7.

[52] J. Thomas, *Cofiant y Parch Thomas Rees, D.D., Abertawy* (Dolgellau, 1888), pp. 99-100.

[53] For example, see A. J. Parry, *The Apostle Paul's Meat Argument and its Bearing upon the duty of Christians in relation to the drinking customs of the present times* (Swansea, 1879).

[54] *The British Temperance Advocate and Journal*, 3, no. 11, 15 November 1841, p. 127.

[55] For example, see *Merthyr Express*, 30 July 1881; 13 August 1881; *The Christian Standard: monthly magazine of Cardiff Evangelistic Movement*, I, no. 10, April 1892, p. 1.

[56] *Merthyr Express*, 26 September 1885.

[57] Rev. Thomas Jones, *Sober Views of the Millenium* (1835), p. 2.

[58] Ibid., pp. 12, 37.

[59] For example, see *Teetotal Essayist*, I, no. 5, 15 May 1847, pp. 38-9; Rev. Rhys Gwesyn Jones, *Courting, Marrying and Living* (Llanidloes, 1867), p. 50.

[60] E. G. Millward (ed.), op. cit., p. 199.

[61] Ibid., p. 125.

[62] Brian Harrison, *Drink and the Victorians*, p. 185.

[63] For example, see *Y Dirwestydd*, no. 7, January 1837, pp. 51-2.

[64] *Teetotal Essayist*, I, no. 5, 15 May 1847, p. 33; see also *Metropolitan Temperance Intelligencer and Journal*, no. 23, 10 June 1843, p. 181.

[65] *Teetotal Essayist*, I, no. 9, 24 September 1847, p. 71; for a similar view see *Cambria Daily Leader*, 13 April 1864.

[66] Rev. R. Jones, *The Claims of the Temperance Movement on Christian Ministers* (Manchester, 1860), p. 9.

[67] G.R.O., Dowlais MSS., 1831 (1), ff, 575-6, T. R. Guest, 'A plain address to such ministers of the Union Lodges as are in connexion with Christian Churches,' 7 November 1831.

[68] See New British and Foreign Temperance Society, *Fourth Annual Report, 1840*, pp. 47-8; P. T. Winskill, *The Temperance Movement and its Workers*, vol. 4, p. 99.

[69] *London Temperance Intelligencer*, I, no. 25, 6 May 1837, pp. 202-3.

[70] Report of the Royal Commission on the Church, *P.P.*, 1911, op. cit., vol. 4, p. 23, Q. 35,033.

[71] *The Treasury*, 5, 1868, p. 279.

[72] *C.M.G.*, 5 December 1840.

[73] Harrison, *Drink and the Victorians*, p. 126.

[74] See, for example, *The Treasury*, 9, 1872, pp. 55-7.

[75] Rev. Joseph Evans, op. cit., p. 158; see also *St. John's (Cardiff) Parochial Magazine*, vol. 1, 1870, pp. 198-9; *Report of the Church Congress, 1879* (Swansea, 1879), p. 283.

[76] See, for example, *Merthyr Express*, 11 December 1875; *Monmouthshire Merlin*, 23 June 1882; 18 April 1884; *The Christian Standard*, I, no. 4, October 1891, p. 7.

[77] *The Treasury*, 6, 1869, p. 395.

[78] *Baptist Chronicle*, 2, no. 7, December 1893, pp. 173-4; see also *Monthly Tidings*, 7, no. 6, June 1891, p. 119; *Merthyr Express*, 19 April, 1879.

[79] W. E. Kochs, op. cit., p. 77.

[80] *The Journal of the New British and Foreign Temperance Society*, 2, no. 3, 18 January 1840, p. 21. Letter from Bagillt.

[81] See H. E. Lewis, *With Christ among the Miners* (1906), p. 31; E. T. Davies, op. cit., p. 62.

[82] *British and Foreign Temperance Intelligencer*, 4, no. 168, 25 January 1840, p. 31; 4, no. 183, 9 May 1840, p. 151; *Journal of the New British and Foreign Temperance Society*, 2, no. 10, 7 March 1840, p. 76.

[83] *The Weekly Journal of the New British and Foreign Temperance Society*, 3, no. 16, 16 April 1841.

[84] See *Y Dirwestydd*, no. 29, November 1838, p. 235.

[85] *Journal of the New British and Foreign Temperance Society*, 2, no. 47, 21 November 1840, p. 381.

[86] Ibid., no. 3, 18 January 1840, p. 22.

[87] See *The Treasury*, 17, 1880, pp. 121-4; B. Wilson. *Sects and Society* (1961), p. 322; E. J. Hobsbawm, op. cit., p. 139; E. T. Davies, op. cit., p. 60; H. R. Niebuhr, *The Social Sources of Denominationalism* (New York, 1960), p. 62. For the transient behavioural lunacy of Welsh revivals see N.L.W., MS. 11,721 C, a letter from John Elias, Llanfechell to F. Carmichael, Amlwch, on the effect of revivals, 25 October 1822.

[88] See J. S. Bushnan, op. cit.; G. O. Jones, 'Cholera in Wales', *National Library of Wales Journal*, 10, 1957-8.

[89] *C.M.G.*, 4 August 1849.

[90] *Morning Chronicle*, 15 April 1850.

[91] Evan Powell, *History of Carmel Baptist Chapel, Sirhowy* (Cardiff, 1933), p. 29.

[92] John Thomas, op. cit., p. 5.

[93] Ibid., pp. 8-9.

[94] *Yr Annibynwr*, February 1858, p. 26; see also *Y Drysorfa*, 1858, p. 371; *Yr Eurgrawn*, 1858, pp. 59-60.

[95] See, for example, *The Revival*, no. 3, 1 October 1859, p. 11; Evan Davies (ed.), *Revivals in Wales: facts and correspondence supplied by pastors of the Welsh Churches* (1859), pp. 8, 60.

[96] Ibid., p. 4.

[97] *Alliance News*, 28 May 1859.

[98] Evan Davies, op. cit., pp. 32, 38, 63, 65, 68.

[99] *Yr Annibynwr*, 1860, p. 60; Eifion Evans, *When he is come* (Bala, 1959), p. 77.

[100] Thomas Phillips, *The Welsh Revival in its origin and development* (1860), p. 19; see also *Western Temperance Herald*, 23, no. 1, 1 July 1859, p. 74.

[101] Thomas Phillips, op. cit., p. 98.

[102] Ibid., p. 30.

[103] *Y Gwladgarwr*, 5 November 1859, p.178.

[104] *C.M.G.*, 26 November 1859.

[105] On this see *The Revival*, no. 5, 15 October 1859, p. 22; *Y Gweithiwr*, 29 October 1859; *Alliance News*, 5 November 1859; *The Nonconformist*, 19, no. 739, 28 December 1859, p. 1,046; S. Couling, op. cit., pp. 263-4.

[106] *Star of Gwent*, 7 December 1861; D. J. Davies, *The Tredegar Workmen's Hall, 1861-1951* (Newport, 1952), pp. 24-5.

[107] Alexander Sharp, *A Narrative of the Great Revival Work in South Wales in 1871* (Cupar Fife, 1871), *passim*.

[108] J. Vyrnwy Morgan, *The Welsh Religious Revival* (1909), xviii.

[109] *Circular Letter of Monmouthshire Particular Baptist Association* (Beaufort, 1870), p. 9.

[110] *The Treasury*, 16, 1879, p. 89; Edward Parry, *Llawlyfr ar hanes y diwygiadau crefyddol yng Nghymru* (Corwen, 1898), pp. 157-8.

[111] J. V. Morgan, op. cit., pp. 164-5.

[112] Harrison, *Drink and the Victorians*, p. 164.

[113] Ibid., p. 187.

[114] Henry Richard, *Letters on the social and political condition of the Principality of Wales*, p. 5.

[115] H.B. A Cardiganshire Voter, *The Welsh Destiny. A Political Triad* (Aberystwyth, 1891), p. 4.

[116] Thomas Jones, *The Welsh Looking-Glass, or Thoughts on the State of Religion in North Wales* (1812), p. 30.

[117] See *Star of Gwent*, 19 August 1857.

[118] See Ibid., 5 September 1857; Thomas Rees, *Miscellaneous Papers on Subjects Relating to Wales* (1867), p. 65; W. R. Lambert, 'Some Working-Class Attitudes Towards Organized Religion in Nineteenth-Century Wales', *Llafur*, 2, no. 1, Spring 1976, 7-8.

[119] *Proceedings of Swansea Conference, September 1862* (Liberation Society, 1862), p. 10.

[120] See *The Treasury*, 18, 1881, p. 239; Childrens Employment Commission, *P.P.* 1842, pp. 370, 374, 383, 386, 412, 416, 421; J. G. Kohl, *Travels in England and Wales* (1844), p. 106.

[121] *Church Quarterly Review*, 15 October 1882, p. 74.

[122] Henry Richard, *Letters and Essays on Wales*, p. 216; see also *The New British and Foreign Temperance Intelligencer*, 2, no. 85, 23 June 1838, p. 206; Rev. Joseph Evans, op. cit., p. 9.

[123] For Hughes, see *North Wales Chronicle*, 2 June 1835; for Pritchard, see *Y Drysorfa*, 1839, p. 55.

[124] Henry Richard, op. cit., p. 217.

[125] W. D. Wills, 'Ecclesiastical Reorganization', *passim*; and 'The Established Church in the Diocese of Llandaff, 1850-70', *W.H.R.*, 4, no. 3, June 1969, 235-73.

[126] *C.M.G.*, 17 November 1838.

[127] Wills, 'Ecclesiastical Reorganization', p. 103.

[128] Alfred Ollivant (ed.), *Substance of the speeches delivered at Bridgend and Newport in 1850* (1851), p. 15.

[129] On this see Rev. Canon Bevan, *The Church in the South Wales Coalfield* (1894), p. 14; Wills, 'Ecclesiastical Reorganization', *passim*.

[130] All the letters are reprinted in Evan Jones, *The Dissent and Morality of Wales* (1847).

[131] Ibid., p. 18.

[132] Ibid., p. 19.

[133] Alfred B. Evans, *Dissent and its Inconsistencies* (1841), p. 132; see also James Owen, *The Free Churches and the People* (1890), p. 14.

[134] Alfred B. Evans, op. cit., p. 134.

[135] *Cambrian*, 13 June 1853.

[136] E. Pughe, *The Religious Statistics of Wales* (Bangor, 1867), p. 14.

[137] *Monmouthshire Merlin*, 25 October 1887.

[138] For this, see 'A Special Correspondent', *Letters from Wales. A Republication of a series of Letters in the 'Times' dealing with the state of Wales in especial relation to the Land, the Church and the Tithe* (1889), p. 11.

[139] *Report of Llandaff Diocesan Conference, 1889* (Cardiff, 1889), p. 45.

[140] *Welsh Weekly*, 1, no. 8, 26 February 1892, p. 10.

[141] *Y Genedl*, 19 February 1892.

[142] P. T. Winskill, op. cit., vol. 2, p. 29; for a similar example at Merthyr Tydfil, see *C.M.G.*, 17 April 1841.

[143] *High Moveable Conference of the Rechabites at Swansea* (Swansea, 1903), p. 55.
[144] *North Wales Chronicle,* 17 March 1835.
[145] Ibid., 17 March 1835, 21 April 1835; *Caernarvon and Denbigh Herald,* 24 December 1836.
[146] *London Temperance Intelligencer,* 1, no. 20, 1 April 1837, p. 161.
[147] *C.M.G.,* 27 July 1845; *The Principality,* 18 August 1848.
[148] See David Williams, *John Frost,* p. 323.
[149] Thomas Thomas, D.D., *The Civil duties of Christians. A Sermon occasioned by the late outrages at Newport, Mon.* (n.d.), p. 27.
[150] See W. D. Wills, 'Ecclesiastical Reorganization', pp. 272, 349-50.
[151] *C.M.G.,* 25 May 1860. Griffith himself was a moderationist, not a teetotaller; his wife's shopping lists reveal such items as whisky, stout and sherry: see C.C.L., MS. 3.504, Box 16, Mrs. J. Griffith's Diaries, Journals and Letters, 1845, 1860-4, 1866-7 and 1870. See also *Merthyr Express,* 19 March 1881 (Griffith's obituary).
[152] *Cambrian,* 28 May 1858.
[153] Ibid., 9 July 1858; *C.M.G.,* 17 July 1858.
[154] *Cambrian,* 10 December 1858.
[155] See Ibid., 1 April 1859, 8 April 1859, 17 June 1859.
[156] *Star of Gwent,* 14 May 1859.
[157] *C.M.G.,* 4 June 1859.
[158] *Alliance News,* 3 December 1859.
[159] *Star of Gwent,* 3 March 1860.
[160] *C.M.G.,* 28 January 1860.
[161] Ibid., 10 December 1859.
[162] *Star of Gwent,* 25 February 1860.
[163] *C.M.G.,* 15 September 1860.
[164] See, in general, G. Kitson Clark, *The Making of Victorian England* (1962), pp. 187-8.
[165] See Thomas Rees, op. cit., particularly the chapter 'The Working Class and Religious Institutions'.
[166] *Alliance News,* 24 February 1866.
[167] See p. 213.
[168] James Hews Bransby, *An Account of the Calvinistic Methodists in Wales* (Caernarfon, 1845), p. 8.
[169] Ibid., p. 11.
[170] Ibid., p. 13.
[171] *Y Drysorfa,* August 1835, p. 23.
[172] Ibid., see also *The British and Foreign Temperance Herald,* 4, no. 45, September 1835, pp. 101-2.
[173] *Y Drysorfa,* March 1837, p. 241. For the views and resolutions on temperance by the North Wales Association up to the early 1890s see Edward Jones, *Y Gymdeithasfa* (1891), chapter 10, 'Dirwest', pp. 186-201.
[174] *Y Drysorfa,* December 1838, p. 371.
[175] Ibid., p. 372. See also *Journal of the Calvinistic Methodist Historical Society,* 11, no. 1, June 1926, p. 9.
[176] *Y Drysorfa,* July 1840, p. 182; see also *Proceedings of the World Temperance Convention* (1846), p. 33.
[177] N.L.W., MS. 5,053 B (Richard I), Lewis Edwards to Henry Richard, 14 January 1879. See also Rev. Joseph Evans, *Biographical Dictionary of the Ministers and Preachers of the Welsh Calvinistic Methodist Body* (Caernarvon, 1907), p. 288.
[178] Caernarvonshire Record Office, M.S. Rhestr Ymgeiswyr am Aelodaeth, 1836-64.
[179] *Y Dysgedydd,* 1833, p. 177.
[180] For example, Rev. William Jones, *The Character of the Welsh as a Nation* (n.d.); *Royal Gordovigion Eisteddfod, Liverpool 1840* (1841), pp. 33-5; Children's Employment Commission, *P.P.,* 1842, p. 509.
[181] See N.L.W., Calvinistic Methodist Archives, 5923, 'Some of the distinguishing characteristics of Calvinistic Methodism'.
[182] See ibid., and Eliezer Davies, *Calvinistic Methodism in Wales: its present position and future prospects: a critical review* (1870), p. 11.
[183] Evan Powell, *History of Tredegar* (Newport, 1902), p. 47.
[184] *The Journal of the new British and Foreign Temperance Society,* I, no. 9, 2 March 1839, p. 77.
[185] *Y Dirwestydd,* no. 5, October 1836, p. 34.
[186] Evan Price, *History of Penuel Calvinistic Methodist Chapel, Ebbw Vale* (Wrexham, 1925), p. 72.
[187] *The National Temperance Magazine,* 2 February 1845, p. 87.
[188] Ibid., p. 88.

[189] Ibid., p. 87.

[190] For example, see N.L.W., C.M. Archives, 5935, Address on Temperance, n.d.

[191] *The History, Constitution, Rules of Discipline and Confession of Faith of the Calvinistic Methodists in Wales* (1850), pp. 29-31; see also *The Treasury*, 10, 1873, p. 202.

[192] Ibid., 8, 1871, p. 197.

[193] Ibid., 10, 1873, p. 119.

[194] See, for example, *Alliance News*, 20 September 1879, p. 602; R. Rae (ed.), *The National Temperance League's Annual for 1881* (1882), pp. 73-4.

[195] *The Treasury*, 15, 1878, p. 114; *Alliance News*, 20 September 1879, p. 602.

[196] *The Treasury*, 18, 1881, p. 247; Royal Commission on the Church, *P.P.*, 1911, vol. 3, Part 2, Q. 25, 499.

[197] *The Treasury*, 16, 1879, pp. 175-6, 217.

[198] See *Reports and Minutes of the Quarterly Association of Calvinistic Methodists of South Wales* (1886), p. 3.

[199] *The Treasury*, 18, 1881, p. 344; *South Wales Daily News*, 5 August 1881; Edward Jones, op. cit., p. 196; Royal Commission on the Church, *P.P.*, 1911, vol. 3, Q. 25,499.

[200] Manchester Public Library, Anti-Corn Law League Letter Book, vol. 4, 28 May 1840, letter 606. I owe this reference to Professor I. G. Jones. See also *Anti-Corn Law Circular*, 4 June 1839; *Anti-Bread Tax Circular*, 2 December 1841.

[201] I. G. Jones, 'Merioneth Politics in mid-nineteenth century. The Politics of a Rural Economy', *Journal of Merioneth Historical and Record Society*, vol. 5, no. 4, 1968, 290-1.

[202] For example, see *Alliance News*, 30 July 1859, 22 September 1866; *The Treasury*, 8, 1871, p. 94; Central Association for Stopping the Sale of Intoxicating Liquors on Sundays, *Fourth Annual Report, 1870*, pp. 14-15.

[203] *Caernarvon and Denbigh Herald*, 29 August 1885; for the 1892 General Election see *Monthly Tidings*, 8, no. 7, July 1892, p. 165.

[204] N.L.W., C.M. Archives, 5924, 'The Forward Movement', n.d., c. 1896.

[205] See the memorandum in C.C.L., 'Cochfarf' Papers (unscheduled); *The Christian Standard*, I, no. 5, November 1891, pp. 3-4.

[206] C.C.L., 'Cochfarf' Papers, memorandum.

[207] *The Christian Standard*, I, no. 8, February 1892, p. 13.

[208] N.L.W., C.M. Archives, 5924, 'The Forward Movement'.

[209] *The Treasury*, 7, 1870, pp. 90-1.

[210] For example, see Rev. Joseph Evans, op. cit., p. 26.

[211] *The Treasury*, 14, 1877, pp. 16-18.

[212] See E. T. Davies, op. cit., p. 51.

[213] Thomas Jones, op. cit., p. 136.

[214] Henry Owen, *Welsh Religion and Welsh Christianity* (Carmarthen, 1896), p. 6.

[215] See N. Curnock (ed.), *John Wesley's Journal* (1909), vol. 3, p. 143, note 2.

[216] See *The Weekly Journal of the New British and Foreign Temperance Society*, vol. 3, no. 37, 10 September 1841, p. 361.

[217] A. H. Williams, *Welsh Wesleyan Methodism, 1800-58* (1935), p. 164.

[218] Lloyd Morgan, *Hanes Wesleyaeth yn Aberystwyth*, pp. 9, 28: quoted in A. H. Williams, op. cit., p. 164.

[219] *Yr Eurgrawn*, 1840, p. 30.

[220] Ibid., 1842, p. 320.

[221] *Monmouthshire Merlin*, 7 December 1888.

[222] R. W. Dale, *History of English Congregationalism* (1907), p. 687.

[223] *North Wales Chronicle*, 7 July 1840; T. H. Williams, op. cit., p. 19.

[224] *Y Dysgedydd*, October 1841, pp. 329-30.

[225] E. T. Davies, op. cit., pp. 31-41.

[226] See R. T. Jenkins, *Hanes Cymru yn y Ddeunawfed Ganrif* (Cardiff, 1928), p. 52.

[227] *Y Gwerinwr*, May 1855, p. 42.

[228] *Y Diwygiwr*, 1859, p. 144.

[229] *Yr Amserau*, 11 August 1852.

[230] J. L. Jones, *Cymanfaoedd yr Annibynwyr. Eu Hanes â'u Llythyrau* (Dolgellau, 1867), p. 449.

[231] *Y Dysgedydd*, July 1837, p. 111.

[232] D. G. Williams, *Llythyrau a Hanes Cymanfaoedd Deorllewin a Deddwyrain yr Annibynwyr, 1845-60* (Llanelli, 1927), pp. 69-70 (translated).

[233] Rev. William Rees, *Memoirs of Rev. William Williams of Wern. Translated by J. R. Jones* (1866), pp. 84-5.

[234] See above, p. 65.

[235] *The Journal of the New British and Foreign Temperance Society*, 2, no. 19, 9 May 1840, p. 150.

[236] See Rev. William Williams, *Cofiant a Gweithiau Ieuan Gwynedd* (Dolgellau, 1876), pp. 5-7, 16-26, 50-66, 311-63; *Dictionary of Welsh Biography*, pp. 432-3.

[237] Evan Jones, 'The Moral Obligation of Total Abstinence', *The Teetotal Essayist*, I, no. 6, 15 June 1847, pp. 41-48; I, no. 11, 22 November 1847, pp. 84-5. See also N.L.W., MS. 2,768 C (Edward Griffith 78).

[238] N.L.W., MS. 1,027 C (Ieuan Gwynedd 3), Evan Jones, An Essay on Intemperance, 1852.

[239] *The Teetotal Essayist*, 15 June, 22 November 1847.

[240] See N.L.W., MS. 1,027 C (Ieuan Gwynedd 3), Evan Jones, An Essay on Intemperance.

[241] Ibid. See also N.L.W., MS. 2,767 C (Edward Griffith 77), Ieuan Gwynedd Miscellany.

[242] See N.L.W., MS. 12,863 F, Journal of Rev. William Rees, Llechryd, 1880-1917: The New Church or the Tabernacle of the Lord at Llechryd; E. D. Jones, 'William Rees, Llechryd (1839-1919). A Welsh Swedenborgian', *National Library of Wales Journal*, 15, no. 2, Winter 1967, 234-5.

[243] See Alphonse Esquiros, *Religious Life in England* (1867), pp. 181-3.

[244] W. Rees, *The Devil's Keys. Cloi Dirwest o dŷ Dduw* (Ystalyfera, 1888), p. 100.

[245] Ibid., p. 103.

[246] Ibid., p. 109.

[247] Ibid., pp. 5-7.

[248] N.L.W., MS. 12,863 F, 3 March 1880; Rees, *The Devil's Keys*, p. 10.

[249] Ibid., pp. 11,113.

[250] Ibid., pp. 20-1.

[251] Ibid., p. 27.

[252] Ibid., p. 14.

[253] Ibid., p. 30.

[254] N.L.W., MS. 12,863 F, 12 April 1880.

[255] *The Devil's Keys*, p. 71; E. D. Jones, op. cit., 235.

[256] *The Devil's Keys*, p. 55.

[257] Ibid., p. 119.

[258] Ibid., p. 24.

[259] *Merthyr Express*, 11 August 1866.

[260] *Welsh Weekly*, I, no. 8, 26 February 1892, p. 10. For similar charges against the Baptists see *Alliance News*, 3 December 1859; *Merthyr Express*, 17 May 1873.

[261] Thomas Jones, op. cit., p. 138.

[262] E. D. Lewis, *The Rhondda Valleys* (1959), p. 223, note 6.

[263] See D. Rhys Stephen, *Memoirs of Christmas Evans* (1847), p. 149; Royal Commission on the Church, *P.P.*, 1911, vol. 7, appendix 20, p. 107.

[264] Rev. J. V. Morgan, *Welsh Religious Leaders in the Victorian Era* (1905), p. 176.

[265] See Rev. Thomas Morgan, *The Life and Work of the Rev. Thomas Thomas, D.D.* (Carmarthen, 1925), p. 86; Winskill, op. cit., vol. 4, p. 100.

[266] Rev. Thomas Thomas, D.D., *A Course of Lectures . . . Lecture No. 6*, op. cit., p. 3.

[267] Evan Powell, *History of Carmel Baptist Chapel*, p. 85.

[268] J. R. and G. Williams, *History of Caersalem, Dowlais* (Llandysul, 1967), p. 49.

[269] Newport Public Library, MS. q MOOO (286). 48,086, Monmouthshire English Baptist Association Minute Book, vol. 1, 1857-1901.

[270] See E. T. Davies, op. cit., p. 93; N.L.W., MS. 10,506 B, 'Anti-Tradition', The distinguishing features of the Baptists, n.d., pp. 15-16. James Owen wrote that, 'We believe that God's will is to be done on earth in the polling booth and in Parliament as well as at the prayer-meeting, in the county council as well as in the missionary committee, on school boards, as well as in churches; that human life in all its relations and interests, belongs to Christ'. *The Free Churches and the People. Address at the Baptist Union of Great Britain and Ireland. Assembly at Cardiff, October 1890*, p. 29.

[271] *Circular Letter of Glamorgan and Carmarthenshire English Baptist Association* (Llanelli, 1866), p. 6.

[272] James Owen, op. cit., p. 28.

[273] For example, see *A Letter from the Ministers and Delegates of the English Association of the Glamorgan Welsh Particular Baptists at Treorchy* (1890), p. 7.

[274] D. Attwater, op. cit., p. 75.

[275] G.R.O., D/DC La/1/-2/13. Historical Notes on Roman Catholics in Glamorgan, file 5, Notes on nineteenth-century Catholicism in Cardiff and Glamorgan.

[276] Ibid., Attwater, op. cit., pp. 72, 137.

[277] Ibid., pp. 33, 38-9, 68-9, 71-2, 91, 101, 115-9, 122, 126, 129-30, 135, 207, 223-4, 275; see also *Franciscan Missions among the Colliers and Ironworkers of Monmouthshire*, pp. 22, 35.

[278] *C.M.G.*, 11 June 1853.

[279] *Monmouthshire Merlin*, 20 November 1858; *C.M.G.*, 30 April 1859.

[280] *Monmouthshire Merlin*, 1 January 1859.

[281] G.R.O., D/D/DX, ha 5/4; *Monmouthshire Merlin*, 20 November 1858; *C.M.G.*, 25 January 1868.

[282] *Monmouthshire Merlin*, 1 January 1859.

[283] *The Reformer and South Wales Times*, 1 November 1861.

[284] *Monmouthshire Merlin*, 1 January 1859; *C.M.G.*, 31 July 1869.

[285] *Monmouthshire Merlin*, 23 May 1863.

[286] *Catholic Opinion*, 5, no. 125, 7 August 1869, p. 327.

[287] See *Swansea and Glamorgan Herald*, 23 November 1859; Rev. Mathias Maurice, *Social Religion* (7th ed., 1860), pp. 235, 241-2; E. T. Davies, op. cit., p. 64; E. R. Wickham, *Church and People in an Industrial City* (1957), p. 194.

[288] E. T. Davies, op. cit., p. 85.

[289] Ibid., pp. 91-2.

[290] *The Ferrett or South Wales Ratepayer*, I, no. 5, 14 January 1871, p. 5.

[291] *South Wales Daily News*, 19 September 1892.

[292] Ibid., 21 September 1892.

[293] See *Report of the Second Triennial Conference of the English Section of the Presbyterian Church of Wales, Liverpool, 1892* (Caernarfon, 1892), p. 25.

CHAPTER V

PROHIBITION IN WALES: THE UNITED KINGDOM ALLIANCE AND THE RESORT TO POLITICAL ACTION

The most intensive political activity of the middle years of the nineteenth century was carried on, not by the traditional parties, but by a wide assortment of special interest groups. Some of these groups sprang from the increasing disillusionment of the hopes of reformers for gaining their ends through coalition with one of the major parties, and many of them saw themselves as direct heirs of the Anti-Corn Law League.[1] Some groups were a defensive reaction to attacks on interests which their supporters had hitherto believed secure. Others, including the United Kingdom Alliance, represented minority opinion and hoped, through propaganda and agitation, to swing public sentiment in their favour or to make a greater impression than their numbers warranted.

The Alliance was established in June 1853 by a group of Mancunian nonconformists headed by cotton manufacturer and Quaker, Nathaniel Card. The original aim of the Alliance was 'the total and immediate legislative suppression of the liquor traffic'.[2] According to Alliance advocates, the era of temperance reform by 'moral suasion'—by education and the provision, in some areas, of counter-attractions to the public house—had failed. 'The fruits received', maintained the evangelical Rev. Canon Evan Jenkins of Dowlais, 'have not been anything in proportion to the seed sown. Very little impression has been made on the drinking masses—very little reform and improvement is visible amongst them'.[3] The existence of the liquor traffic ensured that some reclaimed drunkards would fall back into their bad old ways.[4] Whereas the suasionist temperance societies had sought to suppress drunkenness and drinking, to stop the supply by stopping the demand, the Alliance sought to suppress intemperance by suppressing the traffic in drink— preventing the effects by preventing the supply. The Alliance did not want a law to prevent any man drinking—membership and official positions in the Alliance were open to abstainers and non-abstainers alike—but a law to prevent all men engaging in the sale of liquor. The drinker was free to brew his own beer or to obtain it in any other way

than purchase.[5] The Alliance was afraid of temptation—thus, its first
Secretary, Samuel Pope in 1856: 'It is not the desire for "drink"
which led to its enormous consumption; it is the social circumstance,
the legalised system of temptation, which has created this desire.'[6]

The Alliance complaint was that the law of the country sanctioned,
permitted and fostered drinking and drunkenness and its
concomitant evils. The liquor traffic was legalised by an Act of
parliament and 'nothing but an Act of Parliament can repeal an Act
of Parliament'. The Alliance wanted the state to declare for sobriety
and morality; it believed that the state could never be morally
indifferent: it should not only resist wrong but strive to prevent
wrong. The Alliance did not want to make moral conduct
compulsory: it wanted only to modify the environment in order to
make moral conduct feasible.[7] The recourse to legislation was
justified by the assertion that individual freedom must give way to the
requirements of society. Society guaranteed every individual his life,
property and liberty, but the very moment man used his freedom
improperly and broke the law of the land, then society withdrew its
guarantee and the man's life, property or liberty were restricted.
Strong drink interfered with the life, property and liberty of the
people. Hence society had the right to withdraw its guarantee from
the men who sold the drink.[8] Legislative restriction was necessary in
order to avert social disorganisation as intemperance had become so
great a problem that it had ceased to be under the 'moral control'
provided by society.[9] Thus 'the Temperance Movement is now
assuming a new phase, a bolder and a much more practical character.
The question now assumes a political aspect, and it must be treated in
accordance with the first principles of political science . . . The
question is now changed; total abstinence is held in abeyance, and the
agitation henceforth is to be political rather than moral, legislative
rather than social'.[10]

The move towards the use of electoral power by the temperance
movement is not surprising. Temperance electoral activity was
natural, for the enemy was the drink trade, an interest which was
thoroughly established as a powerful electoral force. It was a standing
provocation to the temperance movement and its influence made it
virtually inevitable that the temperance fight against drink would take
place, in part, within the electoral sphere. Furthermore, temperance
became a complete way of life for many of its supporters, so it was
natural that efforts should be made to include the electoral part of a

temperance advocate's existence. The Alliance made tremendous efforts to organise its voters and give them a thorough temperance political identity. Temperance electoral activity was natural for another important reason. There was a clear parallel between the taking of a teetotal pledge, and the taking of a pledge to abstain from voting for candidates who would not promise to support proposed temperance legislation. Another aspect of the temperance movement which shaped the electoral action in which it engaged was the fact that the major political arm of the United Kingdom Alliance was itself electoral—the establishment of prohibition through local polls or referenda. It was natural that prohibitionists should be greatly interested in opportunities for the utilizing of existing electoral procedures. The clash between temperance and the drink interest at a parliamentary election could be seen as a trial run for the type of electoral situation which they were striving to inaugurate on an official basis throughout Britain.*

It is important to realise that in Wales the transition from the policy of moral suasion to the policy of legislative suppression aroused no overt opposition or controversy. As the Alliance attacked only the trade in drink, Alliance supporters confirmed that moral suasonists would still be needed to fight against the manufacture and consumption of drink. Although suasionists saw that the Alliance's Permissive Bill would not solve the problem of home brewing, would rarely be enforced even if passed, and would probably promote great civic strife, and although the Alliance argued that moral suasion had made a small proportion only of the population into abstainers and had not reduced the number of drink places to any great extent, attempts were made to stress the area of common ground between the two approaches to the drink problem. Indeed, the Alliance sought to win suasionist support when it maintained that the only ground upon which legislative interference with the liquor traffic could be based was that for which temperance societies had always contended, namely, the dangerous nature of intoxicating drinks and the 'moral duty' of total abstinence from their use: 'To ask for prohibition on any other ground would be illogical and absurd.'[11] Nevertheless, by 1861-2 Welsh subscriptions to the National Temperance League, the

---

* See D. A. Hamer, *The Politics of Electoral Pressure. A Study in the History of Victorian Reform Agitations* (1977), p. 13.

national suasionist body, fell away markedly; by 1869 subscriptions from Welsh temperance societies had ceased altogether and the number of individual subscribers had fallen to four.[12]

The Permissive Bill, the instrument of the Alliance reform, was formally adopted at the Alliance annual meeting in October 1857 and was first introduced into the House of Commons by Wilfrid Lawson (Liberal, Carlisle) in 1864. The bill which, remarkably, was first suggested by a brewer, Charles Buxton, in an article entitled 'How to stop drunkenness', which appeared in the *North British Review* in 1854, was the authoritative embodiment of the objects, principles and policy of the Alliance.[13] The bill did not propose to prohibit the liquor traffic by enactment, but provided that on application of any district (parish, township or borough), the votes of the ratepayers should be cast on the question of whether the liquor traffic should exist in that district or not, a majority of two-thirds of the ratepayers being necessary to decide the question. Thus the Alliance, having realised the impracticality of its first total and immediate demand, soon rejected a 'national and imperative' policy in favour of a proposal 'local and permissive'.[14]

The Alliance demand, as embodied in the Permissive Bill, did not meet with any measure of success in parliament. Lawson introduced the bill every year he sat in the House up to 1878, but it never progressed beyond the second reading.[15] However, in 1879 the bill was dropped and in its place Lawson introduced a local option resolution, which was defeated by a much less greater margin than the Permissive Bill had been during the 1870s—and understandably so, as many Liberal M.P.s were happier to vote for a resolution than for an actual piece of legislation. Local option proposed that a tenth of the electors in any district could sign a requisition for a poll and if this in turn produced a two-thirds majority for 'no licence', all licences in the district would, after three years' warning, be withdrawn, though hotels, restaurants and railway refreshment rooms would be exempt. A later version allowed also for 'limitation', with a quarter of the local licences being suppressed after each successful poll. Local option thus came to denote a system of licensing reform, which allowed the ratepayers several choices of policy, rather than the Permissive Bill's 'all or nothing' choice. After the Liberal victory at the General Election of 1880, the tide turned and on 18 June 1880 Lawson's resolution was carried by 229 votes to 203.[16] Although Gladstone promised early action on the question, licensing was not even mentioned in the Queen's speech in 1881 or 1882, and in 1883 Lawson introduced his resolution again. Gladstone spoke in its support and it was carried by 228 votes to 141.[17] But two years later, when the government fell, no bill had yet appeared.

Alliance policy was based upon distrust of the magistrates and confidence in the ratepayers. The feeling was that licensing magistrates were not keeping proper control over the granting of licences. It was argued that borough magistrates, by the very nature of their appointment, were placed under temptations to jobbing and favouritism.[18] At Ffestiniog in the late 1880s, one of the licensing justices was an agent, on commission, of Bass and Company.[19] The granting of a licence in a locality rested with 6-8 people several of whom invariably lived outside that locality, and who were, therefore, not conversant with local conditions.[20] A common complaint was that magistrates often refused to have public houses in or near the localities in which they resided, and placed them instead in the poorer neighbourhoods.[21] Another, that unrepresentative county magistrates, appointed by the Lords Lieutenant for political service, often reversed the decisions of borough magistrates in removing or refusing to allow licences for public houses in some areas.[22] In October 1884 for instance, at Swansea Quarter Sessions, the decision of the Cardiff magistrates to refuse to renew certain licences, was reversed.[23] According to the Alliance the only remedy was to give the people the power to do what they thought fit. Drinking contributed to crime and poverty, and crime and pauperism caused an increase in the rates; ratepayers should therefore have a major say in licensing matters. They were, of necessity, interested in the question, and from their intimate knowledge of the circumstances of their own localities, were best qualified to form a judgment on the subject. The Alliance had no truck with the suggestion of transferring the power of licensing from the magistrates to a district or county board of representatives of the ratepayers, as the profit received from licences would become a great temptation to a board for which the reduction of the rates would be one of the chief aims.[24] The ratepayers must be given a 'special voice' in the matter in the form of a direct and absolute veto.

In a sense, the stress on ratepayer control of licensing embodied a conscious attempt to gain some measure of social equality with landowners, who were able to prohibit the existence of public houses on their own estates. By the mid-1860s in Wales drinking places had been prohibited on the estates of Lords Llanover and Tredegar,

C. R. M. Talbot, M.P., H. Hussey Vivian, M.P., Henry Nevill (Llanelli) and the Neath Abbey Coal and Iron Company.[25] In 1887, T. E. Ellis maintained that the 'present bad law' which regulated the liquor traffic contributed to the 'terrible chasm' between rich and poor, and that the aristocracy's power of preventing drinking places being erected and opened on its land should be extended to 'the democracy'.[26] Thus the strength and influence that the Alliance was to gain in Wales may be attributed to the fact that it was, at least partly, regarded as a vehicle for the campaign against aristocratic and agricultural ascendancy.

During the 1850s and '60s the Alliance made rapid progress in Wales. In the autumn of 1854, the Rev. Owen Jones, a Welsh Mancunian, toured north Wales, holding several meetings to explain the 'Manchester remedy', and forming auxiliaries of the parent society. The first Welsh auxiliary was established at Caernarfon in September.[27] By October, Alliance membership in Wales totalled over 1,000, including 350 electors and over 30 ministers of religion.[28] Dissemination of the cause in north Wales usually took the form of lectures on prohibition by 'exiled' Welsh ministers at chapels—chiefly those of the Calvinistic Methodists. Thus, in late 1854, the Rev. Richard Jones, Independent minister at Manchester, and the Rev. John Thomas, D.D., Independent minister at Liverpool, held a series of meetings in north-east Wales, and recruited hundreds of supporters.[29] In 1854 articles on the prohibition law operating in the state of Maine in the United States appeared in *Yr Amserau* and in *Y Gwerinwr*, which was edited by Thomas. Alliance ideas were first discussed in south Wales at two Aberdare chapels in the spring of 1855, when the Rev. Owen Jones and George Lomax of Manchester undertook a tour of lectures. Meetings were held and members enrolled at Aberdare, Merthyr, Pontypridd and Cardiff, and the Rev. Canon Evan Jenkins of Dowlais and David Davis of Maesyffynnon, near Aberdare, the coal owner, gave the movement their support.[30] By the end of 1855, 42 Alliance auxiliaries had been established in Wales, 34 of them in north Wales.[31] Progress was so marked that the Alliance asserted that Wales was ready for prohibition and that the country could possibly be selected as the 'favoured spot' in Britain where a prohibitory measure could first be tried as a 'British experiment'.[32]

The prohibitionist movement received powerful support from church and chapel in Wales. Doubtless, the church in general, and the Calvinistic Methodists in particular, were attracted by the certainty and comprehensiveness of a total prohibition law in the face of 'weak humanity' and 'brittle good intentions'. A Calvinistic Methodist minister of Minera, Wrexham, conceded the fact that moral suasion had done a great deal of good, but as long as temptation stood in the way their work as temperance advocates was futile.[33] To *Y Gwladgarwr* the Alliance cause was the cause of justice and virtue, philanthropy and religion, truth and sobriety, a cause to which the success of religion, the morals and commerce of Wales was naturally joined.[34] The Calvinistic Methodists embraced the Alliance platform wholeheartedly. Of the 181 Welsh ministers of religion who attended the Alliance's Ministerial Conference on the suppression of the liquor traffic at Manchester in June 1857, 140 were Calvinistic Methodists. The remainder comprised 34 Independents, 4 Baptists, and one each of Primitive Methodist, Wesleyan Methodist and Established Church.[35] Despite its low representation at the conference the most evangelical of the clergy of the Church in Wales supported the Alliance, and indeed, a certain degree of ecumenism was fostered by the co-operation of church and nonconformity on the issue of prohibition.[36] At an Alliance meeting at Dowlais in October 1860, Canon Jenkins came together with several nonconformist ministers and Father Millea, the Catholic priest, to advocate the Permissive Bill, while in north Wales Dean Cotton of Bangor co-operated with the leaders of local nonconformist congregations.[37]

Numerous Alliance meetings continued to be held in Wales during the late 1850s and early '60s. In 1860 Alliance agent Charles Carr delivered 76 lectures on the Alliance in the western valleys of Monmouthshire.[38] Most effort and activity were devoted to the populous industrial towns of south Wales in an effort to explain the Permissive Bill, to distribute tracts, to win the support of electors, and more especially, to augment the funds of the Alliance by subscription.[39] Two important *eisteddfod* essays explaining the prohibition law in operation in the state of Maine appeared in pamphlet form in 1857-8, and were an invaluable means of informing the monoglot Welshman of the ideas and principles of the Alliance; these were 'Cyrus', *Y Maine Law* (Bethesda, 1857) and I. Williams, *Traethawd ar Gyfraith Maine* (Denbigh, 1858). Both pamphlets received an extensive circulation, especially in north Wales. At the Eisteddfod of the Temperate Cambro-Brethren (*Eisteddfod Cymmrodorion Dirwestol*) at Merthyr in December 1856 the Alliance offered a £30 prize for the best essay in Welsh on the legislative suppression of the liquor traffic. In December 1873 the Alliance executive decided to publish a Welsh edition of abstracts from Alliance *Annual Reports* and in 1888 there was a possibility that a special Welsh language edition of *Alliance News* would soon be published. This latter plan did not materialise, but from the autumn of 1888 a special Welsh column appeared in the newspaper.

Owing to the language difficulty, early Alliance organisation in Wales, with the exception of lecturing, was carried out by native Welshmen and not by Manchester-based advocates. At a general conference held at Conway in August 1855, the Alliance executive nominated a number of the most influential supporters of the movement in Wales to act as a consulting and corresponding Welsh Committee.[40] A major task of the committee was to establish auxiliary societies of the Alliance and to convert existing temperance societies to the Alliance viewpoint. By the spring of 1857, 45 of the 64 Alliance auxiliaries in Britain were situated in Wales.[41] Unlike the temperance societies, Alliance auxiliaries had no continuous recreational rôle to play. The Alliance plan was to solicit the co-operation, by subscription, of those temperance societies in Wales which would support permissive legislation, in return for financial subsidies and assistance in the form of prohibition lectures and publications.[42] Later, in November 1882, it was decided that the Alliance grant to local auxiliaries would vary proportionately with the amount raised by subscriptions by the auxiliary.[43]

Throughout the 1870s an annual grant of £50 was made by the Alliance to the North Wales Temperance and Prohibitory Association at Bangor, and an annual grant of £150 to the South Wales Temperance and Prohibitory Association at Merthyr.[44] Such money had to be used for Alliance purposes only. Grants were made in order to enable auxiliaries to work the electoral register, that is, to compile the register of temperance electors in an effort to impress and win the co-operation of local politicians; to pay for the cost of agitation undertaken by local bodies at strategic moments, such as the progress through parliament of the Permissive Bill and the taking of canvasses and collection of petitions; and to pay for the cost of conferences on temperance legislation and the insertion of Alliance advertisements in Welsh periodicals and newspapers.[45] If the Alliance was dissatisfied with the amount of money raised by subscriptions, or with any part of the work undertaken by auxiliaries, grants were refused.[46] Indeed, the Alliance exercised a strict and almost over-bearing control over those auxiliary societies which received grants. In 1873 the Secretary of the Alliance demanded to have a copy of the annual balance sheet of the South Wales Temperance and Prohibitory Association placed before the Alliance executive, and decided that the same procedure be adopted for all the organisations receiving grants from the Alliance.[47]

At the local level the most vital function of the auxiliaries was to work for the return of candidates, at parliamentary and municipal elections, favourable to the legislative suppression of the liquor traffic. The auxiliaries were solely responsible for fighting local elections but at general elections they were very tightly controlled by the Alliance. In north Wales this function was carried out, in the main, by the North Wales Temperance Electoral Association, which was established at Wrexham in March 1868 in order to take 'electoral action to obtain due representation of the great commercial, sanitary, political and moral interests embodied in the Temperance question'.[48] A declaration, signed by 132 ministers of religion and 208 laymen, headed by C. E. Darby, the Brymbo industrialist, and Alliance advocates, William Lester and W. H. Tilston, stated that the Association would co-operate with the Alliance for the legislative suppression of the liquor traffic. The Association quickly organised local electoral committees in order to influence candidates in favour of restrictive and prohibitory measures against the sale of drink. Where contested elections occurred, the electoral committees arranged deputations to the candidates to discover their views on licensing, and the candidate favourable to restrictive legislation was supported.[49]

In 1856 the Alliance suggested the division of England and Wales into districts under superintending agents in order to sustain the interest and activity aroused by Alliance lecturers.[50] However, it was not until 1866 that this plan fully materialised. By that time the whole of England and Wales, with the exception of parts of south Wales, was covered by an organised system of agencies controlled by the Alliance executive committee.[51] The North Wales District, comprising Caernarfonshire, Anglesey, Denbighshire and Flintshire, was placed under William Thomas of Bangor; the Mid-Wales District, comprising Montgomeryshire, Merionethshire, Radnorshire and Cardiganshire, under the Rev. Richard Jones of Llanidloes, while the South Wales District—Carmarthenshire, Breconshire, Pembrokeshire and Glamorgan—was superintended directly from Manchester by the Alliance executive until 1870, when the duty was taken over by the South Wales Temperance and Prohibitory Association at Merthyr.[52] During the late 1870s, the districts were reduced to two: Anglesey, Caernarfonshire, Denbighshire, Flintshire, Montgomeryshire, Merionethshire and Cardiganshire, coming under the superintendence of H. J. Williams ('Plenydd') of Chwilog and, from 1887, his assistant, D. R. Daniel, and Glamorgan, Carmarthenshire, Pembrokeshire, Breconshire, Radnorshire and Monmouthshire, coming under the superintendence of Ebenezer Beaven, a Cardiff town councillor. Both Williams and Beaven were full-time, paid employees of the Alliance.

Intensification of its electoral activity in 1872 caused the Alliance to delegate authority to the two major auxiliaries in Wales to set up a system of electoral agency. It is not surprising that in this era of 'combative dissent' the task in each case was entrusted to a nonconformist minister. Both North and South Wales Districts were therefore divided into sub-districts, to each of which was appropriated an electoral sub-committee and an electoral agent. The agents were directed to compile registers of all borough and county electors in their districts, and to ensure that, as far as possible, parliamentary candidates were 'right' on items of temperance legislation.[53]

Apart from political work, the superintending agents also promoted petitions, acquainted themselves with current temperance literature, collected funds, held meetings and kept a keen watch on the activities of local publicans.[54] Agents had to obtain the permission of the Alliance to engage the speakers they wanted at local meetings and the Alliance always stipulated that at such meetings local option resolutions were to be submitted and later sent to the Home Secretary and local M.P.s, and that subscriptions or collections were to be obtained and forwarded to Alliance funds.[55] An essential task of the agents was to visit London to lobby M.P.s on temperance issues and to mobilise support for any bill dealing with the liquor traffic which was before parliament. Ebenezer Beaven visited London in March 1886 to urge upon Welsh members the necessity of legislation to curb the growth of drinking clubs in Cardiff, while in June 1888 Beaven and John Cory, the Cardiff industrialist, Liberal Unionist and strong Alliance advocate, went to the Commons to interview Unionist members on the compensation clauses of the Local Government Bill.[56] During the early 1890s, the Alliance worked also through two Welsh Liberal M.P.s, T.E. Ellis, who became a Vice-President of the Alliance in 1892, and David Lloyd

George. Both were regarded by the Alliance as 'Temperance Whips'
for the Welsh members, their duty being to ensure a large attendance
of Welsh members in the House when an important licensing bill was
before parliament.[57] Lloyd George was paid by the Alliance for
speaking at several meetings in England during the months
immediately following his election to parliament in April 1890, and in
1889 he had been instrumental in securing the adoption of direct veto
of the liquor traffic by the National Liberal Federation meeting at
Manchester.[58]

An important aspect of Alliance organisation and agitation in
Wales, carried out by auxiliaries and agents, was the taking of
canvasses, or plebiscites as the Alliance preferred to call them, on the
Permissive Bill and on local option. On such occasions the views of
householders, voters and 'other male adults', were tabulated, printed
in the *Alliance News* and the *Annual Report*, and very often sent to
M.P.s. Two examples of Alliance canvasses in Wales are given in
Appendix I. They showed an overwhelming majority in favour of
restrictive legislation on the drink issue. Suffice it to say, however,
that the results of such canvasses should not be taken at their face
value. No canvass could indicate the *intensity* of support for
prohibition. No Alliance canvass in Wales was completely national in
its scope. Moreover, the questions offered few alternatives and may
have been framed in a prejudicial way. Most serious of all, most of
the canvasses were restricted to householders: they did not penetrate
the hard-drinking residuum.[59] Petitions, another device favoured by
the Alliance, were often organised at places of worship where there
was a suspicion that the 'chapel screw' could be applied. The number
of petitions did not correlate with the intensity of feeling on the issue
and their numbers could be turned on and off like a tap.
Nevertheless, canvasses and petitions convinced the Alliance that in
Britain as a whole, it enjoyed the support of an élite among working
men.

Between 1856 and 1895 Alliance income from all British sources
increased from £1,888 to £11,800, a six-fold increase.[60] The greatest
amount subscribed in any one year was £19,013 (1873). During the
same period, Alliance income from Wales increased 22-fold, from
£33 in 1856 to £509 in 1895, the highest annual subscription being
£591, given in 1889 (see Figs. 1 and 2). Welsh subscription to the
Alliance was derived from three major sources: individuals, Alliance
auxiliaries and independent temperance societies and collections

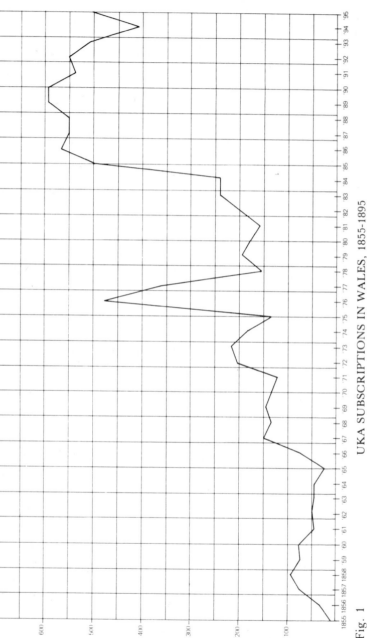

Fig. 1 UKA SUBSCRIPTIONS IN WALES, 1855-1895

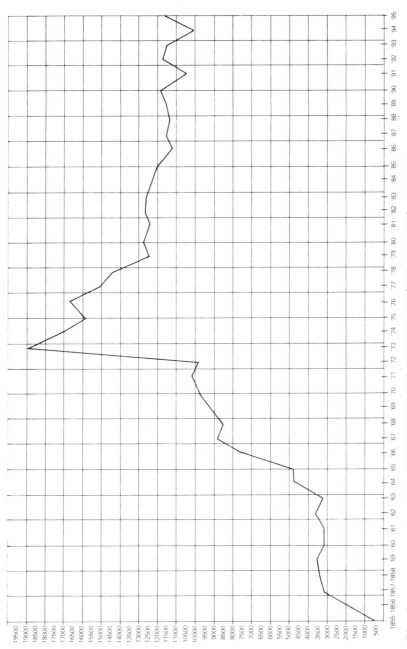

Fig. 2   UKA SUBSCRIPTIONS IN BRITAIN [INC. WALES], 1855-1895

from nonconformist chapels. This last source amounted to only £44, or 0.5 per cent of the Welsh total of £9,490 contributed to the Alliance from Wales between 1856 and 1895. Of this total of £44, over £30 was given during the period 1858-66.

During the years of religious revival, 1859-60, donations from chapels trebled, from £3. 10s. to £15. 5s. From 1866, however, Alliance auxiliaries were formed increasingly in Wales and quite possibly sympathetic chapel members started to donate money through these auxiliaries rather than through chapels. Table 9 below shows the annual Welsh subscription to the Alliance from all three sources of revenue, expressed as a percentage of the British total.

TABLE 9.   UKA SUBSCRIPTIONS FROM WELSH SOURCES, 1856-1895

Year	British Total (£)	Welsh Total	Number of Welsh Subscribers	Welsh Percentage
1856	1,888	33	11	1.9
1857	3,178	78	9	2.4
1858	3,337	92	13	2.9
1859	3,567	75	34	2.1
1860	3,396	78	48	2.4
1861	3,390	49	31	1.3
1862	3,580	50	32	1.2
1863	3,260	46	29	1.7
1864	4,715	45	39	0.9
1865	4,720	26	17	0.6
1866	8,112	74	39	0.8
1867	8,930	149	100	1.8
1868	8,570	136	100	1.5
1869	9,180	146	105	1.3
1870	9,770	133	124	1.2
1871	10,085	121	114	1.1
1872	9,702	205	180	2.1
1873	19,013	216	154	1.1
1874	16,813	183	151	1.1
1875	15,760	138	122	0.9
1876	16,740	477	198	2.9
1877	15,040	362	182	2.4
1878	14,350	158	262	1.1
1879	12,433	195	250	1.5
1880	12,710	179	241	1.4
1881	12,391	160	208	1.3
1882	12,598	201	210	1.6
1883	12,446	238	257	1.9
1884	12,060	237	240	2

TABLE 9.   UKA SUBSCRIPTIONS FROM WELSH SOURCES,
1856-1895—continued

Year	British Total (£)	Welsh Total	Number of Welsh Subscribers	Welsh Percentage
1885	11,998	495	718	4.1
1886	11,205	567	740	5.1
1887	11,398	550	758	4.9
1888	11,305	549	805	4.9
1889	11,400	591	858	5.1
1890	11,800	590	707	5
1891	10,745	536	690	5.1
1892	11,889	552	690	4.9
1893	11,567	505	646	4.2
1894	10,205	406	525	4
1895	11,800	509	611	4.2

From the above statistics the following developments are noticeable. First, Welsh subscriptions doubled between 1866 and 1867, from £74 to £149, while the British total increased only from £8,112 to £8,930. Second, the great British increase between 1872 and 1873, when subscriptions doubled from £9,702 to £19,013, was not mirrored in Wales, where subscriptions increased only from £205 to £216. Third, in Wales between 1875 and 1876 subscriptions more than trebled (£138 to £477), while the British increase was from £15,760 to £16,740 only. Fourth, in Wales between 1877 and 1878 subscriptions were halved from £362 to £158, while the British total was reduced by £700 only. Fifth, between 1884 and 1885 Welsh subscriptions more than doubled, while the British total declined slightly. Sixth, during the decade 1885-95 the Welsh total gradually increased, reaching a peak of £591 in 1889; Tom Ellis wrote to D. R. Daniel in October 1889, witnessing the fact that Welsh temperance organisations 'seem to have had a rekindling of energy with the awakening of Wales'.[61] But during the same period there was no corresponding increase in the British total which, after reaching its peak in 1873, declined and remained steady at an average of £12,400 a year in the early 1880s, and at £11,600 in the late 1880s and early '90s. Last, eleven subscriptions were received from Wales in 1856 and 34 in 1859. Between 1859 and 1864, the average number of Welsh subscribers was 35. In 1865 this number was halved to 17. A great increase is noticeable between 1866 and 1867, from 39 to 100 subscribers; the number of subscribers remained at an average of 110 up to 1871; thereafter the statistics show that between 1871 and 1872 there was an increase from 114 to 180; between 1872 and 1876, an annual average of 150 subscribers; and between 1876 and 1884, an annual average of 240 subscribers. In 1885 the number trebled from 240 to 718, and reached a peak of 858 in 1889. During the early 1890s the number declined to an average of 605 a year.

How can we explain these changes? The Welsh peaks, in amount of money subscribed, were reached in 1867, 1872, 1875 and 1885. There is no doubt that the Reform Acts of 1867 and 1884, with the widening of the franchise, increased people's awareness of the possibility of political action, and therefore increased the number of electors in Wales who would be interested in temperance legislation. In 1884-5 the Welsh county electorate increased from 74,936 to 200,373. It is noticeable that accretions of support came to the Alliance during any great legislative effort that was made at Westminster: the Licensing Act of 1872, the Welsh Sunday Closing Act of 1881 and the Welsh Veto Bills of the early '90s. There is no evidence that fluctuations in funds were connected with the *per capita* consumption of alcohol. The highest Welsh subscription of £591 in 1889 may be attributed to the appeal for funds caused by the Alliance agitation against the proposals for the compensation of publicans in the Local Government Bill of 1888, and to the desire of Welsh temperance supporters to retain the Act they had won in 1881 and to show their solidarity for the commission of inquiry into the Sunday Closing Act, which sat in Wales during 1889. The great increase of 1876 was due mainly to the large contribution of £250 from industrialist David Davies of Llandinam. Except for the year 1885 in Wales, there is, surprisingly perhaps, no correlation between increased subscriptions and years of general elections, both for the British and the Welsh totals.

The area of greatest financial support for the Alliance in Wales in the 1850s was south Wales, where 29 places subscribed between 1856 and 1860; in north Wales, during the same period, 18 places subscribed. In 1861, however, the number of places subscribing in north Wales increased five-fold (from 4 to 20) while the number of places in south Wales only doubled. During the following decade growth was more marked in the north, but from the mid-70s the number of places subscribing in south Wales increased greatly, doubling in 1876 from 17 to 34. Thereafter, subscriptions from south Wales amounted to 55 per cent of the total number of Welsh places subscribing, and north Wales, 45 per cent. The greatest increase during the period was in 1885, when thousands of working-class men were enfranchised and when the number of places subscribing in north Wales trebled from 21 to 64 and the number of places in south Wales doubled from 30 to 65. The dominant growth in south Wales was essentially in the industrial areas, where Newport, Cardiff, Aberdare, Merthyr, Neath, Swansea and Llanelli were the first communities to support the Alliance. The agricultural Vale of Glamorgan was totally unrepresented. In north Wales, the most important large centres of growth and support were Wrexham, which, as a result of the philanthropic activities of the Darby brothers, gave 47 per cent of the Welsh total in 1861, and 49 per cent in 1866, Holywell and Caernarfon. In 1867 the Alliance made inroads in mid-Wales, where first subscriptions were received from Llanidloes, Llanbrynmair, Newtown, Caersws and Machynlleth, and Alliance growth in this area increased during the early 1870s.

Between 1856 and 1878 the average Welsh subscription varied between £1 and £1. 15s., though it reached a peak of £2. 7s. 6d. in 1876. From 1878 the number of subscribers and the places of subscription gradually increased and reached a high plateau between 1885 and 1890, but the total amount of money given did not rise correspondingly; that is, more people in more places were subscribing less money per head: between 1878 and 1895 the average individual subscription was 13s.[62] It may be that this increase in small subscriptions was a result of the Reform and Redistribution Acts of 1884-5, which brought into effective political usefulness working-class social groups such as farm labourers and miners.

Most of the major individual donors to the Alliance in Wales were people whose business lay in industrial manufacture and who were imbued with ideas of self-help and business integrity. Essentially, they were progressive employers, Liberal in political inclination, non-conformist in religion, and restless for social progress. In Glamorgan, for example, John and Richard Cory, and in Denbighshire, Charles and W. H. Darby, opened up new sources of local wealth through exploiting mineral deposits. Several such donors contributed to the Alliance's Special Guarantee Funds of 1867 and 1870-75.

Many of these subscribers shared a common fund of radical ideas. John Cory (1828-1910), a Wesleyan Methodist, became a Vice-President of the Alliance in 1885. He also supported the Liberation Society; during the 1890s his benefactions amounted to nearly £50,000 a year.[63] C. E. Darby (1822-1884), the Brymbo iron and

TABLE 10.   UNITED KINGDOM ALLIANCE SPECIAL GUARANTEE
FUNDS IN WALES, 1867, 1870-5

	1867 (£50,000 fund)	1870-75 (£100,000 fund)
C. E. Darby, Brymbo	100	100
W. H. Darby, Brymbo	25	—
C. and H. Bath, Swansea	100	—
David Davis, Maesyffynnon	—	25
J. and R. Cory, Cardiff	125	85
William Lester, Wrexham	25	10
John Lewis, Haverfordwest	25	—
W. L. Daniel, Merthyr	—	10
James Jenkins, Machynlleth	—	10
William Thomas, Wrexham	—	10
W. T. Raper, Cardiff	—	10
Rev. Richard Jones, Llanidloes	—	10
Robert Nurse, Machen	—	50
Thomas Williams, Gwaelodygarth	20	25
David Davies, Llandinam	—	20
Thomas Owens, Holywell	—	20
Rev. Evan Jenkins, Welshpool	—	15
Edward Phillips, Newport	—	15

coal proprietor and Quaker, was also actively interested in the
Reform League, the Peace Society and the Liberation Society; he
gave £300 to the Liberation Society's Special Welsh fund in 1884. His
brother, W. H. Darby (1819-1882), was a powerful advocate of
prohibition and extremely active in philanthropic work. He served as
president of several temperance organisations in north Wales and
worked for the establishment of British Schools for all denominations.
For some years he was associated with Hugh Owen in the
management of the Normal College at Bangor. A champion of free
trade and a vigorous opponent of church rates, he considerably
improved the Liberal registration in Denbighshire.[64] The self-made
industrialist and Liberal M.P., David Davies of Llandinam
(1818-1890), a Calvinistic Methodist deacon and a rigid puritan, was
the largest single Welsh subscriber to the Alliance in any one year:
£250 in 1876 and the same amount again in 1877; the Alliance made
him a Vice-President in 1876. Together with the Cory brothers and
David Davis, Maesyffynnon (1821-1884), 'the Gladstone of Wales',
he promoted the construction of Barry Docks and railway (1884-89),
which broke the monopoly of the Bute Docks and the Taff Vale
Railway.[65]

The basis of Alliance support in Merthyr Tydfil lay with Thomas Williams, J.P., Gwaelodygarth (1823-1903) and W. L. Daniel (d. 1907), both of whom were Independent deacons and chairman and secretary, respectively, of Merthyr Liberal Association during the 1880s and 1890s. Both were men of considerable standing in the community. Daniel regarded the drink question as 'the first in his political creed'. He held the offices of Official Receiver and High Constable of Merthyr in the 1880s and was the chief organiser behind the efforts to return C. H. James and Henry Richard to parliament as Liberal members at the general election of 1880.[66] Thomas Williams, a director of the Great Western Colliery Company, was a very generous supporter of the Liberation Society and the Peace Society as well as the Alliance. An extremely vigorous nonconformist radical, he became the epitome of combative dissent in nineteenth-century Merthyr.[67]

*   *   *   *

As has been seen the Alliance kept its auxiliary bodies on an extremely tight rein. For this reason Alliance organisation in north Wales did not run very smoothly and the prohibition campaign there was seriously retarded by the quarrel that occurred between Alliance agents, H. J. Williams and D. R. Daniel on the one hand, and the Alliance executive at Manchester on the other. As early as 1877, William Thomas, then the Alliance agent in north Wales, informed the Alliance that he was unable to arrange sufficient meetings to fill up his time, and in January 1882 the Alliance executive expressed dismay at the lack of activity in north Wales.[68] In December 1888 the executive informed H. J. Williams that they were very doubtful of the utility of the meetings held in north Wales; the North Wales District had incurred a loss to the Alliance of over £90 for the financial year 1887-88.[69] Williams maintained that the Alliance expected far too much of him and that his salary was grossly inadequate.[70] The root cause of the difficulty encountered by the Alliance in working the North Wales District was that only two officials—a superintending agent and his assistant—were employed to cover seven counties. A better system would have been to retain the one superintending agent for the whole district but also appoint one assistant agent to each county; however, Alliance funds probably obviated such a scheme.[71]

Several other factors combined to disrupt Alliance work in north Wales in the early 1890s. The funds of the Alliance were in a parlous

condition after the costly struggle against the proposed compensation
to publicans during the period 1888-90, and in north Wales the
problem was exacerbated from 1891 by the serious illness of
Williams, which meant that subscriptions to the Alliance from north
Wales fell away markedly, D. R. Daniel being unable to cope with
the considerable amount of work that was thrust upon him.[72] By the
summer of 1893 the Alliance overdraft reached a new peak and a call
went out to Daniel for increased subscriptions. But little extra
money was raised and in August 1894 the Alliance decided that
Daniel's engagement was to be terminated on 31 December, 'in view
of the financial condition of the organisation'.[73] However, due to the
powerful intervention of his friend and Alliance Vice-President, Tom
Ellis, Daniel was retained.[74] The second disruptive factor was that
the Alliance was incensed with Daniel because of the way in which
William Rathbone was 'allowed' to be returned for Caernarfonshire
at the general election of 1892 without having given a definite pledge
to support the direct veto.[75] Thirdly, Daniel, on Ellis' advice, refused
to institute the Alliance policy of forming direct veto associations in
north Wales constituencies, agreeing with Ellis that there was no need
for special associations and that the conventional temperance societies
and the religious *seiadau* would more suitably perform the function.[76]
Fourthly, great bitterness was engendered by the fact that the
Alliance expected its agents to concentrate with exclusive single-
mindedness of purpose on Alliance tasks, and to reject entirely any
other interests. In October 1876, the Alliance had instructed the
district agents and all other salaried officials of the Alliance not to
enter into any other engagements of a business or professional
character without the express sanction of the Alliance executive.[77]
Consequently, the executive was extremely annoyed when Daniel
was elected to his parish council in November 1891 without first
having consulted the Alliance.[78] Furthermore, in March 1895,
Daniel was elected an alderman of the recently-formed County
Council of Caernarfonshire, became chairman of the parish council
and was elected a delegate for a local Liberal association.[79] The
Alliance voiced strong objections to Daniel's having taken such
offices.[80] Daniel's reaction was to turn to Ellis for advice. He wrote to
Ellis bitterly castigating the Alliance executive as 'pathetic' and
'thoroughly incompetent' to supervise the Welsh section of their
organisation. 'It is high time', he asserted, 'that this should be made
plain to earnest temperance reformers like Lawson. John Herbert

Roberts* has not enough grit in him. Most of their English representatives are local preachers with the Wesleyans or Baptists, and don't you think that *adds* to the prestige of temperance speakers in England? We also in Wales should have the benefit of positions that give us the best standing with the public.' Daniel was determined not to yield: 'A career on the staff of the Alliance means political and civic suicide and the sacrifices they demand of one are more than any self-respecting man can make'.[81] Once more, however, Ellis stepped into the breach and ensured that Daniel would stay in his post; Ellis drafted a letter to the Alliance, written and signed by Daniel, arguing that an aldermanship would give the Alliance cause much prestige in Caernarfonshire, and that if ever the Alliance's local veto bill became law, Daniel, as the chairman of the parish council, would be able to secure the complete application of the act.[82] Under such pressure, the Alliance finally agreed that Daniel should be retained as an agent.

During the 1850s and '60s, the actual political work of the Alliance consisted of demanding pledges from the candidates at elections. The means adopted by local Alliance workers to discover a candidate's views was the Alliance test question: 'Will you, if elected, support a measure to confer upon a majority of two-thirds of the ratepayers of any borough, parish or township, the power to prohibit the sale of intoxicating liquors within their respective district?' At the general election of 1868 the Alliance maintained strict neutrality outside the traditional parties and refrained from spending money in favour of particular candidates out of consideration of the political sensitivities of its subscribers.[83] But it overplayed its hand. The pledge it demanded as a condition of support for a candidate or of refraining from opposing him was a very stringent one because the candidate had to support the particular measure advocated by the Alliance and no other, and this turned out to be more likely to hurt Alliance friends than Alliance foes, for a moderate temperance reformer might boggle at giving their pledge and therefore lose the support of the Alliance, while a candidate who had no interest in temperance reform at all would not be troubled by it since he could never have hoped to gain support from any people whom they influenced.

To make clear both to voters and to parliamentary candidates the existence of a withholdable temperance vote, the Alliance developed

---

* John Herbert Roberts (1863-1955): Liberal member for West Denbighshire, 1892-1918; created Baron Clwyd, 1919.

the idea of committing voters well in advance of an election to vote only for candidates who gave a pledge, and the usual method of doing this was to canvas electors to subscribe their signatures to a pledge. The crucial question was how far temperance voters were prepared to go on withholding their votes altogether when there was no candidate who completely satisfied their demands. Such a strategy meant that the voter might have to abstain and so enable a Conservative candidate who was totally opposed to temperance legislation to win over a Liberal, who was perhaps only partially in favour. The choice was between voting for the better man and refusing to vote for anyone who did not measure up completely to one's standards. Up to 1872, at least, the 'better man' strategy was adopted in contests between a total opponent and a 'lukewarm' supporter.

By 1872 the Alliance had realised these deficiencies in its electoral policy as an Alliance deputation in favour of local option was flatly refused by Lord Kimberley, the sponsor of H. A. Bruce's Licensing Bill of 1872 in the House of Lords, on the ground that the Alliance did not represent the popular view.[84] Consequently, in September 1872 the Alliance adopted a policy of 'direct action'. It was decided that whenever a vacancy occurred in the representation of any constituency the electors would be recommended to nominate a candidate who was in favour of the Permissive Bill, irrespective of party, 'and the Council of the U.K.A. pledges itself to give such candidate every possible support by deputation, lectures and the distribution of publications. In the event of any constituency being unable to procure a suitable candidate the Council pledges itself to find candidates so as to afford every elector an opportunity of recording his vote in favour of the Permissive Bill, until the question be decided.'[85] This was a decision to force the pace in the constituencies; it was a clear commitment to a strategy based on independent candidates rather than on abstention by voters. In future, the electors would have an out-and-out Permissive Bill man for whom to vote, the implication being ˌeven stronger that the Alliance voter would be called upon to put the Permissive Bill or local option before all other public questions, and to vote irrespective of party for the Alliance candidates. In 1873 the Alliance established an electoral department with a full-time organising secretary to devote its attention to the organisation of the constituencies, and established an election fund which was kept distinct from the main body of Alliance funds.[86] In the same year Alliance representatives were

recognised in the registration courts along with the Liberal and
Conservative agents as having an interest in the revision of registers.

The effect of the adoption of 'direct action' as Alliance policy was
to split the temperance movement in Wales. As a voter, the
temperance advocate was asked to make his vote turn entirely on
whether a candidate gave a satisfactory pledge on the temperance
issue and this was to ask the voter to throw away his vote except in so
far as temperance reform was concerned. Unless the voter was
fanatically interested in temperance reform, or had no interest in any
other subject, he would not do this. At the annual meetings of the
North Wales Temperance and Prohibitory Association at Llandudno
in October 1873, a resolution calling upon the temperance electors of
north Wales to vote for Permissive Bill candidates, irrespective of
their party politics, was carried by the narrow majority of two, 51
voting in favour and 49 against.[87] A notable dissentient was the early
Alliance supporter, the Rev. John Thomas of Liverpool, who, in
voting against the motion, maintained that he did not wish to be
compromised on other political questions which he considered to be
as equally important as the temperance question.[88] Thomas was at
pains to stress that he objected, not to the policy of the Alliance, but to
the method of procedure. The Permissive Bill would be made the
major issue in every election and other items of national interest in
politics, such as disestablishment, would be neglected. Moreover,
Thomas realized that more Liberals than Conservatives supported
the Alliance and that the new policy, if carried out to the letter
throughout the country, would have a disastrous effect on the
fortunes of the Liberal party: there would be no point whatsoever in
bringing candidates forward if they had no chance of winning.
Indeed, it was believed by some Liberals that the Alliance was trying
to force its policy on the Liberal party by threatening to split its
vote.[89] Like many other Welsh nonconformists who were also
temperance advocates, John Thomas was not prepared to sacrifice his
radicalism to prohibition, and he maintained that although he himself
would never vote for a Conservative who advocated the Permissive
Bill, the result of the new Alliance policy would indeed be to split the
Liberal vote, and of course a weakened Liberal party would be less
likely and less able to press for other favoured radical issues such as
disestablishment.[90]

On the other hand there were those extreme temperance zealots in
Wales who were determined to give their votes only to the candidate

who would pledge support for Alliance policy. In October 1878, Thomas Cordes, Conservative M.P. for Monmouthshire, was presented with a declaration, signed by 400 burgesses of Newport, which maintained that in any future election, they would not vote for a candidate who refused to support the Permissive Bill. 'The acceptance of our measure', said Newport temperance reformer, Samuel Harse, 'is the one and only condition of our support.'[91]

The Alliance test question was put to a few candidates only for Welsh seats at the 1859 general election. In the Swansea and Merthyr Boroughs, Dillwyn and Bruce respectively refused to support the Permissive Bill, claiming it to be a piece of class legislation. Both were returned at the election as was W. O. Stanley (Liberal, Beaumaris), the only candidate in north Wales who is recorded as having pledged himself to support the bill.[92] The occasion of the 1868 general election witnessed a wider area of operations by the Alliance in Wales. Again, the test question was put to parliamentary candidates by local Alliance workers. The widening of the franchise, as embodied in the Reform Act of 1867, was heavily stressed. At Merthyr, D. E. Williams of Hirwaun and Thomas Williams of Gwaelodygarth, in seeking the views of Henry Richard on the Permissive Bill, emphasized the fact that there were already 200 temperance electors in the constituency and claimed that under the new Act 'we shall have at least ten times the present number while the publican interest will be exactly the same number under the Bill as at present.'[93] The only Welsh member who had voted for the Permissive Bill on its introduction into the Commons in 1864 was John Hanmer (Flint Boroughs), W. O. Stanley not having voted for it at the last moment. But as a result of the 1868 election, a further seven members favourable to the Permissive Bill, or at least to a thorough revision of the licensing system, were returned, all of them from north Wales constituencies. These were Richard Davies (Anglesey County), Stanley, who again promised to support the bill, Captain L. Jones Parry (Caernarfonshire), W. Bulkeley Hughes (Caernarfon Borough), G. Osborne Morgan (Denbighshire), Watkin Williams (Denbigh Borough), and David Williams (Merionethshire). Lord Richard Grosvenor (Flintshire) and C. R. D. Hanbury-Tracy (Montgomery Boroughs) were both described as being 'lukewarm', while C. W. Wynn (Montgomeryshire) was implacably opposed to any temperance legislation.[94]

The weakness of the Alliance position, of course, was that a candidate's pledge was no real guarantee that he would support the Permissive Bill in the division lobby. In 1869 both Jones Parry and Watkin Williams suffered from terminal terror, Parry voting against the bill and Williams abstaining from voting. The failure of Williams to keep his pledge led to an acrimonious correspondence between him and the North Wales Temperance and Electoral Association. In a letter to the Association Williams maintained that his confidence in the Permissive Bill had been shaken by the 'importunate and almost disingenuous manner in which some members of your association endeavoured to draw me into declarations in favour of that measure', and that he had promised to give the bill 'the most deliberate and anxious consideration', which was all the Association had asked of him.[95] The Association replied that Williams had promised to vote for the bill and that the executive of the Association 'took action' upon the faith of that promise 'by which your election was materially assisted'.[96] Feelings remained embittered, for in January 1874 Williams made a public attack on the Permissive Bill, and the Alliance suggested that temperance electors should try to oust Williams at the forthcoming general election.[97] But the Alliance climbed down; after a meeting with Williams, local Alliance supporters decided to support him at the election provided he would not vote against the Permissive Bill and would support Sunday closing. The Alliance executive approved this decision.[98] It seems that either the Alliance was leaning over backwards to support a Liberal candidate, or that George Kenyon, the Conservative candidate for Denbigh, was implacably opposed to any form of restrictive legislation on the drink issue. Watkin Williams, however, despite the help he received from the Alliance at the election, remained intransigent and voted against the bill in June 1874.[99] In 1880, after a difference of opinion with his constituents over the Permissive Bill, Williams left Denbigh and stood for Caernarfonshire.

The Alliance was able to make greater efforts at by-elections when resources could be focused on a particular constituency. Table 11 shows the outcome of the by-elections in which the Alliance played a part. Only for the Montgomeryshire by-election of 1894 do we possess any detail about a campaign. A. C. Humphreys-Owen, the Liberal candidate, was a temperance supporter who had closed a public house on his estate at Berriew, and he strongly advocated the use of legislation in removing the temptation to drink.[100] His opponent, Robert Williams-Wynn (Conservative), was supported by the publicans. The London-based Licensed Victuallers National Defence League rented an office in Welshpool and sent up a staff of agents who went through the county disseminating trade literature in the form of handbills, claiming that the brewers and publicans were the strongest supporters of the farming community and of the national revenue.[101] But Humphreys-Owen was returned by a majority of 225.

In many instances one suspects that the candidates who pledged themselves, if elected, to support Alliance policy, were not totally sincere, and merely went through the motions of promising adherence to Alliance doctrine in order to gain a quick, short-term political advantage. For it must be emphasized that the extreme Alliance policy, as embodied in the Permissive Bill and the policy of 'direct action' after 1872, was not at all popular among some Welsh M.P.s and among other leaders of Welsh opinion. Many voiced the criticism that the Permissive Bill was an item of class legislation in the sense that if it ever became law, the poor, unlike the rich, would be unable to keep a private cellar, and thus be unable to brew their own beer.[102] It was claimed by some, with justification, that the bill was undemocratic, as the majority of voters for the bill would be by no means the majority of the persons who would be affected by the granting or withholding of a licence. The bill was unjust, therefore, because it conferred on two-thirds of the ratepayers the right to legislate for all the people. The rights of non-electors would be swamped. Far from 'elevating' working men, a permissive pro-hibitory liquor law would make slaves of them by 'putting them to do the bidding of a section of the ratepayers'.[103]

At an election meeting at Dowlais in August 1868 Henry Austin Bruce noted that there were two questions only on which he and his constituents differed: the ballot and the Permissive Bill.[104] Bruce had voted against the bill in 1865 in spite of having been presented with a petition signed by 30,000 of his constituents urging him to support the measure, and on 25 July 1865 he met his constituents at the Temperance Hall in Merthyr to explain the reasons for his action. Bruce was convinced that drunkenness was on the decrease and that this was a result of the 'spread of education' and the 'attainment of a higher moral feeling'. For him, the Permissive Bill was far too stringent: hardship would be inflicted upon nineteen sober people in order to save the twentieth from drunkenness.[105] Moreover, at first he was opposed to giving any legislative authority to a majority of ratepayers.[106] Bruce admitted that something had to be done to decrease the number and improve the character of public houses; his plan was to restrict licences to houses of a high rateable value and to take steps to ensure the reality of that value. He considered that if beer could be sold in houses properly rated at £20 p.a., the number of public houses would greatly diminish and the business would pass into more respectable hands.[107] By 1871, however, Bruce, although maintaining that he was still opposed to the Permissive Bill as such, was willing to concede that he thought the measure contained a 'very valuable and wholesome principle', that of ratepayer control.[108] Indeed, his Licensing Bill of 1871 provided for the regulation by ratepayers of the number of public houses and the extent of adulteration of beer.

For Richard Fothergill, who, with Henry Richard, represented Merthyr Tydfil during the 1870s, the Permissive Bill, if enacted, would bring riot and bloodshed. He explained to Alliance supporter W. L. Daniel that in deference to the wishes of his constituents he had not voted against the bill in 1870 but had abstained, and he believed that those M.P.s who voted for the measure did so in order to please a well-meaning section of their constituents as they knew that the bill would never pass.[109] It is possible, however, that Fothergill's real fear was not so much the rather exaggerated spectre of violence following upon the implementation of the Permissive Bill, but the fear that if such a law came into operation in Merthyr and Dowlais, the majority of his workmen might migrate permanently to those neighbouring areas of Monmouthshire—Rhymney, Tredegar and Nantyglo—where work and drink could be obtained.

The most common, but probably the most powerful, argument used against the Permissive Bill was that it was grossly impractical. H. Hussey Vivian (Glamorgan) believed that those who advocated the bill were 'wasting the force' of the temperance movement on an 'unworkable' measure: 'I altogether deny the right of any man or any number of men to say to his neighbour "You shall not eat or drink this particular thing." It may be said I voted for Sir W. Lawson's Bill: true, I have done so in one shape or another. Since I have been in Parliament I have voted in favour of every measure calculated to reduce intemperance, but I have done so in the sense that it is utterly impossible that such a policy as Lawson's should become law, and simply in the sense of entering my earnest protest that stringent legislation on this matter must be undertaken.'[110] Similarly, C. R. M. Talbot, Vivian's fellow-member for Glamorgan, had voted for the measure largely, as he admitted, in deference to the numerous petitions he had received, but he thought that the bill must be improved between the second and third readings; if this was not done he could not vote for it on the third reading. He was convinced that in persevering with the Permissive Bill in its present state 'they were firing a large amount of blank cartridge' against the liquor traffic.[111]

Unable to support absolute prohibition Vivian did intimate that he would support any measure to enable a community to reduce, but not totally prohibit, the number of public houses to any number it pleased, consistent with the legitimate wants of that community.[112] Here, Vivian was resurrecting the ideas contained in the most comprehensive statement on liquor licensing made by a Welshman in the nineteenth century: the views of Thomas Gee, Alliance supporter and editor of *Baner ac Amserau Cymru*.

Gee had been a temperance advocate since 1830, when, at the age of fifteen, he had signed a moderation pledge, and during the 1840s he had been secretary of *Cymdeithas Llwyr-Ymattaliad Dinbych*.[113] In 1866 and 1869 Gee published two pamphlets which publicly questioned the policy of the Alliance: *Our Licensing System considered. Friendly Suggestions for a change in the 'Permissive Bill' of the U.K.A. A letter addressed to the General Council,* and *Suggestions for a change in the Licensing Laws.*[114] He pointed out that the weakness of the Permissive Bill was that it left no option between entire suppression of the liquor traffic and almost indiscriminate licensing.[115] The Alliance should be criticised for not being favourable to a restriction of the traffic or to a gradual change for the better in those areas where immediate and total suppression was considered impractical or inadvisable.[116] Gee agreed with the Alliance that power should be transferred from magistrates and excise officers to the ratepayers alone; but he maintained further that the ratepayers should not be confined to the question of 'immediate and total suppression' but have *'the full and individual control of the system, whether such be for the extinction or the limitation of the traffic'.*[117] Thus Gee proposed to place the word 'control', instead of both 'prevent' and 'prohibit', in the Permissive Bill, so that the bill would be one 'to enable owners and occupiers of property to control the common sale of intoxicating drinks'.

In Gee's scheme, the powers conferred on the ratepayers were to be exercised at a special annual vestry or other meeting held for that purpose before the annual licensing session. The powers included the power of increasing, continuing or diminishing, and also of suppressing, at the ratepayers' own discretion, the number of public houses in their respective parishes or districts, and the power of fixing the conditions of all licences issued, including Sunday trade and the hours of opening and closing.[118] Gee suggested that when the vote of the vestry was for total suppression, the votes of two-thirds of the ratepayers should be required, but that a simple majority would be sufficient for limitation and for all other purposes of the bill.[119] If the vote was in favour of increasing the number of licensed houses or of extending their privileges, the licensing magistrates were to have a power of veto upon the same. The only other power left to the magistrates would be to licence those houses which were approved by the ratepayers.[120] If the vestry voted for a reduction in the number of public houses—say, by ten—the ratepayers would be supplied with lists of all the houses in the parish and they would strike out the ten which they considered the most objectionable.[121] In this way the scheme would ensure that the character of licensed houses would be improved, as their tenants would know that the renewal of their licences depended upon the manner in which their houses were conducted.

As Gee asserted, his scheme possessed several important advantages over the Permissive Bill. Certainly, there would have been less difficulty in obtaining an act embodying his proposals than the Permissive Bill. The propriety of entrusting the vestry or local boards with authority had already been admitted by parliament in poor law acts, highway acts, lighting acts and nuisance removal acts, so that it was probable that there would be no great opposition to that particular proposal.[122] Gee maintained that the passage of a bill such as he envisaged would be helped through the Commons by the fact that it would not, in every parish, necessarily involve great changes but would be considered merely as a transfer of responsibility from the magistrates and excise officers to the ratepayers. Yet his proposal might also secure the extreme Alliance policy of the entire suppression of the liquor traffic as effectually as the Permissive Bill; moreover, it would prepare certain districts for more stringent measures.[123] Gee was convinced that the Permissive Bill would be of no practical value whatsoever to those urban districts which were most in need of it, as a two-thirds majority would be very difficult to obtain in such districts. Conversely, in some rural districts public houses would be closed by the bill, yet these were the districts where the evil effects of drink were least felt. Gee's scheme, on the other hand, would produce satisfactory changes in the largest towns as well as in the thinly populated districts.[124]

Gee received widespread support for his ideas from those temperance reformers who regarded them as more practicable and feasible than the Permissive Bill.[125] During 1868-69 his suggestions were taken as the basis for the establishment of Associations for Reforming the Granting of Licences in Glamorgan, Monmouthshire, Denbighshire and Montgomeryshire, the principles of such associations being to give ratepayers the power to suppress, decrease or to increase the number of public houses.[126] But from 1869 the *Alliance News* and the local press were silent on the progress of these bodies, and one assumes that they were very short-lived. One leading dissentient from Gee's views among prominent Welsh temperance reformers was the member for Flint District, John Roberts of Abergele, who voiced his concern over the fact that, under Gee's scheme, the licensing question would be submitted annually to the ratepayers more in the form of a personal than an abstract question of principle; this might engender very bad feeling: 'I almost fear to contemplate the result of such a strife in my parish of Abergele where the people become almost mad in parochial squabbles.'[127]

Not unexpectedly, the Alliance reaction to Gee's suggestions was to assume a totally uncompromising attitude of opposition. T. H. Barker, the secretary of the Alliance in the 1860s, told Gee that the Alliance 'does not believe in gradual restriction. It is *too late* to attempt to undo the work of a dozen years of teaching and organizing. To lower our flag to "restriction" would be to *disorganise* the U.K.A.'[128] For William Lester, the veteran temperance advocate of Wrexham, 'Gee's plan . . . contains the power to licence an *evil,* and therefore must be wrong in principle'.[129] Of course, the possibility that Gee's proposals would *increase* the existing facilities for drink in some districts, was anathema to the Alliance. The Alliance claimed that his proposals contained nothing new except the proposal to submit the licensing question to a local board or a vestry meeting, and maintained that such meetings, except possibly in small communities, would not express fully the opinion of the inhabitants, and would be liable to 'packing'.[130] The Alliance would not budge from its position of 'total suppression in any district, however small or however large, to which the suppression is applied'. It was argued, further, that Gee's scheme, like the Permissive Bill, contained a full veto power—it was not only controlling but also prohibitory—and consequently it would experience no less difficulty than the Permissive Bill in passing through parliament.[131] To Gee's claim that a Permissive Bill would benefit no towns which did not adopt it, the Alliance replied that in some districts the vote, though falling short of a two-thirds majority, would nearly approach it, and that in such places, the publicans would be obliged to be on their good behaviour since at any time a change in public opinion might involve their 'utter extinction'.[132]

Despite the rebuff from the Alliance some of Gee's essential ideas of licensing reform were embodied later in the several Welsh local veto bills of the late 1880s and early '90s. For instance, the bill of 1891 proposed to enable owners and occupiers in Wales to have effectual *control* over the liquor traffic; the bill allowed for either a reduction of licences, or an end to their increase or total prohibition. As in Gee's plan a majority of two-thirds of the ratepayers was necessary for total prohibition, but only simple majorities for the other alternatives. Dismayed by the continual failure of the Permissive Bill and of local option, the Alliance, as will be seen, did not withhold its support of this and successive measures. Lack of success did indeed force the organisation to lower its flag to 'restriction'.

The Alliance's unreasonable reaction to Gee's licensing scheme was not untypical. The organization seriously lacked political sense. Its all-or-nothing approach grievously retarded the progress of temperance. In this way the Alliance incredibly but effectively destroyed Bruce's Licensing bill of 1871 because it did not embody fully the principle of local option. Indeed, the Alliance regarded the failure of attempts to extend licensing regulations as 'absolute gain' for the prohibitionist cause because such failures discredited the moderate alternative to its policy. The Alliance saw the trade in drink as an all-explaining evil which must be removed before progress could be made in any other sphere of social reform. It never grasped the opportunity for broadening its programme to include other necessary reforms and therefore attract the support of a greater number of politicians. It had no policy whatsoever for immediately palliating the drink problem; it never used its funds to pay for the provision of counter-attractions to drinking places.[133] Moreover, it seems almost certain that had the Permissive Bill become law, its enforcement in

Wales would have been fraught with difficulties. Drunkenness among police forces was not unknown and the police often relied on publicans for information about the criminal world. The Permissive Bill would have been bitterly opposed by a hard core of working men; it would have caused disputes in Wales with which those that followed the Welsh Sunday Closing Act in the 1880s—which, of course, involved the closing of public houses on one day only in the week—could not compare. Later, prohibition in the United States was to foster disrespect for the law and to promote corruption; it is unlikely that people can be civilized through sumptuary laws. However, it is one great virtue of the Alliance that it lifted many nonconformists out of their quietism and encouraged them to participate in political life.[134]

*   *   *   *

In its early years the Alliance had spurned all party allegiance; it had not wished to identify itself too closely with any political party for fear of alienating potential support. But by the 1860s it was fairly clear that the temperance cause aroused more sympathy in the Liberal party rather than the Conservative party, and as the legislative influence of private members waned, the argument for party alignment grew in strength.[135]

The adoption of the Permissive Bill by the Alliance in 1857 attracted many Liberals to the temperance movement if only because the bill possessed certain decentralizing aspects which attracted some politicians who wanted an increase in the amount of local initiative. In 1859, 21 Conservatives and 57 Liberals supported the Permissive Bill; by 1880 only one Conservative supported it as against 145 Liberals.[136] The alignment of the Liberal party with temperance reformers was initiated by the latter. The Liberals alone seemed likely to take up local option and in 1874 the Alliance advocated the infiltration of the Liberal party. In 1891 the policy of direct veto was included in the Liberals' Newcastle Programme.[137] For one thing, the Liberal party was the party associated with religious toleration and therefore nonconformists had gravitated towards it. It was thus natural that a movement which appealed strongly throughout its history to nonconformists should look to the Liberal party for aid. The increased political power of nonconformists after the 1850s forced the Liberal party to pay increasing attention to their demands.

Moreover, the individual candidates who first waged electoral campaigns without using publican assistance were usually Liberals or radicals. On the other hand, Conservatives were identified in the public mind with electoral corruption. Liberal nonconformists, especially Quakers, were the most ardent upholders of electoral sobriety.

It was inevitable that the Liberal party would align itself behind a temperance programme. In Wales, even more so than in England, many temperance advocates were Liberals; the temperance movement had made great progress within the nonconformist denominations, and mid-Victorian working men who voted Liberal were usually imbued with temperance. The Liberalism of the temperance advocate was important because invariably he was a very energetic party worker. 'The best fighting men in the ranks of the Liberal army', said Lloyd George in 1898, 'were the Temperance men, and from an electioneering point of view the Liberals could not afford to quarrel with these men.'[138]

Of major importance in determining the political affiliations of the drink interest during the second half of the nineteenth century were Bruce's licensing proposals of 1871-72. Among the causes of the defeat of Gladstone's government of 1868-74 must be numbered Bruce's licensing bills. Bruce aroused most hostility amongst the drink trade with his proposals for reducing the number of licences; for relating the number of licences to local needs and opinions, thus seeming to adopt the spirit if not the letter of the principle behind the Permissive Bill; and for the proposed sharp reduction in opening hours. The Alliance decided not to oppose the second reading of the 1871 bill but, as we have seen, its obsession with the Permissive Bill ensured that there was no enthusiastic support for Bruce's measure. The government eventually decided to bring in a more modest licensing measure during the next session and Bruce's bill was never given a second reading. The 1872 bill abandoned the local power clause. Again, no help was received from the Alliance. The bill was a non-party measure though critics were more numerous on the Conservative side. In fact, as Dr. Harrison points out, the Licensing Act of 1872 was one of many measures which the Gladstone government passed with Conservative support against radical indifference or hostility.[139]

Even this modified Act was regarded by the drink trade as one of 'pains, penalties and confiscations'. Gladstone's oft-quoted remark,

'We have been swept away, literally, by a torrent of beer and gin',
was an over-simplification, soon retracted, but without a doubt a
significant cause of the Liberal defeat in 1874 was the constant
campaigning that went on against the government in almost every
public house from the time Bruce's first licensing bill was introduced
in 1871. It was the retail trade which was most deeply interested in
the Licensing Act, since the consumption of alcohol continued to
increase in spite of the restrictions, and the publican was in a unique
position to influence votes. His customers were mainly working-class
men who rightly regarded the public house as a centre of recreation
and enjoyment which their homes could not provide. The publican
enjoyed a special status, and it was not unusual for him to be asked to
hold money for organisations or to arbitrate disputes among his
customers. Most certainly, the publicans used their half-business, half-
friendship relationship to agitate for their own interest and exploited
the irritations of the legal closing hours to turn their patrons from the
Liberal party.[140]

It might be noted however that not even in the 1880s was there any
absolutely clear party division on the temperance question. In 1882
Gladstone was still bidding for brewer support with his policy of a
'free mash tun', or the abolition of the malt tax. In Wales at this time
the signs are clearer that temperance was closely aligned with the
Liberal party. In 1885 the temperance reformers of Cardiff
subscribed seven-eighths of the amount of money needed to cover the
election expenses of E. J. Reed, the Liberal candidate, and in 1889
the nonconformist denominations in the town demonstrated against
the sale of drink in any club or institute which bore the name
'Liberal'.[141] From the mid-1880s strong support for temperance in
Wales came from the North Wales and South Wales Liberal
Federations. Both bodies consistently carried resolutions in favour of
ratepayer control and in favour of the successful working of the Welsh
Sunday Closing Act of 1881.[142] Local Alliance supporters joined with
the South Wales Liberal Federation in January 1895 to support the
government's local veto bill 'and as the Government is a Liberal one
its organisations are the proper media by which to bring pressure on
the headquarters staff'.[143] Indeed, in Welsh politics, at both local and
national levels, temperance became almost exclusively a Liberal
concern during the last quarter of the nineteenth century.

NOTES

[1] See P. Hollis (ed.), *Pressure from Without in Early Victorian England* (1974), *passim.*

[2] U.K.A., *First Annual Report, 1853-54*, p. 2.

[3] *C.M.G.*, 10 April 1858.

[4] For example, see *Merthyr Express*, 11 July 1868.

[5] See ibid., 9 September 1865; H. Carter, *The English Temperance Movement. A Study in Objectives* (1933), pp. 76-7.

[6] *The Times*, 2 October 1856, quoted in Carter, op. cit., p. 90.

[7] See Harrison, *Drink and the Victorians*, pp. 204-6.

[8] W. H. Darby, *Reasons in favour of a Maine Law for Great Britain* (Wrexham, n.d.), p. 3; *Cambrian,* 14 September 1860.

[9] See, for example, *Caernarvon and Denbigh Herald*, 12 February 1870.

[10] *C.M.G.*, 10 March 1855; 4 August 1855.

[11] U.K.A., *Tenth Annual Report, 1862*, p. 26.

[12] National Temperance League, *Annual Report, 1862*, pp. 35-41; *1869*, pp. 42-46.

[13] *North British Review*, 25, 1854-5.

[14] See Carter, op. cit., p. 88.

[15] Lawson was defeated at the General Election of 1865 and the bill was not introduced again until 1869. In 1872 the bill was 'talked out' without a division.

[16] *3 Hansard ccliii*, cols. 386-89 (18 June 1880).

[17] Ibid., *cclxxviii*, cols. 1,377-79 (27 April 1883).

[18] See, for example, A. J. Johnes, *A letter written in reply to an invitation to join a conference for a revision of the licensing system* (Welshpool, 1867), p. 6.

[19] J. Williams to T. E. Ellis, 12 September 1890, N.L.W., T. E. Ellis Papers, 2092/1-2; see also *Tarian y Gweithiwr*, 31 August 1884.

[20] For example, see *Alliance News*, 12 September 1868; *The Ferret or South Wales Ratepayer*, 28 March 1874.

[21] See *Cambrian*, 3 December 1880; *Alliance News*, 4 February 1882: *4 Hansard x*, col. 98 (15 March 1891).

[22] *Monmouthshire Merlin*, 20 February 1885; *Alliance News*, 28 February 1885; Report of the Royal Commission on Liquor Licensing Laws, *P.P.* 1897, Q. 10,536. Evidence of J. W. W. Bund, J.P. for Worcestershire and Cardiganshire.

[23] *Western Mail*, 17 October 1884.

[24] See *Caernarvon and Denbigh Herald*, 7 November 1885.

[25] Rev. J. Kirk, *Progressive Suppression of Public House Licences with illustrations of the social result* (n.d.), London School of Economics, Jevons Collection, vol. 20, p. 676.

[26] *Alliance News*, 26 November 1887; see also 30 June 1893; 18 August 1893; 13 July 1895.

[27] Ibid., 23 September 1854; *Bristol Temperance Herald for the West of England and South Wales*, 18 November 1854, p. 170.

[28] *Alliance News*, 24 October 1854.

[29] Ibid., 30 November 1854.

[30] *C.M.G.*, 10 March 1855; *Alliance News*, 31 March 1855.

[31] U.K.A., *3rd Annual Report, 1855*, p. 11.

[32] *Alliance News*, 23 June 1855; *Proceedings of the Ministerial Conference on the Suppression of the Liquor Traffic at Manchester, 1857* (Manchester, 1857), p. 46.

[33] *Alliance News*, 24 February 1866.

[34] *Y Gwladgarwr*, 29 October 1859.

[35] *Proceedings of the Ministerial Conference*, op. cit., pp. 13-14.

[36] Ibid., p. 11.

[37] *Bristol Temperance Herald for the West of England and South Wales*, 18 November 1854; *Alliance News*, 6 October 1860.

[38] *The Temperance Spectator*, 1 April 1860.

[39] For example, see *C.M.G.*, 18 February 1860; *Alliance News*, 19 September 1863; 4 June 1864; *Merthyr Express*, 19 May 1865; 17 November 1866.

[40] U.K.A., *Third Annual Report, 1855*, p. 11.

[41] U.K.A., *Fifth Annual Report, 1857*, p. 27.

[42] See U.K.A., *Fourth Annual Report, 1856*, p. 19.

[43] U.K.A., *Minutes, 1882-84*, 15 November 1882.

[44] Ibid., 1871-73, meetings of 29 November 1871, 27 November 1872.

[45] Ibid., 1880-82, 19 July 1882; 1882-85, 5 December 1883; 1885-87, 12 August 1885; 29 September 1886; 1887-89, 15 September 1888.

[46] Ibid., 1895-97; on 10 April 1895 the regular £10 grant to the North Wales Temperance Association was refused for these reasons.

[47] Ibid., 1873-75, 18 June 1873.

[48] *Alliance News,* 11 July 1868.

[49] See *Caernarvon and Denbigh Herald,* 26 September 1868.

[50] U.K.A., *Fourth Annual Report, 1856,* p. 19.

[51] U.K.A., *Fourteenth Annual Report, 1866,* p. 7.

[52] Ibid., p. 65.

[53] See *Alliance News,* 14 December 1872; *The Treasury,* 10, 1873, p. 162.

[54] See, for example, H. J. Williams to D. R. Daniel, 24 January 1887, N.L.W., D. R. Daniel Papers, f. 2,299; U.K.A. Minutes, 1870-95, *passim.*

[55] See Ibid., 1882-85, 5 December 1883.

[56] Ibid., 1885-86, 10 March 1886, 1887-89, 6 June 1888.

[57] See Ibid., 1889-91, 14 January 1891.

[58] Ibid., 29 November 1889; 5 June 1890.

[59] For the general defects of canvasses see H. Cantril, *Gauging Public Opinion* (Princeton, 1944), p. 3; L. W. Doob, *Public Opinion and Propaganda* (New York, 1948), p. 151; see also Brian Harrison, 'The British Prohibitionists, 1853-1872. A Biographical Analysis,' *International Review of Social History,* XV (1970), part 3, 393.

[60] The analysis which follows is based on statistics abstracted from the annual reports of the Alliance, 1853-95.

[61] T. E. Ellis to D. R. Daniel, 25 October 1889, N.L.W., D. R. Daniel Papers, 335(a).

[62] Cf. I. G. Jones, 'The Liberation Society and Welsh Politics, 1844-1868', *W.H.R.,* 1, no. 2, 1961, 206.

[63] *Welsh Weekly,* 22 January 1892; W. Johnstone, *Notable Men of Cardiff* (Cardiff, 1903), pp. 47-54.

[64] *North Wales Guardian,* 17 November 1882; R. Roe (ed.), *The National Temperance League Annual for 1883* (1884), pp. 142-3.

[65] U.K.A., *Annual Reports, 1876, 1877; Dictionary of Welsh Biography,* sub David Davies.

[66] N.L.W., W. W. Price's Index, *sub* W. L. Daniel; *Merthyr Express,* 3 July 1850; 31 May 1884.

[67] See W. R. Lambert, 'Thomas Williams, J.P., Gwaelodygarth (1823-1903): A Study in Nonconformist Attitudes and Actions', S. Williams (ed.), *Glamorgan Historian,* vol. 11 (1975), and references cited therein.

[68] U.K.A., Minutes, 1876-78, 25 July 1877; 1880-82, 18 January 1882.

[69] H. J. Williams to D. R. Daniel, 14 December 1888, N.L.W., Daniel Papers, 2,360.

[70] Ibid.

[71] For a criticism of temperance organisation in Wales see *Welsh Weekly,* 22 January 1892.

[72] U.K.A., Minutes, 1889-91, 19 February 1890; 1 July 1891.

[73] U.K.A. Executive to D. R. Daniel, 14 July 1893, N.L.W., Daniel Papers, 2,313; U.K.A., Minutes, 1893-95, 22 August 1894.

[74] Ibid., 9 January 1895.

[75] Ibid., 1891-93, 27 July 1892.

[76] Ellis to Daniel, n.d., *c.*1890, N.L.W., Daniel Papers, 397.

[77] U.K.A., Minutes, 1876-78, 4 October 1876.

[78] Ellis to Daniel, 12 December 1891, N.L.W., Daniel Papers, 387.

[79] K. W. Jones-Roberts, 'D. R. Daniel, 1859-1931,' *Journal of the Merioneth Historical and Record Society,* 5 (1965), p. 65.

[80] U.K.A. to Daniel, 30 April 1895, N.L.W., Daniel papers, 2,324.

[81] Daniel to Ellis, 1 May 1895, ibid., 426.

[82] Daniel to U.K.A., 4 May 1895, ibid., 443.

[83] U.K.A., *Sixteenth Annual Report, 1867-68,* p. 33.

[84] Carter, op. cit., p. 184.

[85] U.K.A., Minutes, 1871-73, 30 September 1872.

[86] Ibid., 1873-75, 24 September 1873; U.K.A., *Twenty-first Annual Report, 1873,* p. 5.

[87] *Alliance News,* 25 October 1873.

[88] Ibid., see also *The Templar of Wales,* 1, no, 3, June 1873, p. 5.

[89] For example, see H. H. Vivian to the South Wales Temperance and Prohibition Association, 13 March 1874, N.L.W. Lord Swansea Collection (uncatalogued).

⁹⁰ Owen Thomas and J. Machreth Rees, *Cofiant y Parch John Thomas, D.D., Liverpool* (1898), pp. 279-80.

⁹¹ *Merthyr Weekly Mail,* 2 November 1878.

⁹² *Alliance News,* 7 May 1859; 14 May 1859.

⁹³ D. E. Williams to Henry Richard, n.d., *c.* 1867, N.L.W., MS. 14,022 B, op. cit., f 286.

⁹⁴ *Alliance News,* 12 December 1868. No details of south Wales constituencies are given.

⁹⁵ Ibid., 29 May 1869.

⁹⁶ Ibid.

⁹⁷ U.K.A., Minutes, 1873-75, 14 January 1874.

⁹⁸ Ibid., 26 January 1874.

⁹⁹ *3 Hansard ccxx,* col. 61 (17 June 1874).

¹⁰⁰ *Alliance News,* 30 March 1894; 28 September 1894.

¹⁰¹ Ibid.

¹⁰² See *Monmouthshire Merlin,* 22 October 1859; *Merthyr Express,* 27 March 1875.

¹⁰³ *Monmouthshire Merlin,* 28 May 1864.

¹⁰⁴ *Merthyr Express,* 8 August 1868.

¹⁰⁵ Ibid., 28 July 1865.

¹⁰⁶ Ibid., 4 August 1865; *Letters of the Rt. Hon. Lord Aberdare, vol. 1, 1832-74* (Oxford, 1902), pp. 256-57.

¹⁰⁷ C.C.L., MS. 3,508, H. A. Bruce to Rev. John Griffith, 11 August 1865.

¹⁰⁸ *The Times,* 4 May 1871.

¹⁰⁹ *Merthyr Telegraph,* 23 July 1870.

¹¹⁰ *No case against the U.K.A. and the Permissive Bill* (Manchester 1872), p. 81; see also N.L.W., Lord Swansea Collection, H. H. Vivian to W. L. Daniel, 1 June 1869; Vivian to Swansea Licensed Victuallers Protection Association, 2 June 1871. Vivian had voted for the Permissive Bill in 1864, 1869, 1870 and 1871.

¹¹¹ *Western Mail,* 4 February 1874; 6 February 1874.

¹¹² H. H. Vivian to Rev. J. Owen, 1 July 1878, N.L.W., Lord Swansea Collection.

¹¹³ *Cardiff and South Wales Free Churchman,* April 1899.

¹¹⁴ *Friendly Suggestions* is in N.L.W., MS. 8,320 D (Gee Miscellanea); a summary is printed in *Alliance News,* 22 December 1866. *Suggestions for a change* is in N.L.W., MS. 8,320 D (Gee 16).

¹¹⁵ *Friendly Suggestions,* p. 4.

¹¹⁶ Ibid., see also *Baner ac Amserau Cymru,* 17 Chwefror 1869.

¹¹⁷ *Friendly Suggestions,* p. 5.

¹¹⁸ *Suggestions for a change,* p. 2.

¹¹⁹ *Friendly Suggestions,* p. 7.

¹²⁰ *Suggestions for a change,* p. 3.

¹²¹ Ibid.

¹²² *Friendly Suggestions,* p. 8.

¹²³ Ibid.

¹²⁴ *Baner ac Amserau Cymru,* 5 May 1869; *Caernarvon and Denbigh Herald,* 21 November 1885.

¹²⁵ For example, see N.L.W., MS. 8,308 D (Gee 4), Duke of Newcastle to Gee, 24 November 1866; MS. 8,305 D (Gee 1), John Bright to Gee, 27 December 1866, f. 10.

¹²⁶ *Alliance News,* 2 October 1869; 12 November 1869.

¹²⁷ John Roberts to Gee, 21 June 1869, N.L.W., MS. 8,308 D (Gee 14).

¹²⁸ T. H. Barker to Gee, 2 June 1866, N.L.W., MS. 8,305 D (Gee 1), f. 5.

¹²⁹ *Baner ac Amserau Cymru,* 28 April 1869.

¹³⁰ *Alliance News,* 29 December 1866. The Alliance reply to Gee was translated into Welsh by the Rev. Owen Jones and 10,000 copies were printed: *Yr 'Awgrymiadau Cyfeillgar' Yn cael eu Hadolygu yn Ddiduedd* (Manchester, 1867).

¹³¹ *Alliance News,* 29 December 1866.

¹³² Ibid.

¹³³ Harrison, *Drink and the Victorians,* pp. 374-5.

¹³⁴ Ibid., pp. 376-7, 385.

¹³⁵ Ibid., pp. 242-3.

¹³⁶ D. Burns, *Temperance History,* vol. 1, p. 426; H. Carter, op. cit., p. 200.

¹³⁷ U.K.A., *Twenty-second Annual Report, 1874-75,* pp. 6-7; H. J. Hanham, *Elections and Party Management. Politics in the Age of Gladstone and Disraeli (1961),* p. 122.

¹³⁸ *Alliance News,* 28 January 1898.

¹³⁹ Harrison, *Drink and the Victorians,* p. 281.

[140] See *Licensed Victuallers Guardian,* 14 February 1874; 17 April 1880.

[141] *Western Mail,* 23 November 1885; C.C.L., MS. 4,616, Cardiff Junior Liberal Association, Minute Book, 20 June 1889.

[142] For example, see North Wales Liberal Federation, *Annual Report, 1888,* p. 5; *Annual Report, 1889,* pp. 5-6.

[143] U.K.A., Minutes, 1893-95, 19 January 1895.

CHAPTER VI

THE TEMPERANCE QUESTION IN WELSH LOCAL AND NATIONAL POLITICS, 1853-1895

DURING the period 1853-95, at both local and national levels, Welsh temperance reformers set themselves to the task of putting Alliance policy into practice. At the local level attempts were made to secure the election of temperance supporters to local boards and to town councils and to combat the influence of representatives of the drink trade on such bodies. The burden of town rates in Wales fell heavily upon that social group from which the temperance movement derived a great deal of its leadership: the middle-class rate-paying group. Hence the desire to abolish licences, and also to use the temperance issue in local elections in order to gain control of the administration of the licensing law and the poor law. At Westminster it seemed that the cause of Welsh temperance increasingly became an instrument of a strong nationalistic strain in Welsh political and social life and was no longer championed for primarily physiological and moral reasons. It seemed that during the last two decades of the century the demand for, and the securing of, temperance legislation for Wales became more important than the proposed content of that legislation.[1]

What were the issues at stake in local politics between temperance supporters and publicans and brewers? Temperance reformers believed that the drink trade had a deleterious effect on the community; it did not employ labour to any great extent and was detrimental to working men because it absorbed resources which should have become the capital of the country for the employment of labour. The trade in drink prevented working men improving themselves by obtaining higher wages and a reduction of the hours of labour.[2] Invariably, publicans and brewers were strongly represented on town councils in Wales and therefore on local watch committees. For members of the drink trade, a place on a watch committee had a distinct monetary value, and in some towns police action against licensing infringements was foiled by the number of publicans and brewers on such committees.[3] Cardiff temperance reformers complained in October 1860 that the power of regulating the police in the town had been abandoned to the licensed victuallers on the council and that the police were afraid to do their duty. It was the firmly-held view that the council 'does not represent the worth and business talents of the town'.[4] Similar complaints were made at Swansea. It seemed that the only remedy was to diminish the power of the licensed victuallers on town councils, and replace them by 'men of undoubted business habits, whose moral calling is beyond suspicion'.[5] In 1860-61, for example, there were nine licensed victuallers on the Swansea town council: the council chamber, according to the local ratepayers, once so respectable and respected, had been taken over by a narrow 'class' or occupational interest which worked against the welfare of the town.[6] A Licensed Victuallers Association had been formed at Swansea in 1858 in order to secure equality of water rates with other tradesmen,[7] and in 1861, largely as a result of their influence on the town council, the publicans induced that body to lower the rate from 1s. 9d. to 1s. 6d. in the pound.[8]

Inherent in the situation at the local level was the very real commercial or occupational jealousy aimed at the drink trade. At an Alliance meeting at Newport in 1878 it was stated that if the working classes were more sober the amount of money which would be diverted from the unproductive manufacture of strong drink would go to other productive industries.[9] To many tradesmen the publican appeared as a member of a trade which was legally protected against competition. A publican could oppose the granting of a licence to a new applicant who wished to open a public house in his immediate neighbourhood, and in so doing, was allowed to take with him as many ratepaying friends as he wished in order to endorse his opposition.[10] But drapers, grocers and other tradesmen did not have this power. Moreover, why should the publican be legally licensed to transact his business on Sundays while the grocer or draper be legally compelled to close his shop? The general feeling was that publicans and brewers—intemperately but characteristically condemned by temperance advocates as men who lived, fed and fattened on the wholesale and retail manufacture of paupers, criminals and lunatics—were no longer 'respectable'.[11]

The publicans' reply was to argue that the drink trade had a legitimate stake in the country and was justified in participating in local politics. Publicans claimed that the amount of capital invested in the various branches of the drink trade in Britain was almost as much as the combined capital invested in the cotton, woollen and iron industries of the country, and that the trade in 1861, for example, paid 37 per cent of the gross annual taxation of Britain. [12]

In Wales the earliest political activity by temperance reformers and publicans occurred at Newport and Neath. In October 1859 the Newport and Pillgwenlly Reform Registration League was established as an auxiliary of the Alliance, 'for the purpose of sending fit and proper persons to the Town Council and the House of Commons who will pledge themselves to represent the social and moral necessities, and protect the public interests of the town and neighbourhood, especially from the traffic in intoxicating drinks'. [13] It was decided that at any meeting, if the majority agreed to support any candidate for political office the minority should comply and record its votes together in favour of that candidate. The work of the League was taken up with the registration of two-thirds of the ratepayers of Newport who would vote for the operation of the Permissive Bill.

At the municipal election of 1859 in Newport, Nelson Hewertson, 'a moral, upright character', but not a teetotaller, was brought out by the League to oppose John Hyndman, a wine and spirits merchant, in the East Ward of the town. [14] Every attempt was made to play down the importance of the advent of the drink question in local politics. Hewertson denied that he came forward to oppose Hyndman because the latter was engaged in the drink trade; he maintained that 86 burgesses had signed a requisition asking him to stand, only 22 of whom were members of the League. Hewertson was returned at the head of the poll and Hyndman was placed at the bottom. [15] Local temperance advocates were in no doubt as to the importance of the result. 'We obtained such a glorious victory over the traffic yesterday', wrote a Newport correspondent to the *Alliance News,* 'I believe many boroughs may do likewise if they work as we did yesterday and for the last week.' [16] Again, in January 1860, when a vacancy occurred in the West Ward, Edward Phillips, the League's candidate, was returned at the head of the poll by a substantial majority. [17] The League's choice of Phillips was a controversial one; it seems that four or five extreme temperance zealots took upon themselves the authority of the whole membership of the League in January 1860, for it was claimed by two members of the League that no meeting of League members had been called and that Phillips had been chosen by a few only of the League's members, some of whom were on his election committee. [18]

The municipal elections of 1861 were more contentious. In both wards of the town, the League joined the 'Tredegar Wharf Interest' under the Conservative, Lord Tredegar, against the four Liberals, who were led by brewer and former mayor, James Brown. All four Liberals were returned and the League collapsed. The local Liberal newspaper, the *Star of Gwent,* accused the League of selling its high ideals for political power; the League had been powerless in 'trying to obtrude its nostrums upon public taste'; temperance reformers must 'limit their activity within a narrower sphere of reformation in which they may effect good by precept and example. Political and civic preponderancy is not within their circle of duty or the compass of their power'.[19] There was obviously a considerable amount of consternation in the town at the appearance of a new element in local politics. At the first meeting of the town council after the election the Liberals accused the League of trying to set itself up as 'a great political machine in the town'. The feeling among the Liberals was that temperance reformers had stepped out of line by participating as a group in local politics.[20] Such criticism was refuted, not surprisingly by the Conservative *Monmouthshire Merlin,* which claimed that temperance reformers had a right to unite for the promotion of municipal or political purposes provided that their object was 'moral and constitutional'. It was argued that, basically, the League was not different from the Anti-Corn Law League or the Financial Reform Association.[21] The Liberal complaint that the temperance supporters wanted teetotalism foisted on the public was refuted; Hewertson had been supported by the league in 1859, but he was not a teetotaller.[22] The League claimed that the re-elected Liberal mayor, James Brown, had used and would continue to use his influence in the interests of the drink trade, and that behind temperance activity in Newport in 1861 lay an attempt, however crude, to reform an allegedly corrupt police force, which was the puppet of the drink interest on the town council.[23]

There was little further political activity connected with the temperance issue in Newport until the mid-1880s. After much discussion, in January 1887, Newport Temperance Society decided to amalgamate with the newly-formed Newport and County Temperance and Electoral Association, whose policy was to secure united political action on the temperance issue.[24] The rules of Newport Temperance Society were now amended so as to include political action. A new electoral roll was adopted and an electoral pledge drawn up. An electoral agent was appointed whose main tasks were to organize support for candidates supporting Alliance policy at local elections, and to collect petitions against applications for licences at annual licensing sessions. As an Alliance auxiliary, the society was kept in close touch with the Alliance by subscription and Alliance spokesmen were often obtained for large public meetings and demonstrations.[25] It is likely that this return to political activity was taken as a result of the action of temperance voters at the borough election of 1885, when Edward Carbutt, the temperance Liberal, was defeated by Sir George Elliot, the Conservative candidate. The inference was that certain members of the General Committee of the society had voted for Elliot, and all such persons were now to be 'rigorously excluded' and the new organization constituted 'upon a Radical basis pure and simple'.[26]

The return to political action caused a rift among Newport temperance advocates. Membership of the new society consisted of two sections: a general section consisting of moral suasionists and an electoral section consisting of those who subscribed to the electoral roll.[27] For many years two separate subscription lists were operated. Henry Phillips, J.P., President of the society in its early months, soon relinquished his office, and at the same time gave £200 to the society for 'the advancement of Temperance work in Newport by moral suasion'.[28] Complaints about the political affiliation of the society continued. Conservatives asserted that the society was 'an undisguised Radical Association'; it had withheld support at elections from Conservative candidates who had been life-long teetotallers while it had assisted Liberal candidates who had nothing in common with true temperance principles. In a word, temperance had been 'prostituted to politics'.[29]

To this extent had temperance become a contentious issue and a Liberal concern in Newport politics by the late 1880s. It should be stressed, however, that the Conservative complaint that Conservative teetotallers were not supported by the Newport society might not always be relevant because a teetotaller could well be a suasionist and therefore unwilling to support legislation on the temperance question; and almost invariably, Conservatives who were interested in the temperance movement in the 1880s were suasionists. The leading Welsh suasionist of the 1880s and '90s, the Conservative, T. Marchant Williams, secretary of the National Temperance League, claimed that the coupling of temperance with party politics was the major reason for the parlous state of the temperance movement in Wales in the mid-1890s. The 'constant linking' of temperance with party politics deprived the temperance cause of the active and open support of 'a large, powerful and influential section of the Welsh people': the Welsh Conservatives.[30]

At the same time as the temperance question entered the political arena at Newport, temperance reformers and members of the drink trade were preparing to do battle at Neath. Here, the temperance group met with little success at local elections. In October 1859 two of the four sitting councillors who were offering themselves for re-election were temperance advocates, and opposition to their re-election was organised by the drink interest, which put forward as its candidates an auctioneer who was also a Conservative agent, and a tradesman.[31] Both nominees of the drink interest were elected at the head of the poll. 'The beer did it!', claimed the *Cambrian*. Such was the bitterness as the result was declared that the authorities threatened to call in the police.[32] As a direct result of the election, the Mayor of Neath in 1858-9, James Kenway, a temperance supporter, resigned from the council. In his letter of resignation to the burgesses, Kenway maintained that the result of the election was inimical to the responsibility of the character of the council and to the good government of Neath. 'Men of good position, of education, and tried principles have been ejected from the Council for no cause but to make way for the nominees of a party with whose principles I have no sympathy, and in whose public conduct I have no confidence.'[33] Kenway condemned the drink interest and implied that the burgesses did not act in accordance with their convictions. It seems certain that the root cause of publican activity at Neath in 1859 was that Kenway's conduct as mayor in stringently enforcing the laws relating to disorderly public houses and cases of drunkenness had proved irksome to the trade.[34]

Professor Vincent has remarked that what is particularly noticeable in the electoral behaviour of the drink interest in the second half of the nineteenth century in Britain is 'the vigorous *ils ne passeront pas* with which the trade met the Temperance movement'.[35] In the 1870s the drink trade became a sharply-defined pressure group organised to defend its economic interest. This was in response to the activities of the Alliance and to the appearance, in the early 1870s, of the extreme Independent Order of Good Templars, whose uncompromising attitude was 'a vote for a vote and nothing for nothing'.[36] To fight this threat the Licensed Victuallers National Defence League was formed in 1873. But the League was never very strong or well-organised in Wales and, on the whole, it failed signally to affect the course of Welsh local and national politics. The aim of the League was to encourage brewers and publicans to put the defence of their trade above party political affiliations. At a meeting of Cardiff publicans in January 1874, called to decide what action should be adopted at the forthcoming general election, the chairman maintained that it was not a question of politics but of trade; it was the duty of Cardiff publicans to forget party politics and to support the candidate who came nearest to the requirements of the test questions of the Defence League. [37] Thus, they decided to support the Conservative candidates, Ivor Guest for the county seat and Hardinge Giffarde for the Cardiff seat. Liberal supporters saw such action as an example of a group of men subordinating great political and national questions to their own personal, narrow and selfish interests. [38] In reply, publicans claimed that they were only imitating the tactics of the Alliance and the Good Templars who also had sworn to act apart from party politics. A publican posed the rhetorical question: 'Have not pains and penalties been showered down upon our devoted heads as if we were subjects of some eastern despot, and have we not been exceptionally legislated for unlike every other trade? Can we, like they, go into any court for the recovery of any just debt?' [39] What the publicans were dissatisfied with was, not what had been done, but what had been threatened. They objected to the discretion of the magistrates because they feared that teetotal or temperance magistrates might win seats on the bench and create a majority for measures of a restrictive character, which would make the public houses some of them had purchased become bad bargains.

At the General Election of 1880 the trade made great efforts to safeguard its interests against the temperance threat in south Wales. The Licensed Victuallers National Defence League issued test questions which local licensed victuallers' associations laid before parliamentary candidates. At Cardiff a deputation of the local association put the questions to Arthur Guest (Conservative) and Edward Reed (Liberal). The latter replied that he was in favour of Sunday closing, local option and compensation paid to publicans dispossessed of their licences; he added that he deprecated any organised political action on the part of a 'purely commercial body'. [40] Guest was against Sunday closing and local option and in favour of compensation, and was consequently supported by the trade. The chairman of the association was confident that if the 273 licensed victuallers and beer retailers in the Cardiff Boroughs (Cardiff, Cowbridge and Llantrisant) secured three votes each, they would form 'a great political power' in the borough. [41]

However, the association's directive to local publicans to vote for Guest caused open dissension in their ranks. Liberal publicans maintained that they would vote for Reed despite the decision of the association to support Guest. [42] A Cardiff publican issued a circular addressed to the licensed victuallers of Cardiff in which he asserted that 'Every one of us has a right to his own individual opinion on this point, and I resent indignantly the attempt of any man, or any clique of men, because they happen to carry on the same business as myself to dictate to me as to the direction in which I should give my vote'. [43] He asserted that it would be folly for a Liberal publican to vote against his party merely because of the memory of Bruce's Licensing Act of 1872. That Act, it was alleged, was highly advantageous to the publican. It made it difficult for potential newcomers to the trade to obtain a licence and so prevented competition, while at the same time it afforded means of getting rid of houses of disrepute. It was claimed that since 1872 the licence value of public houses had increased greatly. [44] The unity of the Cardiff publicans was further weakened by the declaration of some of the Liberal working men of Cardiff not to give their custom to those publicans who supported Guest. In several instances, blue placards were torn from publicans' windows. [45] Reed triumphed at the election and the Cardiff publicans were forced to admit that 'after all the trouble and expense, and the persevering energy which we threw into the late parliamentary election, we failed to secure a unanimous trade-vote'. [46]

Similarly, at Merthyr Tydfil the trade attempted and failed to influence the outcome of the election. In 1880 the two candidates at Merthyr were the liberals, Henry Richard and C. H. James, both of whom were pledged to temperance reform. The Merthyr publicans hoped that Richard Fothergill, the local industrialist, would stand also, as he had always opposed Lawson's local option resolutions in the Commons, and had written a letter disparaging the principle of local option to the Licensed Victuallers National Defence League, by whom it had been published in the daily press. [47] However, Fothergill refused to stand, and ultimately, a third candidate was found in the mineral agent of the Marquis of Bute, W. T. Lewis of Mardy (later

Lord Merthyr), ostensibly an Independent, but in reality a Conservative. Lewis refused to support any measure of licensing reform, and Liberals were convinced that he had been brought out by the publicans of the borough. Certainly, the vast majority of publicans in the borough displayed blue posters in their bars and windows, thus making it clear which way they intended to vote.[48] But, like the Cardiff publicans, they reckoned without their host. Some publicans were forced to take down the posters unless they wished to lose a sizeable portion of their custom.[49] During election day a large body of Liberal working men came down to Merthyr from Dowlais, throwing stones and smashing the windows of 'Tory' public houses and singing, to the tune of *Men of Harlech*,

> When the stupid Tory faction
> Failed to give us satisfaction
> We had Liberal reaction
> At the Temperance Hall.
> Chorus: For Merthyr will never have a Tory, etc.[50]

The outcome of the election was the return of Richard and James. 'The publicans have collapsed', proclaimed the *Merthyr Express* gleefully. The newspaper proceeded to analyse shrewdly the rôle of the drink trade in politics since 1874. From that year, and following upon the Liberal licensing legislation, the trade had 'suppressed politics' and 'gone in for interest'. In so doing it had exercised great influence and had decided many elections. But this policy, argued the *Express*, should now be abandoned. Paranoiac publicans and millennial temperance advocates were mistaken if they thought that a Liberal government would legislate the drink trade out of existence. If any licences were taken away, compensation would be given.

> The publican who puts his trade before all things else, and the teetotaller who stakes everything upon his own peculiar shibboleth belong to the same category of unreasonable and unpracticable beings. There are certain broad lines of public policy which must be followed, and within these there is ample ground for fair and equitable treatment of the thousand and one subsidiary subjects of practical politics. The great lesson for the licensed victuallers is that henceforth the safe and prudent course is to let individual members of the Trade determine their course of action by their political convictions. They have no more to fear from Liberals than Conservatives. So powerful an interest as theirs never can be violently interfered with by any government; and the modifications which may be deemed necessary in the regulation of the liquor traffic from time to time will be accompanied with adequate

compensation whenever it can be shown that vested interests are permanently injured.[51]

Such a view, however sane and sensible, reckoned without the evangelical and sectarian zeal, and the upsurge of national consciousness, which marked Welsh politics in the last two decades of the nineteenth century.

The Welsh temperance cause at Westminster, apart from the winning of the Welsh Sunday Closing Act in 1881, did not meet with a great measure of success. Yet the Welsh members of parliament, more especially the Liberal members, gave overwhelming support to temperance legislation. The number of teetotallers in the House of Commons increased from 2 in 1865 to 36 in 1885; at least G. Osborne Morgan (Denbighshire), Henry Richard (Merthyr Tydfil), W. O. Stanley (Beaumaris) and John Pughe (Cardiganshire), all Liberals, claimed to be a part of this increase.[52] At the end of the period covered by this study, 32 of the 34 M.P.s for Wales and Monmouthshire were in favour of local option and it was believed that there were seven teetotallers amongst them: T. P. Lewis (Anglesey), Bowen Rowlands (Cardiganshire), Alfred Thomas (East Glamorgan), Lloyd George (Caernarvon District), J. Herbert Lewis (Flint District), J. H. Roberts (Denbighshire) and Major Evan Jones (Carmarthen District). Apparently, Tom Ellis had 'to abandon this teetotalism owing to the delicate state of his health'; moreover, as will be seen, the claim that Major Jones was a teetotaller cannot be taken seriously.[53] The voting behaviour of the Welsh members on proposed temperance legislation was thus remarkably uniform. In 1869 and 1870 eleven Welsh members in each year voted for the second reading of the Permissive Bill, and five voted against. The voting of Welsh members on temperance bills and resolutions between 1880 and 1893, with the exception of the Welsh Sunday Closing Bill, was as follows:[54]

		For	Against
1880	Local option resolution	23	4
1881	Local option resolution	17	3
1883	Local option resolution	23	2
1889	English Sunday Closing Bill	14	1
1891	Local Veto (Wales) Bill	22	0
1893	Direct Veto (Wales) Bill	28	1

Of the four Welsh members who voted against Lawson's local option resolution in 1880, three were Conservatives: Lord Emlyn

(Carmarthenshire), C. O. Morgan and J. A. Rolls (both Monmouthshire). Lord Richard Grosvenor (Flintshire) was the only Liberal to vote against the resolution. In 1883, however, Grosvenor saw fit to support the resolution, and henceforth, opposition to temperance measures among Welsh members came solely from Conservatives. The only exception was in 1889 when, on the second reading of the English Sunday Closing Bill, 21 Welsh members abstained and the. Bill was defeated by 7 votes.[55]

On the other hand, on the issue of Welsh Sunday closing, there seemed to be no two opinions. The Welsh Sunday Closing Act of 1881 was the most remarkable legislative achievement of the Welsh temperance movement in the nineteenth century.[56] The Sunday closing movement was born out of the co-operation between sabbatarians and temperance reformers. For the latter, the Act represented the apotheosis of their evangelical endeavours in Wales since the 1830s. For the trade in Wales, the Act, following as it did upon Sunday closing for Scotland (1853) and for Ireland (1878), seemed to be 'prohibition by degrees', a further instalment of prohibitory measures aimed against the liberty of the working man and the livelihood of an important economic group in society.[57] The 1880s witnessed a great controversy as to whether the Act had succeeded or failed to reduce Sunday drunkenness, the real issue being the viability of the rôle of legislation in attempting to make men sober.

The dominant influence in the growth of sabbatarian sentiment in Wales was provided by evangelicalism. The evangelicals' blind reliance on the Scriptures was founded on a literal interpretation of the Bible and a thorough-going familiarity, in the strict Calvinist tradition, with its contents. A major tenet of evangelical faith was a strong belief in the proper observance of the Sabbath, founded on a very strict interpretation of the Fourth Commandment.[58] As has been seen, in nineteenth-century Wales religious nonconformity was the basis of the social and cultural pattern of life, and the general picture was of a strict form of puritanism, which insisted on piety and the observance of certain sacraments. Sunday observance became a formal religious practice and was part of the social life of a community, particularly in rural areas. The Lord's Day was the nearest approach to Heaven that was possible on earth. Heaven itself was regarded as an everlasting Sabbath.[59] From the early years of the temperance movement in Wales, Sunday drinking had been condemned by church, chapel and middle-class example-setters. Under the conditions of early industrialisation a man's leisure time came at the weekend, so that drinking and drunkenness were concentrated on Saturdays and Sundays, particularly in the seaports of south and west Wales, which were characterized by a large 'floating' population of single men and lodgers freed from the restraints of a settled and responsible home life. From the 1830s observers were unanimous in alleging that desecration of the Sabbath was the 'crying sin' of Wales. The most common complaint of the respectable religious community was that in some areas public houses and beer houses were kept open during the hours of divine service, and that respectability had often to make its way home from the service through crowds of roaring, swearing drunkards.[60]

What was the reaction of working men in Wales to the attempts of respectability to curtail their opportunities for recreation? J. S. Mill in *On Liberty* (1859) castigated sabbatarian and temperance legislation as examples of 'illegitimate interference with the rightful liberty of the individual'.[61] Certainly, temperance reformers and sabbatarians sought to curtail the pleasures of the working man, but at the same time, expressed concern—and this is what exasperated their opponents—for his happiness and well-being. The feeling was that the working classes could not be trusted to enjoy any means of Sunday recreation, as it would lead inevitably to the desecration of the Lord's Day.[62] Sabbatarians tended to inveigh against 'the working classes' without making any distinction between types of working men. Sabbatarian denunciation was, in fact, directed against the 'residuum' of the working classes: the indifferent, morally degraded, but potentially 'dangerous' class.

Only the public house and the chapel were open on the Welsh Sunday, and any attempt to provide rational counter-attractions to the public house were strenuously resisted by sabbatarians. The 'clergy and inhabitants' of Cardiff met in September 1844 to discuss the desecration of the Sabbath caused by the opening of the Taff Vale Railway on Sundays and the offering of a lower range of prices for working men and their families. Although it was argued that the railway was a counter-attraction to the public house on a Sunday, a memorial was drawn up for the suppression of Sunday travelling. Dissentients presented a counter-memorial arguing that the Sabbatarian memorial was 'adverse to the interests of the poorer classes of south Wales'.[63] The social division was made plain. A working man said: 'The great ones of the country had got rich by the labour of the working classes, and they grudged them the little relaxation which a Sunday trip gave them.'[64] The general complaint was that only working men were blamed for Sabbath desecration, whereas the rich were equally guilty. This was a perfectly justifiable criticism, as in their clubs and homes the better-off had their own independent facilities for recreation, eating and drinking, but the poor had only the public facilities subject to legislative restriction. Sabbatarians were concerned only with public profanation and not with private indulgence. A Merthyr workman wrote to the local press criticising the blindness, arrogance and inhumanity of those who had brought about Sunday closing in Wales:

> How would these very good people like to live days, weeks and months underground without a sight of the sun, and then on a wet Sunday to keep within doors all the sunless hours, except while attending divine worship? Oh, these very generous people have their nice cosy clubs or homes which they enjoy every day. But the collier has to live in discomfort in a small home, and for near six months in every year never sees the sun, except on the first day of the week.[65]

Many anti-sabbatarians who wished the Welsh Sunday to be improved for the working man but without its general character as a day of rest being endangered, argued that education or moral suasion, and not legislative enactments, would be a more successful method of reducing Sunday drunkenness and disorderly conduct; that the Sunday opening of museums, theatres, coffee taverns and newspaper rooms at hours other than those of church service would result in a more knowledgeable and 'improved' working class, amongst which drunkenness would not be so marked; indeed, that Sunday drunkenness was a direct result of the Sunday closing of places of public recreation.[66] However, such enlightened proposals invariably fell on deaf ears. Any effort towards providing rational and harmless recreation for the working man on a Sunday was consistently blocked by sabbatarians, and stigmatized as a conspiracy to deprive the working man of his day of rest. The Sunday Closing Act exacerbated this tendency, for the clause in the Act which permitted *bona fide* travellers on Sunday to obtain drink if they could prove that they had travelled over three miles, led sabbatarians to oppose any form of entertainment on Sunday so as to prevent any inducement to Sunday travelling.[67]

Working-class opposition to sabbatarian views in general, and to the Welsh Sunday Closing Act in particular, was thus very real. However, the Sunday Closing Bill would hardly have become law if it had not had the support of the majority of Welsh working men. During the 1870s the agitation for a Sunday Closing Act for Wales was proceeding apace and the canvasses taken by various interested bodies showed an overwhelming preponderance of working men in favour of Sunday closing. As far as we know, no meeting of working men was held in Wales in opposition to the proposed measure.[68] Again, very few petitions against the proposed Bill were sent to parliament, and the only marked working-class opposition came from Cardiff in a petition organized by Cardiff Licensed Victuallers Association. Some 16,844 signatures were obtained against the bill, including 3,324 labourers and 1,768 seamen (see Table 12). However, Cardiff—an anglicized town with a large impermanent population—was not a typical example of Welsh working-class sentiment on the Sunday closing question. Moreover, the trade in Cardiff was much better organized than anywhere else in Wales to fight against what it saw as an appalling threat to its livelihood.

TABLE 12. CLASSIFIED LIST OF SIGNATORIES TO THE PETITION AGAINST THE WELSH SUNDAY CLOSING BILL, 1881

Accountants	47	Coal merchants	48
Agents and Travellers	737	Coal trimmers	468
Architects	7	Constables	2
Auctioneers	5	Coopers	15
Bakers	154	Coppersmiths	24
Basket makers	1	Coppersmelters	10
Billiard markers	5	Cordwainers	21
Blacksmiths	291	Corn porters	8
Blockmakers	8	Curriers	16
Boilermakers	218	Dock gasmen	12
Bookbinders	5	Drapers	97
Brewers	19	Dyers	8
Bricklayers	92	Engine Drivers	73
Builders	98	Farmers	81
Butchers	220	Firemen	461
Cabdrivers	109	Fitters	598
Carpenters	678	Gardeners	125
Chandlers	7	Gasfitters	41
Chemists	12	Gentlemen	99
Chimney sweeps	19	Grocers	147
Clerks	485	Gunsmiths	3

TABLE 12. CLASSIFIED LIST OF SIGNATORIES TO THE PETITION AGAINST THE WELSH SUNDAY CLOSING BILL, 1881—continued

Hauliers	150	Puddlers	24
Hobblers and Stevedores	85	Railwaymen	231
Hairdressers	48	Saddlers	33
Hawkers	127	Sailmakers	33
Innkeepers	109	Sawmakers and Cutlers	8
J.P.s	2	Sawyers	53
Labourers	3,324	Schoolmasters	6
Locksmiths	4	Seamen	1,768
Major	1	Shipbrokers	12
Machinists	21	Shipwrights	158
Masons	479	Shoemakers	111
Master Mariners	130	Shopkeepers	88
Merchants	213	Soldiers	6
Milkmen	31	Solicitors	18
Millers	26	Surgeons	7
Ostlers	181	Surveyors	4
Painters	322	Tailors	173
Pattern makers	52	Tinsmiths	46
Pawnbrokers	11	Undescribed	475
Photographers	12	Upholsterers	70
Pilots	80	Warehousemen	53
Plasterers	140	Watchmakers	26
Plumbers	78	Watermen	70
Porters	53	Weavers	4
Printers and Compositors	108	Wheelwrights	55
Professionals	64	Women	1,887
		TOTAL:	16,844

Source: *Licensed Victuallers Guardian*, 4 June 1881, p. 269.

Numerous public meetings were held in favour of Sunday closing in Wales during the late 1860s and early '70s, but it was not until 1875 that the demand for a separate legislative enactment was made explicit. Here, it was the English Grand Lodge of the Good Templars in Wales, and not the more autochthonous Welsh Grand Lodge, which played a very important rôle.[69] At the annual meeting of the English Lodge at Swansea on 17 August 1875 it was determined to frame a temperance bill for Wales which would embody not only total Sunday closing but also local option and the abolition of grocers' licences.[70] At a Swansea conference of ministers and laymen in October 1875 a resolution was passed 'that a measure be introduced into Parliament specially for Wales providing for the entire closing of public houses on the Lord's Day'.[71] On 17 November a deputation from the English Lodge of the Good Templars, headed by the Merthyr Liberal, W. L. Daniel, and comprising Dr. Rawlings of Swansea, Rev. Charles Ayliffe of Newport and John Fergusson of Cardiff, waited upon Henry Richard, the member for Merthyr, at Zoar Schoolroom in the town, to discuss the proposal to introduce a temperance bill for Wales, which would cover the licensing question in general.[72] At the meeting, Richard expressed himself in favour of a separate bill for Wales respecting any temperance legislation, and promised to confer with other Welsh members. However, the Welsh members and the temperance organizations in Wales restricted their demand to Sunday closing alone, realising, presumably, that a proposed item of temperance legislation for Wales would have a better chance of becoming law if it were confined solely to Sunday closing, which was in consonance with the religious sentiment of Wales, and which would stand a better chance of success in parliament.

The near-unanimous feeling in Wales in favour of a Sunday closing bill was shown by the many canvasses and meetings held by the Good Templars and the Manchester-based Central Association for Stopping the Sale of Intoxicating Liquor during the Whole of the Twenty Four Hours of a Sunday (C.A.S.S.I.L.S.). These two bodies, along with the support of church and chapel, were responsible for the intense agitation of the 1870s. The precautions about using this type of evidence have been mentioned in the previous chapter. Most serious of all, most of the canvasses were restricted to householders: members of the hard-drinking residuum were left largely untouched. The sheer number of petitions may not necessarily have connoted strong feelings on the issue and such numbers could be determined almost at will.

Strenuous efforts were made during the period 1878-80 to carry out a comprehensive canvass of opinion among the householders in nineteen Welsh towns.[73] The results showed that 38,443 householders were in favour of Sunday closing, 717 against and 1,202 remained neutral.[74] At Aberdare the canvassing committee analysed the returns, 'that the public might know the opinion of householders in different social positions'. The only detailed returns given were those for the working class, and the analysis showed that 92 per cent of the collier-householders and 93 per cent of the artisan-and labourer-householders who were canvassed were in favour of Sunday closing.[75] At Mountain Ash too, the returns of the canvass showed the depth of working-class householder support for the proposed measure (see Table 13).

TABLE 13. CANVASS OF HOUSEHOLDERS AT MOUNTAIN ASH ON THE QUESTION OF STOPPING THE SALE OF INTOXICATING LIQUOR ON SUNDAYS, 14 MAY 1878

				Percentage of Each 'Class'		
Occupation	For	Against	Neutral	For	Against	Neutral
Colliers	438	12	15	94.2	2.6	3.2
Labourers	194	18	6	89.2	8.2	2.6
Mechanics	84	13	8	79.6	12.6	7.8
Tradesmen	58	5	5	85.2	7.4	7.4
Widows	50	—	2	96.1	—	3.9
Engine drivers and Firemen	35	2	—	94.6	5.4	—
Unemployed	29	5	2	80.6	14.8	5.6
Colliery Managers, Overmen and Weighers	26	3	—	89.7	10.3	—
Railway Employers	10	—	1	91	—	1
Ministers	7	—	—	100	—	—
Professionals	6	1	2	66.7	11.1	22.2
Publicans	3	5	1	33.3	55.6	11.1
Farmers	1	1	—	50	50	—
TOTAL	941	65	42	89.9	6.1	4

Source: D. M. Richards to H. H. Vivian, 25 May 1878. N.L.W., Lord Swansea Collection: 'Sunday Closing and Permissive Bill, Correspondence, c. 1875' (an enclosure).

Considering the fact that publicans stood to lose a considerable part of their trade—the working man had more money in his pocket on a Sunday than on any other day in the week—those who were questioned during the canvass of 1878-80 did not come out in any strength against the proposed Sunday closing measure. Many remained neutral. Thus, 423 pronounced themselves in favour of an Act, 100 were against, with 160 neutral.[76] In all, between 1875 and 1881, 1,173 publicans in Wales declared their opinion: 792 for total Sunday closing, 152 against and 229 neutral.[77] Temperance and sabbatarian advocates had, of course, to make much of the argument that they were fighting also for the welfare of the publican, who must have his day of rest every week.[78] Sunday opening, it was argued, contributed to over-work. Publicans and their staffs worked over a hundred hours per week, whereas the Factory Acts prescribed fifty-six-and-a-half hours a week. A stock temperance claim was that, according to insurance companies, publicans were a short-lived group. Temperance reformers received the support of many local tradesmen and shop-keepers who were incensed that the publican should be legally licensed to transact his business on a Sunday while they should be legally compelled to close. The feeling was that publicans must be put on the same footing as other trades.[79]

Only the publicans at Cardiff, Newport and a few other large towns made efforts to organize petitions and memorials against Sunday closing. The licensed victuallers at Cardiff maintained that the vindictive Liberal government was seeking to punish publicans for having given their votes to the Conservatives in 1874, and they decided to boycott nonconformist places of worship.[80] But no thoroughly organized opposition amongst the trade manifested itself. No separate trade canvass was undertaken and very few representatives from the Licensed Victuallers National Defence League came into Wales. Moreover, the publicans had no friends among the Welsh M.P.s, and during the various stages of the Sunday Closing Bill's passage through parliament they had to rely on English members, notably Edward Warton, member for Bridport, to oppose the measure.

In September 1879 John Roberts, the member for Flint District, gave notice of introducing a Sunday Closing Bill for Wales, maintaining that the feeling in Wales in favour of such a measure was so strong 'that the continuance of the Sunday traffic is impossible without doing violence to the Welsh nation generally'.[81] The bill was read a first time on 6 February 1880 and was endorsed by Roberts, Henry Richard, Samuel Holland (Merioneth), H. H. Vivian, Watkin Williams and Osborne Morgan. During the second reading, on 30 June, Roberts stated that Welsh feeling was so unanimous, and there were so many difficulties connected with the question of closing public houses in England on Sundays, that he felt it his duty to ask the House to pass a bill 'which would be distinctly applicable to the Principality of Wales', and which would be modelled on the Irish Sunday Closing Act of 1878.[82] The only opposition to the measure came from Warton, a constant spokesman of the trade in the Commons, who argued that Wales was a part of England, and gave voice to the real fear of the trade that the bill 'was an attempt to let in by a kind of side wind the principle of Local Option'.[83] But his argument that the 'very excellence' of the Welsh people rendered the measure unnecessary was met with the answer that the temptation was always present and should be removed.

The bill passed its second reading without a division and was put down for the committee stage on 12 July. In the meantime, hostile tactics were employed by the trade. Amendments were placed on the notice paper by Warton and Onslow (Guildford) and the bill could not get into committee without the help of the government. However, the end of the session was approaching and other business proved too pressing; the bill was withdrawn on 2 September.

At the opening of the 1880-81 session Roberts' Bill was the first in the ballot among private members, and was read a first time on 7 January 1881. During the debate on the second reading on 4 May supporters of the Bill stressed the Irish precedent, and the support for the measure, not only from the people of Wales, but from their parliamentary representatives, of whom only Lord Emlyn (Carmarthenshire) was against it.[84] The most notable feature of the debate was the claim that Wales was justified in demanding separate legislation on the issue. Osborne Morgan, the Judge-Advocate-General, maintained that parliament had legislated 'departmentally' on the drink question in fixing different hours of closing time for London, for provincial towns and for rural districts. He continued, 'I think it is time that people should understand that in dealing with Wales you are really dealing with an entirely distinct nationality, a nationality more distinct than that of the Scotch or Irish, because Wales is separated from England not merely by race and by geographical boundaries, but by a barrier which interposes at every turn of life—I mean the barrier of language'. Moreover, the whole social, moral and religious atmosphere of Wales was different from that of England; the Welsh, it seemed, were ready for Sunday closing.[85]

Of decisive importance was the support of Gladstone, who spoke for fifteen minutes in favour of the Bill.[86] He noted that not one of the speeches against the Bill had come from Welsh members, and that those who opposed it had not said anything that could influence the House in its rejection. He admitted that in the past it had not been the custom of parliament to consider Welsh opinion as 'a distinct independent factor', and that Wales had been regarded as being in a closer relationship to England than either Scotland or Ireland.

> But I am bound to say that it appears to me that we have pushed these considerations too far. . . . Where there is a distinctly formed Welsh opinion, as in the present case, upon a given subject which affects Wales alone, and the acceptance of which does not entail any public danger or public inconvenience to the rest of the Empire, I know no reason why a respectful regard should not be paid to that opinion.[87]

Gladstone's justification was that the Sunday closing question was not a question involving constitutional, political or parliamentary control but a question of local police enforcement and supervision, and on this question parliament had distinguished already between England and Scotland, England and Ireland, and between different parts of England.[88] The Bill easily passed its second reading by a majority of 146, only 17 voting against.

In committee, attempts were made by both sides to amend the Bill. The attempt by Edward Carbutt (Monmouthshire) to get his county included in the Bill was unsuccessful. He argued, quite correctly as events were to show, that the boundary between Wales and Monmouthshire was densely populated and determined drinkers would be able to cross the River Rhymney into Monmouthshire, where the public houses would be open, whereas if Monmouthshire was included in the Bill, the boundary would consist of a largely agricultural district which would offer fewer difficulties over enforcement. However, the Attorney-General argued that Monmouthshire, although a predominantly Welsh-speaking county, was legally a part of England.[89] Similarly, the attempt of Hardinge Giffarde (Cardiff District) to obtain the exemption of Cardiff from the provisions of the Bill, on account of its large migratory population, also failed, and the Bill passed through committee on 15 June.[90]

During June and July it seemed as if the Bill would suffer the same fate as its predecessor of the previous year. The Irish Land Bill dominated. Although the Welsh Bill was down for its third reading on 6 July, Gladstone had inimated the night before that no time could be found for it.[91] However, on Saturday, 20 August, in highly controversial circumstances, the Bill finally passed its third reading intact.[92] The 'trade' was in uproar. Its spokesmen in the House complained bitterly that the third reading had been sprung upon the House—a 'trick of legislating by surprise'—near midnight, when only seventy members were present, and on that day of the week when sittings of the House were traditionally called for government business only, and that the sitting of 20 August had been called for supply. It was also a tradition that 'blocking' did not apply on a Saturday at the end of a session.[93] It seems likely then that the passing of the third reading of the Bill was very well stage-managed by the Liberal government, though there is no direct contemporary evidence to support this contention. Under the guidance of Lord Aberdare the Bill passed rapidly through the House of Lords, and received the Royal Assent on 27 August.

The operation of the Sunday Closing Act aroused intense controversy, but of more importance was the underlying principle of the Act: for the first time in its history, the Imperial Parliament had sanctioned separate legislative treatment for Wales. Although there had been many 'Welsh Acts' in the past, 'never before had a distinctive legislative principle been applied to Wales, as distinct from England'.[94] Such separate treatment seemed to be justified, as England and Wales did not form an indivisible whole on the Sunday closing question: Sunday closing for Wales seemed to be a national demand, whereas sabbatarian restrictions on the sale of liquor in England had resulted in immense opposition and, in 1855, serious riots.[95]

The principle of separate treatment for Wales naturally aroused consternation among Anglicans, and some clergymen refused to sign petitions in support of the Act.[96] Opponents of the idea of separate legislation for Wales saw clearly that 'the Dissenters are going in for disestablishment, and if they get Sunday closing first, they will try for closing ever day in the week, with I don't know what else besides, immediately after'.[97] In 1889 the *Western Mail*, a Conservative newspaper, maintained that the Act was merely a means to an end in that it was the first instalment of Home Rule.[98] This was exactly the view and the hope of politically-active Liberals, nonconformists and nationalists in Wales. They saw, with Thomas Williams of Gwaelodygarth, that 'that measure would bring very radical reforms about in Wales in time to come'.[99] Williams said he regarded the Act as a precedent for the disestablishment and disendowment of the Church of England in Wales. The will of the people had won Sunday closing: it would also win disestablishment. Gladstone was embarrassingly reminded of his remarks in favour of Welsh Sunday closing when, in August 1885, Henry Richard, who had played an important rôle from the outset in pushing the claim of Wales to separate legislation on the temperance question, referred Gladstone to his 'kind and most generous speech' on the second reading of the Sunday Closing Bill in May 1881. Gladstone, Richard maintained, had then laid down the *principle* that a 'respectful regard' should be paid to 'a distinctly formed Welsh opinion upon a given subject', and intimated that, on the basis of this statement, Gladstone should surely support a measure for Welsh disestablishment.[100] Similarly, the Sunday Closing Act was used in 1888 to support the argument for the establishment of a Welsh Grand Committee 'for the consideration of all Bills relating to Wales'.[101] As Osborne Morgan asserted during the second reading of the Local Veto (Wales) Bill in March 1891, arguments used by the opponents of the Bill and founded on the premise that Wales was an integral part of England, had 'come too late'.[102] Distinctive treatment had been given to Wales over Sunday closing and, in 1889, over intermediate education: Wales was not to be regarded as being a mere part of England.

The 1880s witnessed an immense controversy over the efficacy of the Act, and great statistical warfare was joined as to whether the Act had resulted in an increase or a decrease in Sunday drunkenness. Generally speaking, the Act was successful in rural areas and in the towns of north Wales, where it was least needed, but met with a great amount of evasion in the urban communities of south Wales. The inconvenience and hardship of a closed public house on a Sunday was acutely felt in parts of Wales, as beer, the national drink, was not as portable nor as easily preserved fresh as was, for example, whisky, the national drink of Scotland and Ireland, where Sunday closing was also in operation. Consequently, the demand for drink on a Sunday manifested itself more clearly in Wales than in Scotland and

Ireland.[103] Border smuggling, the opening of clubs and the abuse of the *bona fide* traveller clause of the Act were among the most popular forms of evasion of the Act.

Publicans estimated that the closing of their houses on the day which, they claimed, was the most profitable in the week, would mean an average loss to them of £300 per head per year.[104] Indeed, a major effect of the Act was to divert business from the more scrupulous to the less scrupulous publicans, who were willing to run the police gauntlet.[105] This was especially noticeable at Merthyr Tydfil, where 85 of the 125 licensed houses in 1889 were 'tied houses', occupied by tenants who went into the business with little capital and who risked very little when they violated the law. Their insecurity of tenure fashioned the attitude that they had to make all the money they could while they were thus employed.[106] To circumvent the Act, casks of beer were sold to Saturday-night customers for Sunday consumption.[107] Of course, the effect of this was to transfer drinking from the public houses to the homes of the people, with a consequent increase in female drunkenness, and a danger that more over-indulgence would occur in private homes than in public houses, where landlords stood to lose heavily if they permitted drunkenness on their premises.

A major effect of the Act was to create a demand for drink at public houses situated a little over three miles from populous centres. The clause of the Licensing Act of 1874 which had been incorporated in the Welsh Sunday Closing Act, had provided that a person 'shall not be deemed a *bona fide* traveller unless the place where he lodged the previous night is at least three miles from the place where he demands to be supplied with liquor'. It had been decided that a person was not a *bona fide* traveller if he travelled for the sole purpose of obtaining drink, but if the person who served him with liquor believed that he was a traveller, he ought not to be convicted. This situation inclined magistrates to take the view that a three-mile journey was the test of being a *bona fide* traveller under the Act. This, however, was not the correct interpretation of the law, but as the real test was the intention of the purchaser and the knowledge of the seller, it was very difficult to apply. A test case in 1882 gave the decision that a person who went to a public house on a Sunday for refreshment while in the course of a journey, whether for business or pleasure, was entitled to demand drink, and the publican was justified in supplying it.[108] Naturally, temperance advocates took the view that a *bona fide* traveller was a person who, in the course of business only, was compelled to travel on Sundays. There is little doubt that the overwhelming majority of so-called *bona fide* travellers were travelling solely to obtain a Sunday drink: from Cardiff to Penarth and Barry; from Swansea to the Mumbles; from Pontypridd to Porth; from Bethesda to Bangor, and from Bangor to Beaumaris.[109]

Few *bona fide* travellers were found in those communities in south Wales where the result of the Act was the proliferation of clubs and shebeens. Temperance advocates correctly maintained that clubs had been in existence for some years before 1881, but there is no doubt that the Act increased the number, the sale of drink being diverted to clubs from properly regulated and police-controlled licensed houses.[110] The shebeen, or bogus club, existed at Cardiff, Barry and Dowlais, and was similar to the old *cwrw bach* in that it was 'a [private] place where beer is taken in casks from a wholesale dealer and consumed upon premises which are unlicensed'.[111] It is not surprising, therefore, that the growth of clubs and shebeens was vigorously opposed by publicans. It was not necessary to register clubs nor to obtain a licence; there were no fixed hours, and clubs often took more money on a Sunday than most licensed houses took in the whole week.[112] Between June 1882 and June 1883 over 3,000 working men joined clubs in Cardiff: an increase of 900 per cent over the previous year.[113] There is no doubt that such clubs supplied a real social need in a large community like Cardiff after 1881. A census undertaken by David Davies, assistant editor of the *Western Mail*, in the summer of 1889, revealed that the total number of shebeens in Cardiff was in excess of 480, and these were concentrated in Grangetown (40), Cathays (79), Newtown (45), Canton (38), Roath (91), Dockland (57), and in the central part of the town, including, ironically, Temperance Town (137).[114] Many were run by peripatetic workmen, mostly Irish navvies engaged on the construction of Barry Docks, and invariably, they sold a highly adulterated beer—described by one consumer as 'a cross between senna and vinegar'—which was bought at 8*d.* a gallon and sold at 6*d.* a quart: a 300 per cent profit.[115]

Nevertheless, temperance reformers insisted that Sunday drunkenness decreased after 1881, and that the Act was a 'great boon' to Wales. The opposition, headed by the *Western Mail* of Cardiff, declared that the effect of the Act had been an increase in Sunday drunkenness and a decrease in week-day drunkenness. Both sides quoted statistics of drunkenness at each other, but these were of little value as there was often little relation between figures for arrests for drunkenness and the incidence of drunkenness. As Lord Aberdare admitted to the *Western Mail* in January 1889:

> It is a commonplace to say that statistics are misleading. It is true to say that of all statistics those on drunkenness are the most misleading. . . . It is no exaggeration to say that the number of convictions may be doubled or halved in accordance with the instructions of the chief constable or the bench, the numbers of drunkards remaining the same. . . . Yet, after all, they certainly supply the best prima facie evidence we possess.[116]

Most statistical returns are unreliable, but it is likely that the least inaccurate statistics were placed before the Royal Commission in 1889-90. These statistics contained all those cases of 'simple drunkenness' as well as those of 'drunk and disorderly', between 6 a.m. on Sunday morning and 6 a.m. on Monday morning. The Commission was at pains to mention facts which might have affected the statistics: varying police enforcement, changes in the size and movement of the population, prosperity or depression in trade and industry, and the presence of large works in process of construction during the 1880s.[117] The statistics show that the Act led to an increase in Sunday drunkenness in Glamorgan and the borough of Cardiff, but a general reduction in drunkenness in rural areas where the Act was least necessary.

On the other hand, the *Western Mail,* armed with its own particular body of statistics, argued vehemently that the Act had been a total failure. On 31 December 1888 the newspaper published a set of returns which showed that, during 1885-87, week-day drunkenness had decreased, but Sunday drunkenness had increased. This prompted Lord Aberdare to challenge the editor, Lascelles Carr, to institute an enquiry into the true state of affairs. Accordingly, a 'Special Commissioner' was appointed by the *Western Mail,* who was to make periodical Sunday tours in the area extending from Carmarthenshire to the English border, and comprising agricultural, mining and purely urban districts, to collect all available information bearing on the effect of the Act, and to report impartially on what he saw and heard.[118]

The enquiry painted a very black picture: Sunday drunkenness had increased as a result of the imposition of restrictions which were not capable of absolute enforcement.[119] Temperance advocates claimed that the enquiry was biased: it was conducted by one man, David Davies of the *Western Mail*, the mouthpiece of the drink trade in Wales; no attempt had been made to assess the situation in north and west Wales; and most of those interviewed by Davies were publicans and policemen.[120] Nevertheless Lord Aberdare felt himself obliged to admit the failure of the Act: 'The effect . . . on my mind of the picture presented by your correspondent is such, that were a Bill introduced into Parliament for the repeal of the Welsh Sunday Closing Act, I could not, unless evidence were adduced of better effects produced by a better administration of the law, vote against it.'[121] Although he was undecided as to whether the failure of the Act was due to its 'inherent impolicy' or to 'causes within public control', Lord Aberdare's 'frank admissions . . . caused the most profound sensation in the minds alike of the friends and foes of Temperance legislation'.[122] The efforts of the *Western Mail* to prove the Act a failure and the admission of its failure by the man who had piloted the Bill through the House of Lords, were major factors causing a Royal Commission to be set up in March 1889 to enquire into the effects of the Act.

On 19 March 1889, J. M. Maclean, Conservative M.P. for Oldham and a proprietor of the *Western Mail,* called the attention of the Home Secretary to the recent statement of Lord Aberdare on the Sunday Closing Act, and demanded an enquiry. It was decided to hold a Royal Commission, the members of which were to be Lord Balfour (the Chairman), Lord Emlyn, J. T. Hibbert, Judge Horatio Lloyd, Richard Harrington and Professor John Rhys (the Secretary).[123] Welsh nonconformist opinion erupted. The *Western Mail* was compared to Balaam who was hired to curse the children of Israel.[124] The demand for a Royal Commission had come from 'a Lancashire Tory': no Welsh members had asked for such 'a futile and superfluous enquiry'.[125] Moreover, the request of the Welsh members for the appointment of Lord Herschell, a Liberal, as chairman of the Commission, had been ignored.[126] The composition of the Commission was held to be a public scandal. It had been blatantly 'packed' with four Tories and a weak Liberal, and no true Welshman or nonconformist at all. The dominant feeling was that the Commission would 'sell a nation to please a party': there was a real prospect of another *Brad y Llyfrau Gleision.*[127]

The view that the Commission would report against the successful working of the Act was not realized. Once again, intense agitation by temperance supporters brought in numerous memorials, resolutions and petitions, this time in favour of the working of the Act, especially from churches and chapels, and efforts were made to prepare sympathetic witnesses to give evidence before the Commission. Later, the Commissioners were to admit that the value of the evidence they had taken was 'seriously affected' by the 'scarcity of witnesses prepared to approach the question in a judicial manner, and not rather as advocates of the one side or the other'.[128] But as the historian of the English temperance movement has noted, nineteenth-century enquiries into the temperance question too easily relied on interested pressure groups to provide their witnesses; consequently it was difficult to proceed from subjective impression to objective statistical analysis.[129] Few working men appeared or were called before the Sunday Closing Commission, while temperance partisans of the middle and upper classes, whose callings did not bring them into contact with the people affected by the Act, were represented too strongly among the witnesses and gave evidence consisting largely of opinions and not facts.[130] The first hundred witnesses before the Commission comprised only six working men but also thirty-four magistrates and police officials.[131] Doubtless, many working men could not afford to lose work in order to appear before the Commission, but if there had been widespread opposition among working men to the measure, it surely would have found an outlet. The large towns and ports of south Wales with their large population of lodgers might seem likely places where serious opposition could have manifested itself. Lodgers relied on public houses for food and recreation because they were usually unwelcome at their lodgings except to sleep. Yet, the only demonstration against the Act was held at Cardiff in October 1889 when 2,000 working men marched through the town demanding 'British Rights for British Working Men', and 'No Compulsory Sunday Closing'.[132] In the following month, the Sunday closing question was the major issue in the municipal election in the West Ward of the town. The Conservative platform was 'Reasonable Sunday Opening' and 'The Liberty of the Working Man'. The leading Tory candidate, E. J. Smith, President of Cardiff Licensed Victuallers Association, was returned by a substantial majority.[133]

What were the recommendations of the Royal Commission? The Commissioners maintained that it was very difficult to decide whether the Act had increased or diminished Sunday drunkenness. In the rural areas of Wales it had aided the cause of temperance by removing a temptation from the weak minority. In some urban areas, notably most of the towns of Glamorgan, the Act had not been accepted, but constantly evaded and defied. The view of the Commissioners was that recreative counter-attractions, combined with the limited opening of public houses on Sunday, would be more likely to bring a greater degree of sobriety to such areas than the Sunday Closing Act. But this the Commissioners gave as their own opinion, and they did not place it among their suggested amendments.[134] They stated that limited opening on Sunday would be unwelcome to the majority of the Welsh people, and in this, they were probably influenced more by the absence of any general demand by working men for Sunday opening than by a belief in the success of the Act.

On the vexed question of the *bona fide* traveller, the three-mile limit was abolished altogether, and instead, every person who applied for drink, on the ground of his being a traveller had to be able to prove that he was travelling for some other purpose than that of obtaining drink, and that he had not remained in a public house on a Sunday longer than was absolutely required for the transaction of his business, or of obtaining refreshment. The traveller was obliged to give his name and address to the publican, who entered it in a book open to police inspection. A publican who neglected to do this had the privilege of supplying travellers absolutely forfeited.

As far as clubs and shebeens were concerned, the police were to have their power of search greatly extended, and every club in which liquor was sold or supplied to its members was to be registered with the local authority of the district in which the club was situated, the register and rules of the club being open for inspection by the police. Shebeens and those 'clubs' existing only for the purpose of supplying intoxicating drinks to the members were to be declared absolutely illegal. Thus, the Commissioners approved of the Act in general, but criticized it in detail.

What of the criticism voiced before the Commission that the Act constituted an unwarrantable interference with the legitimate liberty of the minority—that it was unjust to punish by legislation the many moderate drinkers for the few who drank to excess? As far as the *Western Mail* was concerned, the Act was a piece of 'grandmotherly' legislation which affirmed that Welshmen were unable to take care of themselves, and unfit to be entrusted with the regulation of their own private conduct on one day out of seven. That the majority of Welsh people wanted the Act was a reason for not passing it, because 'to assume a majority in favour of such an Act is to assume the existence of a state of things which rendered the Act unnecessary'.[135] A legal enforcement compelled moderate drinkers to abstain, but 'unless the conscience of the individual goes freely with the legal restraint, it partakes of the degradation of slavery'. To temperance advocates, however, restrictions on the sale of Sunday drink were entirely justifiable. For them, the Welsh Sunday Closing Act was a practical manifestation of Gladstone's dictum that the 'Government should legislate so as to make it easy to do right and difficult to do wrong'. Liberty did not mean freedom to follow a man's own recklessness and vice irrespective of the good of his neighbours or of himself, but meant the privilege enjoyed by a people of governing themselves, and that privilege included the power of the majority to coerce a 'selfish' minority by measures of 'punishment' and 'repression'. It was impossible to claim that restrictive laws were good or bad in themselves, but that in each case the merit or demerit of such laws depended upon the practical question whether the result would be a balance of good or evil for the community. Individual liberty, then, was not an argument in favour of non-interference by the state. If men who drank to excess formed a society by themselves and injured none but themselves, then non-interference would be justified. But this was not the case. The drinker and the abstainer had to live side by side in society and had equally to conform to its rules if they wished to live in comfort.

On balance, the Welsh Sunday Closing Act seems to have resulted in increased sobriety in Wales on Sunday, with the notable exceptions of Glamorgan in general and Cardiff in particular, where the alcohol dripped through the dotted line. The Act set a legal seal on what was respectable and what was not respectable. The effect of the Act, it could be argued, was to create a *malum prohibitum* which was not a *malum per se,* and the result was to bring the law into disrepute. The Act demoralized the publicans, who were forced to do that which was against the law and run the risk of detection. Moreover, in some areas the irony was that publicans had to work harder on Sundays than before 1881 as, until 1890, no limit was placed on the hours during which a *bona fide* traveller or alleged *bona fide* traveller might be, or endeavoured to be, supplied.[136] The Act demoralized those young children who were used as agents for procuring liquor and as street-corner spies to watch for the police. The Act demoralized the police, who were forced to engage in ludicrous forms of espionage in order to discover illicit drinking practices. The Act demoralized the bench, in the sense that some magistrates could afford to keep a private cellar and consume drink on a Sunday, whereas the next morning they might be obliged to condemn and punish a working man for Sunday drinking. Despite its shortcomings, the Welsh Sunday Closing Act was upheld and was extended to Monmouthshire in 1921. It remained inviolable until the Licensing Act of 1961.

After the passing of the Welsh Sunday Closing Act, Welsh temperance reformers felt there was good reason to go to the government and ask for a local option bill for Wales.[137] At a temperance conference at Rhyl in October 1886 representatives of the Alliance and Welsh temperance bodies formed themselves into a committee to draft a Welsh local option bill.[138] The nature of the bill decided upon represented a defeat for the Alliance, for the bill allowed for either the reduction of licences or the stopping of the increase of licences or total prohibition, instead of the one choice only of immediate and total prohibition which the Alliance favoured. In defending the draft bill the Rev. John Thomas of Liverpool pointed out that as sensible people they were considering not so much what they should wish to do as what they could do. He maintained that he believed wholeheartedly in prohibition but 'if they were going to stand on that ground they would only delay the question for thirty years'; it was better to try to secure what they might have a chance of obtaining rather than aim at what appeared impracticable.[139]

There seems little doubt that the Welsh local option and direct veto bills of the late 1880s and early '90s were intended, in part, to secure the recognition of Welsh nationality. The Sunday Closing Act was a precedent and an inspiration. Henry Richard—no root and branch separatist—admitted that in matters of temperance and education Wales possessed a 'distinct nationality', and that special circumstances justified the Welsh people in demanding separate legislation: 'It is mere pedantry to adhere to an articifial uniformity when some variation of law and administration may be just and useful.'[140]

In the opinion of the more radical members of *Cymru Fydd* (the Young Wales movement), such as Tom Ellis and Lloyd George, Wales must wash its hands of the responsibility of keeping up the revenue of England by degrading its men, women and children through the use of strong drink. Why must stern, dutiful Wales be tacked on to demoralized England? Speaking at Brighton in March 1891 Lloyd George maintained that 90 per cent of the inhabitants of Wales were in favour of the direct veto and 75 per cent in favour of total prohibition. Why didn't they get it? He feared England blocked the way. Drink was a great national evil 'and yet they spent night after night in the House of Commons discussing trivial, slight—he might say idiotic—pottering little questions with that great question unsettled'.[141] Ellis believed that the Welsh must use their influence 'as a people' to control the liquor traffic so as to purify their lives, to increase their self-respect, self-control, self-conquest and thrift.[142] He was dubious whether this could be done by local option. Indeed, in 1889, Ellis came out in favour of a 'definite temperance policy' for Wales in view of the forthcoming report of the Sunday Closing Commission. Ellis wanted to introduce temperance bills for Wales to combat the most glaring evils and not 'yet another Direct Veto Bill for Wales which is the same as those for England, Scotland and Ulster'.[143] To persist with local option and direct veto, Ellis argued, did not enable Wales to give any real lead or guidance in temperance reform. However, his proposals were not taken up and the principle of local option was persevered with.

A local option bill for Wales was first introduced into the Commons by Bowen Rowlands in 1887. The bill provided for a direct popular veto on the liquor traffic throughout the various parishes and districts in Wales. It involved a system of licensing reform which allowed the ratepayers several choices of policy, rather than the Permissive Bill's all or nothing choice. Under the terms of the bill a two-thirds ratepayer majority could obtain the prohibition of the sale of intoxicating liquor in a district and a simple majority was required for the reduction of the number of licences to a specified number and for the proposal that no new licences should be granted. Opponents of the bill were quick to point out that it was restrictive only; that to be just in principle the bill should confer the power of increasing what people regarded as conveniences as well as the power of suppressing what they regarded as evils or nuisances. The bill received its first reading on 14 February but no further progress could be made, and it was withdrawn for the session on 16 July. A similar bill, introduced in February 1889, met with the same fate. A third bill, introduced in November 1890, met with more success, and its second reading was fixed for 18 March 1891.

The Alliance strongly supported the bill and urged Lloyd George—in his capacity as 'Temperance Whip' for the Welsh members—to do his utmost to secure a large attendance of Welsh members on that day.[144] Lloyd George determined that an effort should be made to prevent supporters of the bill from 'pairing', and to induce them to be present in the House and to vote.

> Men like Kenyon* and West** may not like to vote against the Bill straight but they would rather like to get out of it by pairing *generally* in favour of the Government. That is my point and if it is well urged throughout England we may yet carry our Welsh Bill. I have endeavoured to get the Alliance to press their agents throughout the U.K. to get influential *Unionists* in every constituency—men who happen to be Temperance supporters—to write to their respective members to vote for the Bill. This will at least have the effect of preventing their voting against the Bill and in the case of *liberal* unionists it may induce them to cast their vote for it. A small majority would to a great extent answer our purpose.[145]

During the debate on the second reading of the bill, familiar arguments were reiterated by both sides. Particularly noticeable was the speech of Osborne Morgan in support of the bill. He asserted that the arguments used by opponents of the measure in the debate and founded on the idea that Wales was a part of England had been made too late in the day, as Wales had already received separate treatment over Sunday closing and intermediate education. He openly admitted that the bill was an item of experimental legislation and the thin end of the disestablishment wedge.[146] It was finally carried by 6 votes.[147] The government did not attempt to oppose the measure and remained neutral.[148] Lloyd George wrote exultantly to Tom Ellis of 'our splendid victory', which was 'quite unexpected as the Welshmen were all absent with the exception of six staunch teetotallers amongst them'.[149] This was not an accurate statement, as 22 Welsh members had voted for the second reading. For the Alliance, 'the outpost has fallen and the capture of the main citadel is but a question of time'.[150] On 19 March the House went into committee on the bill and the Marquis of Carmarthen, a director of Hollands Gin, moved a sweeping amendment of the measure. But no further stage was reached. The bill stood as a first order on 27 May but on 26 May Lord Elcho moved an adjournment of the House until 28 May, the 27th being Derby Day. This aristocratic motion was opposed by

---

* Unionist M.P. for Denbigh District.
** Liberal M.P. for Denbighshire: Liberal Unionist for Denbighshire after 1892.

Bowen Rowlands, Wilfrid Lawson and W. V. Harcourt, but was carried by a majority of 28. The bill was kept on the notice paper until 14 July, when there was no possible chance left, and it became a dropped order.[151]

In March 1893 the Welsh-American, Major Evan Jones (Carmarthenshire) introduced another local option bill for Wales side by side with W. V. Harcourt's more general local option measure. During the summer of 1892 the Welsh Party had re-cast the Welsh local option bill so as to make it more extreme and hence, as events were to show, more unrealistic.[152] It was decided to frame a bill which proposed to grant virtually complete rights of prohibition to a local two-thirds majority, without compensation for publicans and with no other options of reducing the number of licences or of prohibiting new licences. Unlike the government's measure, the Welsh bill made no exception in favour of hotels, restaurants and refreshment houses. Major Jones, who had been successful in the private members' ballot, regretted that chance 'should have placed a Bill of such deep interest and far-reaching importance in his 'prentice hand'. His doubts may well have concerned his own qualifications for supporting the bill: the following spring he was absent from a meeting of the Welsh Party because he was 'stupidly drunk about the House' and had to be taken home. His wife said that 'when he had these attacks on he could not be restrained—there was only one thing to be done and that was to keep him from appearing too much in public'.[153]

The advent of the Welsh bill placed the government and the Alliance in an embarrassing position. Harcourt's bill, which applied to both Wales and England, was wholeheartedly supported by the Alliance and received its first reading on 1 March, while the claims of the Irish Sunday Closing Amendment Bill had also to be considered. On 6 March Lloyd George wrote to D. R. Daniel:

> We are in a fix. The Alliance crowd are extremely anxious we should withdraw our bill in favour of the Irish measure which comes second on the orders of the day. Ellis and I are strongly opposed to such a course. We consider the question tomorrow.[154]

Two days later Lloyd George informed Daniel:

> We succeeded today at our meeting to proceed with our Bill Wednesday next. Raper [the Parliamentary Agent of the Alliance] and Co. came foaming and spitting. They threaten to desert us in the division lobby. We'll see about that. Whyte [the Secretary of the Alliance] is very angry.[155]

The meeting of the Welsh Party referred to by Lloyd George voted unanimously to carry on with the Welsh bill.[156] Apparently, Jones had received no official communication from the government voicing its disapproval, and Ellis, the Junior Whip, who was present at the meeting, maintained that he knew nothing of supposed government opposition.[157]

The Alliance argued that whereas Wales was included in the government's local option bill, there was no provision in the bill for Ireland, and if the Welsh measure, as first order of the day for 15 March, were out of the way, the Irish Sunday Closing Amendment Bill, as second order, would come to the front with a fair assurance that its second reading would be secured, as had been the case in 1892, by a large majority.[158] Although refusing to give way, the Welsh members indicated their willingness to shorten debate on their own bill in order to leave time for the Irish measure; but this was felt to be impracticable and beyond their power.

On 15 March the Welsh bill secured its second reading by a majority of 36, Harcourt being compelled to speak in its support.[159] Lloyd George's speech in the debate was an uncompromising plea for prohibition. He contended that where they could 'get the co-operation of a majority of the people in the forcible removal of temptations to intemperance from their midst', they should 'avail themselves of it'. In Llŷn there were fifteen parishes with no public houses; in these parishes there was only one pauper to 41 of the population, compared with one to 18 in parishes with public houses: 'I do not want to go to Maine or Canada, for within a day's journey of this House honourable members can test the effect of prohibition.'[160] Owing largely to the efforts of Ellis, who in the sphere of Welsh temperance reform at least, showed that his mouth had not been 'gagged by a bag of English gold', the government had issued a whip in favour of the bill.[161] Ellis was congratulated on his 'delicate handling' of the bill which showed that he was 'not lost to Wales'.[162]

As in 1891 the bill did not progress beyond the committee stage. According to J. Herbert Lewis (Flintshire), 'every cubic inch of the House of Commons atmosphere is charged with obstruction, so we cannot be sanguine'.[163] In Lewis' view, Welsh temperance reformers should take every opportunity to urge upon their English counter-parts the importance of bringing pressure to bear upon the government to carry the Welsh bill during the 1893 session, as the government could not possibly carry its own measure any further: 'That is understood by every Parliamentarian. But it is not so well understood by the Temperance Party in the country, and the Government would go a long way to conciliate them if they were to give an earnest of their intention in regard to the larger measure by passing the smaller one which is applicable to Wales.'[164] As far as positive action by the Welsh Party was concerned, disestablishment barred the way: 'The Welsh Party cannot very well press the Government on this question, because they are pledged to exert all their strength on the side of disestablishment. To press for disestablishment *and* temperance would weaken their demand in each case and would really do no good to either cause.'[165] On 5 April, W. S. Caine, Alliance supporter and M.P., confidentially informed J. Herbert Lewis, his son-in-law, that there was no chance whatsoever of the government bill being passed in the present session but that the Welsh bill, if properly supported, might have a chance of passing.[166] But the Welsh Party could not give its undivided attention to it, and Lewis informed Daniel on 10 August that the prospects for the Welsh bill 'are not at all roseate. We are now so much absorbed in the Disestablishment question that the present is an inopportune time for any forward movement on Temperance. It may be that our insistence with regard to Disestablishment will help the prospects of the Welsh Direct Veto Bill.'[167]

No help was forthcoming from the Alliance which remained firmly committed to the government bill and refused all overtures from Daniel to help the passage of the Welsh measure. The Alliance informed Daniel: 'It is not possible for us to stop the agitation in favour of the Government Bill even if it were desirable. Petitions are everywhere in progress. You must not discourage the sending up of petitions in favour of the Government Bill.'[168] The only hope rested with the government, and in early August a temperance deputation from south Wales conferred with several Welsh members with a view to inducing Harcourt to take up the Welsh bill and to drop his own. The Welsh members claimed that Wales was 'in advance of England' on the temperance question, that the Welsh bill had reached the committee stage and that the government bill would not even secure a second reading during the 1893 session.[169] But to no avail, for Harcourt refused to support the Welsh bill in committee and it was subsequently lost.[170]

As we have seen, the progress of the temperance question in Welsh politics was seriously affected in the late 1880s and early '90s by the predominance of disestablishment as the major radical political issue.[171] 'Feelings ran high', wrote D. Miall Edwards, 'and much valuable energy was withdrawn from constructive spiritual and social work into the channels of bitter controversy.'[172] Disestablishment was a more emotive and contentious issue than temperance reform and was therefore—to borrow Lloyd George's phrases in reference to the tithe agitation, but which would apply equally aptly to disestablishment—a more likely issue to 'raise the spirit of the people' for the 'impending national upheaval'.[173] As Lloyd George pointed out in 1891 the temperance movement seemed to be making little real progress, as there was 'too general an agreement in favour of restrictive measures upon the question'. Few politicians allowed themselves to differ in public on the temperance issue and thus 'it is not a question upon which you can get up a keen party fight'.[174] Moreover, on practical grounds it seemed more likely that Wales would secure a disestablishment measure than a temperance measure. Temperance reformers were notoriously divided amongst themselves as to what they really wanted: Sunday closing only, direct veto, total prohibition, the abolition of grocers' licences, whereas as far as disestablishment was concerned, there were no two opinions.[175]

Throughout the late 1880s and early '90s the Welsh Liberal members insisted on putting disestablishment first. In October 1887 it was suggested by the Alliance and Welsh temperance bodies that a memorial to Gladstone should be organized by the Welsh members, setting forth the claim that Wales was ready for prohibition.[176] But Ellis, who had previously promised to assist in the matter, now advised against proceeding with it because at the instance of the Welsh National Council, Wales had 'definitely made its first united appeal to the Liberal Party on disestablishment, and the Welsh members would feel that they were stultifying themselves if they made another collective appeal before submitting the former to Parliament'.[177] The Alliance grudgingly accepted Ellis' advice.[178] What particularly incensed the Alliance was the abstention of so many of the Welsh members during the second reading of Stevenson's English Sunday Closing Bill in February 1889.[179] D. A. Thomas, when explaining his abstention to his constituents, maintained that one of the aims of the Welsh Party was not to promote or assist in passing measures relating solely to England against the wishes of the English members, the implication being that the Welsh Party hoped to encounter no obstruction from English members on Welsh disestablishment.[180] On the other hand, fanatical temperance supporters suggested that if Gladstone would give the Welsh people a 'clear sound' on the drink question, then most Welshmen would 'more readily abide' with the 'careful course' he was taking on Welsh disestablishment.[181]

The view of the temperance zealot was that reforms such as disestablishment and home rule were trifling and that temperance, as a long-deferred social question which was, allegedly, above party, should come first. At the meetings of the Welsh Baptist Union at Caernarfon in August 1892, Lloyd George maintained that the drink question was more important than home rule and disestablishment, and that the enormity of the evil fully justified the unity of nonconformists in the political arena.[182] Possibly, Lloyd George was not as extreme as he pretended to be on the temperance question. Certainly, temperance achieved a symbolic importance for him during his career and he retained a zealous devotion to its outward forms for decades. His first appearance on a public platform was at a temperance meeting at Machynlleth in 1883, and his maiden speech in the Commons on 13 June 1890 was made on the issue of proposed compensation to publicans who might be dispossessed of their licences.[183] In his public pronouncements Lloyd George may have overrated the importance of temperance legislation: it seems unlikely that he really considered temperance legislation *per se* as being of greater importance than disestablishment and home rule in the early and mid-1890s. Indeed, at a conference of the South Wales and Monmouthshire Temperance Association at Tredegar in September 1894 Lloyd George was taken to task by the ever-sensitive Alliance for having given much greater prominence to disestablishment and home rule and to have 'left the Veto Bill in the rear'.[184] The effect of his speech, claimed the Alliance, was to put a 'regular wet blanket' on Harcourt's general veto scheme.[185] Lloyd George insisted, however, that he had always regarded the temperance question as one of the truly fundamental social and political questions of the day and that what he had suggested in his Tredegar speech was 'that the speediest and surest means for Wales to secure a comprehensive and effective measure was by securing for herself the right to legislate in her own domestic affairs. Seeing that Wales has for over fourteen years returned a proportion of nine-tenths of her representatives to demand from Parliament the Local Veto simply to be either voted down or checkmated by the brewers' ring which seems to govern England, my suggestion is not an unreasonable one for a Welshman to make under the circumstances.'[186] For Lloyd George the proposals in his speech which advocated the abolition of the House of Lords—a body that would mutilate into impotence any extreme temperance legislation—and the abolition of the social wrongs that led people to drink were not, as the Alliance seemed to think, ends in themselves that would be given greater priority over temperance legislation, but essential prerequisites for the success of the struggle to make men sober.

Tom Ellis, an Alliance Vice-President in 1892, believed that temperance was of 'second-class importance. Disestablishment, like Home Rule, was of first-class importance.'[187] Similarly, D. A. Thomas, as President of the South Wales Liberal Federation in 1894, declared himself in favour of temperance legislation, but stressed that the efforts of Welsh politicians should be directed towards temperance only after diestablishment had been gained.[188] The Alliance could do little but protest. 'I may tell you quite candidly', wrote the Alliance Secretary to D. R. Daniel, 'that my personal fear about the Welsh people is this: that you are so completely off your heads on the question of disestablishment that in order to get that passed in a fashion that will suit you, you will be disposed to huddle up the Temperance question in almost any fashion.'[189] The *Alliance News* was critical of Welsh members who 'care more for the little finger of Disestablishment than they do for the whole body of the Liquor Traffic (Local Control) Bill . . . In the Government nursery the baby that cries loudest is attended to first, and meanwhile the rest may suck their thumbs.'[190] Surely it was better to disestablish the publican first and take the parson afterwards, for, after all, as Alliance President, Wilfrid Lawson, pointed out in Cardiff in 1895, one Welsh publican did far more harm than ten Welsh parsons. But the Alliance wish was not fulfilled and Lawson, in his own words, became the Jonah who was swallowed by Young Wales.[191]

*   *   *   *

Since 1868 the course of Welsh history had seemed to point to 'a complete recognition of the national status of Wales'.[192] The *Cymru Fydd* or Young Wales movement had begun after 1886 as essentially a movement of cultural aspirations. However, in the eyes of Lloyd

George it became an anti-landlord, anti-parson and anti-brewer movement which he hoped would help to realize the political aim of national self-government. But by 1895-6 the disunity within the ranks of the Welsh members of parliament and the disintegration of *Cymru Fydd* meant that radicalism in Wales had come to lose its nationalist leanings.[193] Lloyd George's call in 1895 that Welsh demands for reform, including temperance, should be concentrated in one great agitation for national self-government could not be realized with the collapse of *Cymru Fydd*.[194] Unlike Ellis, Lloyd George failed to perceive that it was the nonconformity of Wales that created the unity of Wales, not a national demand for home rule.[195]

The advent and progress of the temperance question in Welsh politics helped to facilitate the developing political-religious alignment in Wales between nonconformists, Liberals and temperance reformers on the one hand, and Anglicans, Conservatives and the drink interest on the other. In Welsh nonconformist mythology, the Parliament of 1874 became the 'beer and parson parliament', in which the two main objects of Conservative policy were to retard education and to promote drinking, as 'the less people know and the more they drink, the more Torified they will be'.[196] Nonconformists professed themselves unable to expect any social or religious amelioration from Conservatives and they flocked to the Liberal party because they saw in Liberalism religious liberty and a 'political system based on ethics—a system of morals applied to political life'.[197] For such nonconformists, Liberals and temperance reformers citizenship was a solemn responsibility, the vote a sacred trust and one's religion and one's vote inseparable.

NOTES

[1] Cf. nonconformist demands in J. H. S. Kent, 'Hugh Price Hughes and the Nonconformist Conscience', G. V. Bennett and J. D. Walsh, op. cit.

[2] *Alliance News*, 3 September 1870; 21 December 1878.

[3] See A. T. Davies, *The Relation of Municipal Action to Morals* (1899), p. 8; *Alliance News*, 24 February 1872.

[4] *C.M.G.*, 6 October 1860.

[5] *Cambrian*, 7 October 1859.

[6] Ibid., 1 November 1861; *The Ferret or South Wales Ratepayer*, 10 April 1875.

[7] *Cambrian*, 5 November 1858.

[8] *Swansea and Glamorgan Herald*, 30 October 1861.

[9] *Alliance News*, 21 December 1878.

[10] See *South Wales Daily News*, 28 February 1874.

[11] *Alliance News*, 2 November 1861; W. H. Darby, op. cit., p. 6.

[12] *Cambrian*, 1 November 1861; *Licensed Victuallers Guardian*, 22 June 1872.

[13] *Monmouthshire Merlin*, 15 October 1859; *Alliance News*, 29 October 1859.

[14] *Monmouthshire Merlin*, 22 October 1859.

[15] Ibid., 29 October 1859; 5 November 1859.

[16] *Alliance News*, 12 November 1859.

[17] *Monmouthshire Merlin*, 14 January 1860; *C.M.G.*, 18 February 1860.

[18] *Star of Gwent*, 14 January 1860.

[19] Ibid., 23 November 1861.

[20] *Alliance News*, 23 November 1861.

[21] *Monmouthshire Merlin*, 16 November 1861.

[22] *Newport Gazette*, 16 November 1861.

[23] *Alliance News*, 2 November 1861; *Monmouthshire Merlin*, 30 November 1861.

[24] Newport Temperance Society Minutes, 1885-93, 28 January 1887.

[25] Ibid. See also Newport and County Total Abstinence Society and Gospel Temperance Union, *Annual Report, 1887*, pp. 3, 5-6, 9; *Annual Report, 1888*, pp. 5, 10, 12; D. J. Thomas, op. cit., pp. 66-8.

[26] Newport Temperance Society Minutes, 1885-93, 16 July 1886; *Evening Star of Gwent*, 15 January 1887.

[27] Newport Temperance Society, *Annual Report, 1887*, p. 3.

[28] Ibid., Minutes, 1885-93, 6 April 1887.

[29] *South Wales Daily Times and Star of Gwent.* 3 May 1889; D. J.Thomas, op. cit., p. 65.

[30] *Proceedings of the National Temperance Congress at Chester, 1895* (1896), pp. 166-7.

[31] *Cambrian*, 21 October 1859.

[32] Ibid., 4 November 1859.

[33] Ibid., 18 November 1859.

[34] *Swansea and Glamorgan Herald*, 21 December 1859.

[35] J. Vincent, *Pollbooks. How Victorians Voted* (Cambridge, 1967), pp. 17-18.

[36] *Licensed Victuallers Guardian*, 22 June 1872.

[37] *Western Mail*, 31 January 1874.

[38] N.L.W., Lord Swansea Collection, South Wales Temperance and Prohibition Association to H. H. Vivian, 12 March 1874; *South Wales Daily News*, 2 and 4 February 1874; *Western Mail*, 12 February 1874; *The Workman's Advocate. Amddiffynydd y Gweithiwr*, 21 March 1874.

[39] *Western Mail*, 24 February 1874.

[40] *South Wales Daily News*, 16 March 1880.

[41] Ibid., 19 March 1880.

[42] Ibid., 25 March 1880.

[43] Ibid., 31 March 1880.

[44] Ibid., 5 April 1880.

[45] Ibid., 26 March 1880.

[46] Ibid., 9 August 1880.

[47] *Merthyr Express*, 13 March 1880.

[48] Ibid., 3 April 1880.

[49] Ibid.

[50] Ibid., 3 and 27 March 1880.

[51] Ibid., 17 April 1880.

[52] A. A. Reade, *The House of Commons on Stimulants* (1885), p. 6.

[53] T. Marchant Williams, *Welsh Members of Parliament, 1894* (Cardiff, 1894), pp. 17, 21, 23, 25, 49, 51, 59.

[54] *3 Hansard ccliii*, 18 June 1880, cols. 386-89; *3 Hansard cclxii*, 14 June 1881, cols. 562-4; *3H cclxxviii*, 27 April 1883, cols. 1377-9; *Cymru Fydd*, January 1889, p. 47; *3H cccli*, 18 March 1891, cols. 1339-40; *4H x*, 15 March 1893, col. 111; *Explanation and Notes of the Temperance (Wales) Bill* (Brecon, n.d., c. 1931), p. 8.

[55] *Cymru Fydd*, January 1889, p. 47.

[56] For a discussion of the Act which is somewhat more detailed than that which can be given here see W. R. Lambert, 'The Welsh Sunday Closing Act, 1881', *W.H.R.*, 6, no. 2, December 1972, 161-89.

[57] *Licensed Victuallers Guardian*, 27 August 1881; 3 September 1881; *The True Templar*, March 1888, p. 39; *The Welsh Review*, November 1891, p. 23.

[58] For example, see Evan Jenkins, *Funeral Sermon Upon the Death of Sir John Guest* (1852), pp. 23-4; *Y Dyngarwr*, I, 1879, p. 20.

[59] See Bennett and Walsh, op. cit., p. 185.

[60] *C.M.G.*, 19 December 1835; 27 February 1836; 3 March 1838.

[61] J. S. Mill, *On Liberty* (paperback edn., 1962), pp. 221-2.

[62] For example, see *C.M.G.*, 7 September 1844.

[63] Ibid.

[64] Ibid.

[65] *Merthyr Express*, 30 July 1881.

[66] C.C.L., MS. 2.560, Cardiff Society for the Impartial Discussion of Political and Other Questions, Minutes, vol. 1, 1886-8. Meeting of 17 January 1887; H. M. Thompson, *Our English Sunday* (Cardiff, 1887), pp. 3, 5; J. P. Thompson, *Sunday Emancipation* (Cardiff, 1887), p. 11.

[67] See Report of the Commissioners appointed to inquire into the operation of the Sunday Closing (Wales) Act, 1881. *P.P.*, 1890, op. cit., q. 11,034. Hereafter cited as *S.C.Rept.*

[68] *The Sunday Closing Reporter*, June 1883, p. 256.

[69] *Alliance News*, 30 April 1881; *Proceedings of the National Temperance Congress, Birmingham 1889* (1889), p. 165.

[70] *South Wales Daily News*, 20 August 1875; *Alliance News*, 28 August 1875.

[71] *Western Mail*, 12 December 1884.

[72] U.K.A., Minute Book, vol. 2, 1873-5, meeting of 17 November 1875; *Sunday Closing Reporter*, February 1883, p. 242.

[73] Ibid., March 1879, p. 109. The towns were Abercarn, Aberdare, Bala, Blaenavon, Caernarfon, Corwen, Dolgellau, Fishguard, Haverfordwest, Hirwaun, Llanidloes, Machynlleth, Milford Haven, Mountain Ash, Neath, Newtown, Pembroke Dock, Pwllheli and Wrexham.

[74] C.A.S.S.I.L.S., *Eleventh Annual Report (1878)*, p. 12; *Twelfth Annual Report (1879)*, pp. 12-14; *Thirteenth Annual Report (1880)*, pp. 12-17.

[75] *The Treasury*, 16, 1879, p. 108; E. T. Davies, op. cit., p. 64.

[76] C.A.S.S.I.L.S., *Annual Reports, 1878-80*; *Monmouthshire Merlin*, 11 July 1879.

[77] *3 Hansard cclx*, 4 May 1881, col. 1478; *Western Mail*, 10 January 1885.

[78] See, for example, *Merthyr Express*, 14 May 1870.

[79] See, for example, ibid., 2 April 1881; *Cambrian*, 2 October 1875.

[80] *South Wales Daily News*, 30 August 1881.

[81] *Alliance News*, 13 September 1879.

[82] *3 Hansard ccliii*, 30 June 1880, col. 1168.

[83] Ibid., cols. 1176-77.

[84] Ibid., *cclx*, 4 May 1881, col. 1750.

[85] Ibid., cols. 1761-62.

[86] U.K.A. *Twenty Ninth Annual Report (1881)*, p. 14.

[87] *3 Hansard cclx*, 4 May 1881, col. 1772.

[88] Ibid., col. 1773.

[89] Ibid., *cclxii*, 15 June 1881, cols. 614, 616.

[90] Ibid., cols. 621-22.

[91] *South Wales Daily News*, 6 July 1881; the editorial reminded Gladstone that 'Ireland is not everything'.

[92] *3 Hansard cclxv*, 20 August 1881, col. 603.

[93] *Cambrian*, 26 August 1881; *3 Hansard* cclxv, 20 August 1881, cols. 603, 623-24.

[94] K. O. Morgan, 'Gladstone and Wales', *W.H.R.*, I, no. 1 (1960), 10; *Wales in British Politics*, p. 43.

[95] For example, see *Cambrian*, 16 April 1880; Brian Harrison, 'The Sunday Trading Riots of 1855', *Historical Journal*, 8, 2 (1965), *passim*.

[96] Owen Thomas and J. Machreth Rees, op. cit., p. 405.

[97] *Merthyr Express*, 2 April 1881.

[98] *Western Mail*, 1 November 1889.

[99] *Merthyr Express*, 27 October 1883. For Williams see W. R. Lambert, 'Thomas Williams', loc. cit.

[100] H. Richard to W. E. Gladstone, 7 August 1885, N.L.W., MS. 14,022 B, f. 238.

[101] *3 Hansard cccxxiii*, 3 November 1888, col. 472.

[102] Ibid., cccli, 18 March 1891, col. 1326.

[103] *S.C. Report*, Q. 16,666; *Western Mail*, 21 August 1889.

[104] N.L.W., Calvinistic Methodist Archives, 5935: Address on Temperance, n.d.; *Merthyr Express*, 7 October 1882.

[105] [David Davies], *The Welsh Sunday Closing Act* (Cardiff, 1889), p. 31; *Western Mail*, 11 January 1889.

[106] Ibid., 14 February 1889.

[107] *Merthyr Express*, 28 January 1882; *Alliance News*, 2 September 1882.

[108] *Western Mail,* 12 September 1882.

[109] Ibid., 28 February 1883; 27 March 1885.

[110] *3 Hansard cclxii,* 15 June 1881, col. 1850; Cardiff Temperance and Prohibition Association, *Annual Report (1884),* p. 7; *S. C. Report,* QQ. 15,638, 15,881.

[111] Ibid., Q. 15,676. In contrast to a genuine club, a shebeen 'had no printed rules, no stated object or purpose, no books, no furniture, musical instruments or accommodation for dining, no treasurer, no fund, no credit, no banker'. See *The Welsh Sunday Closing Act: an Epitome of Opinions.* Cardiff Licensed Victuallers and Beerhouse Keepers Association (Cardiff, 1884), pp. 10-11.

[112] *Western Mail,* 5 June 1883; 6 March 1889; Cardiff Temperance and Prohibition Association, *Annual Report (1883),* p. 23.

[113] *Western Mail,* 5 June 1883.

[114] *S.C. Report,* QQ. 16,656-57.

[115] *Western Mail,* 27 February 1889.

[116] Ibid., 2 January 1889. For details of the controversy see W. R. Lambert, 'Sunday Closing Act', 175-83.

[117] *S.C. Report,* pp. 20-21.

[118] [D. Davies], op. cit., p. 7.

[119] *Western Mail,* 7 March 1889.

[120] *Sunday Closing Reporter,* March 1889, p. 2.

[121] *Western Mail,* 7 March 1889.

[122] Ibid.

[123] Ibid., 4 June 1889.

[124] *Tarian y Gweithiwr,* 6 May 1889. On 21 March Lord Aberdare had informed his wife that the editor of the *Western Mail* was 'moving heaven and earth, and another quarter against it [the Sunday Closing Act] with the insidious appeal to the interests of "the poor" '. *Letters of the Rt. Hon. Henry Austin Bruce* (Oxford, 1902), vol. 2, p. 258.

[125] *Cymru Fydd,* 2 July 1889, p. 387.

[126] Newport Public Library, MS. M000 (328), 39193, Welsh Liberal Members Committee, Minute Book, August 1886-July 1889: meeting of 3 April 1889; *Western Mail,* 4 April 1889.

[127] N.L.W., J. Herbert Lewis Papers, Group I, no. 1, p. 106. Minutes of Liverpool Welsh Liberal Association: annual meeting, 24 May 1889. I am grateful to Mrs. Idwal Jones, Plas Penucha, Caerwys, for granting me permission to see these papers. See also *Western Mail,* 4 June 1889.

[128] *S.C. Report,* p. 7.

[129] Harrison, 'Sunday Trading Riots', 236.

[130] *Western Mail,* 10 April 1889; 24 October 1889. For general criticism of nineteenth-century Royal Commissions and Select Committees see G. Kitson Clark, *The Critical Historian* (1967), pp. 78-9.

[131] *S.C. Report, passim; Western Mail,* 17 June 1889.

[132] Ibid., 24 October 1889.

[133] Ibid., 2 November 1889.

[134] See *Alliance News,* 4 April 1890. For the detailed recommendations of the Commissioners see *S.C. Report,* pp. 40-3.

[135] *Western Mail,* 16 May 1883; 1 June 1883.

[136] *S.C. Report.* QQ. 15,051, 16,198.

[137] For example, see Cardiff Temperance and Prohibition Association, *Annual Report (1884),* p. 6.

[138] U.K.A. Minutes, 1885-87, meeting of 1st November 1886.

[139] *Alliance News,* 5 November 1887.

[140] *Merthyr Express,* 20 September 1884.

[141] *Alliance News,* 13 March 1891.

[142] Ibid., 26 November 1887.

[143] *Y Goleuad,* 5 Rhagfyr 1889.

[144] U.K.A. Minutes, 1891-93, 14 January 1891.

[145] Lloyd George to D. R. Daniel, 6 February 1891, N.L.W., Daniel 2759. See also James Whyte (U.K.A.) to Daniel, 29 January 1891, ibid., 2,362a.

[146] *3 Hansard cccli,* 18 March 1891, cols. 1326-7.

[147] Ibid., col. 1342.

[148] *Alliance News,* 27 March 1891.

[149] Lloyd George to T. E. Ellis, 11 April 1891, N.L.W., Ellis 683.

[150] *Alliance News,* 27 March 1891.

[151] See U.K.A. *Thirty-Ninth Annual Report (1891),* pp. 15-17.

[152] U.K.A. Minutes, 1891-3, 31 August 1892.

[153] D. Lloyd George to Margaret Lloyd George, 25 and 31 April 1894; quoted in J. Grigg, *The Young Lloyd George* (1973), p. 133. See also K. O. Morgan (ed.), *Lloyd George. Family Letters, 1885-1936* (Cardiff and London, 1973), p. 73.

[154] Lloyd George to D. R. Daniel, 6 March 1893, N.L.W., Daniel 2,762.

[155] Ibid., 8 March 1893, N.L.W., Daniel 2,763. See also D. R. Daniel, Diary 1893, *sub* 9 March 1893, N.L.W., Daniel 516.

[156] *South Wales Daily News*, 10 March 1893.

[157] Ibid.

[158] Ibid., 15 March 1893.

[159] *4 Hansard X*, 15 March 1893, col. 112. See also H. W. Lucy, *A Diary of the Home Rule Parliament, 1892-95* (1896), p. 86.

[160] *4 Hansard X*, 15 March 1893, cols. 116-22.

[161] *Y Goleuad*, 1 Medi 1892; *South Wales Daily News*, 15 March 1893.

[162] Owen Williams to T. E. Ellis, 21 March 1893, N.L.W., Ellis 2,062.

[163] J. H. Lewis to D. R. Daniel, 28 March 1893, N.L.W., Daniel 1,979.

[164] Ibid.

[165] Ibid.

[166] Ibid., 6 April 1893, N.L.W., Daniel 1,980.

[167] Ibid., 10 August 1893, N.L.W., Daniel 1,981.

[168] U.K.A. to Daniel, 13 April 1893, N.L.W., Daniel 2,310.

[169] Press-cutting appended to J. H. Lewis to Daniel, 10 August 1893, N.L.W., Daniel 1,981.

[170] See U.K.A. to Daniel, 30 August 1893, N.L.W., Daniel 3,311.

[171] Kenneth O. Morgan, *Freedom or Sacrilege? A History of the Campaign for Welsh Disestablishment* (Penarth, 1965), p. 34.

[172] D. Miall Edwards, *Religion in Wales* (Wrexham, 1926), p. 4.

[173] Lloyd George to T. E. Ellis, 19 May 1887, N.L.W., Ellis 679.

[174] *Alliance News*, 20 March 1891.

[175] See, for example, Rev. J. Eiddon Jones, Llanrug, to T. E. Ellis, 18 January 1893, N.L.W., Ellis 1,119.

[176] U.K.A. Minutes, 1887-9, 19 October 1887.

[177] Ibid., 23 November 1887, Ellis to Daniel, 19 November 1887, N.L.W., Daniel 338(a).

[178] U.K.A. to H. J. Williams, 24 November 1887, N.L.W., Daniel 338a/3.

[179] The bill was defeated by seven votes. See *Cymru Fydd*, January 1889, p. 47.

[180] *Merthyr Express*, 9 March 1889.

[181] For example, see N.L.W. Rendel Papers, 19,456 D, IX, 557.

[182] *North Wales Chronicle*, 20 August 1892.

[183] K. W. Jones-Roberts, op. cit., 65.

[184] *Alliance News*, 21 September 1894.

[185] Ibid., 28 September 1894.

[186] Ibid.

[187] *South Wales Daily News*, 20 January 1893.

[188] U.K.A. Minutes, 1893-5, 19 December 1894.

[189] James Whyte to Daniel, 1 September 1892, N.L.W., Daniel 2,304.

[190] *Alliance News*, 18 August 1893.

[191] Ibid., 25 January 1895.

[192] K. O. Morgan, *Wales in British Politics*, p. 120.

[193] See ibid., pp. 162-4.

[194] Lloyd George to Thomas Gee, 9 October 1895, N.L.W., Gee MS. 8,310E, 501.

[195] K. O. Morgan, *Wales in British Politics*, p. 164.

[196] *Cambrian*, 8 January 1874.

[197] A Nonconformist, *Liberalism and Liberty* (1891), pp. 3-4. See also Henry Richard, *The Political Relations of the Nonconformists to the Liberal Party* (Manchester, 1872), *passim* but especially pp. 15-16.

CHAPTER VII

CONCLUSION

FROM the 1890s the temperance movement in Wales, as in Britain generally, declined, together with the decline of drunkenness and nonconformity. The drink problem lost its distinct identity in the face of the advance of the twentieth-century welfare state, which aimed at improving the total environment of working people by obtaining welfare legislation.[1] Nonconformity in Wales was on the decline from the 1890s. The influence of the chapel in Welsh life weakened and the Welsh language began its slow decline. There was, now, a much greater concern with secular matters such as the relationship between capital and labour, than with the fundamentalist, unphilosophical and other-worldly church and chapel crusade against intemperance.[2]

Many Welsh working men came to have no great liking for the Calvinistic tenets of Welsh nonconformity, which taught that blessings and rewards were only to be found in a future state of existence. As a working man complained in 1891: 'A religion which is put into the pocket on Sunday night, to lodge there for six days at a time, is not likely to interest those who find their six-day work no sham, while the·seventh is only dressed up for the occasion.'[3] The general feeling was that the Christianity preached from the pulpit was not the Christianity practised on the streets and in the place of work. The chapels and churches seemed not to take sufficient interest in the social and economic affairs of working-class members and sometimes made abusive comments on the drinking habits of union members. The *South Wales Labour Times* in March 1893 noted that working men increasingly could not reconcile the 'smug sentiments of brotherly love', which emanated regularly from the pulpit, with the 'fawning' of the ministers on the prosperous deacons and their 'lofty condescension' towards the poorer members. A working man said: 'They compare the silky tones and sanctimonious expression of the churchman on Sundays with his scowling face and brutal sneers among his workmen on Monday.'[4] During the 1890s working men were increasingly bound to see organized religion in such social and political terms.

Although many early Labour men were temperance reformers before joining the labour movement (if only because, like some Chartists, they believed that temperance would enable working men to strengthen their political position), by the 1890s most socialists considered that the temperance movement was diverting the working man from his proper concerns. The idea of isolating the drink problem from other social problems was increasingly questioned. Socialists thought that the temperance movement was turning working men from the real causes of social evils to some of their minor effects. In Wales, the predominance of Calvinistic theology meant that temperance reformers concentrated on the effects of drunkenness while paying scant attention to its causes. It was, as Dr. Harrison has written, a 'symbolic event' when in October 1908, during a licensing debate, Victor Grayson moved that the Commons adjourn to consider the question of the unemployed: 'There are thousands of people dying in the streets, while you are trifling with this Bill.'[5]

During the 1880s and '90s, then, increasing numbers of urban workers in Wales were losing confidence in the churches as a means of social improvement and were becoming committed instead to trade unionism and political action. Welsh nonconformity did not give a lead to the aspirations of the workers; the evidence the present writer has found would tend to support Canon Davies' view expressed fifteen years ago that the English nonconformist churches of Wales took a greater interest in social amelioration, more especially during the last two decades of the century. Welsh nonconformity's antagonism to the early workers' unions, the benefit clubs and to certain manifestations of Chartism is well known. The concentration of Welsh nonconformity on disestablishment during and after the 1880s became less and less relevant to the problems of an industrial society. By the end of the century workers concluded that they could best achieve their aspirations through their own industrial and political organizations, and they ceased to look to the chapels as their political allies. During the last two decades of the century, miners' unions were comparatively weak. This was a period of co-operation between the owners and the workers during which most miners' leaders came from the ranks of nonconformity. Mabon was the key figure. The bitter strike of 1898 brought this phase to a close. Thereafter, the struggle was for a minimum wage, and socialism and class warfare were the keynotes of the new industrial gospel. Thus the politics of Welsh nonconformity became irrelevant to many working men. Disestablishment had no place in workers' politics. Gradually they became less impressed by the nonconformist social pathology, which traced the evils of man to drinking, gambling, whoring, a landed aristocracy and the lack of international arbitration.

Nonconformity helped to commit the Liberal party to causes which were now becoming increasingly uncongenial to large numbers of people. In 1895 Lord Rosebery testified that the Liberal party was becoming hamstrung by measures which challenged vested interests.[6] The temperance question was conspicuous as an aspect of the 'Old' Liberalism which was rapidly becoming a shibboleth, unsuitable to winning over the mass democracy.[7] To many observers at the turn of the century, nonconformity and Liberalism resided in Crotchet Castle, whence there had issued for far too long tedious, teetotalling nonconformists launching raids on pubs, theatres, music halls, and politicians cited in divorce cases. At the same time, nonconformity's almost exclusive absorption in political activity connoted a loss of spiritual power. The growing secularism and hedonism in society increasingly isolated puritanical nonconformists. It was, indeed, the Liberal government's bills for local veto on the sale of drink which helped to bring about the heavy Liberal defeat in the general election of 1895. When Barebones came again in 1906, and the Commons included the largest-ever body of nonconformists, their most notable fight against the Education Act of 1902 only served to make nonconformity more political than ever before.[8] In truth, the composition of the 1906 parliament flattered to deceive, for it reflected the social complexion of Liberalism rather than the power of nonconformity. The great Welsh religious revival of 1904-5 was quickly followed by backsliding; as early as February 1906 there were predictable reports that drunkenness had reared its ugly head in the Rhondda valleys. In June 1907 the Rev. Thomas Phillips heard 'from a London layman who has paid a visit to the field of the late Revival . . . that many of the young converts have relapsed, because of the lack of shepherding and care, due to the pachydermatous conservatism of some of the elder brethren'. As apparent was the 'crumbling machinery of Liberalism in the constituencies' in Wales, where there was a strong threat from the nascent forces of Labour.[9]

Did the temperance movement produce any noticeable decline in the level of drunkenness in Wales? It would be wrong to assume that when a social evil declines, the movement aiming to promote that decline necessarily deserves the credit. In so far as any change was produced in Wales' drinking habits by the 1890s, the extension of recreational facilities, the provision of better water supplies and non-intoxicants, the gradual improvement of the police and the arrival of the railway, probably achieved at least as much for sobriety as temperance societies and temperance legislation. Certainly, the provision of counter-attractions—better housing, the growing popularity of the motor car, the cinema, and a systematic communal provision of those amenities which were so lacking for most of the nineteenth century, such as recreation grounds and allotments—did a great deal to curb drunkenness. The cardinal errors of the temperance movement were that it gave scant attention to the environmental factors creating drunkenness and that it was too sectarian. Because Welsh teetotallers believed that they could explain social ills in terms of individual moral failure they failed to investigate the drink problem systematically and without bias, and they were relatively uninterested in financing counter-attractions to the drinking place. Admittedly, the temperance movement provided halls, temperance hotels and excursions and various other forms of entertainment, but only for those who had already been saved from drink. Temperance reformers did comparatively little to help to relieve the anomie of urban life. Indeed, they had a strong contempt for the popular culture of the hard-drinking residuum, and they did not study working-class drinking habits objectively. Nonconformists and temperance advocates tried hard to avoid contamination from evil by shunning all contact with it. In this way they showed themselves so anxious to advertise the miseries of drunkenness that they even resisted publicans' attempts to support other recreations besides drinking. By depriving the public house of its many auxiliary attractions, temperance reformers made it more of a drinking place than it need have been.[10]

Of the major campaigns against drink and drunkenness in Wales, teetotalism, with its one-eyed intolerant creed, was not likely to prove particularly effective for very long. Teetotallers assumed that sudden character transformations could be produced merely by the sinner's exertion of will-power. Although they tried to impose their standards of conduct on society at large, in practice their appeal was directed at the sober only, and their advocacy merely served to confirm the respectable in their respectability. A further manifestation of hypocrisy was that teetotallers' harsh condemnation of drunkenness made the spread of the vice more likely; severe denunciation of the drunkard's weakness could facilitate his slide into alcoholism.

During the 1850s the 'legislative compulsion' of the United Kingdom Alliance usurped 'moral suasion' as the temperance panacea, and the temperance question became embroiled in party politics. In particular, two distinctive features of the Liberal political outlook attracted prohibitionists: the desire for moral progress and the belief in popular control. Furthermore, Liberals were always suspicious of monopolies and, therefore, at first they welcomed into their fold prohibitionists who opposed the licensing system. A major disadvantage for the temperance movement of the link with politics, however, was that gradualist and practicable temperance legislation was now discouraged. The Alliance's extremist approach, shown in its Permissive Bill, seriously retarded the temperance movement, the most striking illustration being the way in which it effectively destroyed Bruce's licensing bill of 1871. The organization seriously lacked political skills as well as political sense: the direction towards pragmatic ends, and 'wheeling and dealing'—that pejorative phrase that covers a wide array of human connections and collaborations without which there can be few accomplished deeds—were not a part of the Alliance's methods. Prohibitionists showed that exclusive devotion to one panacea which characterizes the crank. They never tried to broaden the Alliance programme by including other necessary reforms which might attract the support of politicians.

Those temperance reformers who, like Thomas Gee, advocated an eminently more practicable licensing policy were condemned by the Alliance as apostates. Not only did parliament's votes on temperance legislation bear little relation to its opinions (as the views of Hussey Vivian and H. A. Bruce on the Permissive Bill testify), but it is also almost certainly likely that had the Permissive Bill become law, it would never have been enforced properly in Wales, largely owing to small, inefficient and often drunken police forces. The often farcical disputes and problems which followed the application of the Welsh Sunday Closing Act in the 1880s give a hint of the disputes which a Permissive Bill would have brought, particularly if it was not enacted throughout the whole of Wales.

Whereas the Alliance as an organization was highly sectarian in its relationships with other reforming causes, its individual supporters were catholic in their reforming relationships.[11] The mass membership of prohibitionist organizations in Wales remains somewhat obscure, but of great importance for the prohibitionist cause was the leadership of several powerful Liberal, nonconformist patriarchs, active in numerous radical causes and dominating figures in their localities. These men were often rugged, self-reliant and progressive individualists, also largely industrialists, and genuinely attached to mid-Victorian Liberalism. Men like the Cory brothers of Cardiff, W. H. and C. E. Darby of Brymbo, David Davis, Maesyffynnon, Thomas Williams of Gwaelodygarth, Merthyr Tydfil, David Davies, Llandinam, and D. A. Thomas, later Lord Rhondda, were prominent representatives of advanced class-conscious radicalism and militant dissent during the second half of the nineteenth century.

Deprived of social status for much of the nineteenth century these nonconformists saw in a progressive cause like temperance a means of confirming their separateness from the world. Such separateness was a positive attraction to nonconformists, who were keen to show their contempt for traditional social habits and aristocratic immorality, and who wished to construct a godly community in a corrupt world. As nonconformists these men revelled in conflict against sin and worldly oppression.[12] They could not be 'at ease in Zion', and must, like Pilgrim, spend their lives fighting. To these men, conflict in life's battles—for which they shared a common fund of radical attitudes—positively developed the character.

The most important single influence fashioning their views was religion. For them, the 'two nations' of Anglicanism and nonconformity were as important as the 'two nations' of Disraeli. They stressed the efficacy of Welsh nonconformity as an agent of social control; it was an undisputed fact that nonconformity had made Wales a religious and law-abiding country. They firmly believed in absolute religious equality attainable only by the separation of church and state, supported the Liberation Society to achieve this end and urged the removal of nonconformist disabilities and opposition to all Anglican political privileges. Militant nonconformists who supported the temperance movement conducted their social pathology in terms of aristocratic and Anglican oppression. They regarded the licensing system as the tool of an aristocracy keen to avoid taxation by levying indirect taxes and eager to increase the price of the barley grown on its estates by imposing drinking places on respectable working men in the poorer areas. This would enable the people to be held in subjection, would discourage them from self-improvement and deprive them of religious liberty and political instruction. Thomas Williams of Gwaelodygarth, for example, believed that public order could no longer be achieved through the servility to the aristocracy which traditional types of religion and recreation had fostered. Rather, public order must come through self-improvement in the citizen. By encouraging sober, self-improving recreation the middle class hoped to gain allies from the lower parts of society for its attack on aristocratic rule, whereas by encouraging popular drunkenness at festivals and elections, Tories and aristocrats hoped to perpetuate their dominance.[13] As supporters of decentralization and as opponents of monopoly, militant nonconformists were more closely linked to temperance after the appearance of prohibition in 1853, for the temperance movement could now hold out the bait of legislation which would testify to the power and worth of nonconformist culture.

The peace movement was another contemporary radical agitation that attracted nonconformists and temperance reformers. They believed in international arbitration and the end of 'meddling'; foreign policy should be based on the principles of peace and non-intervention in the internal affairs of other countries. Such men wanted to set high moral standards in foreign affairs. They eagerly supported the *Risorgimento,* the principle of anti-slavery and the cause of the North in the American Civil War, and they vigorously condemned the Bulgarian Atrocities. In short, they were Cobdenite and Gladstonian supporters of opponents of cynical, aristocratic diplomacy.

From the vantage point of the last quarter of the twentieth century it is evident that the nineteenth-century Welsh temperance movement was important for the way in which it trained many Welshmen for public life as, on an exalted level, the careers of Lloyd George and Thomas Jones testify. It played an important part in the process of self-improvement and of enabling ordinary working-class people to become respectable. Although it also made many people self-righteous and censorious, it produced a large number of responsible, serious-minded citizens. As Professor T. J. Morgan remarked, the motto of the movement, encapsulating its drive and urge for self and mutual improvement, could well be a line from one of the temperance hymns of Ben Davies of Panteg, Ystalyfera, meaning 'To lift the peasant class'.[14] The movement also raised the status of women by defending wives against husbands. In particular, in its attack on *laissez-faire* attitudes, it paved the way for a society which would treat its humblest citizens as worthy of consideration.

The temperance movement has endured up to the present day in parts of Welsh-speaking Wales, albeit on a small scale. In 1960 even George Thomas, M.P. for Cardiff West, was forced to confess that to be a temperance worker seemed 'a funny thing in this House'.[15] Slowly, the temperance movement—to borrow David Ogg's expressive comment on the Peace of Westphalia—has been relegated to the limbo of an antiquarian curiosity.

NOTES

[1] See Brian Harrison, 'Temperance Societies', *The Local Historian*, 8, no. 4 (1968), 136.

[2] See, for example, K. O. Morgan, *Freedom or Sacrilege?*, p. 22.

[3] *South Wales Daily News*, 19 February 1891.

[4] *South Wales Labour Times*, 4 March 1893.

[5] *4 Hansard 194*, 15 October 1908, c. 495; 16 October 1908, cc. 631-4; quoted in Harrison, *Drink and the Victorians*, p. 405.

[6] Earl of Rosebery, *The Pressing Question for the Liberal Party* (1895), cited in K. O. Morgan, *The Age of Lloyd George. The Liberal Party and British Politics, 1890-1929* (2nd edn. 1978), p. 23.

[7] Ibid., p. 26.

[8] For this, see G. O. Pierce, 'The "Coercion of Wales" Act, 1904', H. Hearder and H. R. Loyn (eds.), *British Government and Administration. Studies presented to S. B. Chrimes* (Cardiff, 1974).

[9] *South Wales Daily News*, 8 February 1906; *Baptist Times*, 14 June 1907, quoted in S. Koss, *Nonconformity in Modern British Politics* (1975), p. 91. For the weakening of Liberalism in Welsh constituencies, see K. O. Morgan, *Wales in British Politics*, pp. 243 ff.

[10] See Harrison, *Drink and the Victorians*, pp. 358, 360.

[11] See Harrison, 'The British Prohibitionists, 1853-72', *passim.*

[12] See Harrison, ' "A world of which we had no conception." Liberalism and the English Temperance Press', *Victorian Studies*, XIII (December 1969), no. 2, p. 147.

[13] See Harrison, 'The British Prohibitionists', 392.

[14] T. J. Morgan, 'Peasant Culture of the Swansea Valley', p. 107.

[15] *5 Hansard 631*, 26 March 1960, col. 81, quoted in J. M. Lee, 'The Political Significance of Licensing Legislation', *Parliamentary Affairs*, 14 (1960-61), 211.

APPENDIX I

PERMISSIVE BILL CANVASSES, 1859, 1889

Locality	For	Permissive Bill Against	Neutral
Dinas, nr. Pontypridd	225	17	21
including — Householders	160	9	18
Other adults	65	8	3
Dukes Town, Brecon	180	9	18
including — Householders	140	8	0
Others	40	1	18
Ystradyfodwg	258	22	18
including — Householders	108	12	13
Male adults	150	10	5
Voters (included in householders)	20	1	3
Holyhead	1,111	38	116
Llanpumpsaint	74	0	6
Llanfrechfa	227	24	37
Gyfeilton, nr. Pontypridd	275	22	23
Margam	67	10	11
Penrhyndeudraeth	322	3	20
including — Householders	185	3	20
Male adults	137	0	0
Voters	12	2	0
Tonyrefail	208	7	22
including — Householders	90	1	14
Publicans	1	2	3
Other male adults	117	4	5
Voters	25	1	2
Trecynon, nr. Aberdare	1,613	156	79
Householders	786	73	73
Other adults	827	83	6
Tref Herbert, nr. Ystradyfodwg	144	7	11
Tredegar	1,978	61	58
Householders	1,589	39	0
Other male adults	389	22	58
Machen	432	90	55
Housholders	238	86	34
Other male adults	194	4	21
TOTALS	6,115	466	495

SOURCE: U.K.A., *Seventh Annual Report, 1858-59,* p. 36: *Alliance News,* 12, 19, 26 March, 9 April 1859.

A similar canvass was conducted in 1889 in Merionethshire by the Merioneth Temperance Association which submitted two questions to the ratepayers of selected districts: '1. Are you in favour of giving the ratepayers the power of deciding by direct veto the number of licences to be granted within your district? 2. Are you in favour of the prohibition of all licences for the common sale of intoxicating liquor?' There were 10,904 inhabited houses in Merionethshire in 1889, and in comparing the number of persons who voted with the total number of houses in the county it should be kept in mind that many of the voters voted on one question only.

Name of Town, Parish or Locality	First Question			Second Question		
	Yes	No	Neutral	Yes	No	Neutral
Llanegryn	48	0	1	45	1	2
Llwyngwril (District)	100	3	13	92	8	16
Pennal	134	2	1	71	26	24
Abergynolwyn	132	3	5	90	43	7
Bryncrug	99	1	0	92	4	2
Arthog and Friog	68	1	4	63	5	5
Llanbedr	49	0	0	41	2	4
Esgairgeiliog	42	1	0	39	3	0
Llanfrothen and Croesor	96	1	0	81	2	4
Corwen (town)	190	14	12	144	35	37
Penllyn (5 parishes)	885	28	39	731	96	5
Corris (part of the parish)	262	3	9	251	7	12
Towyn (town)	80	3	9	49	27	8
Nantmor (part of Beddgelert)	57	1	1	57	4	3
Dolgellau (parish)	483	27	27	384	54	36
Maentwrog	146	6	10	135	15	30
Ffestiniog (parish)	1,935	71	94	1,808	128	85
Trawsfynydd (parish)	271	8	21	237	16	26
Penrhyndeudraeth	354	8	15	286	30	18
Aberdovey (village)	149	2	2	131	9	9
Llanfachreth	22	0	2	38	2	3
Hermon (part of Llanfachreth)	10	3	0	9	2	0
Llanymawddwy and Mallwyd	240	7	11	163	35	22
Gwyddelwern and part of Bettws	72	2	3	69	3	4
Bettws Gwerful Goch	36	0	0	29	4	3
Harlech	94	3	1	81	9	3
Glyndyfrdwy	59	3	1	49	22	11
Pantperthog (part of Pennal)	51	0	1	43	8	1
Llandrillo	97	7	11	81	19	11
Llangor Cynwyd	125	9	17	92	38	19
Bontddu	70	3	2	50	6	0
TOTAL	6,476	186	312	5,531	662	463

SOURCE: U.K.A. *Thirty-seventh Annual Report, 1889*, pp. 58-9.

APPENDIX II

WELSH OFFICE-HOLDERS OF THE ALLIANCE, 1853-95

Year	Office	Name
1855	Vice-President	Very Rev. Dean Cotton, Bangor
1855	'Officer'	Rev. Canon E. Jenkins, Dowlais
1855	'Officer'	W. H. Darby, Brymbo
1855	Executive Committee	Rev. Richard Jones, Manchester
1855	Executive Committee	Rev. Owen Jones, Manchester
1856	'Officer'	Rev. Augustus Morgan, Machen
1860	Vice-President	Rev. Canon E. Jenkins
1861	Vice-President	Rev. A. Morgan
1861	Positions on General Council	Dean Cotton
		C. Darby
		W. H. Darby
		Rev. Owen Evans, Maentwrog
		Rev. Simon Evans, St. Clears
		Rev. T. Edwards, Caernarfon
		Rev. William Edwards, Aberdare
		Rev. R. F. Griffiths, Caernarfon
		Rev. J. Griffiths, Neath
		Rev. D. Hughes, Tredegar
		Rev. D. Jones, Caernarfon
		Rev. John Jones, Talysarn
		Rev. Canon E. Jenkins, Dowlais
		Rev. Thomas Lewis, Bangor
		Rev. W. Lloyd, Wrexham
		F. Levick, J.P., Blaina
		Rev. T. Levi, Ystradgynlais
		Joseph Maybery, Llanelli
		Rev. A. Morgan, Machen
		Rev. John Phillips, Bangor
		Henry Phillips, Newport
		Rev. Robert Parry, Ffestiniog
		Rev. D. Phillips, Maesteg
		R. C. Rawlins, Wrexham
		Rev. Samuel Roberts, Llanbrynmair
		Rev. David Rees, Llanelli
		W. T. Rogers, Beaumaris
		George Smart, Cardiff
		Rev. Dr. Thomas Thomas, Pontypool
		Rev. Owen Thomas, Talybont
		Thomas Williams, Gwaelodygarth, Merthyr Tydfil
1876	Vice-President	D. Davies, M.P., Llandinam
1876	Vice-President	Thomas Williams, J.P., Gwaelodygarth, Merthyr Tydfil
1876	Vice-President	P. H. Chambres, J.P., Denbigh

Year	Office	Name
1884	Vice-President	Sir Llewellyn Turner, J.P., Caernarfon
1885	Vice-President	John Cory, J.P., Cardiff
1892	Vice-President	T. E. Ellis, M.P., Llandderfel

SOURCE: U.K.A., *Annual Reports, 1853-95.*

BIBLIOGRAPHY

1. MANUSCRIPTS

Aberdare Public Library.
Henry Richard MSS. Minutes of Merthyr and Aberdare Nonconformist Election
Committee, 1867-68; 1872.

Alliance House, Caxton Street, London.
Minutes of the Executive Council of the United Kingdom Alliance, 1872-1895. 20
volumes.

University College of North Wales, Bangor.
Bangor MSS. 434 (167, 169, 195), 737 (136-141), 2,000 (19), 2,434 (117, 157),
2,546 (2), 5,757 (37), 411.
Edern MS, 11(E), 35(11), 35(44).
Gabriel Hughes MS, 14-15.
Caianydd MS, 8-11.
Newell MS, 42, 57.
Porth-yr-Aur MS, 4429, 4434-4474A.
Shankland MS, 13.

Gwynedd Record Office, Caernarfon.
The Town Accounts of Caernarvon, 1632-33.
Rhestr Ymgeiswyr am Aelodaeth, 1836-1864.
M/008, Rhaglen Cymanfa Ddirwestol Gogledd Cymru, 1850.
Police Committee Minute Book, 1856-1888.
County Analysts' Reports on Food and Drugs, 1879-1887.
Minutes of Caernarvon Licensing Committee, 1883.
Returns of Licences from Petty Sessions, 1878-1881.
Petitions from Caernarvonshire for the Early Closing of Public Houses, 1872.
Returns of General Inquiries concerning Licensed Houses, 1891, and published
Report thereon, 1892.

Cardiff Central Library.
1.521, E. P. Williams, Journal of a Tour in Glamorganshire, 1836.
1.543, Henry Allgood, Notes on Dowlais (1910).
1.548, 1.587, Sermons of the Rev. John Griffith, Rector of Merthyr Tydfil. *c.* 1875.
1.699, Rheolau Cymdeithas Cymedroldeb, Pentyrch, 1837-1841.

2:329, 'A Cambrian Literary Gentleman', The Social, Industrial and Literary State of the Cambrian Nation in 1880.

2.580, Cardiff Society for the Impartial Discussion of Political and Other Questions. Minute Books, 1886-1906.

2.651, Cardiff Discussion Union. Minute Book, 1889-1891.

2.731, William Rees, Llandovery. Miscellaneous Letters and Papers.

2.1205, Rev. John Owen, Caerffili, Address on Temperance (1891).

3.330, 'Hugo', The Dignity of Labour. Aberdare National Eisteddfod, 1885.

3.386, 'Aurelian', The Dignity of Labour. 1885.

3.492, Cefn English Wesleyan Sunday School Minute Book, 1889-1910.

3.504, Mrs. John Griffith, Merthyr. Diaries and Journals, 1845, 1860-64, 1866-67, 1870.

3.508, Letters and Diaries of John Griffith, Rector of Merthyr, 1845-1868.

3.512, The Diaries of John Davies (Brychan).

3.674, Llanfabon Parish. Churchwardens Minute Book, 1866-1895.

3.742, R. T. Evans, The Economic and Social Evolution of the Rural Population of Carmarthenshire (typescript).

4.137, D. W. Jones, Merthyr and South Wales Miscellany, 1865-73.

4.138, D. W. Jones, Merthyr, its Eisteddfodau and History, 1901-2.

4.522, Eiddie Ifor, Blaina (Thomas Evan Watkins, 1801-1889), At y Werin Weithyddol.

4.616, Cardiff Junior Liberal Association. Minute Book, 1886.

4.683, Henry Murton, Recollections of Dowlais, 1808-1812.

4.762, A List of all Friendly Societies in Glamorgan, 1836.

4.813, Cardiff Election Papers, 1866-68.

4.851, E. T. John, The History of Certain Merthyr Chapels.

4.1049, Bute MSS, Glamorgan Magistrates, 1836-47.

4.1050, Bute MSS, Glamorgan Police, 1839-46.

4.1112, Edgar Chappell, Historical Notes on Labour Unions and the Truck System in South Wales, n.d., c.1940 (typescript).

5.153, Return of Nonconformists in Glamorgan, 1830.

South Wales Temperance and Band of Hope Union, Cardiff.
Cardiff Temperance and Prohibition Association. Minutes, 1879-1884.
Cardiff Temperance and Band of Hope Union. Minutes, 1879-1895.
MS. Memoir of the Rev. Morris Morgan of Morriston (1837-1917).

Carmarthenshire Record Office, Carmarthen.
Dynevor MSS, Box 126, f.13. Poster, Evils of Country Ale-Houses, c.1833.
Museum Collection, Police Records, no. 111, Police Book of Summonses and Warrants, 1856-61.
Museum Collection, MS 179, Miscellaneous Ale and Spirits Account Book of Alcwyn Evans, publican, of Carmarthen, 1859-1889.
Museum Collection, no. 326, Register of Carmarthen Temperance Society with the names of those who signed the 'pledge', and additional memoranda, 1841-1859.

Glamorgan Record Office, Cardiff.
D/DX ib. 10. Robert Drane, Eating and Drinking in Times Past (1901).
D/DX ja, 1-10. Certificate and awards to James Beddoe, including the certificate of the Temperance Society. 1891.
D/DX ha,
    File 3, no. 4. The Welsh Ancestry of Father Theobald Mathew (d.1843).
    File 4, no. 1. History of the Merthyr and Dowlais Missions.

File 4, no. 2. A Brief History of the Catholic Church in Dowlais. 1920.

File 4, no. 10. Extract from 'Sundays in Wales', 1859.

File 5, no. 1. Catholicism in the Archdiocese of Cardiff a century ago. 1929.

    nos. 2-4. Three essays on Catholicism in Cardiff and Glamorgan in the nineteenth century.

    no. 5. The Catholic Revival in South Wales in the nineteenth century.

    no. 6. Cardiff Diary of the Fathers of the Institute of Charity. c. 1857.

D/D Xes, 1-20. Records of Brecon Road (Merthyr) Liberal Association.

D/D Xj, Unrest in Merthyr. Number of men on Poor Rate. 1875.

Dowlais MSS (D/DG).

    Section C, Box 5. Menelaus Memorandum on the Employment of Women and Children in the Iron Works of South Wales.

    Rules and Regulations to be observed by all employed in the collieries of the Dowlais Iron Company, 1861.

    Notice to Workmen employed in Dowlais Works setting out penalties to be imposed upon wages for absenteeism. 1853.

    Dowlais Iron Company. Incoming Letter Books, 1795-1869 (selected volumes only).

D/D Vau, Elections in Merthyr, 1888-1910.

Merthyr Urban District Council. Rules, minute books and annual reports of Building Societies and Merthyr Working Mens Society, 1881-1914.

The United Kingdom Temperance and General Provident Institution for Mutual Life Assurance, 1889-96.

Merthyr Tydfil Welsh Temperance Society. Trust Deed, 1877.

D/D GV/35. Vivian Collection. Sunday Closing Act. Correspondence, 1889.

D/D Wes/CR, Wesleyan Methodist Records. Cardiff Roath Circuit.

U/M, Board of Guardians. Merthyr Union. Cholera Committee Minute Book, 1866.

Rhymney Iron Company MSS, D/D Rh, 1-265.

QE, Box 7, 1/9F, Chief Constable of Glamorgan. Reports and Quarterly Returns, 1842-60, 1868-88.

Lambeth Palace Library, London.

The Archives of the Church of England Temperance Society.

Manchester Public Library.

Anti-Corn Law League MSS. Letter Books, 1840-46.

Merionethshire Record Office, Dolgellau.

M/1/238. Register of Dolgellau Temperance Society, 1875-77.

QA/P. Merionethshire Constabulary. Register of Charges for Towyn and Barmouth, 1875-95. 2 vols.

Merthyr Tydfil Central Library.

Merthyr Tydfil Parish Minute Books, 1799-1833, 1833-1896. 2 vols.

National Library of Wales, Aberystwyth.

1,025 C (Ieuan Gwynedd 1), Essay on the elevation of the working classes. c. 1850.

1,026 C (Ieuan Gwynedd 3), An essay on intemperance (1852).

2,397 A (D. S. Davies 17), Nodiadau ar Ddirwest.

2,741 B (Edward Griffith 51), Cymdeithas Dirwestol Ieuanctyd Dolgellau.

2,768 C (Edward Griffith 78), Cuttings from *The Teetotal Times and Essayist* (Jersey, 1847-48), including three essays by Evan Jones (Ieuan Gwynedd).

4,943 B, Merthyr in 1860. Merthyr Missionaries Report.

6,528 E, Mines and Mining Population of South Wales, 1859.

7,995 A, Undeb Cerddorol Dirwestwyr Ardudwy, Minute Book, 1870-77.

8,305 C-11 D, Thomas Gee MSS.

8,320 D, Gee Miscellany, including Permissive Bill, 1866, 1869.

8,322 B (Matthews 2), A Roll of Members of the Aberystwyth Auxiliary Temperance Society, formed 31 August, 1835.

8,323 B (Matthews 3), Minute Book of the Aberystwyth Auxiliary Temperance Society, 1835-37; 1855-56.

8,324 D (Matthews 4), A Roll of 3,226 persons from Aberystwyth and District who signed the Total Abstinence Pledge between 21 October 1836 and 13 August 1855, with their addresses and occupations.

8,325 D (Matthews 5), Rules and Resolutions of the Aberystwyth Temperance Society, and minutes of committee meetings, 29 May-14 July, 1837.

8,371 D (Neuadd Wen 42), Temperance activities at Llanuwchllyn, 1838-40.

8,373 B (Neuadd Wen 44), Draft Minutes of Temperance meetings at Llanuwchllyn, 1836-38.

8,374 A (Neuadd Wen 45), Miscellaneous notes of sermons and minutes of temperance meetings, taken by John Jones, Llanuwchllyn.

8,391-93 A-C, Diaries and Letters of Eben Fardd.

9,165 D (Hobley Griffith 15), Address from Llanrwst Good Templars, c. 1875.

10,187 C, Temperance Poems. Temperance Eisteddfod, Merthyr, 1860.

10,275-6 E (Solva 1-2), Llythyrau at Hugh Jones a Thomas Pierce a Owen Jones, Liverpool, 1837-42.

10,291 B (Solva 17), Account of ministers at Tredegar for food and beer, 1829-39.

10,362 E (H. O. Evans 55), Temperance Miscellanea.

10,461 D (Evan Owen 19), Papers relating to temperance meetings at Liverpool, 1879.

10,506 B, Essay on 'The Distinguishing Features of the Baptists' by 'Anti-Tradition'.

10,507 C (Evan Owen 65), Draft letters by Evan Owen on Liverpool Welsh Baptist subjects, 1873-80, and on behalf of the Temperance Committee of the Denbigh, Flint, Montgomery and Merioneth Welsh Baptist Association, 1897-99.

10,519 E (Evan Owen 77), Miscellaneous Papers relating to the work of the Temperance Committee of the Denbigh, Flint and Merioneth Baptist Association, 1897-1901.

10,520 C-1 B (Evan Owen 78-79), Notes relating to temperance activity at Liverpool.

10,546 A—7 E (Evan Owen 104-5), Letters to Evan Owen relating to his activities in connection with the temperance movement in Liverpool and North Wales.

10,854 A (Frondirion), Letter from Sir John Rhys relating to the Royal Commission on Sunday Closing in Wales, 1890.

11,161 B, Minutes of Côr Undebol Dirwestol Dolgellau, 1867.

11,489 B, A Register of membership, 1836-39, of Llanbrynmair Temperance Society (est. 16 Sept. 1836). A section of the volume is in the hand of Samuel Roberts ('S.R.', 1800-1885). A variant register is preserved in MS 16,734 B.

11,614 E (D. Morgan Lewis 1), Album of Clwydwenfro.

11,721 C, Letter of the Rev. John Elias on the effects of revivals, c. 1822.

12,059 C (D. D. Williams, 7), The Influence of the Methodist Movement in Wales on Social Life.

12,072 A, Llyfr Cymdeithas 'Ddirwestaidd' Corris, August-December 1836.

12,184 C, Cofnodion Temlwyr Da Penrhyndeudraeth, 1892-98.

12,293 C, Llythyrau D. R. Daniel.

12,652 D, Lleyn and Eifionydd District Lodge of Good Templars. Minute Book, 1875-85.

12,695 B, Undeb Dirwestol Uwch Llifon. Minute Book, 1892-1904.

12,863 F, Journal of the Rev. William Rees, Llechryd, 1880-1917.

14,199 C (Rees Jenkins Jones), Unitarianism in South Wales.

14,205 B (Rees Jenkin Jones), A Reply to 'Chartism Unmasked' (1841).

14,268 B (Oakford, 26), A General Revival of Religion (essay).

14,696 D, D. T. Eaton, The Mechanics Institutes of South Wales (1948).

15,339 A, Dowlais Works Beer Book, 1894.

15,371 A, Evan Jones, A Diary and Temperance Notes.

15,405 A, Letters of Rev. William Williams, Caledfryn.

15,439 B-42 C, Cardiff Nonconformist Union. Minutes, 1867-94.

16,050 B, Llyfr Cofnodion Cymdeithas Ddirwest Llandderfel, 1872-86.

16,146 B (E. C. Powell), Register of Llandinam Calvinistic Methodist Temperance Society, n.d.

16,157 B, E. I. Williams, Notes for a history of Blaina and Nantyglo, Parish of Aberystruth, Monmouthshire.

16,212 C, Some Reminiscences of T. E. Ellis, M.P.

16,219 B, Addresses on Temperance (1858-85) by Rev. John Williams, Aberystwyth.

16,652 B, Thomas Gee, 'The Origins of Moral Evil' (1837).

16,734 B (Bontdolgadfan 8), Lists of signatories to pledges drawn up by the Llanbrynmair Temperance Society, 1836-51.

16,735 B (Bontdolgadfan 9), Temperance Miscellanea, 1858-78.

16,861 C, Lord Clwyd, Some Memories of My Life.

17,253 C, Minutes of Glamorgan Baptist Association, 1870-95.

17,271 A, Rev. Thomas Evans, Ruabon, Autobiography of a Congregational Minister, n.d.

17,535 B (Thomas Levi 5), Addresses on Temperance (1869-88) by Rev. Thomas Levi.

18,313 A, Temperance Songs by Ellis Jones, Dowlais, c.1846.

18,342 C, Three Essays on 'The Effects of Alcoholic Drinks on the Human System', submitted to the National Eisteddfod at Pwllheli, 1875.

18,740-41 D, Letters to Sir Llewelyn Turner, 1860-1901.

19,255 B, Cofnodion Temlwyr Da Croesor, 1873-76.

19,256 A, Addresses on Good Templary, 1874-75.

19,643 B, Cardiganshire Election, 1885.

19,658 C, Aberystwyth Womens Liberal Association. Minute Book, 1894-97.

19,911 B (Padarn Davies), Minute Book of Pabell Padarn, Independent Order of Rechabites, 1842-46.

Calvinistic Methodist Archives.

52, Returns of Monthly Meetings: temperance statistics, n.d.

70, The Church and Social Problems (1919).

874, Address to Pontypridd Good Templars by Daniel Davies, 27 March 1874.

3,441, E. O. Davies, 'The Sunday School'.

5,836, J. M. Howell, 'What Nonconformity stands for' (1917).

5,923, Characteristics of Calvinistic Methodism.

5,924, The Forward Movement (1901).

5,926, 'Temperance', n.d.

5,929, Araith Ddirwestol.

5,935, Address on Temperance.

6,306 Address on Temperance.

6,945, Dylanwad y Ddiod Feddwol ar y Meddwl.

6,947, Dirwest fel Egwyddor.

6,955, Band of Hope Register, Siloh Chapel, Lampeter, 1875-84.
7,306-7,342, Letters of the Rev. David Charles, Bala.
7,750-7,751, Letters of the Rev. J. Eiddon Jones, Llanrug.
8,925, Temperance Oaths, 1853.
10,059-61, Three Lectures on Temperance, 1876.
10,063-66, Four Lectures on Temperance, n.d.
16,024, The Sufferings of Nonconformity, n.d.
16,194, Temperance reports and resolutions, 1888-95.
16,196, Committee on Temperance and Purity: Lower Montgomery Presbytery, 1896.
16,514, Notes and Addresses on Temperance, n.d.
16,540, Hanes dirwest ym Mhontrobert, Mafod.
17,850, Dr. Thomas Rees, A Lecture on Edward Matthews, Ewenny (1884).

Deposited Collections.
Cwrt Mawr MSS, 8, 58-61, 96, 122, 414, 481.
637-42 A, Minute Books of the North Wales Womens Temperance Union, 1892-98.
Roll MSS, Bay 31, Shelf 3, Garn (Bow St.) Band of Hope and Juvenile Temperance Society Pledge Roll, 1856-67.
  Aberystwyth Juvenile Temperance Society Pledge Roll, 1852-66.
D. R. Daniel Papers.
T. E. Ellis Papers.
Ellis Griffiths Papers.
Glansevern Collection (papers of A. C. Humphreys-Owen).
David Herbert (Resolven) Collection.
J. Herbert Lewis Papers.
Stuart Rendel Papers.
Lord Swansea Papers.

Newport Public Library.
MS q M000 286, Monmouthshire English Baptist Association Minute Books, 1857-1901.
MS M000 (328). 39193, Welsh Liberal Members Committee Minute Book, August 1886-July 1889.

Newport Temperance Society.
MS Minutes of Newport Temperance Society, 2 vols., 1887-95.

Public Record Office.
H[ome] O[ffice] 40/57, 45/54, Cuttings from *The Advocate and Merthyr Free Press.*
HO 40/30, Part 3, Disturbances in Wales.
HO 40/57, 45/54, Translations of *Udgorn Cymru,* 1841.
HO 45/9527/36620, Liquor Licensing. The Working of the Welsh Sunday Closing Act, 1881.
HO 45/454, Part 1, Thomas Yates, 'The Organisation of Teetotallers in Wales', incorporated in Edwin Chadwick, Memorandum on disturbances in Wales, 11 July 1843.
HO 73/8, Returns from Poor Law Guardians, 1836.
FS 1/917/296-1/917/301, Friendly Societies in Wales, 1820-38.

British National Temperance League, Sheffield.
National Temperance League. Minute Books, 1856-1877.
MS, A Homely Talk with Total Abstainers with a Few Suggestions for the Successful Working of a Temperance Society.

Royal Institution of South Wales, Swansea.
The Glamorgan Election of 1826, Expense Account.
Public Houses and Beer Shops in the Borough of Swansea, July 1853.

2. PRINTED SOURCES (place of publication London, unless otherwise stated)

A. *Works of Reference*

Dictionary of Welsh Biography (1959).
Dod's Parliamentary Companion, 1832 to date.
J. Evans, *Bibliographical Dictionary of the Ministers and Preachers of the Welsh Calvinistic Methodist Body* (Caernarvon, 1907).
I. G. Jones and D. Williams (eds.), *The Religious Census of 1851. A Calendar of the Returns Relating to Wales,* vol. 1. South Wales (Cardiff, 1976).
R. T. Jenkins and William Rees, *A Bibliography of the History of Wales* (second edn. Cardiff, 1962).
Kelley's Directory of Monmouthshire and the Principal Towns and Places in South Wales (1884).
F. H. McCalmont, *Parliamentary Poll Books* (Nottingham, 1910).
B. R. Mitchell and P. Deane, *Abstract of British Historical Statistics* (Cambridge, 1962).
Rev. J. V. Morgan (ed.), *Welsh Religious Leaders in the Victorian Era* (1905).
Owen's Directory for Glamorgan, Monmouth, Shropshire, Hereford, and Radnor (1878).
T. R. Roberts, *A Dictionary of Eminent Welshmen* (Cardiff, 1908).
T. Marchant Williams, *The Welsh Members of Parliament* (Cardiff, 1894).
W. R. Williams, *Parliamentary History of Wales, 1541-1895* (Brecknock, 1895).
G. B. Wilson, *Alcohol and the Nation. A Contribution to the Study of the Liquor Problem in the United Kingdom for 1800-1935* (1940).

B. *Official Papers*

Hansard's Parliamentary Debates, Third and Fourth Series, 1830-1895.
Report of the SCHC on the Sale of Beer, P[arliamentary] P[apers], 1830, X(253).
Account of the number of brewers, licensed victuallers and persons licensed under the Act 'to permit the general sale of beer by retail in the United Kingdom', PP 1831, XVII(60); 1831-32, XXXIV(78).
Report of the SCHC on the Sale of Beer, PP 1833, XV(416).
Report of the SCHC on the causes and consequences of the prevailing vice of intoxication among the labouring classes, 1834, VIII(559).
Report of the SCHC appointed to inquire into the laws and practises relating to the observation of the Lord's Day, 1831-32, VII(253).
Report on the State of Elementary Education in the Mining Districts of South Wales, 1840, XL(182).
Return of the number of persons taken into custody for drunkenness and for disorderly conduct by the police force in each city and town, 1841-51. 1852-53. LXXIX(242).
Report of the SCHC on the Payment of Wages in Goods. 1842, IX(471).
Report of the Royal Commission appointed to inquire into the employment of children, 1842, XV-XVII(380-382).
Report on the Sanitary Condition of the Labouring Population, 1842, XXVI(430).
Reports of H. Seymour Tremenheere on the State of the Population in the Mining Districts.

1844	XVI(592).
1845	XXVII(670).
1846	XXIV(737).
1847	XVI(844).
1847-48	XXVI(993).

1849	XXII(1109).
1850	XXIII(1248).
1851	XXIII(1406).
1852	XXI(1525).
1852-53	XL(1679).

Report of the Health of Towns Commission into the Sanitary Condition of the Labouring Population of Britain, by Sir Henry de la Bêche, 1845, XVIII(981).

Report of the SCHC on Railway Labourers, 1846, XIII(530).

Report of the Commissioners of Inquiry into the State of Education in Wales, 1847, XXVII(870).

Report of the SCHL on the Bill regulating the Sale of Beer and other liquors on the Lord's Day, 1847-48, XVI(501).

Report of the SCHL to consider the operation of the Acts for the Sale of Beer, 1850, X(398).

Report to the General Board of Health on a Preliminary Inquiry into the Sewerage, Drainage and supply of water, and the Sanitary Condition of the inhabitants of Merthyr Tydfil, 1850, XI(311).

Return of the number of persons taken into custody for drunkenness and disorderly conduct, 1851, 1861, 1871, and 1876. 1877, LXIX(401).

Report of H. S. Tremenheere on the operation of the Truck Act in the Mining Districts. 1852. XXI(in 1525).

Report of the SCHC on Public Houses, 1852-53, XXXVII(855), 1854, XIV(231).

Report of the SCHC on the Payment of Wages Bill, 1854, XVI(382).

Report of the SCHC on the Sale of Beer, 1854-55, X(407), First report; 1854-55, X(427), Second report.

Report of the SCHC on Mines, 1866, XIV(431): 1867, XIII(496).

Report of the SCHC on the Sale of Liquors on Sunday Bill, 1867-68, XIV(402).

Report of the Commissioners appointed to inquire into the Truck System, 1871, XXXVI(326-7).

Report of the SCHC on Habitual Drunkards, 1872, IX(242).

Reports from Borough authorities in England and Wales relating to the Licensing Act (1872), 1874, LIV(180).

Report of the SCHL on Intemperance, 1877, XI(171), XI(271), XI(418); 1878, XIV(338); 1878-79, X(113).

Returns for England and Wales of the total number of convictions in respect of drunkenness, 1885-89, 1889, LXI(363).

Report of the Royal Commissioners appointed to inquire into the operation of the Sunday Closing (Wales) Act, 1881, 1890, XL(1).

Evidence, Report and Appendices of the Royal Commission on Land in Wales and Monmouthshire. 1894, XXXVI, XXXVII; 1895, XL, XLI; 1896, XXXIII-XXXV.

Royal Commission on the Liquor Licensing Laws, 1897, XXXIV(8356); 1897, XXXV(8523-1); 1898, XXXVI(8694), XXXVII(8696), XXXVIII(8822); 1899, XXXIV(9075), XXXV(9379, 9379-1).

Report, Evidence and Indexes of the Royal Commission appointed to inquire into the Church and other Religious Bodies in Wales, 1910, XIV-XIX.

C. *Newspapers, Periodicals and Reports*

NEWSPAPERS

The Advocate and Merthyr Free Press.
Baner ac Amserau Cymru.
Caernarvon and Denbigh Herald.
Cambrian.

Cambria Daily Leader.
Cardiff Reporter.
Cardiff Times.
Cardiff Figaro.
Cardiff and Merthyr Guardian.
Cardiff and South Wales Whip.
Carmarthen Journal.
Evening Star of Gwent.
Y Goleuad.
Merthyr Express.
Merthyr Telegraph.
Merthyr Weekly Mail.
Monmouthshire Merlin.
Morning Chronicle.
Newport Gazette.
North Wales Chronicle.
North Wales Gazette.
The Principality.
The Reformer and South Wales Times.
Silurian.
South Wales Daily News.
South Wales Labour Times.
Star of Gwent.
Swansea and Glamorgan Herald.
Tarian y Gweithiwr.
The Times.
Western Mail.

PERIODICALS

(a) *General*

Aberdare Banner of Faith 1884-86.
Aberdare Dawn of Day, 1886-89.
Yr Adolygydd, 1850-1853.
Yr Annibynwr, 1836-1864.
Anti-Corn Law Circular, 1838-1841.
Anti-Bread Tax Circular, 1841-1843.
The League, 1843-1846.
Baptist Chronicle, 1892-1895.
Y Bedyddiwr, 1842→.
Y Beirniad, 1859-1879.
Brewers Journal, 1872-1874.
Bye-Gones, 1880-1881.
Cardiff Congregational Magazine, 1868-1875, 1890.
Cardiff Review and Monthly Record of Christian Work, 1894.
Catholic Opinion. 1867, 1869-1873.
Christian Standard. The Monthly Magazine of the Cardiff Evangelistic Movement, 1891.
Churchman in Wales, 1873.
Congregational Magazine for the counties of Glamorgan and Carmarthen, 1873.
Cymru Fydd, 1888-1892.
Y Cylchgrawn, 1851.
Cambrian Journal, 1854-1864.
Y Diwygiwr, 1835→.
Y Drysorfa, 1833→.

Y Dysgedydd, 1833→.
Yr Eurgrawn Wesleyaidd, 1833→.
The Evangelist for Cardiff, 1886-1887.
The Ferret or South Wales Ratepayer, 1870-1875.
The Friend: Religious, Moral and Political Intelligencer for Shropshire and North Wales, January-March, 1838.
Y Geninen, 1883→.
Y Gweithiwr Cymreig, 1885-1889.
Y Gwerinwr, 1855-1856.
Y Gwladgarwr, 1833-1841.
Greal y Bedyddwyr, 1833-1837.
Yr Haul, 1833→.
Hygiene. A Monthly Journal for the promotion of public and domestic health, 1889-1891.
Licensed Victuallers Guardian, 1869-1889.
Y Lladmerydd, 1885-1895.
Transactions of Liverpool and Welsh National Society, 1885-1904.
Merthyr Tydfil Parish Magazine, 1887-1891.
Methodist Recorder and General Christian Chronicle, 1861, 1865.
Meliora: a quarterly review of social science in the ethical, political and ameliorative aspects, 1858-1869.
Monmouthshire Baptist, 1886.
Monmouthshire Congregational Magazine, 1868.
Monthly Herald, 1857-1859.
Monthly Tidings: A Record of Christian work among the Calvinistic Methodists of Wales, 1885-1893.
The Millennial Harbinger and Voluntary Church Advocate, 1835-1836.
The Nonconformist, 1845, 1859.
North Wales Congregational Magazine, Sept.-Dec. 1891.
Pembrokeshire Congregational Magazine, 1837-1838.
Red Dragon, 1882-1887.
The Revival, 1859-1862.
Seren Gomer, 1833→.
Y Seren Ogleddol, 1835-1836.
Seren Cymru, 1851-1858.
St. Johns (Cardiff) Parochial Magazine, 1870-1895.
Y Traethodydd, 1845→.
The Treasury, 1864-1884.
Udgorn Cymru, 1841.
The Universe, 1846-1848.
The Welsh Calvinistic Methodist Record, 1852-1854.
Y Wawr, 1850→.
Y Winllan, 1848→.
Welsh Weekly: an independent journal of religious and social life in Wales, 1892.
Wales (ed. O. M. Edwards), 1894-1896.
Welsh Review, 1892.
Western Vindicator, 1839.
Weekly Register, 1881-1886.
Workman's Advocate. Amddiffynydd y Gweithiwr, 1873-1875.

(b) *Temperance*

The Abstainer. Monthly Magazine of Cardiff Band of Hope Union, 1890-1895.
Yr Adolygydd, 1838-1839.

Alliance News, 1854-1895.
Yr Athraw, sef cylchgrawn llenyddol, crefyddol, dirwestol, 1836-1844.
Blue Ribbon Gazette and Gospel Temperance Herald, 1882-1886.
British and Foreign Temperance Herald, 1832-1835.
British and Foreign Temperance Advocate, 1834-1835.
British Temperance Advocate and Herald, 1839-1841, 1852-1855.
New British and Foreign Temperance Intelligencer, 1836-1838.
British and Foreign Temperance Intelligencer, 1839-1842.
Journal of the New British and Foreign Temperance Society, 1839-1843.
Cambrian Temperance Chronicle, 1891-1892.
Church of England Temperance Magzine, 1864-1867.
Cardiff Methodist Temperance Magazine, 1877.
Crickhowell Temperance Advocate, 1836.
Y Cymedrolwr, 1835.
Y Cerbyd Dirwestol, 1837-1838.
Cyfaill Rhinwedd, 1846.
English Chartist Circular and Temperance Record for England and Wales, 1841-1844.
Y Dirwestydd, 1836-1839.
Y Dirwestwr, 1840-1845.
Y Dirwestydd Deheuol, 1840-1841.
Y Dirwestwr Deheuol, 1838.
Y Dyngarwr, 1843, 1879-1888.
Methodist Temperance Magazine, 1871, 1873-1874.
Metropolitan Temperance Intelligencer and Journal, 1843-1845.
Preston Temperance Advocate, 1834-1837.
Y Rechabydd, 1840-1842.
Temperance Spectator, 1859-1866.
Sunday Closing Reporter, 1874-1895.
Y Seren Ddirwestol, 1837.
Y Tremlydd Cymreig, 1873-1878.
Western Good Templar, 1871-1873.
Templar of Wales and Good Templar's Advocate, 1873.
Templar Record. English Grand Lodge of Wales, 1883-1885.
True Templar, 1888-1889.
Templar Clarion, 1894-1895.
Teetotal Times and Essayist, 1846-1852.
National Temperance Chronicle, 1843-1850, 1851-1856.
Udgorn Dirwest, 1850.
Weekly Record of the Temperance Movement, 1856→.
Western Temperance Herald, 1859-1869.
Working Man's Teetotal Journal, 1844.

REPORTS

Abercarn Teetotal Association, *Annual Report, 1878.*
Cardiff Temperance and Prohibition Association, *Annual Reports, 1882-1892.*
Cardiff and District Band of Hope Union, *Annual Reports, 1888-1895.*
Newport and County Total Abstinence Society and Gospel Temperance Union, *Annual Reports, 1884-1895.*
Newport and District Band of Hope Union, *Annual Reports, 1889-1895.*
Swansea Temperance Society, *Annual Report, 1872.*
South Wales Temperance Association, *Annual Reports, 1887, 1890-91.*
United Kingdom Alliance, *Annual Reports, 1854-1895.*

National Temperance League, *Annual Reports, 1856-1890.*
National Temperance League, *Annuals, 1881-1895.*
New British and Foreign Temperance Society, *Annual Reports, 1836-1842.*
British and Foreign Temperance Society, *Annual Reports, 1840-1841.*
Church of England Temperance Society, Llandaff Diocesan Branch, *Annual Report, 1888.*
National Union for the Suppression of Intemperance, *Annual Reports, 1872-1895.*
Central Association for Stopping the Sale of Intoxicating Liquors during the Whole of the 24 hours of Sunday, *Annual Reports, 1887-1895.*
Cardiff Town Mission, *Annual Reports, 1880-1886.*
Undenominational Christian Mission and Ragged Schools, Pontymoile, Pontypool. A Brief Record of Work Among the Colliers and Iron Workers. *Annual Reports, 1891-1898.*
South Wales and North Wales Liberal Federations, *Annual Reports, 1885-1895.*
Swansea Benevolent Visiting Society, *Annual Report, 1839.*
Reports of the North and South Wales Conferences of the English Churches of the Presbyterian Church of Wales, 1881-1893.
Annual Reports of the North Wales and South Wales Associations of the Calvinistic Methodists.
Report of the Proceedings of the English Congregational Union of North Wales, 1893.
Reports of the Church Congress at Swansea, 1879; . . . at Cardiff, 1889; . . . at Rhyl, 1891.
Reports of the Llandaff Diocesan Conference, 1884-1895.
Proceedings of the World's Temperance Convention, 1846.
Annual Directory and Rechabite Reference Book, 1892-1893 (Manchester, 1893).
United Kingdom Alliance. Report on Special Conference for Wales at Cardiff, 1954 (typescript).
Congregational Union of England and Wales. The Aberdare Addresses, 1830.
The Established Church and Nonconformity in Wales. Proceedings of Swansea Conference, 1862.
Proceedings of the International Temperance Convention at London, 1862.
Proceedings of the First – Third Annual Sessions of the English Grand Lodge of Wales. (Merthyr Tydfil, 1872-1874).
Proceedings of the Ministerial Conference on Temperance, Manchester, 1874.
Proceedings of the United Temperance Mission at Newport, Monmouthshire, 1879.
Proceedings of the National Temperance Congress, Liverpool, 1884; . . . Birmingham, 1889, . . . Chester, 1895.
Proceedings of the High Moveable Conference of the Independent Order of Rechabites, Swansea, 1903.
Monmouthshire Baptist Association, Circular Letters, 1832 ff
Thomas Richards, *Monmouthshire Baptist Association. Circular Letters, 1832-1945* (Newport, 1947).
Glamorgan and Carmarthenshire Baptist Association, Circular Letters, 1866.
Adroddiad Cyfarfodydd Undeb Bedyddwyr Cymru, 1878-1895.
Undeb yr Annibynwyr Cymraeg. Adroddiad Cyfarfodydd yr Undeb, 1872-1895.
History and Rules of Discipline of Calvinistic Methodists in Wales, 1850.
Y Gymanfa Gyffredinol. Minutes of the General Assembly of Calvinistic Methodists, Vol. 1, 1864-1895.
Presbyterian Church of Wales. Report on Conference of English Churches at Cardiff, 1895.

D.　*Pamphlets*

Address and Rules of Newport Working Mens Association for benefiting politically, socially and morally, the useful classes (Newport, n.d., *c*.1838).

Adroddiad o'r Ddadl ar Ddirwest, a gynhaliwyd yn Llantrisant, Tachwedd 18, 1842, rhwng John Jones (Llangollen) ac Evan Davies, 'Ieuan Myfyr' (Pontypridd) (Llanelli, 1842).

Awen-Gerdd Debygawl a Dynwaredawl ar destun-ymadrodd Teetotalaidd (Merthyr Tydfil, 1839).

Awgrymiadau am Gyfraith er atal y Fasnach mewn Diodydd Meddwol: fel y cytunwyd arnynt gan gynghor cyffredinol cyngrair y deyrnas unedig (Manchester, n.d., *c.*1867).

W. Bailey, *The Higher Socialism. Paper read at the Cardiff Free Methodist Improvement Class* (Cardiff, 1889).

T. H. Barker, *Yr 'Awgrymiadau Cyfeillgar' yn cael eu Hadolygu yn ddiduedd. Llythyr at . Gyfaill yng Ngogledd Cymru* (United Kingdom Alliance, Manchester, 1867).

W. L. Bevan, *The Church in Wales* (1885); *Is the Church in Wales an advancing Church?* (1893); *The Church in the South Wales Coalfield* (1894).

B.H. (A Cardigan Voter), *The Welsh Destiny. A Political Triad* (Aberystwyth, 1891).

G. Bird, *Observations on Cholera* (Swansea, 1849).

S. Bowly, *Total Abstinence in its proper place. Addressed to the religious portion of the community* (Gloucester, n.d.).

James Hews Bransby, *An Account of the Calvinistic Methodists in Wales* (Caernarfon, 1845).

C. E. Breese, *Welsh Nationality* (Portmadoc, 1895).

O. Bromley, *A ydyw y 'Permissive Bill' yn gyson a Rhyddid? Attal y llifeiriant neu y fasnach feddwol ar 'Permissive Bill'* (United Kingdom Alliance, Manchester, 1870).

H. A. Bruce, *On Amusements, as the means of continuing and extending the education of the working classes* (Cardiff, 1850); *The Present Position and Future Prospects of the Working Classes in the Manufacturing Districts of South Wales* (Cardiff, 1851); *Merthyr in 1852* (Cardiff, 1852).

John Burns, *Labour and Drink* (1904).

J. S. Bushnan, *Religious Revivals in relation to Nervous and Mental Diseases* (1860).

J. C. Campbell, *A Lecture on the Social State of the Mineral Districts* (Cardiff, 1849).

Cardiff and District Temperance and Band of Hope Union. Fifty years of Safeguarding the Young Life of Cardiff, 1879-1929. Jubilee Souvenir (Cardiff, 1930).

Joseph Chamberlain, *Licensing Reform and Local Option* (Birmingham, 1876).

Characteristics of Welsh Preaching (Glasgow, 1853).

Club Life in Cardiff: the fruits of the Welsh Sunday Closing Act (Cardiff, 1883).

W. J. T. Collins and F. Townsend, *Life in Earnest at Pontymoile, 1878-1897* (Newport, n.d.).

W. J. T. Collins, *A Mission of Mercy: a record of the work done by the Undenominational Christian Mission at Pontymoile* (Newport, n.d.).

The Two Colliers: a dialogue between a Gloucester and a Blackwood, Mon. collier (Newport, 1840).

Cyfansoddiad ac emynau Uwch Deml Cymru. Merthyr Tydfil, 1872, 1873 (Aberdare, 1874).

Cyfrifon o Draul Anghymmedroldeb er annogaeth i Ddirwest (Caerleon, n.d., *c.*1834).

Cymdeithas Gerddorol Ddirwestol y cyfansoddiadau buddugol yn nhrydedd Eisteddfod Aberdâr (Aberdare, 1861).

'Cyrus', *Y Maine Law* (Bethesda, 1857).

J. Dalbey, *Treial Alcohol* (Llanfaircaereinion, 1938).

W. H. Darby, *Reasons in favour of a Maine Law for Great Britain* (Wrexham, n.d.).

A. T. Davies, *The Relation of Municipal Actions to Morals* (1899).

[David Davies], *The Welsh Sunday Closing Act: Lord Aberdare's Challenge to the Western Mail* (Cardiff, 1889).

D. S. Davies, *Anerchiad yn erbyn rhoddi aelodaeth eglwysig i werthwyr pethau meddwol* (Merthyr Tydfil, 1877).

D. J. Davies, *The Tredegar Workmen's Hall, 1861-1951* (1951).

J. Davies, *Anerchiad Difrifol y Rechabiaid Annibynawl* (Merthyr Tydfil, 1839).

Eliezer Davies, *Calvinistic Methodism in Wales: its present position and future prospects* (1879).

E. Davies, *Revivals in Wales* (1859).

E. Davies, J. Evans and D. Lewis, *Anthem, Canig a Thôn, sef cyfansoddiadau arobryn yn 8fed gylchwyl Cymrodorion Dirwestol Merthyr, Christmas 1854* (Merthyr Tydfil, 1855).

J. J. Davies, *Y Gronfa Ddirwestol* (Caernarfon, 1838).

Joseph Davies, *Epistol at y Llwyrymatalwyr yn Cynnwys Adolygiad ar Draethawd y Parch. William Williams, Caernarfon* (Denbigh, 1836).

R. R. Davies, *Prize Essay on the desirability of recreation grounds for Swansea* (Swansea, 1875).

D. Miall Edwards, *Religion in Wales* (1926).

Rev. Ebenezer Edwards, *Pregeth ar Ddirwest* (Brynmawr, 1858).

Rev. William Edwards, *Traethawd ar Ddirwest* (Aberdare, 1860).

D. Elias, *Anerchiad Dwys yn Dangos Buddioldeb Cymdeithas Cymmedroldeb a Dirwest* (Caernarfon, 1857).

Rev. J. Elias, *Ymddiddan am Gymdeithas Cymmedroldeb* (Bangor, 1836).

A. B. Evans, *Dissent and its Inconsistencies* (1841).

Christmas Evans, *Y Cynhyrfiad Dirwestol. Sylwadau ar Lwyrymattaliad* (Caernarfon, 1837); *Y Cynhyrfiad Dirwestol, neu ddiwygiad mawr yr oes* (Dolgellau, 1837).

Evan Evans, *A Duoglott Guide for Making Temperance Drinks* (Cowbridge, 1838).

Explanation and Notes of the Temperance (Wales) Bill (Brecon, n.d. *c.*1931).

J. C. Fowler, *On Public Libraries* (Swansea, 1871).

J. Francis, *A Sermon to the Working Classes* (Newport, 1839).

'Freeman', *How Jeremy Chisselpence solved the bona-fide Traveller Question* (1880).

J. S. Gavin, *Poverty, its cause and cure* (Manchester, 1898).

Thomas Gee, *Our Licensing System Considered. Friendly Suggestions for a change in the Permissive Bill of the United Kingdom Alliance* (Denbigh, 1866); *Suggestions for a change in the Licensing Laws* (Denbigh, 1869).

Good Templary in Wales. Diamond Jubilee, 1874-1934 (Gowerton, 1934).

W. Griffith, *Thomas Edward Ellis, 1859-1899* (Llandybie, 1959).

William Harries, *Gwirf, neu Alcohol, ei natur a'i effeithiau* (Caernarfon, 1870).

A. F. Harvey, *The Royal Commission and Sunday Closing in Wales, Scotland and Ireland* (1899).

S. H. Hobson, *Possibilities of the Labour Church* (Cardiff, 1893).

Holwyddoreg ar Egwyddorion a Rheolau y Gymdeithas Cymmedrolder (Liverpool, 1834).

Thomas Horne, *Our own poor* (Newport, 1884).

G. J. Holyoake, *The Social Means of Promoting Temperance* (1859).

M. Hughes, *Ffrwyth y Profiad, neu waedd yn erbyn meddwdod* (Wyddgrug, 1837); *Traethawd ar Lwyrymwrthodiad: yn cynwys adolygiad ar Draethawd y Parch William Williams, Caernarfon* (Wyddgrug, 1837); *Traethawd ar Annghymedroldeb* (Wyddgrug, 1844).

Rev. J. Hunter, *Temperance Legislation in 1871. Mr. Bruce's Bill: What it was and why it was abandoned* (Glasgow, n.d.).

'Ignotus', *The Last Thirty Years in a Mining District* (1867).

C. H. James, *A Lecture on Wages delivered before the Total Abstainers of Merthyr Tydfil* (Cardiff, 1851); *What I remember about myself and old Merthyr* (Merthyr Tydfil, 1894).

E. Jenkins, *Chartism Unmasked* (Merthyr Tydfil, 1840); *A Sermon Upon the Death of Sir John Guest* (Merthyr Tydfil, 1853).

A. J. Johnes, *A Letter written in reply to an invitation to join a Conference for a Revision of the Licensing System* (Welshpool, 1867).

A. E. Jones, *Diseases produced by drink* (1888).

Rev. B. Jones, *Temperance versus Teetotalism. Cymedroldeb. Total Overthrow of Teetotalism. Llwyr-Ddymchweliad Titotaliedyddiaeth* (Llanrwst, 1838).

D. Jones, *A Tee-totaler's Defence. An address to the inhabitants of the Parish of Llansaintffraid* (Oswestry, 1837).

D. Jones, *How to bring to Church those who habitually stay at home on Sunday* (Bangor, 1895).

Evan Jones, *The Dissent and Morality of Wales* (1847); *A Vindication of the educational and moral conditions of Wales* (Llandovery, 1848).

E. K. Jones, *Jiwbili deddf cau tafarndai ar y Sabboth yng Nghymru* (Conwy, 1931).

H. Jones, *Wales and its Prospects* (1889).

Hugh Jones, *Ffrwyn i Asyn: yn cynnwys yr Achosion a'r Rhesymau fod William Williams o Gaernarfon, yn gwrthwynebu y Llwyrymwrthodwyr* (Caernarfon, n.d., c. 1837).

J. I. Jones, *Why are we Nonconformists?* (Brecon, 1881).

J. Jones, *Y Sabboth* (1852).

J. D. Jones, *Dylanwad y Groes: yn nychweliad ac argyhoeddiad Dafydd Sion, Meddwyn Diwygiedig: yng nghyda Darlith gan Belzebub, ar y Symudiad Dirwestol yn Tredegar* (Tredegar, 1860).

Rev. Richard Jones, *The Claims of the Temperance Movement on Christian Ministers* (Manchester, 1860).

Rev. R. Gwesyn Jones, *Courting, Marrying and Living* (Llanidloes, 1867).

R. W. Jones, *How to make our Sunday Schools more efficient* (1884).

Robert Jones, *Traethawd ar Sobrwydd a Meddwdod* (Caergybi, 1837).

T. Jones, *Meddwdod yn cael ei ystyried* (Swansea, 1835).

Thomas Jones, *The Welsh Looking-Glass, or Thoughts on the State of Religion in North Wales* (1812).

Rev. Thomas Jones, *Sober Views of the Millennium* (1835).

G. S. Kenrick, *The Population of Pontypool and the Parish of Trevethin, situated in the so-called 'Disturbed Districts'* (1840).

W. E. Kochs, *A Short Treatise on Labour, Strikes, Liberty, Religious, Political and General Public Questions* (Cardiff, 1892).

H. Ladd, *The Vital Question of the day, or How to Suppress Drunkenness from a Publican's Point of View* (Carmarthen, 1877).

Thomas Levi, *Casgliad o Areithiau at wasanaeth y Band of Hope* (Aberystwyth, 1866).

F. R. Rees, *Liberalism and its Mission* (1879).

Liberal Policy and Tory Tactics, being an Inquiry into the reasons why, at the last General Election, the Liberal Party, led by Mr. Gladstone, was defeated (1878).

J. Livesey, *Free and Friendly Remarks upon the Permissive Bill, Temperance Legislation and the Alliance* (1862).

J. Livesey and J. Price, *Darlith ar Ddirwest* (Llanidloes, 1837).

M. G. Lloyd and G. F. Thomason, *Welsh Society in Transition. A Survey of Recent Researches into the Social Structure of Wales* (Cardiff, 1963).

J. Malins, *Legislation on Sunday Closing: Progress and Results* (1889); *The Temperance Party and the New Parliament* (1892).

B. H. Malkin, *Tracts of the Society for the Improvement of the Working Population in Glamorgan* (Cowbridge, 1831).

J. Morgan, *Curates and Colliers* (Cardiff, 1873).

K. O. Morgan, *Freedom or Sacrilege? A History'of the Campaign for Welsh Disestablishment* (Penarth, 1965).

Rev. W. Morgan, *The Rechabites* (Bradford, 1841).

W. Morgan, *Ymgom y Glowyr* (Aberaman, 1867).

A. E. Morris, *The Christian Use of Alcoholic Beverages* (Risca, n.d., c. 1963).

W. Morris, *The Working Man's Garden* (Swansea, 1869).

A. V. Murray, *The Ethics and Techniques of Persuasion. Fourth Murray Hyslop Memorial Lecture* (Cardiff, 1953).

A Nonconformist, *Liberalism and Liberty* (1891).

Alfred Ollivant, *A Missionary Agency among the Mining Population. An Appeal (1860); Three Addresses delivered to the Clergy of the Diocese of Llandaff at His Visitation, July-August, 1875* (1875).

Evan Owen, *Workmen's Libraries in Glamorgan and Monmouthshire* (Cardiff, 1895).

H. Owen, *Welsh Religion and Welsh Christianity* (1895).

J. Owen, *The Free Churches and the People* (n.d., c.1894).

L. Page, *Easy Lessons in Alcoholic Liquors* (Cardiff, 1890).

T. Page, *An Earnest Appeal to the Nation at large on the mischievous effects of beer houses* (1846).

Papurau ar Ddirwest (Caernarfon, 1836).

Rev. A. J. Parry, *The Apostle Paul's Meat Argument and its bearing upon the duty of Christians in relation to the Drinking Customs of the Present Times* (Swansea, 1879).

G. A, Parry, *Drink and Industrial Unrest* (1919).

J. H. Phillips, *An Essay on the advantages of Free Libraries* (Cardiff, 1867).

Thomas Phillips, *The Welsh Revival* (1860).

David Pearce, *Dirwestiaeth* (Llanrwst, 1838).

Francis Place, *The Improvement of the Working People* (1834).

D. Price, *Y Catecism Cyntaf, neu yr Holwyddoreg Ddirwestol* (Merthyr Tydfil, 1840).

R. Pritchard, *Darlith ar Ddirwestiaeth* (Llanrwst, 1837).

R. H. Prichard, *Asaph Bach; sef argraffiad newydd o'r Fasged Gerddorol Cyflwynedig i'r Band of Hope* (Cardiff, 1861).

E. E. Probert, *The Attitude of our Churches to the cause of Total Abstinence* (Cardiff, 1896).

J. W. Pugh, *An Address on the Pernicious Effects of Theatrical Amusements* (Llanidloes, 1842).

E. Pughe, *The Religious Statistics of Wales* (1867).

David Rees, *The Moral Conflict* (Llanelli, 1851).

H. Rees, *Pregeth ymroddiad calon o blaid cymedroldeb* (Bangor, 1836).

William Rees, *Llwyr-ymattaliad yn cael ei ystyried* (Caernarfon, 1836).

R. Rees, *A Lecture on how to save and prolong life* (Cardiff, 1896).

Rev. T. Rees, *Miscellaneous Papers on subjects relating to Wales* (1867).

Revivals of Religion in Scotland, Ireland and Wales (1840).

J. T. Rhys, *Wales and its Drink Problem* (Aberystwyth, 1912).

Henry Richard, *The Political Relations of the Nonconformists to the Liberal Party* (Manchester, 1872).

D. M. Richards, *Aberdare in 1837* (Aberdare, 1897).

G. C. Richards, *The Evils of Indiscriminate Charity* (1894).

Evan Richardson, *Holwyddoreg Ddirwestol* (Llanrwst, 1837).

E. F. Roberts, *A Visit to the Iron Works and Environs of Merthyr Tydfil in 1852* (1853.).

Samuel Roberts, *Pleadings for Reforms, published fifty years ago* (Conwy, n.d., c.1881).

E. Scourfield, *Farmhouse Brewing* (Cardiff, n.d., c.1977).

Alexander Sharp, *A Narrative of the Great Revival Work in South Wales in 1871* (Cupar-Fife, 1871).

'Sianco'r Criws Bach', *Y Gynddaredd Wrthddirwestol, yn cynnwys Ardystion a Phenderfyniadau Wil Dalcen Pres a Huwcyn Bentarw yn erbyn Dirwest a Dirwestwyr* (Merthyr Tydfil, 1838).

Thomas Stephens, *The Congregationalists: their Principles and Ideals* (1890).

Talfyriad o adroddiad Cynghrair y Deyrnas gyfunol ar ddiddymu y fasnach mewn diodydd meddwol am y flwyddyn 1867 (U.K.A., Manchester, 1868).

Temperance Drinks for Harvest and Home (Denbigh, 1913).

The Templar and the Tippler, or the Hypocrite Trapped (Caernarfon, n.d.).

D. Lleufer Thomas, *Labour Unions in Wales. Their early struggle for existence* (Swansea, 1901).

Rev. D. J. Thomas, *The Temperance Movement in Newport, Mon., 1837-1937* (Newport, 1937).

J. Thomas, *Llythyr ar Ditotaliedyddiaeth a chrefydd* (Llanrwst, 1838).

Rev. John Thomas, *Y Meistr a'r Gweithiwr* (Pontypridd, 1859).

John Thomas, *Sunshine on the 'Hills', being a narrative of a revival of the Lord's Work at Tredegar during the visitation of the cholera in the year 1866* (n.d., c.1867).

John Thomas, *Pwysigrwydd Dirwestiaeth* (Wyddgrug, 1870); *Ffug-Chwedl Ddirwestol, Arthur Llwyd y Felin* (Liverpool, 1893).

[Paul Thomas], *'Pearl Fisher'. 'He's done it, Sir.' The Story of God's Work amongst the colliers and tinplate workers in South Wales* (1894).

P. S. Thomas, *Industrial Relations. Relations between employers and employed in Swansea, 1800-1940* (Swansea, 1940).

W. Thomas, *The River Side Hymns for the labouring classes* (1845).

Rev. Thomas Thomas, *A Course of Lectures on the present duties devolving on Christian Professors as members of a Civil Community, Lectures 1-6* (Newport, 1846-7).

H. M. Thompson, *Our English Sunday* (Cardiff, 1887).

J. P. Thompson, *Sunday Emancipation* (Cardiff, 1887).

Rev. C. F. Tonks, *Sunday and the Drink* (1923).

Traethawd ar egwyddorion a dybenion y Gymdeithas Gymmedroldeb (Llanrwst, 1836).

Traethodau ar y rhwystr pennaf i lwyddiant y Gymdeithas Ddirwestol yn y dyddiau hyn (Bangor, 1843).

United Kingdom Alliance, *A Vindication of the Principles and Policy of the United Kingdom Alliance, in reply to recent objections* (Manchester, 1862).

United Kingdom Alliance, *Drinking and Cholera* (Manchester, 1866).

The Victorian Society, *Social Change and Taste in Mid-Victorian England* (1963).

Welsh Nonconformity and Welsh Representation (Liberation Society, 1866).

The Welsh Sunday Closing Act: an epitome of opinions as to its operation (Cardiff Publicans and Beerhouse Keepers Association, Cardiff, 1884).

G. B. Wilson, *The Liquor Problem in Wales: an historical survey.* (Cardiff, 1942).

David Williams, *Thomas Francis Roberts, 1860-1919* (Cardiff, 1961).

Rev. E. G. Williams, *'Move On' or, Church progress in Swansea and suburbs during the last fifty years* (Swansea, 1889).

J. Williams, *Traethawd ar Gyfraith Maine* (Denbigh, 1858).

John Williams, *Rechabiaeth yn cael ei Hegluro* (Wyddgrug, 1842).

Richard Williams, *Pregeth Ddirwestol* (Llanrwst, 1842).

T. D. Williams, *Penillion Arobryn, Eisteddfod y Cymrodorion Dirwestol Merthyr, 1854* (Merthyr Tydfil, 1855).

Rev. William Williams, *Cymedroldeb a Llwyrymataliad. Sylwadau ar y ddwy egwyddor* (Caernarfon, 1834).

William Williams, *Ystyriaethau Ychwanegol ar Lwyrymwrthodiad* (Caernarfon, 1837).

William Williams, *Crynodeb o'r Pynciau Sylfaenol ac Ymarferol a ddelir gan yr Annibynwyr* (Caernarfon, 1838).

William Williams, *Robyn Ddu. Copi o Lythyr a ddanfonwyd gan James Williams* (Merthyr Tydfil, 1839).

William Williams, *Robyn Ddu Eto. Sylwadau ar gopi o lythyr diaconiaid y taihirion* (Caernarfon, 1840).

William Williams, *Amddiffyniad yr ymrwymiad gan Gymanfa Ddirwestol Gwynedd* (Caernarfon, 1844).

Rhisiart Owain Wiliam, *Egluryn Dirwestiaeth* (Caernarfon, 1842).

D. Yellowlees, *Insanity and Intemperance* (Swansea, 1874).

E. Young, *The House of God and the People's Palace. A reply to a letter of Rev. John Griffith of Aberdare* (Cardiff, 1853).

E. *Other Works*

A *Gentleman's Tour in North Wales* (1794).
Lord Aberdare, *Letters of the Rt. Hon. Henry Austin Bruce*, 2 vols. (Oxford, 1902).
W. E. Adams, *Memoirs of a Social Atom*, 2 vols. (1903).
J. P. Addis, *The Crawshay Dynasty* (Cardiff, 1957).
R. D. Altick, *The English Common Reader. A Social History of the Mass Reading Public, 1800-1900* (1957).
A. M. Allchin, *The Silent Rebellion. Anglican Religious Communities, 1845-1900* (1958).
P. Armstrong, *The Church of England, the Methodists and Society, 1700-1850* (1973).
D. Attwater, *The Catholic Church in Modern Wales* (1935).
H. Ausubel, *In Hard Times. Reformers among the Late Victorians* (New York, 1960).
E. Beaven, *The History of the Welsh Sunday Closing Act* (Cardiff, 1885).
D. W. Bebbington, *The Nonconformist Conscience* (1982).
G. V. Bennett and J. D. Walsh (eds.), *Essays in Modern Church History in Memory of Norman Sykes* (1966).
Earl of Bessborough (ed.), *Lady Charlotte Guest. Extracts from her Journal, 1832-1852* (1950).
T. Brennan, E. Cooney and H. Pollins, *Social Change in South-West Wales* (1954).
J. Briggs and I. Sellers (eds.), *Victorian Nonconformity* (1973).
D. Burns, *Temperance History. A Consecutive Narrative of the Rise, Development and Extension of the Temperance Reform*, 2 vols. (n.d., c. 1889).
M. J. Daunton, *Coal Metropolis. Cardiff, 1870-1914* (Leicester, 1977).
J. Davies, *Cardiff and the Marquesses of Bute* (Cardiff, 1981).
W. Davies, *The Agriculture and Domestic Economy of North Wales* (1811).
W. Davies, *The Agriculture and Domestic Economy of South Wales*, 2 vols. (1815).
A. E. Dingle, *The Campaign for Prohibition in Victorian England* (1980).
Ethel Drus (ed.), *A Journal of Events during the Gladstone Ministry, 1868-74, by John, First Earl of Kimberley* (Camden Miscellany, vol. 21, 1958).
J. Dunlop, *The Philosophy of Artificial and Compulsory Drinking Usage* (Greenock, 1839).
Ebbw Vale Literary and Scientific Institute. The History of a Hundred Years, 1849-1949 (Pontypool, 1949).
H. W. J. Edwards, *The Good Patch. A Study of the Rhondda Valley* (n.d.).
N. Edwards, *The Industrial Revolution in South Wales* (1924).
W. Edwards, *Four Centuries of Nonconformist Disabilities, 1500-1912* (1915).
M. Elsas (ed.), *Iron in the Making. Dowlais Iron Company Letters, 1782-1860* (1969).
F. Engels, *The Condition of the Working Class in England* (translated and edited by W. O. Henderson and W. H. Chaloner, Oxford, 1958).
A. Esquiros, *Religious Life in England* (1867).
D. Evans, *The Sunday Schools of Wales* (1883).
Rev. Joseph Evans, *Arrows from a Temperance Quiver* (Carmarthen, 1864).
L. W. Evans, *Education in Industrial Wales, 1700-1900* (Cardiff, 1971).
T. Evans, *The Background of Modern Welsh Politics, 1789-1846* (Cardiff, 1936).
M. W. Flynn and T. C. Smout (eds.), *Essays in Social History* (1974).
Franciscan Missions Among the Colliers and Iron Workers of Monmouthshire (1876).
C. K. Gloyn, *The Church and the Social Order* (1942).
P. H. J. H. Gosden, *The Friendly Societies in England, 1815-1875* (Manchester, 1961).
S. L. Greenslade, *The Church and the Social Order* (1948).

Wyn Griffith, *The Welsh* (1950).

R. B. Grindrod, *Bacchus. An Essay on the Nature, Causes, Effects and Cure of Intemperance* (1839).

J. R. Gusfield, *Symbolic Crusade. Status Politics and the American Temperance Movement* (Urbana, 1963).

A. and Z. B. Gustafson, *Foundation of Death. A Study of the Drink Question* (5th edn., 1888).

B. H. Harrison, *Drink and the Victorians. The Temperance Question in England, 1815-1872* (1971).

J. F. C. Harrison, *The Second Coming. Popular Millenarianism, 1780-1850* (1979).

D. A. Hamer, *The Politics of Electoral Pressure. A Study in the History of Victorian Reform Agitations* (1977).

F. E. Hamer (ed.), *The Personal Papers of Lord Rendel* (1931).

J. L. and B. Hammond, *The Village Labourer* (1911).

J. L. and B. Hammond, *The Town Labourer, 1760-1832* (1917).

H. J. Hanham, *Elections and Party Management. Politics in the time of Disraeli and Gladstone* (1959).

M. H. C. Hayler, *The Vision of a Century: 1853-1953. The United Kingdom Alliance in Historical Retrospect* (1953).

K. Heasman, *Evangelicals in Action* (1962).

G. W. Hilton, *The Truck System* (Cambridge, 1961).

E. J. Hobsbawm, *Primitive Rebels* (1959).

E. J. Hobsbawm, *Labouring Men* (1964).

P. Hollis (ed.), *Pressure from Without in Early Victorian England* (1974).

D. W. Howell, *Land and People in Nineteenth-Century Wales* (1978).

W. Hoyle, *Crime in England and Wales in the Nineteenth Century* (1876).

W. W. Hunt, *'To guard my People'. An Account of the Origin and History of the Swansea Police* (Swansea, 1957).

K. S. Inglis, *Churches and the Working Classes in Victorian England* (1963).

Jabez Inwards, *Memorials of Temperance Workers: Containing Brief Sketches of nearly a hundred deceased and worthy labourers* (1879).

C. H. James, *Seven Lectures on Various Subjects* (Merthyr Tydfil, 1892).

J. L. James, *Cymanfaoedd yr Annibynwyr. Eu Hanes a'u Llythyrau* (Dolgellau, 1867).

D. Jenkins, *Congregationalism* (1949).

Edward Jenkins, *The Devil's Chain* (1880).

J. A. Jenkins and R. E. Jones, *History of Nonconformity in Cardiff* (Cardiff, 1921).

R. T. Jenkins, *Hanes Cymru yn y Bedwaredd ganrif ar bymtheg, vol. 1* (Cardiff, 1933).

R. T. Jenkins, *Hanes Cymru yn y Ddeunawfed ganrif* (Cardiff, 1945).

R. T. Jenkins, *Bardd a'i Gefndir* (1948).

H. Jennings, *Brynmawr: A Study of a Distressed Area* (1934).

A. J. Johnes, *A Prize Essay on the causes which have produced Dissent in Wales from the Established Church* (1835).

A. H. John, *The Industrial Development of South Wales, 1750-1850* (Cardiff, 1950).

D. J. V. Jones, *Before Rebecca. Popular Protests in Wales, 1793-1835* (1973).

D. J. V. Jones, *Chartism and the Chartists* (1975).

Edward Jones, *Some Contributions to the Economic History of Wales* (1928).

Goronwy Jones, *David Davies, Llandinam* (Wrexham, 1913).

G. J. Jones, *Wales and the Quest for Peace* (Cardiff, 1969).

Sir Henry Jones, *The Working Faith of the Social Reformer, and other essays* (1910).

Sir Henry Jones, *Social Powers: three popular lectures on the environment, the press and the pulpit* (1913).

I. Jones, *Printing and Printers in Wales and Monmouthshire* (Cardiff, 1925).

J. O. Jones, *The History of the Caernarvonshire Constabulary, 1856-1950* (Caernarfon, 1963).

R. Merfyn Jones, *The North Wales Quarrymen, 1874-1922* (Cardiff, 1981).

Thomas Jones, *Rhymney Memories* (Newtown, 1938).

Thomas Jones, *Welsh Broth* (1951).

T. Gwynn Jones, *Cofiant Thomas Gee* (Denbigh, 1913).

T. Gwynn Jones, *Welsh Folklore and Folk Custom* (1930).

Rev. W. Jones, *The Character of the Welsh as a Nation* (Liverpool, 1841).

J. G. Kohl, *Travels in England and Wales* (1844).

S. Koss, *Nonconformity in Modern British Politics* (1975).

R. Lee and M. E. Marty (eds.), *Religion and Social Conflict* (New York, 1964).

Letters from Wales: a republication, by permission, of a series of letters in 'The Times' dealing with the state of Wales in especial relation to the land, the church and the tithe (1889).

E. D. Lewis, *The Rhondda Valleys* (1959).

H. E. Lewis, *Nonconformity in Wales* (1904).

H. E. Lewis, *With Christ among the Miners* (1906).

Herman Levy, *Drink: An Economic and Social Study* (1952).

E. Lhuyd, *Parochialia* (1911).

John Lloyd, *Old South Wales Ironworks* (1906).

W. Logan, *Early Heroes of the Temperance Reformation* (Glasgow, 1873).

H. W. Lucy (ed.), *A Diary of the Salisbury Parliament, 1886-1892* (1892).

H. W. Lucy (ed.), *A Diary of the Home Rule Parliament, 1892-1895* (1895).

J. M. Ludlow and L. Jones, *The Progress of the Working Class, 1832-1867* (1867).

T. Mainwaring, *Glimpses of Welsh Politics* (Llanelli, 1881).

B. H. Malkin, *The Scenery, Antiquities and Biography of South Wales*, 2 vols. (1807).

N. Masterman, *The Forerunner* (Swansea, 1972).

Mass Observation, *The Pub and the People. A Worktown Study* (1943).

Z. Mather, *Bywyd a Gwaith yr hynod Ddr. Arthur Jones o Fangor* (n.d.).

P. Mathias, *The Brewing Industry in England, 1700-1830* (Cambridge, 1959).

R. G. McCarthy (ed.), *Drinking and Intoxication. Selected Readings in Social Attitudes and Controls* (Glencoe, 1959).

Edward Miall, *The British Churches in relation to the British People* (1849).

E. Morgan, *Valuable Letters and Addresses of John Elias* (Caernarfon, 1847).

G. Osborne Morgan, *The Church of England and the People of Wales* (1895).

H. A. Morgan, *Church and Dissent in Wales* (Cambridge, 1895).

Kenneth O. Morgan, *David Lloyd George: Welsh Radical as World Statesman* (Cardiff, 1963).

Kenneth O. Morgan, *Wales in British Politics, 1868-1922* (3rd edn., Cardiff, 1980).

Kenneth O. Morgan, *Lloyd George, Family Letters, 1885-1936* (Cardiff and Oxford, 1973).

Kenneth O. Morgan. *The Age of Lloyd George. The Liberal Party and British Politics, 1890-1929* (2nd edn., 1978).

Kenneth O. Morgan, *Rebirth of a Nation. Wales, 1880-1980* (Oxford and Cardiff, 1981).

J. V. Morgan, *The Welsh Religious Revival, 1904-1905* (1909).

J. V. Morgan, *The Church in Wales in the light of History* (1918).

Rev. T. Morgan, *The Life and Work of the Rev. Thomas Thomas, D.D.* (Carmarthen, 1925).

David Morgans, *Music and Musicians of Merthyr and District* (Merthyr Tydfil, 1922).

J. H. Morris and L. J. Williams, *The South Wales Coal Industry, 1841-1875* (Cardiff, 1958).

Thomas Nicholas (ed.), *Social Religion*, by Mathias Maurice (7th edn., 1860).

H. R. Niebuhr, *The Social Sources of Denominationalism* (New York, 1960).

C. O'Leary, *The Elimination of Corrupt Practices in British Elections, 1868-1911* (Oxford, 1962).

T. M. Owen, *Welsh Folk Customs* (Cardiff, 1978 edn.).

Prize Essay on the Operative Classes of Great Britain: their existing state and its improvement (1850).

Robert Parry, *Teithiau a Barddoniaeth Robyn Ddu Eryri* (Caernarfon, 1857).

D. Parry Jones, *Welsh Country Upbringing* (1948).

C. H. Patrick, *Alcohol, Culture and Society* (1952).

I. Peate, *The Traditional Welsh House* (Liverpool, 1946).

H. Pelling, *Popular Politics and Society in Late Victorian Britain* (rev. edn., 1979).

H. Pelling, *Social Geography of British Elections, 1880-1910* (1967).

Sir Thomas Phillips, *Wales: the language, social condition, moral character and religious opinions of the people considered in their relation to education* (1849).

Pioneers of Welsh Education (Swansea, n.d.).

D. J. Pittman and C. R. Snyder (eds.), *Society, Culture and Drinking Patterns* (New York, 1962).

Evan Powell, *History of Tredegar* (Newport, 1902).

Evan Powell, *History of Carmel Baptist Chapel, Sirhowy* (Cardiff, 1933).

Evan Price, *The History of Penuel Calvinistic Methodist Chapel, Ebbw Vale* (Wrexham, 1925).

A. D. Rees, *Life in a Welsh Countryside* (Cardiff, 1950).

D. B. Rees, *Chapels in the Valley* (Wirral, 1975).

J. Machreth Rees and J. Owen, *Cofiant y Parch. John Thomas, D.D.* (Liverpool, 1898).

Rev. Thomas Rees, *History of Protestant Nonconformity in Wales* (2nd edn., 1883).

Rev. Thomas Rees and Rev. Dr. John Thomas, *Hanes Eglwysi Annibynol Cymru*, 4 vols. (1871-5; 1891).

Rev. William Rees, *The Devil's Keys. Cloi Dirwest o Dy Dduw* (Ystalyfera, 1888).

Sir J. Rhys and D. Brynmor Jones, *The Welsh People* (1900).

Henry Richard, *Letters on the Social and Political Condition of Wales* (1867).

Henry Richard, *Letters and Essays on Wales* (1884).

Rev. J. Roberts, *The Calvinistic Methodism of Wales* (Cardiff, 1933).

Joseph Rowntree and A. Sherwell, *The Temperance Problem and Social Reform* (1899).

E. Royle, *Radical Politics, 1790-1900. Religion and Unbelief* (1971).

G. W. E. Russell, *Sir Wilfrid Lawson. A Memoir* (1909).

Mark Rutherford [pseud. W. H. White], *The Revolution in Tanner's Lane* (7th edn., n.d.).

A. Shadwell, *Drink, Temperance and Legislation* (1902).

Wirt Sikes, *Rambles and Studies in Old South Wales* (1881).

M. B. Simey, *Charitable Effort in Liverpool in the Nineteenth Century* (Liverpool, 1951).

Lewis Snow, *Practical Essays on Popular Subjects written for the National Eisteddfodau of Wales* (1866).

R. Souttar, *Alcohol: its place and power in legislation* (1904).

J. N. Stearns, *Temperance in all Nations*, 2 vols. (New York, 1893).

W. C. Sullivan, *Alcoholism: A Chapter in Social Pathology* (1906).

Ivor Thomas, *Top Sawyer* (1938).

Rev. John Thomas, D.D., *Jwbili y Diwygiad Dirwestol yng Nghymru* (Merthyr Tydfil, 1885).

Rev. John Thomas, D.D., *Cofiant y Parch Thomas Rees, D.D., Abertawy* (Dolgellau, 1888).

J. A. Thomas, *The House of Commons, 1832-1901. An Analysis of its Economic and Social Character* (Cardiff, 1953).

M. I. Thomis, *The Town Labourer and the Industrial Revolution* (1974).

D. Thompson, *Nonconformity in the Nineteenth Century* (1972).

E. C. Urwin, *Methodism and Sobriety. The Story of a Great Transformation* (1943).

John Vaizey, *The Brewing Industry, 1886-1951* (1960).

H. M. Vaughan, *The South Wales Squires* (1926).

Victorian South Wales—Architecture, Industry and Society (The Victorian Society, 1971).

J. E. Vincent, *The Land Question in North Wales* (1896).

J. E. Vincent, *The Land Question in South Wales* (1897).

J. R. Vincent, *The Formation of the Liberal Party, 1857-1868* (1966).

J. R. Vincent, *Pollbooks. How Victorians Voted* (1967).

J. L. Ward and T. Coe, *Father Jones of Cardiff. A Memoir* (Cardiff, 1907).

S. and B. Webb, *The History of Liquor Licensing in England, principally from 1700 to 1830* (1903).

Charles Wilkins, *The History of Merthyr Tydfil* (Merthyr Tydfil, 1867).

Charles Wilkins, *The History of the Iron, Steel, Tinplate and Other Trades of Wales* (Merthyr Tydfil, 1903).

A. H. Williams, *Welsh Wesleyan Methodism, 1800-1858* (Bangor, 1935).

David Williams, *John Frost* (Cardiff, 1939).

David Williams, *The Rebecca Riots* (Cardiff, 1955).

Rev. D. D. Williams, *Hanes Dirwest yng Ngwynedd* (Liverpool, 1921).

Glanmor Williams, *S.R.* (Cardiff, 1950).

Glanmor Williams (ed.), *Merthyr Politics. The Making of a Working-Class Tradition* (Cardiff, 1966).

Rev. J. Williams, *Notes and Narratives of Thirty Years Missionary and Ministerial Labours in England and Wales* (Machynlleth, 1885).

J. R. Williams and G. Williams, *History of Caersalem, Dowlais* (Llandysul, 1967).

Rev. William Williams, *Cofiant a Gweithiau Ieuan Gwynedd* (Dolgellau, 1876).

B. Wilson, *Sects and Society* (1961).

G. B. Wilson, *Drunkenness* (1893).

P. T. Winskill, *The Comprehensive History of the Rise and Progress of the Temperance Reformation to 1881, with biographical sketches* (1881).

P. T. Winskill, *The Temperance Movement and its Workers*, 4 vols. (1892).

P. T. Winskill, *Temperance Standard Bearers of the Nineteenth Century*, 2 vols. (1897-8).

P. T. Winskill and Joseph Thomas, *History of the Temperance Movement in Liverpool and District* (Liverpool, 1887).

Rev. D. Young, *A Noble Life. Incidents in the Career of Lewis Davies of Ferndale* (1913).

F. *Articles*

G. M. Ashton, 'Dirwest ynteu Llwyrymwrthod'? *Y Traethodydd*, CXXIII, no. 528, 1968.

S. L. Bethell, 'The Theology of Social Action', *Faith in Wales*, 1944.

J. D. Bollen, 'The Temperance Movement and the Liberal Party in New South Wales Politics, 1900-1904', *Journal of Religious History*, 1, no. 1, 1960.

E. D. C. Brewer, 'Church and Sect in Methodism', *Social Forces*, 30, 1951-52.

Charles Buxton, 'How to stop drunkenness', *North British Review*, 22, 1854-5.

Thomas Darlington, 'The Church in Wales, An Alien Church', *Contemporary Review*, LXIII, June 1893.

A. H. Dodd, 'The Nonconformist Conscience in Public Life', *Hibbert Journal*, January 1938.

M. S. Edwards, 'The Teetotal Wesleyan Methodists', *Proceedings of the Wesley Historical Society*, 33, September-December 1961.

J. F. Glaser, 'English Nonconformity and the Decline of Liberalism', *American Historical Review*, LXIII, no. 2, 1958.

H. J. Hanham, 'Liberal Organizations for Working Men, 1860-1914', *Bulletin of the Society for the Study of Labour History*, no. 7, Autumn 1963.

C. C. Harries, 'Church, Chapel and the Welsh', *New Society*, 21 February 1963.

B. Harrison, 'Drunkards and Reformers. Early Victorian Temperance Tracts', *History Today*, 13, no. 3, March 1963.

B. Harrison, 'Philanthropy and the Victorians', *Victorian Studies*, June 1966.

B. Harrison, 'The Sunday Trading Riots of 1855', *Historical Journal*, 8, 2, 1965.

B. Harrison, 'Religion and Recreation in Nineteenth-Century England', *Past and Present*, no. 38, December 1967.

B. Harrison, 'Drink and Sobriety in England, 1815-1872. A Critical Bibliography', *International Review of Social History*, 12, part 2, 1967.

B. Harrison and P. Hollis, 'Chartism, Liberalism and the Life of Robert Lowery', *English Historical Review*, 82, July 1967.

B. Harrison, 'Temperance Societies', *The Local Historian*, 8, no. 4, 1968.

B. Harrison, 'The Power of Drink', *The Listener*, 81, no. 2081, February 1969.

B. Harrison, 'The British Prohibitionists, 1853-1872. A Biographical Analysis', *International Review of Social History*, XV, part 3, 1970.

B. Harrison, 'Teetotal Chartism', *History*, 58, 1973.

J. F. C. Harrison, 'The Victorian Gospel of Success', *Victorian Studies*, 1, 1957-8.

J. Hart, 'Nineteenth-Century Social Reform: a Tory interpretation of History', *Past and Present*, no. 31, 1963.

E. J. Hobsbawm, 'Economic Fluctuations and some social movements since 1800', *Economic History Review*, 1952.

W. D. Johnson, 'The Inn as a Community Centre', *Amateur Historian*, 2, no. 5, May 1955.

E. D. Jones, 'William Rees, Llechryd (1839-1919): a Welsh Swedenborgian', *National Library of Wales Journal*, 15, 2, Winter 1967.

G. P. Jones, 'Cholera in Wales', *National Library of Wales Journal*, 10, 1957-8.

K. R. Jones, 'Yr Eglwys a Dirwest', *Faith in Wales*, 1934.

I. G. Jones, 'The Liberation Society and Welsh Politics, 1844-1868', *Welsh History Review*, I, no. 2, 1961.

I. G. Jones, 'Dr. Thomas Price and the Election of 1868 in Merthyr Tydfil. A study in Nonconformist Politics. Parts 1 and 2. *Welsh History Review*, 2, no. 2, 1964; 2, no. 3., 1965.

I. G. Jones, 'Cardiganshire Politics in Mid-Century', *Ceredigion*, 1965.

I. G. Jones, 'Merioneth Politics in mid-nineteenth century', *Journal of Merionethshire Historical and Record Society*, 5, no. 4, 1968.

I. G. Jones, 'The Anti-Corn Law Letters of Walter Griffith', *Bulletin of the Board of Celtic Studies*, vol. XXVIII, Part 1, Nov. 1978.

H. Jones, 'Alcoholism and Society', *New Society*, 21 March 1963.

K. Jones-Roberts, 'D. R. Daniel, 1859-1931', *Journal of the Merioneth Historical and Record Society*, 5, part 1, 1965.

W. R. Lambert, 'The Welsh Sunday Closing Act, 1881', *Welsh History Review*, 6, no. 2, 1972.

W. R. Lambert, 'Drink and Work-Discipline in Industrial South Wales, c.1800-1870', *ibid.*, 7, no. 3, 1975.

W. R. Lambert, 'Thomas Williams, J.P., Gwaelod-y-garth (1823-1903): A study in Nonconformist Attitudes and Actions', S. Williams (ed.), *Glamorgan Historian*, vol. 11 (Cowbridge, 1975).

W. R. Lambert, 'Some Working-Class Attitudes towards Organized Religion in Nineteenth-century Wales', *Llafur*, 2, no. 1, Spring 1976.

L. Levi, 'The Limits of Legislative Interference with the sale of Fermented Liquors', *Journal of the Statistical Society*, 35, 1872.

C. Leys, 'Petitioning in the Nineteenth and Twentieth Centuries', *Political Studies,* 3, no. 1, February 1955.

J. M. Lee, 'The Political Significance of Licensing Legislation', *Parliamentary Affairs,* 1961.

R. M. Macleod, 'The Edge of Hope: Social Policy and Chronic Alcoholism, 1870-1900', *Journal of the History of Medicine and Allied Sciences,* 22, no. 3, July 1967.

D. G. Mandelbaum, 'Alcohol and Culture', *Current Anthropology,* June 1965.

N. C. Masterman, 'T. E. Ellis: Pre-Romantic Statesman', *Anglo-Welsh Review,* 14, no. 34, Winter 1964-65.

P. Mathias, 'The Brewing Industry, Temperance and Politics', *Historical Journal,* 1958.

H. McCready, 'The 1874 Election', *Canadian Journal of Economic and Political Science,* 20, 1954.

S. Meacham, 'The Evangelical Inheritance', *Journal of British Studies,* 3, no. 1, November 1963.

Kenneth O. Morgan, 'Gladstone and Wales', *Welsh History Review,* 1, 1, 1960.

Kenneth O. Morgan, 'Liberals, Nationalists and Mr. Gladstone', *Transactions of the Honourable Society of Cymmrodorion,* 1960.

Kenneth O. Morgan, 'Cardiganshire Politics: The Liberal Ascendancy, 1885-1923', *Ceredigion,* 5, 1967.

W. T. Morgan, 'Chartism and Industrial Unrest in South Wales in 1842', *National Library of Wales Journal,* 10, 1957-58.

J. Morris, 'Evan Evans and the Vale of Neath Brewery', *Morgannwg,* 9, 1965.

M. L. Pendered, 'The Psychology of Amusement in its relation to Temperance Reform', *The Socialist Review,* 3, no. 16, June 1909.

S. Pollard, 'Factory Discipline in the Industrial Revolution', *Economic History Review,* 1963.

F. R. Salter, 'Political Nonconformity in the 1830s', *Transactions of the Royal Historical Society,* 1953.

I. Sellers, 'Nonconformist attitudes in later nineteenth-century Liverpool', *Transactions of the Historical Society of Lancashire and Cheshire,* 114, 1962.

N. St. John-Stevas, 'The Victorian Conscience', *Wiseman Review,* Autumn 1962.

B. Thomas, 'The Migration of Labour into the Glamorgan Coalfield, 1861-1911', *Economica,* 1930.

C. R. Williams, 'The Welsh Religious Revival, 1904-5' *British Journal of Sociology,* 1952.

David Williams, 'Rural Wales in the Nineteenth Century', *Journal of the Agricultural Society,* 1953.

David Williams, 'The Pembrokeshire Elections of 1831', *Welsh History Review,* 1, 1, 1960.

Glanmor Williams, 'Chartists, "Rebecca" and the Swansea Police', *Gower,* 12, 1959.

Gwyn A. Williams, 'Friendly Societies in Glamorgan, 1793-1832', *Bulletin of the Board of Celtic Studies,* 18, 1958-60.

Gwyn A. Williams, 'The Making of Radical Merthyr, 1800-1836', *Welsh History Review,* 1, 2, 1961.

W. D. Wills, 'The Established Church in the Diocese of Llandaff, 1850-1870: A Study of the Evangelical Movement in the South Wales Coalfield', *ibid.,* 4, 3, June 1969.

3. UNPUBLISHED THESES

G. H. Armbruster, The Social Determination of Ideologies (University of London Ph.D. thesis, 1940).

J. Burnett, The History of Food Adulteration in Great Britain in the Nineteenth Century with special reference to Bread, Tea and Beer (University of London Ph.D. thesis, 1958).

B. L. Crapster, 'Our Trade, Our Politics.' A Study of the Political Activity of the British Liquor Industry, 1868-1910 (University of Harvard Ph.D. thesis, 1949).

I. W. R. David, Political and Electioneering Activity in South-East Wales, 1820-1851 (University of Wales M.A. thesis, 1959).

A. C. Davies, Aberdare, 1750-1850. A Study in the Growth of an Industrial Community (University of Wales M.A. thesis, 1963).

G. M. Ellis, The Evangelicals and the Sunday Question, 1830-1860. Organized Sabbatarianism as an Aspect of the Evangelical Movement (University of Harvard Ph.D. thesis, 1951).

C. Evans, The Rise and Progress of the Periodical Press in Wales up to 1860 (University of Wales M.A. thesis, 1926).

J. F. Glaser, Nonconformity and Liberalism, 1868-1885. A Study in English Party History (University of Harvard Ph.D. thesis, 1948).

P. E. H. Hair, The Social History of British Coalminers, 1800-1845 (University of Oxford D.Phil. thesis, 1955).

B. Harrison, The Temperance Question in England, 1829-1869 (University of Oxford D.Phil. thesis, 1965).

J. V. Hickey, The Origin and Growth of the Irish Community in Cardiff (University of Wales M.A. thesis, 1959).

R. L. Hugh, The Theological Background of Nonconformist Social Influence in Wales, 1800-1850 (University of London Ph.D. thesis, 1951).

G. R. Hughes, Bywyd Caledfryn a'i Weithgarwch fel Gŵr Cyhoeddus (University of Wales M.A. thesis, 1958).

A. G. Jones, The Economic, Industrial and Social History of Ebbw Vale, 1775-1927 (University of Wales M.A. thesis, 1929).

J. O. Jones, The History of the Caernarvonshire Police Force, 1856-1900 (University of Wales M.A. thesis, 1956).

W. R. Lambert, Drink and Sobriety in Wales, 1830-1895 (University of Wales Ph.D. thesis 1970).

R. T. Lewis, Religious Organizations in Wales considered in relation to economic conditions, 1850-1930 (University of Wales M.A. thesis, 1965).

B. J. Mason, The Rise of Combative Dissent, 1832-1859 (University of Southampton M.A. thesis, 1958).

K. McNab, Aspects of the History of Crime in England and Wales in the Nineteenth Century (University of Sussex M.A. thesis, 1965).

G. E. Owen, Welsh Anti-Slavery Sentiment, 1795-1865. A Survey of Public Opinion (University of Wales M.A. thesis, 1964).

R. I. Parry. The Attitude of the Welsh Independents towards Working-class Movements, 1815-1870 (University of Wales M.A. thesis, 1931).

D. Pritchard, The Slate Industry of North Wales (University of Wales M.A. thesis, 1935).

G. Richards, A Study of Theological Developments among the Nonconformists of Wales in the Nineteenth Century (University of Oxford B.Litt. thesis, 1956-57).

T. Ridd, The Development of Municipal Government in Swansea in the Nineteenth Century (University of Wales M.A. thesis, 1955).

J. Rowlands, A Study of some of the Social and Economic Changes in the town and parish of Amlwch, 1750-1850 (University of Wales M.A. thesis, 1961).

K. T. Weetch, The Dowlais Ironworks and its Industrial Community, 1760-1850 (London School of Economics M.Sc. (Econ.) thesis, 1963).

L. Williams, Movements towards Social Reform in South Wales, 1832-1850 (University of Wales M.A. thesis, 1933).

T. H. Williams, Wales and the Corn Laws, 1815-1846 (University of Wales M.A. thesis, 1952).

W. D. Wills, Ecclesiastical Reorganization and Church Extension in the Diocese of Llandaff, 1830-1870 (University of Wales M.A. thesis, 1965).

INDEX